Blavatsky Unveiled

First published in 2020 by Martin Firrell Company Ltd

Unit 2 City Limits, Danehill, Reading RG6 4UP, United Kingdom.

ISBN 978-0-9931786-9-6

Text is set in Baskerville, 12pt on 17pt.

Baskerville is a serif typeface designed in 1754 by John Baskerville (1706–1775) in Birmingham, England. Compared to earlier typeface designs, Baskerville increased the contrast between thick and thin strokes. Serifs were made sharper and more tapered, and the axis of rounded letters was placed in a more vertical position. The curved strokes were made more circular in shape, and the characters became more regular.

Baskerville is categorized as a transitional typeface between classical typefaces and high contrast modern faces. Of his own typeface, John Baskerville wrote, 'Having been an early admirer of the beauty of letters, I became insensibly desirous of contributing to the perfection of them. I formed to myself ideas of greater accuracy than had yet appeared, and had endeavoured to produce a set of types according to what I conceived to be their true proportion.'

moon laramie blavatsky unveiled

The writings of H.P. Blavatsky in modern English. Volume I.

martin firrell company
MODERN THEOSOPHY

The Zombie Inside
A Practical Guide to the Law of Attraction

Spirit of Garbo

Theosophy and the Search for Happiness
(with Annie Besant)

Moon Laramie is a member of the Theosophical Society in England. He is editor of the *Modern Theosophy* series: short volumes re-presenting important texts from the history of the theosophical movement, paired with writing by contemporary theosophists. He is the author of *Spirit of Garbo*, a spiritual biography of the legendary Swedish film star. *Blavatsky Unveiled Volume I* is the beginning of an ambitious publishing project to present all of Madame Blavatsky's writing in modern English.

Introduction

In September 1877, H.P. Blavatsky published her first occult masterwork, *Isis Unveiled*. At almost 1400 pages long, the book covered a wide range of topics including cosmogenesis, ancient Egyptian Mystery schools and the conflict between science and spiritualism. On its release, *Isis Unveiled* sparked a huge amount of interest. While some newspapers dismissed it as 'discarded rubbish' and 'a large dish of hash', others were wildly enthusiastic.[1]

The *North American Review* saw the book as a 'monumental work . . . about everything relating to magic, mystery, witchcraft, religion, spiritualism, which would be valuable in an encyclopedia.'[2] *The Evening Post* described it as 'a mine of curious information.' According to *The Daily Graphic*, *Isis Unveiled* was 'a marvellous book both in matter and manner of treatment' with an index of subjects 'never before compiled by any human being.'

'One who reads the book carefully through, ought to know everything of the marvellous and mystical,' suggested *The New York Herald*. The *Herald* went on to add that with 'its striking peculiarities, its audacity, its versatility, and the prodigious variety of subjects which it notices and handles, it is one of the remarkable productions of the century.'

Other journals heaped praise on the book's author. The *New York Tribune* took the view that H.P. Blavatsky was 'an adept in secret science . . . a hierophant in the exposition of its mystic lore.' The New York *Independent* described her erudition as 'stupendous' while the *Boston Evening Transcript* believed her to be 'a remarkable woman, who has read more, seen more and thought more than most wise men.'

The first edition of *Isis Unveiled* was sold out within one week and the book has remained in print ever since. In spite of this runaway success, Blavatsky would later go on to criticize her own work: 'Of all the books I have put my name to, this particular one is, in literary arrangement, the worst and most confused.'[3] In her opinion, *Isis Unveiled* had 'no system in it,' was full of 'misprints and misquotations,' 'useless repetitions' and 'most irritating digressions.'[4]

Blavatsky made no apologies for making her views public: 'I have never ceased to say what I thought . . . and to give my honest opinion of *Isis* whenever I had an opportunity for so doing. This was done to the great disgust of some, who warned me that I was spoiling its sale. But as my chief object in writing it was neither personal fame nor gain, but something far higher, I cared little for such warnings.'[5] Although not her magnum opus, ultimately Blavatsky still considered the book to be a work of great importance. She insisted that '*Isis Unveiled* contains a mass of original and never hitherto divulged information on occult subjects.' She went on to 'defend the ideas and teachings in it' and to maintain 'that both are of the greatest value to mystics and students of Theosophy.'[6]

To the modern eye, the linguistic style of *Isis Unveiled* can appear dense, convoluted and over-wrought. In the *Oxford Guide To Plain English*, Martin Cutts recommends that contemporary writers make their average sentence between 15 and 20 words long. In common with numerous publications of the time, *Isis Unveiled* contains sentences often double or triple that length. One sentence in Chapter Seven is 205 words long with ten subordinate clauses, 15 commas, six semicolons and reference to six different historical events. Such elaborate and elongated prose can present a major stumbling block for the 21st-century reader.

Blavatsky Unveiled aims to address the original book's linguistic challenges by rendering Blavatsky's text into easily accessible modern English. For example, the following sentence appears in Chapter One of *Isis Unveiled*:

'The great kingdoms and empires of the world, after reaching the culmination of their greatness, descend again, in accordance with the same law by which they ascended; till, having reached the lowest point, humanity reasserts itself and mounts up once more, the height of its attainment being, by this law of ascending progression by cycles, somewhat higher than the point from which it had before descended.'

In *Blavatsky Unveiled* this has been rendered into four shorter sentences:

'The great kingdoms and empires of the world are subject to a cyclical law of rise and fall. They reach a peak of civilisation and then decline again. When they have reached their lowest point they rally and rise again. The cyclical law of rise and fall ensures that each new peak of civilisation rises higher than its predecessor.'

Another obstacle for the modern reader is the obscure nature of many of Blavatsky's references. The sheer number of mesmerists, mediums, scientists, philosophers, alchemists, eastern adepts, supernatural occurrences and mystical texts can leave modern readers scratching their heads in bewilderment. For the first time, exhaustive scholarship has been applied to the text of H.P. Blavatsky's debut work of occultism. *Blavatsky Unveiled* includes a detailed 10,000-word, easy-to-read notes section and a comprehensive 'Who's Who' detailing every person mentioned in the text, as well as all religious and mythical figures (over 650 entries in total).

All of Blavatsky's references have been meticulously researched and, where possible, verified from their primary source material. Throughout the book, non-uniform spellings of foreign names have been rendered into their current standardized English equivalents. The original spelling used by Blavatsky is noted in the reference sections, prefixed by the letters 'HPB'.

I began working on *Blavatsky Unveiled* on a warm spring afternoon in April 2016. It has taken four years to complete the first volume. I am now working on volume two. So far it has been a fascinating journey into the world of theosophy and Helena Petrovna Blavatsky. The pages of *Blavatsky Unveiled* present a psychedelic rollercoaster ride through a land of Gnostics, Brahmins, Kabbalists, *Chaldean Oracles*, Phrygian Dactyls, cataclysmic floods, spiritualist seances, skeptical scientists, perpetual lamps, phantom dogs and Indian conjurors, to name but a few. Along the way the reader encounters such figures as Pythagoras, Paracelsus, Darwin, Schopenhauer, Isaac Newton, Julius Caesar, Plato, Galileo, Giordano Bruno, the spirit entity Katie King, Franz Mesmer, Aristotle, Eliphas Levi and many others.

As *The New York Sun* said when reviewing the contents of *Isis Unveiled*: 'They give evidence of much and multifarious research on the part of the author, and contain a vast number of interesting stories. Persons fond of the marvellous will find in them an abundance of entertainment.'

Moon Laramie
NORFOLK, APRIL 2020

Notes

1. Gary Lachman, *Madame Blavatsky: The Mother of Modern Spirituality*, Tarcher, 2012.

2. H.P. Blavatsky, 'My Books,' *Lucifer Volume VIII*, May 1891.

3. Ibid.

4. Ibid.

5. Ibid.

6. Ibid.

Blavatsky Unveiled

VOLUME I

Chapter One

Ego sum qui sum.
I am who I am.
A TRUTH OF HERMETIC PHILOSOPHY

We began research where modern science failed to go.
And in our research we concentrated on elements of science
which the wise men of today dismiss as illusions
or unsolvable mysteries.

ZANONI, EDWARD BULWER-LYTTON

Somewhere in the world there is an ancient book. This book is so old that experts could examine it forever and still not agree on the materials used to make it. It is the only copy left in existence. It was used to compile the *Hebrew Book of Concealed Mystery (Siphra Dzeniouta)*, which is itself understood to be immensely old. One of its illustrations shows the divine cycle of God-consciousness emanating from Adam. It appears like an arc of light. It forms a circle and, at the highest point of the circumference, it arcs back to earth bringing a higher form of humanity in its wake. As it approaches closer and closer, the God-consciousness becomes darker and darker until it turns black as it touches the earth's surface.

All Hermetic[1] philosophers share a belief founded on 70,000 years of experience. They believe that sin has made matter denser since man first appeared on earth. In the beginning, the human body was semi-physical in nature. Before the fall, mankind was able to interact with other invisible universes. But since then, matter has become a barrier between man and the spiritual plane. Esoteric tradition teaches that there were also many races of men before Adam. Each race died out to give birth to another. Were these earlier races superior? Did any of them belong to the winged race described by the Greek philosopher Plato in his dialogue *Phaedrus?*[2] Science should be able to answer these questions. Cave paintings in France and Stone Age artifacts provide a good starting point. As the cycle of God-consciousness progressed, men came to know the difference between good and evil just as surely as the gods themselves. The cycle reached its apex and then began to descend. When its arc became parallel with the terrestrial plane, man was clothed in skin.

The earliest traditions of most cultures suggest that a more spiritually developed race preceded modern humanity. The French ethnographer Charles-Étienne Brasseur de Bourbourg published a French translation of the Popol Vuh[3] or Mayan Book of the People in 1861. According to the Popol Vuh, the first men could reason and speak, had unlimited sight and simultaneous knowledge of all things. The Jewish philosopher Philo Judaeus describes the air as filled with invisible spirits. Some are pure and eternal. Others are wicked and mortal. Humanity is descended from godlike beings and will become godlike again. This belief is echoed in the Gospel of St. John. An esoteric reading of this text suggests that those who follow Jesus will become godlike themselves. 'Don't you know that you are gods?' said Jesus. Plato makes the same point in *Phaedrus* suggesting man lived among the gods as a god himself before losing his wings and becoming mortal. The oldest religious philosophies teach that the universe was filled with spiritual beings and it is from one of these that Adam evolved.

The Kalmucks[4] and other Siberian tribes also have myths describing beings that preceded the human race. These earlier beings had almost limitless knowledge and they threatened to rebel against their god, the great chief spirit. To prevent the rebellion, he incarcerated them in physical bodies, imprisoning their senses. They could only escape the limitations of their bodies through a long journey of spiritual evolution. The Kalmucks believe that the shamans of their tribes can access the divine powers of those earlier beings.

The Astor Library in New York has recently acquired a copy of an Egyptian medical treatise written in 1552 BC. This date is generally regarded as the year of Moses' 21st birthday. The treatise is written on papyrus and has been verified as genuine by the German botanist August Schenk. It consists of a single sheet, 30 centimeters wide and more than 20 meters long, forming one scroll divided into 110 numbered pages. It was acquired in Egypt in

1872-3 by the German Egyptologist Georg Ebers. *The New York Tribune* claims the papyrus is one of the six Hermetic books on medicine described by the Christian theologian Clement of Alexandria.

According to the *Tribune's* editor, Egyptian priests in 363 AD attributed 42 books to the Greco-Egyptian mystic Hermes Trismegistus. 36 of these contained the history of all human knowledge. The remaining six dealt with anatomy, pathology, eye conditions, surgical instruments and medicines. The Tribune's editor claims that the Ebers Papyrus is indisputably one of these Hermetic books.

Ebers' purchase of the papyrus brought the world's attention to ancient Egyptian science. Who knows what other lucky and important discoveries might be made in the future.

Modern science confirms the claims made by the oldest traditions that humanity is immensely ancient. In the last few years geology has found proof that humans existed over 250,000 years ago before the last glaciation of Europe. Christian theologians find this difficult to reconcile with the Bible but it was a fact readily accepted by the ancient philosophers.

The fossil record shows that man hunted and built fires in the distant past but the origin of humanity still remains a mystery. Science has come to an impasse and waits for further evidence. No anthropologist or psychologist has been as visionary as the French paleontologist Georges Cuvier, who refuted the idea of evolution, believing that creation occurred in cycles and species became extinct through global catastrophes. Geologists and archeologists have been unable to piece together from the fossil record the perfect threefold model of man - physical, intellectual and spiritual. When archeologists discover crude implements they assume that the further back in time human beings lived, the more primitive they were. This is flawed logic. Suppose humanity became extinct and an archeologist from some future race uncovered simple tools from a tribe on a remote island. He would be mistaken in thinking that everyone in the 19th Century lived in a similarly primitive way.

It is fashionable to think that all ideas from the primitive past are themselves primitive. This devalues the past and yet it is only by looking to the past that so many modern thinkers have made their reputations.

The Irish physicist John Tyndall is always ready to ridicule the ancient philosophers even though many leading scientists have gained acclaim by rehashing their ideas. Increasingly, geologists seem to take for granted that all ancient races were equally barbaric. But not all contemporary scientists agree. Some take the opposite view. For instance the German-born language scholar Max Müller says, 'When we investigate the past, hieroglyphic records only show part of the picture of what man was. The more closely we study him, even as we explore the distant past, we perceive an intellect that belonged to him from the very beginning and it seems impossible that humanity could have emerged merely from brute animals.'

The study of first causes is considered unscientific. Consequently, scientists concentrate on the study of the physical effects of those first causes. The scientific method is inextricably linked to the physical world. When the limits of the physical world are reached, the limits of scientific inquiry are also reached. Scientists are like hamsters on a wheel. They are destined to turn the same problems of physical matter over and over again. Science is immensely powerful and it is not for the mere man in the street to question it. But to question an individual scientist is another thing entirely. No scientist would take a layman's word for the geographical layout of the dark side of the moon. But suppose a lunar accident sent an inhabitant of the moon to earth. Suppose he arrived at the door of the British astronomer James Carpenter. If Carpenter failed to investigate, that would be a dereliction of duty.

It is inexcusable for any scientist to refuse to investigate a new phenomenon. It doesn't matter whether it is a man from the moon or a ghost manifested by the American mediums William and Horatio Eddy.

It is claimed that ancient scholars understood the inner and outer natures of man. They may have followed Plato's philosophical method of inquiry or the scientific approach of Aristotle. How they came to their understanding doesn't really matter. Geologists have been quick to conclude from the fossil record that early man was primitive. But evidence emerges almost daily that the ancient scholars were as sophisticated as is often claimed.

They divided periods of human existence into cycles. They believed that mankind reached a pinnacle of civilization in each cycle and then declined into barbarism again. Ancient monuments reveal the peaks of civilization reached by mankind. Those impressive monuments now lost can be read about in the works of the Greek historian Herodotus. Even in his time many pyramids and world famous temples were already in ruins. He described them as important witnesses to the achievements of earlier civilizations. He stops short of claiming the existence of the Minotaur but has left a basic description of the labyrinth in the city of Knossos[5] where the remains of king-initiates are hidden.

Histories of Egypt's Ptolemaic era[6] convey a sense of how refined past civilizations became. That said, the arts and sciences were acknowledged even then to be in decline and many skills in the arts had already been lost. The French archeologist Auguste

Mariette excavated exquisite wooden statues from the foot of the pyramids. These proved that the Egyptians created art as refined as the Greeks long before the first Egyptian dynasties. The American author Bayard Taylor describes the statues as being unsurpassed with beautiful heads, eyes of precious stones and copper eyelids.These statues are much older and yet finer than the artifacts collected by the Prussian Egyptologist Karl Lepsius, the English collector Henry Abbot and the British Museum.[7] This provides tangible proof of the Hermetic idea that civilization develops and declines in cycles.

The pioneering German archeologist Heinrich Schliemann conducted excavations on the Biga Peninsula in Turkey, formerly known as the Troad.[8] Here he uncovered evidence of the same development from barbarism to civilization and from civilization back to barbarism. If the ancients were able to create superior works of art using skills that are now lost, might they have been equally advanced in other fields including human psychology? Until there is evidence to the contrary, this theory seems as reasonable as any.

It's generally accepted that human knowledge is still in its infancy. Perhaps the present cycle of humanity began comparatively recently. The Chaldeans[9] migrated into Mesopotamia sometime between 940 and 860 BC. According to their philosophy, cycles of human development do not involve the whole of mankind at one and the same time. The American scientist John Draper supports this view when he observes that man's development doesn't occur uniformly around the world or involve the entire population. He cites the example of nomadic Native American tribes, describing them as only now emerging from the Stone Age. This is just another example of a modern scientist drawing the same conclusions as the ancients.

A Kabbalist is a student of Kabbalah,[10] the esoteric school of Judaism. Any Kabbalist familiar with Pythagoras' mathematical theories can show that Plato's metaphysics was based on strict mathematical principles. In his book *The Magicon*,[11] published in New York in 1869, Dr Paulus says that true or higher mathematics is connected to all higher sciences whereas common or everyday mathematics is misleading and illusory. This everyday math seems foolproof precisely because it is limited to the everyday. Aristotle's approach to scientific inquiry was based on the study of things that exist or happen in the world. From these examples, he aimed to derive knowledge of universal principles. By contrast, Plato began by considering universal principles or forms. From these universal principles, he aimed to understand particular examples of these principles as they existed in the world. Scientists adopt Aristotle's approach and reject Plato's on the basis that it is not robust. John Draper complains that visionary mystics like the Greek philosophers Ammonius Saccas and Plotinus have overshadowed the strict mathematicians of the old Musaeum of Alexandria.[12] But Draper forgets that geometry is the only science that proceeds from universals to particulars and it is precisely this method that was used by Plato. Science cannot fail as long as it confines itself to studying physical conditions using Aristotle's approach. But the universe is infinite whereas material science is limited and can only go round and round in circles. Egyptian priests taught Pythagoras the cosmological theory of numerals, the only theory that can reconcile the two units of matter and spirit and equate them mathematically.

Esoteric mathematics explains the origin of the universe, describing the radiation[13] of spiritual material from God and the cyclical nature of these emanations.[14] Physical beings have their origin in the higher spiritual plane which degrades to create the material world. They undergo a journey of evolution until they reach a turning point and are reabsorbed once more into the infinite.

Like everything else in the world, human understanding of physiology evolves cyclically. Just as it seems in its infancy now, it may be proven one day to have been at its most advanced many years before Pythagoras.

The Phoenician proto-philosopher Mochus the Sidonian taught anatomy long before Pythagoras lived. Mochus' disciples and descendants conveyed his sacred wisdom to Pythagoras. Pythagoras was a pure philosopher, someone deeply familiar with nature's fundamental mysteries, and committed to freeing the human soul to realize its full potential. For these achievements, he must always be remembered.

Strict secrecy surrounded the ancient sciences as they were passed down. This is why the ancient philosophies are undervalued in modern times. The Jewish philosopher Philo Judaeus and even Plato have been accused of inconsistencies but a clear pattern lies beneath the metaphysical contradictions of a work like Plato's dialogue *Timaeus*.[15] Have classicists ever read Plato perceptively enough? This is the question begged by the work of authors including the German classicist Johann Gottfried Stallbaum, the German philosopher Friedrich Schleiermacher, the Italian philosopher Marsilio Ficino, the English translator Thomas Taylor, the German philologists Ludwig Heindorf and Philipp Buttmann and the English classicists Floyer Sydenham and George Burges. Plato's hidden allusions to esoteric truths have clearly escaped these authors entirely. In response they suggest that difficult passages were really meant to be worded in a different way. They then have the audacity to change the text to suit their interpretation. There is a line in a poem about Orpheus which reads: 'Of the song, the order of the sixth race close.' This line can only be interpreted as a reference to the sixth root race (the theory of root races will be explained in a future volume).

But in his book *The Works of Plato* George Burges says the line was evidently taken from a cosmogony where mankind was thought to have been created last. If Burges is going to edit another author's works, he should at least understand the author's intention.

Contemporary scholars generally believe that the ancient philosophers had no knowledge of modern science. They even question whether they understood the basic scientific principle that nothing comes from nothing. If the ancients had grasped the concept that matter is indestructible, scholars suggest they did so through intuition rather than by reference to strict scientific principles.

The opposite is true. When these philosophers speculated on the nature of matter, their work was open to public criticism. But their teachings on spiritual questions were profoundly esoteric. They went to great lengths to conceal their views on the relationship between matter and spirit because they had sworn themselves to secrecy.

Scientists and theologians reject metempsychosis (the transmigration or re-birth of the soul after death) but it is a compelling theory if it is regarded in relation to the indestructibility of matter and the principle of the immortality of spirit. Before metempsychosis is dismissed, it should be understood from the standpoint of the ancients. Understanding eternity is not the province of religious superstition or materialist science. Only Pythagoras' esoteric mathematics can describe the harmony and mathematical similarity of spiritual and physical evolution. Pythagoras based his system of esoteric mathematics on the sacred poetic meters of the Hindu Vedas.[16] The German Sanskrit scholar

Martin Haug translated the previously unknown Aitareya Brahmana[17] of the Rigveda.[18] This translation reveals the correspondence between the Pythagorean and Brahmanical systems. In both systems, numbers are the source of esoteric significance. In the Pythagorean system esoteric significance is derived from the relationship between every number and everything intelligible to the human mind. In the Brahmanical system significance is derived from the number of syllables in each verse in the mantras. Plato, follower of Pythagoras, realized the esoteric significance derived from numbers to the extent that he claimed the demiurge[19] (the maker or creator of the world) used the geometric figure of the dodecahedron to construct the universe. Some numbers were particularly significant, for instance four was regarded as sacred by Pythagoreans. (The dodecahedron has twelve faces which is three times four.) Four is the perfect square with four perfectly equal sides. It expresses, geometrically, moral justice and divine fairness and impartiality. The perfect square expresses the power and harmony of physical and spiritual nature. Four in the form of the tetraktys[20] (a triangular figure of ten points arranged in four rows) constituted the ancient mystics' most solemn oath. It was used in place of the name of God because it was forbidden to speak God's name directly.

If the Pythagorean theory of metempsychosis were set alongside the modern theory of evolution, it would provide the missing links in evolution's chain. But no modern scientist will waste time exploring the ideas of the ancients. Scientists don't accept that the ancients knew the earth went round the sun in spite of proof to the contrary. Christian apologists like the Venerable Bede, Augustine of Canterbury and Lactantius discredited the knowledge of pre-Christian theologists. But the study of language and the study of Sanskrit literature have restored those theologists' reputations. For instance, the Vedas provide proof that Hindu sages and scholars understood the physical universe. As long ago as 2000 BC, they knew that the earth was round and orbited the sun. Consequently both Pythagoras and Plato were well aware of these facts - Pythagoras obtained this knowledge in India (or from people who had traveled there) and Plato faithfully echoed Pythagoras' teachings. Two passages from the Aitareya Brahmana are particularly significant:

The sacred text of the Serpent Mantra[21] declares that this was the mantra used by Sarpa-Rajni, the queen of the serpents. The earth is the queen of the serpents because the earth is the mother and queen of all that moves. In the beginning she (the earth) was one head (round), without hair (bald), i.e without vegetation. She then became aware of the mantra that gives those who know it the power to assume any form. She chanted the mantra i.e sacrificed to the gods and as a result her appearance changed. She became variegated, producing any form she liked, changing one form into another. The mantra begins with the words 'ayam gauh pris'nir akramit.'

It describes the earth in the shape of a round, bald head. The head was soft at first and solidified only when the god Vāyu, the lord of the air, breathed on it. This strongly suggests that the authors of the Vedas knew that the earth was round. It also suggests they knew the earth was molten at first and gradually cooled with time. At least 2,000 years before Christ, the Hindus understood that the sun stands at the center of the solar system. The evidence for this claim is as follows:

In the second passage of the Aitareya Brahmana, the hotar (Vedic priest) is taught how the shastras, or sacred texts, should be repeated and how sunrise and sunset should be explained. The text reads, 'Agnishtoma[22] is the god who burns. The sun never sets or rises. When people think the sun is setting they are mistaken. When the sun arrives at the end of the day it creates two opposite effects. It brings night to what is below and day to what is on the other side. When people think the sun rises in the morning they are also mistaken. At the end of the night, the sun, again, creates two opposite effects making day to what is below and night to what is on the other side. In fact the sun never sets nor does it set for him who has such knowledge. . .'

The passage is conclusive. The translator Martin Haug even comments, 'This text explains that the appearance of sunrise and sunset is an illusion. Its author expresses the idea that the sun always stays in a fixed position.'

In one of the Vedas' earliest nivids, or group of mantras, the Hindu sage Kutsa explains the allegorical story of how the planets were set in motion. In the story, the fertility goddess Anahita (called Anaitis by the Romans and Nana by the Persians) represents the earth and is sentenced to revolve around the sun. The sattras, or sacrificial sessions, prove without doubt that the Hindus had considerable knowledge of astronomy as early as 1700 or 1900 BC. The sattras consisted of set periods designated for making offerings to the gods. They lasted one year, following the earth's yearly rotation around the sun. Haug says the sattras were divided into two parts each consisting of six months with thirty days in each month. The Vishuvan, or equinox, cut the whole sattras into two halves. Haug places the composition of the bulk of the Brahmana texts in the period 1400 to 1200 BC. But he believes the oldest may have been created at the very beginning of Vedic literature, as long ago as 2400 to 2000 BC. According to Haug, the Vedas may even be as old as the sacred literature of China. The Chinese *Book of History* or *Shu-King*[23] and the sacrificial songs of the *Book of Odes* or *Shi-King*[24] have both been dated as early as 2200 BC. In light of this, philologists may have to admit that the ancient Hindus had greater knowledge of astronomy than modern science.

There is evidence to suggest that astronomical calculations were made just as accurately by the Chaldeans as they are now. For example, Julius Caesar ordered the Roman calendar to be revised because it no longer corresponded with the seasons. (Summer had merged into the autumn months and the autumn into midwinter.) The Greek astronomer Sosigenes corrected the calendar by putting the 25th of March back by 90 days until it corresponded again with the spring equinox. He also fixed the number of days in each month. Sosigenes' calendar is the one still in use today.

In America, the Aztec calendar allotted an equal number of days and weeks to each month. The Aztecs' astronomical calculations were so accurate that, to this day, no errors have been found in their computations. Compare this with the Europeans who landed in Mexico in 1519 - their Julian calendar was eleven days ahead of the actual time.

Martin Haug's scholarship and his translations of Vedic literature make it possible to corroborate the claims of the Hermetic philosophers. For example, it can easily be proved that the Iranian prophet Zoroaster lived an immensely long time ago. The texts of the Brahmanas[25] (which Haug estimates to have been written 4,000 years ago) describe the religious war between the ancient Hindus living in the pre-Vedic period and the Iranians. The texts describe at length the battles between the Devas (or devils) representing the Hindus and the Asuras representing the Iranians. Since Zoroaster was the first to describe the Hindus as Devas, he must have lived some time before the Brahmanas were written. This raises the question, how old was the religious war they describe?

Haug suggests that the battle felt as old to the authors of the

Brahmanas as the legend of King Arthur did to English writers in the 19th Century.

The esoteric principle of metempsychosis was taught by the Brahmin[26] priests, Buddhists and later the Pythagoreans. Every worthwhile philosopher believed in the principle whether he expressed it or not. Believers included the Greek scholar Origen, the Christian theologian Clement of Alexandria, the Greek bishop Synesius and the Christian philosopher Calcidius. The Gnostics[27] were also believers, described as knowledgeable and enlightened men by the English historian Edward Gibbon in his *Decline and Fall of the Roman Empire*. Socrates held the same beliefs about metempsychosis as Pythagoras and both were put to death as a consequence of their philosophical views. The behavior of the mob never changes. Materialism has been and always will be blind to spiritual truths. Socrates and Pythagoras shared with the Hindus the belief that God animated every particle in the universe with a spark of his own divine spirit. They taught that men have two separate and different souls. One of these souls is perishable - the astral soul. The other is incorruptible and immortal - the augoeides or spark of the divine. They taught that the mortal or astral soul disintegrates as it moves through the after death states and it becomes purer each time it is reconstituted in a new physical incarnation. The astral body is intangible and invisible to our physical senses but it is still part of the material world - its material is simply too fine to detect. For political reasons, Aristotle remained silent about certain areas of esoteric thought but he was clear about his views on metempsychosis. He believed that human souls emanate from the divine and ultimately return to it. The founder of Stoicism, Zeno of Citium, taught that there were two essential qualities in nature. The active quality was male. The passive quality was female. The male was pure divine spirit. The female was inert until united with the male. The divine spirit acting on inert matter produced fire, water, earth and air. Zeno taught that it is the male principle that animates all nature. The Stoics, like the Hindus, believed that the human soul is ultimately reabsorbed by the divine. Saint Justin Martyr believed that human souls were emanations from God and Justin's disciple, Tatian the Assyrian, declared that 'man was as immortal as God himself.'

Every scholar capable of reading Genesis in the original Hebrew will notice a mistranslation in this deeply significant verse: 'And to all the beasts of the earth and all the birds in the sky and all the creatures that move along the ground - everything that has the breath of life in it . . .' The mistranslation is 'everything that has the breath of life in it' which should read instead 'I give a living soul.'

Translators repeated this error throughout the Bible. The Scottish philosopher William Drummond demonstrates that translators even changed the spelling of the name of God. The name of God written as 'El' should in fact read 'Al' - אל in the original Hebrew. According to the religious historian Godfrey Higgins the word 'El' actually means the god Mithra, the sun, the preserver and savior. In his book *The Jewish Oedipus (Oedipus Judaicus)*, Drummond maintains that 'Beth-El' means the House of the Sun and not the House of God. 'El, in the composition of these Canaanite names, does not signify Deus, but Sol.' In this way, theology has distorted ancient theosophy and modern science has distorted the scientific knowledge of the ancients.

Modern science is unable to appreciate the philosophical principle that all matter is animated by a spark of the divine. Its investigations, however accurate, lead nowhere. No branch of science can demonstrate the beginning or the end of things. Instead of tracing phenomena from their primal source, it works in reverse.

It teaches that everything is evolved from the primitive upwards. It starts with the most primitive thing and follows its development as it evolves through the natural world. As soon as this chain of development breaks and the thread is lost, modern science is stymied and can go no further. This was not the case for Plato and his students. In Platonic thought the material is simply a concrete manifestation of a higher and pre-existing abstract image. The immortal soul has its beginning in the divine properties of numbers. The body has its beginning in the divine properties of geometry. The beginning of body and soul is the reflection of the archeus[28] or *anima mundi* (world soul). It arises spontaneously, emanates from the center and suffuses the whole body.

These observations forced the physicist John Tyndall to acknowledge the limitations of modern science even when it comes to understanding the physical world. In Tyndall's view, the force which first arranged atoms into matter is incomprehensible and unobservable by material science. The complexity of the origin of matter is so great that the most powerful scientific imagination is bewildered, and scientific observation can shed no light on the problem. It is enough to make scientists doubt the power of observation itself and to question whether any human mind can understand the ultimate structure of nature and the universe.

There is a fundamental geometric figure in the Kabbalah, which esoteric tradition maintains was given by God to Moses on Mount Sinai. This figure contains the key to understanding the origins of the universe and it contains in itself all other figures. Anyone who can master the use of the key has no need for scientific speculation. No scientific method can compare with the clarity of spiritual perception.

For someone unfamiliar with esoteric geometry, there is still a better alternative to modern science. Psychometry is the ability to receive impressions from an object held in the hand or against the forehead. A child psychometer[29] can give a better indication of the true origins of a grain or a crystal, for example, than any scientific instrument.

Tyndall calls Darwin a 'soaring speculator.' But there may be more truth in Darwin's bold hypothesis of pangenesis[30] than in Tyndall's work where imagination is hampered by too much cautious rationality. In pangenesis, a microscopic germ contains within itself a world of other lesser germs. In some ways the theory suggests progression to the infinite, going beyond the material world and beginning to address the spiritual.

Accepting Darwin's theory of pangenesis is like standing in front of an open door. We have the choice to stay inside or cross the threshold to the limitless, the incomprehensible, to God. The human soul can only vaguely anticipate eternity and there are no words on earth to express the unfathomable infinite. But in timeless eternity our spirit will evolve to realize what it now only barely perceives.

The same cannot be said for the theory promoted by the English biologist Thomas Huxley in his pamphlet *On the Physical Basis of Life*. In spite of opposition from fellow scientists, he proposes the existence of a universal protoplasm and suggests that all life springs from its cells. He claims these cells are the same in a living man, a lamb chop, a stinging nettle and a lobster. He shuts the spark of life inside the cell of the protoplasm and shuts out the influence of the divine. He then closes the door against any further speculation. He uses laws and facts to challenge every question according to the philosophical principle of necessity. He then casts doubt on the principle itself calling it 'an empty shadow of my own imagination.'

Huxley says the essential truths of spiritualism lie beyond the reach of scientific inquiry. On the contrary, it could be said that they are better subjects for scientific study than Huxley's protoplasm. They provide concrete evidence for the existence of spirit whereas the protoplasmic cells offer no evidence of being the source or foundation of life as Huxley would like us to believe.

The ancient Kabbalists accepted no hypothesis until it could be proven by controlled experiment.

But depending too much on physical proof led to the growth of materialism and the decline of spirituality and faith. This was true in Aristotle's day. The commandment from the oracle at Delphi[31] to 'know thyself' was still part of Grecian thought. Some scholars still believed that to know what man is, it is necessary to know what man was. But in spite of this, materialism had already begun to undermine faith. Even the Mysteries, the ancient rituals of the Egyptians, had degenerated into speculation and fraud. Only a few true adepts and initiates remained - the descendants of displaced peoples from earlier invasions of ancient Egypt.

This was the time predicted by the mystic Hermes Trismegistus in his dialogue *Asclepius* when secular outsiders would accuse the Egyptians of devil worship and nothing but the hieroglyphics on Egyptian monuments would survive - as indecipherable enigmas. The scribes and interpreters of the hieroglyphics became refugees. They were afraid that their sacred mysteries would be violated so they sought asylum among the Essenes[32] and buried their esoteric knowledge deeper than ever. Alexander the Great's invasion of Egypt swept away every last trace of the ancient religion. Even though Aristotle himself had been instructed in the secret science of the Egyptians, he knew hardly anything of their profound achievements in esoteric studies.

Both the ancient Egyptian philosophers of the Psammetic Dynasty[33] and contemporary scientists can be said to 'lift the veil of Isis' since Isis is merely a metaphor for nature. But modern science only studies nature's physical aspects. Nature's soul escapes scrutiny and Isis gives nothing away. Anatomists lift layers of muscles and nerves with a scalpel but detect no sign of a spirit. They then claim that man has no soul. They are as blind to the truth as the student who researches the strict letter of the Kabbalah and decides it has no spirit. The surgeon must use different eyes to perceive the real man who once inhabited the body lying on the dissecting table. In the same way, the esoteric truth contained in ancient papyri will only be revealed to someone with intuition. If reason is the eye of the mind, intuition is the eye of the soul.

Science acknowledges a supreme power or universal principle but not a supreme being or personal god. But it is reasonable to ask if there is, in fact, any difference between the two. The power and the being are one and the same. People find it hard to imagine an intelligent supreme power without also associating it with the idea of an intelligent being. The public can never be expected to imagine the omnipotence of god without projecting their own personality onto it. But Kabbalists have never regarded the manifesting God or invisible Ein Sof[34] as anything other than a power.

It seems the ancients anticipated positivism,[35] or the modern scientific method, long before it was developed. According to Hermetic adepts, common sense dictates that the universe cannot be the product of mere chance. To claim as much would be as absurd as saying that a monkey playing with geometric shapes could come up with Euclid's geometric formulas.

Very few Christians understand Jewish theology. The Talmud[36] is immensely difficult to comprehend even for most Jews. The Hebrew scholars who do understand it are not completely certain of their knowledge. They understand even less about the books of the Kabbalah because contemporary Christian scholarship has obscured their esoteric truths. Even less is known for certain about the oriental Kabbalah. There are very few adepts of the oriental Kabbalah and they are the heirs of the Chaldean sages who first discovered 'the starry truths which shone on the great heaven (shemaia) of Chaldean lore.' They have solved the problem of the absolute and are now resting after their enormous efforts. They cannot know more than it is possible for a mortal to know and no one, not even these adepts, can cross into the domain of divinity itself. Travelers have met them on the shores of the Ganges, in the silent ruins of Thebes and in the mysterious deserted chambers of Luxor. They have been glimpsed in masonic halls, the walls of which are decorated with strange signs indecipherable to the casual onlooker. These adepts have been seen there but rarely recognized as such. History records that they were present in the salons of the European aristocracy. They have been encountered in the Sahara and in the caves of Elephanta Island in Mumbai harbor. They can be found everywhere but they only make themselves known to people who have devoted their lives unwaveringly to selfless study.

The medieval Jewish philosopher Maimonides was a great Torah scholar. At one time idolized, he was later treated as a heretic. According to Maimonides, the occult meaning of the Talmud becomes more awe-inspiring the more absurd and meaningless its text appears to be. He has successfully demonstrated that Chaldean magic - the science of Moses and other ancient magicians - was based on long-lost knowledge of the natural sciences. Adepts had a deep understanding of the vegetable, animal and mineral kingdoms. They were experts in occult chemistry and physics. They were psychologists as well as physiologists. It is no wonder, then, that they could perform feats that would seem supernatural even in this day and age.

It is a mistake to dismiss magic and occult science as deception. To discredit it in this way is like saying one half of humanity has been deceiving the other. It is the same as saying that the human race is composed only of con men and gullible fools. Historically, magic has been practiced in every country without exception. When was it forgotten?

The Vedas and the older laws of the Chaldean god Manu are the oldest documents in existence. They contain many magical rites practiced and permitted by the Hindu priests or Brahmins. The clergy of Tibet, Japan and China teach the same lessons today that were taught by the earliest Chaldeans. These clergy prove what they teach - the practice of moral and physical purity supports the development of self-knowledge. These practices allow man to control his own immortal spirit which gives him power over the elementary spirits inferior to himself. There is magic in the West just as old as the magic of the East. The Druids of Great Britain practiced ancient magic in deep caves, and the Roman philosopher Pliny writes extensively in his book *Natural History (Naturalis Historia)* about the wisdom of Celtic leaders.

The Semothees, or Gallic Druids, taught the physical as well as the spiritual sciences. They taught the secrets of the universe, the motion of celestial bodies, the formation of the earth and the immortality of the soul. Their initiates assembled at midnight in sacred groves to learn what mankind once was and what he will become. They needed no artificial illumination or gas to light their temples because the moon goddess illuminated their heads crowned with oak leaves. And the white robed figures of the Druid priests knew how to converse with the queen of the sky.

Modern materialism obscures the spirituality of the Druids but for students of the occult, their knowledge is still evergreen and full of sacred truth. Magic is as old as mankind. Determining when magic first appeared is as impossible as determining when the first man was born. A writer may try to link the appearance of magic in a certain country with a historical figure. But further research proves the writer wrong. Some scholars thought the Scandinavian priest and monarch Odin started the practice of magic in 70 BC but the mysterious rites of the priestesses known as voilers or valas[37] originated much earlier than this. Modern authors tried to prove that Zoroaster was the founder of magic because he founded the Magian religion, Zoroastrianism. Ammianus Marcellinus, Arnobius, Pliny and other ancient historians proved that he was merely a reformer of the magic practiced by the Chaldeans and the Egyptians.

According to the greatest teachers of divinity, all ancient books were written symbolically in a language only the initiated could understand. The biography of the Greek philosopher Apollonius of Tyana is a good example. It encompasses the whole of the Hermetic tradition as every Kabbalist knows. In many respects, it is a counterpart to the stories of King Solomon. Like the tales of King Solomon, it reads like a fairy story but gives facts and historical events as part of the narrative. It presents the travels of Apollonius to India as an allegory of the trials of an initiate. Apollonius has long discussions with the Brahmins, receives their wisdom and converses with his student Menippus. If these passages were interpreted correctly they would reveal esoteric knowledge. Many of the secret teachings of Hermeticism are explained symbolically in Apollonius' visit to Greece and his conversations with the Athenian king Hiarchas and the oracle of Amphiaraus.[38] If these writings were properly understood they would reveal some of the most important secrets of nature. The French occult author Eliphas Levi points out the resemblance between Hiarchas and

Hiram, the architect who built Solomon's temple and gave to Solomon the cedars of Lebanon and the gold of Ophir. Today, members of masonic lodges enact a ritual to avenge Hiram's death but it's doubtful whether even the Grand Lecturers, Freemasonry's senior officiates, really understand who Hiram was.

Put aside the purely metaphysical teachings of the Kabbalah for a moment. A study of physical occultism, especially the occult manufacture of medicines, could benefit modern chemistry and medicine. Commenting on the scientific writings of the Saracens, John Draper said, 'Sometimes we encounter ideas that we thought originated in our own times.' This remark applies even more to the secret theoretical writings of the ancients. Modern medicine has made great advances in anatomy, physiology, pathology and the development of medicines but it is diminished by its narrowness of spirit, rigid materialism and dogmatism. One school of medicine ignores whatever is developed by another and all of them ignore every transcendent idea of man or nature suggested by mesmerism or the study of the brain. They reject every idea that doesn't conform to the requirements of materialism. Physicians from these competing schools of medicine would have to cooperate before all the latest medical knowledge could be assembled in one place. All too often, after the best doctors have failed to help a patient, a mesmerist or healing medium will produce a cure. Medical literature from the time of Hippocrates to the time of Paracelsus and van Helmont, contains a vast number of physiological and psychological healing methods that modern physicians ignore. Even in the field of surgery, modern practitioners are unable to equal the skill of the ancient Egyptians. In Paris, leading surgeons studied the sophisticated bandaging of Egyptian mummies. Even though they had the examples in front of them, they were unable to replicate them with the same degree of accuracy.

The Abbott Egyptological Collection in New York contains many examples of ancient skill in various handicrafts, for example lace making. Some pieces in the collection, like artificial hair and gold ornaments of different kinds, reveal humanity's continuing interest in personal appearance. When the *New York Tribune* reviewed the Ebers papyrus, it reported, 'There is nothing new under the sun . . . Chapters 65, 66, 79 and 89 include hair restorers, hair dyes, pain killers and flea powders, proving that these items were available 3,400 years ago.'

John Draper questions how many so-called modern discoveries were in reality first discovered by the ancients. His book *History of the Conflict Between Religion and Science* gives many examples to prove his point (and is a better book than the title suggests). On page 13, he describes the ancient Greeks' admiration for the achievements of much earlier scientist-philosophers. In Babylon, the Chaldeans held a record of astronomical observations stretching back 1,903 years. These records were sent by the Greek historian Callisthenes to Aristotle. The Egyptian astronomer Ptolemy had a Babylonian record of eclipses going back to 747 BC. Draper comments, 'These ancient astronomical records are the result of sustained close observation of the heavens. The Babylonians' calculation of the tropical year was accurate to within 25 seconds. They estimated the sidereal year to be just two minutes longer than it actually is. They had detected the steady change in the orientation of the axis of the earth's rotation, known as the precession of the equinoxes.[39] They understood the cause of eclipses and used the period of time called a saros[40] to predict their occurrence. The saros is more than 6,585 days in length and the Babylonians' calculations of it were only nineteen and a half minutes out.

'These facts prove that astronomy was patiently and skilfully developed in Mesopotamia. With only basic astronomical instruments, astronomy reached an advanced level. The Mesopotamians had catalogued the stars, divided the zodiac into twelve signs and divided day and night into twelve hours each. According to Aristotle, the Mesopotamians had observed for a long time how stars were obscured by the moon. They had understood the structure of the solar system and knew the order of the planets. They constructed sundials, clepsydras (water clocks) and astrolabes (astronomical calculators).'

Draper says a world of eternal truths lies within the world of fleeting delusions. He says, 'That world of truth is not revealed by myths and superstitions from man's earliest time on earth. It cannot be discovered in the dreams of mystics who thought they were inspired. It is only discoverable through investigations of geometry and the practical study of nature.'

Draper makes a good point. He touches on a profound truth but he doesn't share the whole truth because he doesn't know it. He is unfamiliar with the knowledge imparted during the ancient Egyptian rites of the Mysteries. No one since the Egyptians has equaled their ability in geometry as demonstrated in the construction of the Pyramids and other great monuments. Equally, no one has ever rivaled the Egyptians in the practical investigation of nature.

Their skill as investigators is demonstrated by their use of symbols. Every one of these symbols embodies an idea combining knowledge of the divine with the earthly and physical. Divine knowledge is derived from earthly knowledge by analogy according to the Hermetic formula: 'as below, so it is above.' Egyptian symbols show great knowledge of natural science and a practical understanding of the forces at work in the cosmos.

More is known for certain about the study of esoteric

geometry than ever before. For today's students, there are teachers like the American Egyptologist George Felt, a man who may one day be acknowledged as the world's leading geometer. He has worked with mathematics first devised by the ancient Egyptians to produce the following results. He has discovered the fundamental geometric formula, which provides the key to all elementary geometry including planes and solids. He has produced a geometrical formula of proportion, verifying it in the remains of ancient architecture and sculpture, and showing that the original designs of these structures were based on it precisely. He has established that the Egyptians used this formula as the basis of all their astronomical calculations (on which they founded the majority of their religious symbolism). He has found traces of it in all ancient Greek art and architecture. He has concluded that it must have originated in Jewish sacred records because so many instances of it are found there. He has ascertained that the whole system of calculation was discovered by the Egyptians after tens of thousands of years of research into the laws of nature. He has described it as the science of the universe. This formula also enabled him to solve problems in physiology which had previously been insurmountable. It made the development of a masonic philosophy possible and demonstrates that Freemasonry is the first and last science and religion. In addition, he used visual demonstrations to prove a further point. He shows that the figures placed on temples by Egyptian sculptors and architects were not inspired by their own imaginations. Instead they were based on the invisible beings of the air and other elements, which Felt claims he could make visible, just as the Egyptians had, using chemical and Kabbalistic processes.

In his book *Introduction to Mythology Through Natural History*, the German physicist Johann Schweigger demonstrates that the symbols of all mythologies are science-based. Recent advances have enabled experts to trace the relationship between each divine myth and some aspect of electromagnetism with great accuracy. Along with Schweigger, those experts include the physician Joseph Ennemoser and the author C.C. Bart in Germany, Baron Jules du Potet and the mesmerist Antonio Regazzoni in France and Italy respectively. One example is the Idaeic finger, mentioned in references to the Greek island Samothrace around 600 BC. This artifact was an iron object attracted and repelled by magnetic forces. It was important in the magic art of healing and was used to treat organs, restoring their normal function.

C.C. Bart goes deeper than Schweigger into the significance of the old myths. He studies the subject from both spiritual and physical viewpoints. He talks at length about the Phrygian Dactyls,[41] a mythical race of male beings who were metalworkers. He describes them as 'magicians and exorcists of sickness.' He also refers to the Cabeirian theurgists, metalworking gods who practiced white magic. He says, 'It is true that the Dactyls are closely associated with magnetism but not necessarily solely with magnets. A deeper understanding of magnetism as a whole makes it possible to see how the Dactyls astonished people with healing miracles. In addition to healing, ancient priests practiced many other things - working the land, moral development, the advancement of art and science and occult practices. The Cabeirians followed similar practices and who's to say they weren't guided by the spirits of nature?' Schweigger shares the same opinion and shows that the effects of theurgy[42] were produced by magnetic forces 'guided by spirits.'

Although they appeared to worship many gods, ancients of the educated class worshiped only one. And this was many ages before Moses received the Commandment 'Thou shalt have no other gods but me.' The Ebers Papyrus confirms this as fact in the following words translated from the first four lines of Plate I. 'I came from the city of Heliopolis[43] with the priests of Het aat, the lords of protection, the masters of eternity and salvation. I came from the town of Sais[44] with the mother-goddesses who granted me protection. The Lord of the Universe told me how to cure the gods of all deadly diseases.' The ancients called prominent men 'gods' but it would be a mistake to conclude from this that they were polytheistic. Christians make statues of their heroes but that doesn't mean they worship them as deities. It would be absurd for future generations to believe that Americans worshiped Washington simply because there are so many statues of him. Hermetic philosophy is obscured by mystery. For example the Comte de Volney, the French philosopher and orientalist, asserted that the ancients worshiped material symbols as divine in their own right. But in fact the symbols were only regarded as representing esoteric principles. The French professor Charles-François Dupuis made a similar mistake. After studying Hermetic philosophy for many years, he misinterpreted the symbol of the circle and consequently considered Hermeticism to be nothing more than astronomy. Writing in the magazine *Berliner Monatsschrift*,[45] the physician Johann Peter Eberhard dismisses magic out of hand. The same is true of many other German writers. They regard magic as nothing more than a fictional idea invented by Plato in the *Timaeus*. They have no knowledge of the Mysteries and are not as intuitive as a man like Jean-François Champollion. They have little chance of discovering the esoteric truth concealed behind the veil of Isis and known only to the initiated few.

Jean-François Champollion is universally admired as an expert Egyptologist. According to him, all the evidence suggests that the Egyptians worshiped only one god. He corroborates the accuracy of Hermes Trismegistus' writings, which are widely recognized as immensely ancient and esoterically significant. Joseph Ennemoser also says, 'Egypt was the center of learning for Herodotus, Thales, Parmenides, Empedocles, Orpheus and Pythagoras. They went there to learn about natural philosophy and theology.' It was here that Moses acquired his wisdom and Jesus spent the early years of his life.

Students of all nationalities were drawn to Egypt before the city of Alexandria was founded. Ennemoser goes on to say, 'How come so little is known of these Mysteries even though so many different people studied them at so many different times? So little is known because the initiated kept silent. The destruction of written records may be another cause.' The Roman historian Livy described books on natural philosophy found in the tomb of Numa Pompilius, the second king of Rome after Romulus. They were deliberately suppressed in case they revealed secret mysteries of the state religion. On the orders of the Senate they were burned in public.

Magic was considered a divine science that led to an involvement in the workings of divinity itself. In his treatise *The Special Laws*, Philo Judaeus says, 'It unveils the operations of nature and leads to the contemplation of celestial powers.' Later, magic was misused, degenerated into sorcery and was subsequently violently rejected. So magic should be considered in its original sense when every true religion was based on knowledge of the occult powers of nature. Magic was not originated by the priesthood in ancient Persia as is commonly believed but by the Magi[46] who took their name from it. The Zoroastrian priests or mobeds,[47] are still called 'Magoi' in Pehlvi,[48] the written form of the Middle Persian language. Magic first appeared in the world much earlier than is often believed. The Christian theologian John Cassian describes a magical treatise which was well known in the

4th and 5th Centuries. It was credited to Ham, the son of Noah. And Ham was thought to have received it from Jared, the fourth generation from Seth, the son of Adam.

Thermuthis, the daughter of the Pharaoh's wife Batria, rescued Moses from the Nile. Moses acquired his wisdom from Batria, who was herself an initiate. She was instrumental in turning him into a great prophet 'learned in all the wisdom of the Egyptians and mighty in words and deeds.' Saint Justin Martyr describes Joseph of Canaan receiving knowledge of magic from the high priests of Egypt, citing the Roman historian Pompeius Trogus as his source.

The ancients had greater knowledge of certain scientific disciplines than modern scientists. More than one scientist has reluctantly acknowledged this. The Scottish physician Anthony Todd Thomson edited the two-volume work, *The Occult Sciences (Des Sciences Occultes)*, by the French poet Eusèbe Salverte. Thomson says, 'Scientific knowledge was more advanced in earlier societies than modern scientists would like to admit but this knowledge was confined to the priesthood and hidden from ordinary people.' The German theologian Franz von Baader refers to the Kabbalah, saying, 'The Jews gave us not only our Savior but also our science.' This begs the question: 'Where did the Jews get their wisdom?'

The Greek scholar of the Alexandrian school of Platonists, Origen states that Moses shared the teachings of the Covenant with 70 elders gathered together on God's instruction. Besides the Covenant, he also communicated to them important secrets 'from the hidden depths of the law.' He told the elders to share these secrets only with people they thought deserved to know.

Saint Jerome identifies Jewish elders from the cities of Tiberias and Lydda as the only teachers of the mystical interpretation of Jewish law. Finally, Joseph Ennemoser asserts that the writings of the Christian theologian Dyonysius Areopagita were based substantially on the Jewish Kabbalah. This is hardly surprising since the Gnostics or early Christians were merely followers of the Jewish Essenes under a new name. In his book *Philosophy of History and Traditions (Philosophie der Geschichte oder über die Tradition)*, the philosopher Franz Joseph Molitor stresses the importance of the Kabbalah in particular. He says:

'The revolution of rationalism has destroyed everything positive leaving nothing behind but its own emptiness. Now is the time to refocus our attention on mystery as a source of insight. The Mysteries of ancient Israel also contain all the secrets of modern Israel. These Mysteries would reshape theology based on deep theosophical principles and provide a firm basis for all spiritual sciences. This would open a new path to the myths, mysteries and guiding principles of ancient nations. The wisdom of the school of the prophets is contained in these traditions. This ancient school was not founded by the prophet Samuel but only reopened by him. It aimed to lead scholars to wisdom and highest knowledge and reveal deeper mysteries to the most worthy. One of these mysteries was magic which had a double nature. There was divine magic and evil magic or the black art. These two kinds of magic are divisible into two again - active and seeing. In divine magic man attempts to place himself in sympathy with the world to learn its hidden secrets and perform good deeds. In evil magic he attempts to gain power over spirits in order to perform diabolical and unnatural acts.'

The Greek, Roman Catholic and Protestant churches reject every spiritual phenomenon that manifests through so-called mediums. It is not long since the Catholic and Protestant churches burned, hanged or murdered anyone who manifested spirits or other unexplained forces of nature. The Roman Catholic church is the most powerful of all. The Pope's hands are scarlet with the blood of countless innocent victims murdered on his authority. Catholicism is ready and eager to begin its tyranny again but the Church is prevented from doing so by the 19th-century spirit of progress and religious freedom. The Greco-Russian church is the most gentle and Christ-like, expressing simple blind faith. There has been no consensus between the Greek and Latin churches and the two went their separate ways centuries ago but the Roman church simply ignores these facts. Rome assumes authority over both the Greco-Russian church and all Protestants as well. John Draper says, 'The Church insists the state has no rights over anything in the Church's domain. It claims Protestantism is a mere rebellion and has no rights at all and even in Protestant communities the Catholic bishop has absolute spiritual authority.' The decrees of Rome have been ignored. Papal letters have been left unanswered. Invitations to ecumenical councils and excommunications have been laughingly dismissed. All this has made no difference to the behavior of the Roman Catholic church. Their persistence has only been matched by their insolence. The height of absurdity was reached in 1864 when Pope Pius IX excommunicated the Russian emperor. He cursed the emperor publicly as a 'schismatic cast out from the bosom of the Holy Mother Church.' But neither the emperor nor his ancestors had ever agreed to join the Roman Catholic church in the first place. Though Russia itself became a Christian country a thousand years ago, it had never submitted to the church of Rome. The Pope might as well claim authority over Tibetan Buddhists or the ghosts of the Hyksos people[49] of ancient Egypt.

For generations, spirits have possessed mediums in Russia as well as in other countries. The phenomenon of possession ignores religious and national differences and anyone can be possessed without warning whether they are a beggar or a king.

Not even the present 'Vice-God,' Pope Pius IX could avoid possession. For the past 50 years the Pope has been known to suffer from extraordinary fits. Inside the Vatican, they are called 'divine visions.' Outside, doctors call them epileptic seizures. Popular myth explains them away as the retribution of ghosts - the revenge of soldiers who died in uprisings against the papal army at Peruggia, Castelfidado and Mentana.

The lights burn blue: it is now dead midnight,
Cold fearful drops stand on my trembling flesh,
Methought the souls of all that I caused to be murdered
Came . . .
RICHARD III, SHAKESPEARE

Prince Alexander of Hohenlohe was himself a great medium, in recent times famous for his healing abilities. It's true to say that mediumship and healing are not confined to any particular era or country. They are part of the essential psychological attributes of man - the microcosmos.

For centuries, people have suffered from strange disorders that the Russian clergy and the general public attribute to demonic possession. These unfortunate sufferers gather at the entrances of cathedrals but don't go inside in case their inner demons fling them to the ground. These unwitting mediums are found in the cities of Voronezh, Kiev, Kazan and all other spiritual centers where the relics of saints are located. They congregate in groups around the gates and porches. When the clergy come to a certain part of the Mass, such as the sacraments or the beginning of the prayer and chorus 'ejey cherouvim,' these half-maniacs, half-mediums begin crowing like cockerels, barking, bellowing and braying, and finally collapse into convulsions. 'The devil inside them can't bear to hear the holy prayer' is the religious explanation. Some people feel pity for them, try to help them, and give them money. Occasionally a priest is asked to exorcise one of them. He conducts the ceremony motivated by love and charity or the payment of a twenty copeck silver coin. Some of these apparently afflicted people are fakes. But the genuine ones are mediums with the power of prophecy, sometimes seeing visions. These are never persecuted because of their condition. Why would the clergy persecute them or why would people denounce them as witches or wizards when they are victims who cannot help themselves? Any punishment should go instead to the demon controlling them. The worst that happens to these poor people is that they catch cold from the holy water thrown on them by a well-meaning priest. They are left to the will of God and taken care of with love and pity. A faith based on love and pity certainly deserves respect. It may be superstitious and blind but it can never be offensive to people or the true God. This is not true of the Roman Catholic faith. This is why their treatment of Hindus, Chinese spiritualists and Kabbalists should be questioned. The Protestant clergy should be similarly challenged with the exception of some of their most forward-thinking members. Why do they feel they have the right to damn Hindus, Chinese spiritualists and Kabbalists to the fires of hell?

No irreverence or disrespect is intended toward the divine power that created all things. Its perfection is beyond human comprehension. It is enough to know that it exists and is infinitely wise, enough to know that all living things contain a spark of its divine essence. It is the boundless and endless one. It is the great 'central spiritual sun.' Everything is surrounded by its visible light and the effects of its imperceivable will. It is the god of the ancient and modern seers. The nature of God can be studied only in the worlds manifested by God. God is revealed in the sacred geometry written across the cosmos. This is the only infallible gospel.

In his *Life of Theseus*, the Greek biographer Plutarch says that ancient geographers 'depict unknown regions of the world at the edges of their maps. They put notes in the margin saying nothing lies beyond but deserts full of wild beasts and impassable bogs.' Theologians and scientists do the same. Theologians fill the invisible world with angels or devils. Scientists claim that where matter is absent there is nothing at all.

Many skeptics belong to masonic lodges in spite of their materialist beliefs. The influence of the Brothers of the Rose Cross[50] continues in modern masonic initiations but in name only. Masons ritualize the murder of their Grand Master Hiram Abiff but they have no idea of the actual location of his grave which legend says is marked by a sprig of myrtle. They follow the rituals to the letter but fail to grasp the spirit. They are like an English or German chorus singing the Italian opera *Ernani*. In the fourth act they descend into the crypt of Charlemagne singing about conspiracy in words they don't understand. Similarly modern masons may descend in ritual 'through the nine arches into the bowels of the earth' where the name of God was hidden. Yet in actuality they will not find the 'delta of Enoch'[51] - the golden triangle inscribed with God's true name. The masons observe the Egyptian Rite of Memphis,[52] trying to assure themselves that they are becoming enlightened. As they progress in masonry they hope their minds are freed from superstition and tyranny. But these are all empty words if they neglect magic and turn their backs on spiritualism. Masons have good reasons to feel grief and resent their fate. Since Philip IV of France suppressed the Knights Templar, no one has appeared to rally them in spite of claims to the contrary. They are wanderers looking for the lost delta of Enoch. They have not found it because the pillars of the temple have been destroyed. They must 'wander in darkness' and 'travel in humility,' looking for the lost name of God. They keep looking but will never find it so long as they limit themselves to ritual. They are traveling in darkness. Only the descendants of Ahura Mazdā, the sole god of Zoroastrianism, can offer the light of truth. Only they can teach masons how to pronounce the name of God. Masons must be careful and keep their own counsel until the Rathbone Sisters of the World,[53] the female masons, can turn night into day or good into evil.

When the ancients divided human history into cycles, their calculations were based on scientific principles to some degree. This can be demonstrated by referring to one of the oldest theories of the earth's evolution.

In this theory, the earth is subject to a profound physical change at the end of each time period called a 'great year.' Each great year consists of six sars where each sar is 3,600 years, making 21,600 years in total. According to the Roman writer Censorinus, Aristotle called this year 'the greatest.' The polar and equatorial climates change places at the end of each great year. The polar climate moves slowly toward the equator. The tropical zone, with its rich vegetation and abundant animal life, replaces the frozen landscape at the polar caps.

This climatic change is marked by earthquakes and other natural disasters. The ocean beds shift, causing a semi-universal flood, like the flood of Noah, at the end of every decimillenium and about one neros[54] (10,000 years plus 600 years). This length of time was called 'the heliacal year' by the Greeks but no one outside the priesthood knew anything for certain about its nature or duration. The winter of this year was called 'the cataclysm' or 'the deluge.' The summer was called 'the ecpyrosis.'[55] Popular myth taught that the world was destroyed by fire during the ecpyrosis and by flood during the cataclysm. This information is found in the surviving astronomical writings of Censorinus and the Roman philosopher Seneca. Commentators were uncertain about the length of the heliacal year. Only Herodotus and the Greek poet Linus came close to the truth. Herodotus calculated its length at 10,800 years. Linus estimated it to be 13,984 years. According to the claims of Babylonian priests, the city of Babylon was founded by people saved from the Flood. This is corroborated by the Jewish historian Eupolemus. The city's founders were giants and they built the tower of Babel. They were great astrologers and received esoteric instruction from their fathers, 'the sons of God.' They in turn instructed the priests and left records in the temples of the periodic flooding that they had witnessed themselves. This is how the high priests gained knowledge of the great years. In the *Timaeus*, Plato recounts an old Egyptian priest's criticism of the Athenian statesman Solon. The priest berates him for not knowing that there were several floods like the Great Flood during the reign of the Greek king Ogyges. From this we can deduce that initiated priests the world over believed in the principle of the heliacal year.

It would take a life's work to understand the calculations of time used by the ancients. The Chaldeans used time periods called neroses. The Hindus referred to the Brhaspati[56] (the orbit of Jupiter) and other time periods called yugas[57] and kalpas.[58] A mathematician would be astounded by the number of codes used in Buddhist calculations and by the Hindus to calculate the time period they called the satya yuga. The Buddhists' largest unit of time is the maha kalpa, encompassing countless epochs before the Great Flood. The Buddhist system calculates a kalpa or grand period of 4,320,000,000 years using four yugas as follows:

1st. Satya yuga 1,728,000 years

2nd. Tretya yuga 1,296,000 years

3rd. Dvapa yuga 864,000 years

4th. Kali yuga 432,000 years

Total 4,320,000 years

Four yugas make one divine age or maha yuga. 71 maha yugas make 306,270,000 years. Add to this a period of change (called a sandhi) with the duration of a satya yuga (1,728,000 years) and that makes a manvantara,[59] a Hindu astronomical period of 308,448,000 years. 14 manvantaras make 4,318,272,000 years. Add to this a period of change of 1,728,000 years at the beginning of the kalpa to give a total for the kalpa or grand period of 4,320,000,000 years. Presently we are in the kali yuga of the 28th age of the seventh manvantara of 308,448,000 years. This means there is still plenty of time to go before we have reached even half of the total life span of the world.

These calculations are not based on fantasy. According to the English orientalist Samuel Davis, writing in the journal *Asiatic Researches*, they are based on practical astronomical calculations. Many scientists, including the sociologist Godfrey Higgins, have investigated these computations but been unable to determine which of them is the secret cycle. The German diplomat and scholar Christian von Bunsen has shown that the Egyptian priesthood kept all their calculations hidden. The question is complicated further because the calculations applied to the spiritual as well as the physical progress of humanity. The ancients perceived a close connection between the rhythms of nature and the fortunes of mankind. This is understandable given that they believed the planets constantly influenced the fate of humanity. Higgins suggested that the key to the secret cycle is the Hindu time period of 432,000 years (the kali yuga). But he failed in his attempt to decipher it. It is the most indecipherable of all because it relates to the mystery of creation. It was only recorded in symbols in the *Chaldean Book of Numbers*. The original of this book, if it still exists, is certainly not available in any library. This is because it was one of the oldest of the books that make up the *Hermetica*[60] and their total number is currently unknown.

Some Kabbalists, mathematicians and archeologists used the secret period of the great neros and the Hindu kalpas to estimate the length of the great year. They were unaware of the earlier computations that had put its length at 21,000 years. Instead they calculated it to be 24,000 years because they thought the last period of 6,000 years applied only to the renewal of the earth. Godfrey Higgins accounts for the discrepancy as follows. The ancients thought that the precession of the equinoxes passed through each zodiacal sign at a rate of 2,000 years rather than 2,160. This made the length of the great year four times 6,000 or 24,000 years. Their overestimation of the length of the cycle comes from this error. Just like an ordinary year, the great year must return to its starting point once it is over. So until the great year completes its immensely long cycle, it is impossible to verify that it has returned to the original point in the expected time. Higgins goes on to explain the calculation of 24,000 years as follows: take the angle that the ecliptic plane[61] makes with the equatorial plane[62] - until very recently it was thought that it decreased constantly. If this were true, the two planes would have coincided in about 6,000 years. In a further 6,000 years the sun would have appeared at the same angle in the southern hemisphere as it does now in the northern hemisphere. In a further 6,000 years the two planes would coincide again. In another 6,000 years the sun would appear in the northern hemisphere as it does now. A total period would have passed of about 24,000 to 25,000 years in all. When the sun arrived at the equator, the period of 6,000 years would end and the world would be destroyed by fire. When the sun arrived at its farthest point in the southern hemisphere, the world would be destroyed by water. Either way, the world would be destroyed at the end of every 6,000 years or ten neroses.

Using the neroses to make these calculations produced huge errors. This is because the calculations were made without a full understanding of the secret knowledge held by the ancient priest-philosophers. The errors led the Jews and some Christian Platonists to believe the world would be destroyed completely at the end of 6,000 years. According to the nonconformist theologian Theophilus Gale, this belief was firmly held by the Jews in particular. It has led modern scientists to discredit ancient knowledge in its entirety. It has also prompted the formation of different religious sects including the Adventists who live with the constant expectation that the world is about to end.

The earth revolves once a year around the sun. At the same time, it turns on its own axis every 24 hours. The smaller cycles of day and night occur within the larger cycle of the year. In the same way, smaller cycles of time operate within the greater cycle or great saros.

According to ancient beliefs the evolution of the physical world is accompanied by a similar evolution in the world of the intellect. The world's spiritual evolution proceeds in cycles just as its physical evolution does.

In this way we see a regular ebb and flow in the tide of human progress throughout history. The great kingdoms and empires of the world are subject to a cyclical law of rise and fall. They reach a peak of civilization and then decline again. When they have reached their lowest point they rally and rise again. The cyclical law of rise and fall ensures that each new peak of civilization rises higher than its predecessor.

It is a fact that the history of mankind is divided into golden, silver, copper and iron ages. The same principle is at work in literature. An age of great inspiration and unselfconscious productivity is always followed by an age of criticism and self-consciousness. The age of creativity provides the material for the following age of critical reflection to analyze.

Take the examples of prominent figures in the history of mankind. Consider the spiritual leaders Buddha-Siddartha and Jesus and the military leaders Alexander the Great and Napoleon. These figures were recurring human archetypes which had existed 10,000 years before. They recurred, produced by the mysterious powers controlling the destinies of the world. The prototype of all prominent figures in history can be found in the half-fictitious and half-real traditions of past religions and mythologies. A star shining in the sky above is reflected in the smooth waters of a lake. Similarly, the archetypes of prominent men from the past are reflected in more recent history.

'As above, so it is below. That which has been, will return again. As in heaven, so on earth.'

The world never fully appreciates its great men. Florence has erected a statue to Galileo but hardly even mentions Pythagoras. Galileo was able to draw on the work of Copernicus who had already challenged the then accepted Ptolemaic system.[63] Copernicus showed that the earth was not at the center of the solar system as Ptolemy had believed but that it orbited the sun. But neither Galileo nor modern astronomy were the first to map the positions of the planets. Thousands of years earlier, scholars of Central Asia confirmed the position of the planets based on observation rather than speculation. Pythagoras brought this knowledge to the West. According to the Syrian philosopher Porphyry, the numerals employed by Pythagoras were hieroglyphical symbols and he used them to explain the essential nature of the universe.

The origins of all knowledge can be found in antiquity. The British author and esotericist Hargrave Jennings is particularly eloquent on the subject of the Pyramids. His arguments are compelling when he asks us to consider the era of the ancient Egyptians. Human knowledge was highly advanced. Compared with our own times human powers were exceptional. The Egyptians had been able to build structures on an incredible scale. Given these facts, Jennings asks if it is reasonable to conclude that the sum total of the Egyptians' achievements were devoted to nothing more than a mistake? Is it reasonable to conclude that the people of the Nile were fools laboring in the dark? Or that the mysticism of the elders was merely forgery? Or that modern man has a monopoly on wisdom and can dismiss ancient Egyptian beliefs as nothing more than superstition? Jennings declares the answer is 'no' despite the modern tendency to deny ancient belief systems. In his book *The Rosicrucians* he maintains there is much more to these old religions than most people suppose. 'We do not understand antiquity . . . The Romans and Greeks, the heathens, the Gentiles and the Jews, mythological and Christian doctrine all share a faith in magic.' The teaching of his book, Jennings tells us, is that magic is indeed possible.

It certainly is. Thirty years ago, the first knockings or rappings during a spiritualist seance in Rochester[64] alerted people to the reality of an invisible spiritual world. The gentle shower of raps gradually became a torrent across the world. Spiritualists had to contend with only two sources of opposition - theology and science - but theosophists have to contend with the world at large and in the first place with the spiritualists themselves.

The Christian preacher claims there is a personal God and a personal Devil. Anyone who contradicts this is to be despised. The materialist claims there is no personal God except rational thought and there is no Devil. Anyone who believes otherwise is a congenital idiot. The occultists and true philosophers pay no attention to either of these views but persevere in their work. None of them believes in the absurd, passionate and fickle God of superstition but all of them believe in good and evil. Human reason is the product of the finite human mind. Divine intelligence is an endless and infinite entity. It follows that our limited human reason must be incapable of understanding limitless divine intelligence. Logically anything beyond our understanding, and imperceptible to our senses, cannot exist for us. Therefore divine intelligence does not exist in any meaningful sense. So far, simple reason agrees with science - there is no God. But we each have a 'higher ego' that lives and thinks and feels independently of our mortal bodies. This higher ego does more than believe. It knows that God exists in nature because this God-of-all lives in us and we live in God. This is an intuitive feeling inherent in mankind. Faith and science cannot destroy this realization once someone has fully grasped it.

Nature abhors a vacuum and human nature is no exception. It yearns instinctively for a God. Without God the cosmos would seem like a soulless corpse. But man has been forbidden to search for God in the esoteric traditions where God might actually be found. Instead man fills the void with the idea of a personal God. This idea has been created for him by spiritual teachers using the remains of ancient myths and philosophies. This explains the appearance of many new sects and wildly unbelievable cults. Mankind craves proof of his own immortality. The theology of Christianity doesn't supply any categoric proof. Any religion hoping to replace Christianity would have to satisfy this craving. The English polymath Thomas Browne wrote that the most disheartening thing a man can be told is that his life is limited and there is no future immortal state beyond death. If any religion could supply scientific proof of immortality then the established belief system of the day would either have to use those same facts to support its own dogmas or become obsolete. Ultimately, man has no actual evidence that any future state of immortality exists and many Christian theologians have been forced to admit this. How then has the belief in immortality persisted? Mankind must have experienced proof of some other kind. The persistent belief in immortality suggests that men must have had direct sensory experience of a spiritual dimension. In some cases physical illness may have caused the illusion. But in thousands of instances a spiritual apparition has been seen and heard by a group of individuals who could not all have been hallucinating.

The greatest thinkers of Greece and Rome regarded the existence of spiritual beings as proven. They distinguished between different classes of spirits using the names *manes, anima* and *umbra*. The *manes* is the spirit of the dead dwelling in the underworld. The *anima* is pure spirit ascending to heaven. The *umbra* is an earthbound spirit lingering at its grave. The *umbra* is prevented from ascending to higher regions by its attraction to the world of matter and love of its earthly body. This verse, attributed to the Roman poet Ovid, describes the soul's three aspects:

> *Terra legit carnem tumulum circumvolat umbra,*
> *Orcus habet manes, spiritus astra petit.*

> *The earth covers the flesh; the umbra hovers around the tomb,*
> *The manes goes to the underworld and the anima seeks the stars.*

But all ideas of this kind must be analyzed carefully. Too many people forget that translators and commentators may have been misled by a great many factors. There have been numerous changes in language over the centuries. Old mystic writers were under oath never to reveal their secrets. Their allegorical language may have been misinterpreted. The writing of medieval alchemists has often been read literally and Plato's cryptic use of symbols is commonly misunderstood by modern scholars. One day they may come to know better. They may learn that the necessarianism of modern philosophy (the belief that everything is predestined) was also embraced by the ancients. They may learn that everything mankind is permitted to know was in the possession of the priests of the temple since the beginning of human history. They may come to understand that the differences in beliefs and religions were only external. They may realize that the guardians of the original divine revelation had solved every problem that human intellect is capable of solving and were members of a universal freemasonry of science and philosophy. This freemasonry was a united worldwide movement. It requires the skill of linguists and psychologists to begin to unravel this occult knowledge. Understanding even a small part of the old religions will allow the whole mystery to be revealed.

In the absence of other proofs of immortality, scientists like the American chemist Robert Hare and the British naturalist Alfred Russel Wallace have turned to spiritualism. At the same time, others without a spiritual inclination have turned to materialism under various names.

But none of this really matters because we won't lose faith, even though most contemporary thinkers believe that modern knowledge is superior to all that came before. We won't be deterred even though modern scientists ignore the evidence of ancient and medieval thinkers as if the world began in 1 AD and all important knowledge is recent. There has never been a better time to explore old philosophies. The time is approaching when archeologists, linguists, astronomers, chemists and physicists will need to consider ancient wisdom. Physical science has already gone as far as it can go. Dogmatic theology is running out of inspiration. The world will soon realize that only ancient religions were in harmony with nature and ancient science encompassed everything knowable. Long-kept secrets may be revealed. Forgotten books and lost arts may be rediscovered. Men will find incredibly important papyri and parchments in Egyptian tombs or subterranean crypts. Tablets and pillars may be excavated and interpreted, and their inscriptions will stagger theologians and mystify scientists. Who knows the possibilities of the future? An era of disillusionment and re-evaluation will soon begin. Or has already begun. The cycle has almost completed its course. A new cycle is about to begin. In future, historical records may prove:

> *If ancestry can be in aught believed,*
> *Descending spirits have conversed with man,*
> *And told him secrets of the world unknown.*

Chapter Two

Pride, where wit fails, steps into our defence
And fills up the mighty void of sense . . .
ALEXANDER POPE

But why should the operations of nature be changed?
There may be a deeper philosophy than we dream of - a
philosophy that discovers the secrets of nature, but does not
alter, by penetrating them, its course.
ZANONI, EDWARD BULWER-LYTTON

Is it enough merely for a man to know that he exists? Does he deserve the name 'man' simply by being a human being? Surely the name 'man' implies a spiritual being and to become a genuine spiritual entity man must first recreate himself. He must completely remove self-interest, superstition and prejudice from his mind and spirit. In this context, prejudice means something very different from the usual definition of liking or hating something. Our prejudices are shaped by the people and the ideas around us. Moral cowardice or fear of public opinion prevent us from escaping our own biases. People rarely make up their own minds about the value of something. Quite the reverse. Most people form their conclusions influenced by the opinions of other people. A church member will not pay an absurdly high rent for his pew just because he thinks it is the right thing to do (any more than a materialist will go twice to the same lecture on evolution). He does it because the powerful and influential 'Joneses' do it.

The same is true of everything else. If there had been an equivalent of Darwin in psychology, he might have shown that the descent of man, as it relates to his moral development, progressed in parallel with the changes in his physical form. A keen observer, watching one man 'ape' another man's ideas, might see how similarly men and apes behave. And this similarity may be even stronger than the physical resemblances pointed out by Darwin.

The different species of ape - 'caricatures of ourselves' - appear to have been evolved deliberately so that Darwin's fans can play at making family trees.

Science is making rapid advances in chemistry and physics, medicine and anthropology. Scientists should have no preconceptions and prejudices. Thought and opinion are now free. But scientists are still only human. Human nature doesn't necessarily change as new ideas develop. Inside any scientist, however brilliant, there is still only a man with all the usual human flaws.

Not long ago, theologians were all-powerful and anyone who questioned their authority was denounced as a heretic. How the mighty have fallen . . . ! Science has triumphed. Now science claims the same infallibility even though it is equally unable to prove its case. As the Holy Roman Emperor Lothar I said, 'Times change and we change with them.' Nevertheless it seems only right to question these new 'high priests of science.'

For many years the world has seen the steady growth of the modern spiritualist movement. Spiritualist literature has been produced in both Europe and America, and there have been endless controversies and contradictory hypotheses. Many educated men and women have tried and failed to understand spiritualism's unpredictable phenomena. They may have failed because their investigations were flawed or because spiritualism's secret force is impossible to comprehend. Either way they came to the conclusion that the more psychological manifestations there are, the harder it is to understand their origin.

There is no point denying that phenomena actually occur. Their origins are mysterious and they are called 'spiritual' even though that may not be the right word to describe them. Even if many phenomena are disregarded as fraud, there are still examples that warrant serious scientific investigation. The church forced Galileo to renounce his own theory that the earth revolves around the sun. Afterward he went on to say, *E pur se muove* (And yet the earth moves) implying that whatever one believes, the facts are the facts. Nowadays Galileo's theory is taken as read by the Academy of Sciences.[1] The existence of psychological phenomena may be next.

Mediums produce certain mysterious phenomena, a fact

acknowledged by modern scientists. However these phenomena could be simply the result of an abnormal nervous condition in the medium. Until this has been proven true or false, scientists have no reason to investigate whether the effects are produced by spirits of the dead. This seems logical. It is up to the spiritualists to prove that spirits act in the physical world. Scientists would be on safe ground if their investigations into spiritualism were unbiased and based on a genuine desire to explain the phenomenon. But instead, they treat the subject with contempt. It's true that a great majority of spiritual communications are unconvincing and an insult to the intelligence. Even when genuine, they are often trivial, ordinary and sometimes crude. Over the past 20 years mediums have supposedly relayed messages from Shakespeare, Byron, Franklin, Peter the Great, Napoleon and Josephine, and even Voltaire. The general impression from these messages was that Napoleon and Josephine had forgotten how to spell; Shakespeare and Byron had become drunks; and Voltaire had turned into an idiot. When there is so much blatant trickery involved, who can blame any reasonably intelligent person for concluding that spiritualism is just one big hoax? Famous names and idiotic messages are bandied about. Scientists have become so wary of the subject that they don't have the stomach to investigate further. They judge spiritualism by its superficial scams and frauds. It is like seeing an oil slick and assuming there is no clean water in the sea below. No one can blame them for being dubious but it's fair enough to criticize them for not exploring deeper. Pearls and cut diamonds are not found lying loose on the ground. These scientists are like the hapless diver who discards an oyster without opening it, when he might have found a precious pearl inside.

A number of leading figures criticize the lack of proper investigation but it makes no difference. Scientists are still reticent to investigate such an unpopular subject and that reticence now seems to have turned into a general panic. 'The phenomena chase the scientists and the scientists run away from the phenomena,' observes the Russian journalist Alexander Aksakov in an article about the St. Petersburg Scientific Committee[2] and its investigation into mediumship. The committee carried out the investigation in a way that was disgraceful. Their report was published so quickly that its content must have been pre-decided. It was evidently partial and inconclusive, provoking criticism even from people with no belief in spiritualism.

The American philosopher and historian John Fiske points out the inconsistency of his fellow scientists' opposition to spiritualism. In his philosophical work *The Unseen World* he shows that the existence of spirit cannot be demonstrated to the senses. By definition, 'matter' exists on the material plane and 'spirit' on the non-material plane. It follows that no theory of spiritualism can be tested by material science. In the same book, Fiske criticizes his colleagues as follows:

'It is impossible for the living to have experience or proof of life after death. However rich the afterlife may be we cannot see it. Consequently no evidence is possible but that is not proof in itself that the afterlife doesn't exist. Viewed in this way, belief in an afterlife has no scientific basis and doesn't need any. It is outside the scope of scientific inquiry. No matter how advanced science becomes it will never be able to disprove the existence of the afterlife. Belief in life after death is not irrational in any way. A scientist can believe without compromising his logic or being influenced in his scientific work. Scientists should accept the fact that spirit is not matter and it is not governed by material laws. They should stop trying to investigate spiritualism using their limited material knowledge. This would end the friction between science and spirituality.'

But scientists won't accept this argument and they reject any scientist who does. They angrily dismiss eminent men like Alfred Russel Wallace and refuse to accept the cautious approach of the English physicist William Crookes.

The ideas contained in this book are important because they are based on many years' study of ancient magic and its modern form, spiritualism. Ancient magic is commonly dismissed as sleight of hand even though the rituals of ancient magic are familiar to many people. Spiritualism is dismissed as a universal hallucination even though there is enough evidence to challenge the assumption that spiritualism is simply a hoax.

This book's authority comes from many years of traveling among 'heathen' and 'Christian' magicians, occultists, mesmerizers and the Who's Who of the white and black arts. Fakirs, the holy men of India, have been scrutinized as they consult with the spirits of their departed ancestors. The rituals and techniques of the whirling dervishes have been observed. The hermits and holy men of Europe and Asiatic Turkey have shared their experiences. Nearly all the secrets of the snake charmers of Damascus and Benares have been studied. Scientists who have never had an opportunity of living among these oriental magicians can only judge the surface. They say there is nothing to their performances but sleight of hand. These snap judgments are not to be trusted. Scientists claim to have thoroughly analyzed the powers of nature and yet they fail to investigate the physiology and psychology of the oriental magicians. They reject astounding phenomena out of hand without examining them properly. They are inconsistent and fail in their scientific duty.

Some years ago, the English scientist Michael Faraday said: 'Many dogs are more capable of coming to logical conclusions than some spiritualists.' And yet the subject of spiritualism is still worth pursuing. Abuse is not argument or proof. Scientists like Thomas Huxley and John Tyndall call spiritualism 'a degrading belief' and describe oriental magic as 'jugglery.' But they can't stop truth being true just by hurling insults. If the human soul is immortal, skepticism can't make it mortal and it makes no difference whether that skepticism is based on science or ignorance. Aristotle says, 'Reason is subject to error.' The same is true of opinion. The personal views of the most prominent philosopher are more likely to be questionable than the common sense of his uneducated cook. In the *Tales of the Impious Khalif*,[3] the Arabian sage Barrachias-Hassan-Oglu, says wisely, 'Be careful of being too full of yourself. It is dangerous because it can go to your head. Benefit from your own judgment but learn to respect the judgment of those older and wiser than you. And remember that it is often easier for wisdom to fill an empty head than one so full of knowledge that there is no space left . . . as is the case with the most educated people.'

Scientists have become even more hostile toward spiritualism since William Crookes began to investigate the subject in London. He was the first scientist to oversee a public display of an alleged 'materialized' spiritual entity. Following Crookes' example several other scientists began studies in the field. This required integrity and a degree of courage given the widespread prejudice against serious consideration of spiritualism.

Unfortunately the majority of scientists abandoned their investigations because of the threat of ridicule. This left Crookes as the only scientist prepared to continue the work. Crookes wrote three pamphlets published as *Researches in the Phenomena of Spiritualism*. In these texts, he described the public reaction to the results of his investigations and the response of the scientific community.

Thirty-three members were appointed to the committee of the Dialectical Society[(4)] in London to collect evidence about the phenomena of spiritualism. Crookes applied scientific principles to the study of mediums and shared the results of his work with the society. The public clamored for a verdict. Both the society and Crookes responded by reporting their findings in plain language. They were duty-bound to report nothing other than the truth. The first of their findings was that the phenomena they witnessed were genuine and couldn't be simulated - some unknown force was behind the manifestations. The committee's second finding was that manifestations occurred that defied the laws of nature. But it was unclear whether the manifestations were the result of disembodied spirits or equivalent entities. The third finding was that the phenomena were undeniably real but however hard they tried they could not explain them. Or as the fictional Count de Gabalis put it, they 'could make neither head nor tail on't!'

Now this was definitely not what the skeptical public was expecting. They had expected spiritualism's believers to be embarrassed when Crookes, the engineer C.F. Varley and the Dialectical Society announced their findings. Even scientists who had refused to take part were embarrassed by the fact that the investigation couldn't explain the phenomena. Spiritualism had always been regarded by the well-educated as vulgar, simply a fairy tale to amuse impressionable housemaids and a source of revenue for Vaudeville hypnotists. The Academy of Sciences and the Institute of Paris[(5)] had dismissed it out of hand. So it was regarded as outrageous when scientific experts were incapable of explaining the spiritualist phenomena they had observed.

A tornado of indignation followed. Crookes describes it in his pamphlet *Experiments on Psychic Force*. He begins pointedly with a quotation from the Italian physician Galvini, 'I am attacked by two polar opposite groups - the scientists and the know-nothings, yet I know that I have discovered one of the greatest forces in nature . . .' Crookes then goes on to say:

'Everyone assumed that the results of my experiments would support their assumptions. What they really wanted was not the truth but to have their own preconceived ideas confirmed. When the results of the investigation didn't suit them, they simply rejected those results. They said, 'The medium Daniel Dunglas Home is a clever conjuror who has fooled us all.' 'Mr Crookes may just as well have examined the performances of an Indian magician.' 'Mr Crookes must get better witnesses before he can be believed.' 'The whole thing is too absurd to be taken seriously.' 'It is impossible and an impossible thing cannot exist.' . . . (I never said it was impossible, I only said it was true.) 'The researchers' investigations are amateurish and they think they saw things that were never really there,' etc, etc, etc.'

Scientists attempted to explain away spiritualist phenomena with fatuous theories such as 'unconscious cerebration' (group hallucination), 'involuntary muscular contraction' (to account for the seance table rotating) and the sublimely ridiculous 'le muscle craqueur or cracking knee-joints' (to explain spirits tapping). None of these attempts to discredit spiritualism worked. Having failed to debunk it, they abandoned the subject altogether. They quietly walked away and left their fellow scientists to face public ridicule. It's unlikely they will ever investigate spiritualism again. It's easier to ignore it from a safe distance. It's much harder to categorize it in the context of the natural phenomena recognized by science. How can spiritualist manifestations be classified when they are inner, non-physical phenomena and unknown territory to modern science? Scientists are powerless to explain something related to the nature of the human soul (which most of them deny exists anyway). Rather than admit their ignorance, they attack any non-scientists brave enough to accept the evidence of their own senses.

In an old Russian tragedy, the poet Trediakovsky observes that a kick from God is nevertheless something sweet because it comes from God. Scientists may sometimes be irritable and condescending but they still deserve respect because of their vast scientific knowledge. Unfortunately it is usually the minor scientific thinkers who shout the loudest.

The Christian author Tertullian describes Satan and his imps as the 'monkeys of God.' Perhaps it's lucky that there's no modern Tertullian to call out minor scientists as the 'monkeys of science' and consign them to the dustbin of history.

In his article 'Phenomena of Mediumism,' Alexander Aksakov says, 'Genuine scientists can't deny the existence of objective phenomena. They are obliged to investigate and explain them. But when asked to identify the origins of spiritualist phenomena they are totally at a loss. The subject of spiritualism seems to make them abandon their highest principles - respect for the truth and verification by scientific experiment! . . . They feel that there is something too serious underlying it. They are put into a panic by the findings of investigators such as the British mathematician Augustus de Morgan, the Russian chemist Alexander Butlerov, Robert Hare, William Crookes, C.F. Varley, and Alfred Russel Wallace. They worry that if they give even a little credence to these investigations, the world will be turned upside down. Long-established scientific principles and theoretical frameworks are all at stake.'

Crookes, the Dialectical Society, Wallace and Hare have all verified the phenomenon of spiritualism. The response from leading scientists is itself another phenomenon. It is as if they suffer from some kind of fear-inducing psychological disorder - something like the strange and contagious condition known as hydrophobia, associated with rabies. It's possible that a new disease has been discovered, best described as 'scientific psychic-phobia.'

Scientists should have learned by now that science has its limits. As long as there remains just one unexplained mystery in nature, 'impossible' is a dangerous word for science to use.

In *Researches On The Phenomena of Spiritualism*, William Crookes puts forward eight theories to explain the phenomena he observed.

These are as follows:

First Theory - The phenomena are all tricks, produced by clever mechanical apparatus or sleight of hand. The mediums are confidence tricksters and the attendees are gullible.

Second Theory - The people at a seance are gripped by some sort of collective hysteria or delusion and imagine phenomena which are not there.

Third Theory - The whole thing is the result of mental activity which may be unconscious or consciously directed.

Fourth Theory - It's the result of the medium's spirit acting alone or in combination with the spirits of the people present in the room.

Fifth Theory - It's evil spirits or demons taking the shape of people or things to undermine Christianity. (This is the theory put forward by theologians).

Sixth Theory - It's the actions of beings from other earthly planes of existence which are undetectable to us. They are able to make their presence felt occasionally and are known in almost all cultures as demons (not necessarily evil), gnomes, fairies, kobolds or sprites, elves, goblins, Puck, etc. (This is consistent with the beliefs of the Kabbalists).

Seventh Theory - It's the actions of deceased human beings. (This is the ultimate spiritualist theory).

Eighth Theory - There exists a psychic force that can act in the world whatever its source - a medium's spirit (4th theory), devils (5th theory), fairies (6th theory), departed souls (7th theory).

The first theory has been shown to be true only in exceptional fraudulent cases (though these are unfortunately still too frequent). This theory can be ruled out because it has no relevance to genuine phenomena. Theories two and three are the last-resort objections of skeptics and materialists. And the jury is still out. In William Crookes' opinion, the eighth theory is simply an addition to two and three. That leaves theories four, five, six and seven to deal with.

Even scientific opinion can be mistaken. This can be clearly seen by comparing articles written by Crookes between 1870 and 1875. In one of his early articles he says, 'Greater use of a scientific approach will produce more precise observations and a thirst for the truth. Researchers will come to dismiss spiritualism as so much superstition.' But by 1875, he was the author of detailed and fascinating descriptions of the spirit Katie King, renowned for materializing at seances.

It's hardly likely that Crookes was hallucinating for two or three consecutive years. The 'spirit' Katie King appeared in his own house, in his library, under controlled test conditions. She was seen, felt and heard by hundreds of people.

But Crookes denies that he ever believed the manifestation Katie King was a disembodied spirit. What was it then? Crookes confirms it was not the medium Florence Cook. In that case it was either the spirit of a deceased person or one of the spiritual entities described in the sixth theory; fairies, kobolds, gnomes, elves, goblins or a Puck.

Katie King must have been a fairy - like Shakespeare's Titania. Crookes quotes a Byron poem to describe her. The following lines could only be applied to something as mercurial as a fairy:

Round her she made an impression of life;
The very air seemed lighter from her eyes;
They were so soft and beautiful and rife
With all we can imagine of the skies;
Her overpowering presence makes you feel
It would not be idolatry to kneel.

In 1870, Crookes wrote a damning indictment of spiritualism. He said he believed the whole subject was the product of superstition or at the very least an unexplained trick or a delusion. But by 1875, he concluded his book *Researches In The Phenomena Of Spiritualism* saying, 'Believing Katie King is a fake is more unreasonable than believing her to be the spirit she says she is.' This last remark is firm evidence that:

1. Crookes believed that Katie King was not produced by the medium or an accomplice but was some unknown and unstoppable force of nature. 2. He also believed that he had first-hand experience of this force. In spite of these facts Crookes remained skeptical about spiritualism throughout his investigation. In summary, he believed in the phenomenon but not in the idea that it involved the spirit of a deceased person.

It seems that Crookes solves one mystery by creating another. He describes one obscurity by referring to something even more obscure. In other words he rejects spiritualism's claim to contact the dead and plunges into fresh unknown territory because he cannot say what Katie King really is.

Science can only explain a small number of objective spiritualist phenomena. It has proven that an unknown force produces certain visible effects but scientists are still unable to control the phenomena. They haven't yet discovered the underlying cause. Just like their predecessors, the ancient magicians, scientists must study the triple nature of man in depth - his physiological, psychological and divine aspects. Even people who have investigated spiritualism as rigorously as William Crookes have concluded that the cause is undiscoverable. Similarly, even though they observe and classify the physical effects of the universe, they have made no attempt to discover the first cause that stands behind it. Their method is simply not robust. If someone wants to discover the source of a river there is absolutely no point exploring the river's mouth. Their approach has narrowed their view of the laws of the universe so that anything occurring outside those parameters has the appearance of a miracle. This means very simple forms of occult phenomena have to be rejected as scientific absurdities and consequently modern science has been losing credibility. If scientists had studied so-called miracles instead of dismissing them, they would have rediscovered occult universal laws long understood by the ancients. As the English philosopher Francis Bacon puts it: 'Conviction comes not through arguments but through experiments.'

One of the things that made the ancients so remarkable was their commitment to developing every branch of science. This was especially true of the Chaldean astrologers and the Magi. Like modern naturalists, they tried to understand the natural world by the only practical method - experimental research and logical reasoning. Modern scientists find it hard to believe that the ancients' knowledge of the universe was deeper than our own. But just because they find it hard to believe doesn't make it untrue. Nor is it a reason to dismiss the ancients as simply superstitious. Every new archeological discovery suggests otherwise. The ancients were unrivaled in chemistry. In his famous lecture, *The Lost Arts*, Wendell Phillips says that ancient chemistry had reached a level of development that modern chemistry cannot match. The example of malleable glass illustrates this point well. If a piece of this glass is supported at one end it will stretch under its own weight. Over a period of 20 hours it will become a fine thread flexible enough to wrap around the wrist. Modern science would find it easier to send a man to the moon than to replicate this glass.

A craftsman made a cup of flexible glass and took it to Rome. He presented it to the emperor Tiberius. When the emperor tried to break it, it dented but it did not shatter. The craftsman then beat out the dent with a small hammer. These are historic facts. Nowadays, people believe flexible glass is a myth because modern science cannot manufacture it. In Samarkand[6] and some Tibetan monasteries flexible glassware is still in use. There are people who claim they can produce it because they are familiar with the universal solvent, alkahest.[7] Paracelsus and van Helmont described the alkahest as a naturally occurring fluid that 'can reduce any physical material to its primary essence. It is just as effective with a single material as with several different materials combined. Or it can reduce any material into a uniform and stable liquid that is safe to drink. This liquid will mix with water or other fluids but it will not be altered by them. If it is mixed with itself it will turn into pure water.' What makes this idea so difficult to accept? Why does it seem so fantastic? Is it because modern chemistry cannot reproduce the same results? It doesn't take a huge stretch of the imagination to see that everything must originate from some primary substance. According to the lessons of astronomy, geology and physics this first substance must have been a fluid. Take gold as an example - scientists know very little about its origins - why shouldn't it have existed originally as a fluid and solidified later 'through the cohesion of its particles' as van Helmont maintains?

It seems reasonable to believe in a universal essence that reduces all forms of matter to their underlying primary substance. Van Helmont calls this universal essence 'the most highly refined and pure salt. Only this salt remains unaffected when mixed with other substances. Only it can dissolve the densest materials like stones, gems, glass, earth, sulfur, metals etc. It dissolves them into an amount of red salt equal to their original weight and does this as easily as hot water melts snow.'

The makers of malleable glass claim that ordinary glass becomes malleable when it has been immersed in the alkahest for several hours.

Concrete proof exists that this is possible. A correspondent of the Theosophical Society managed to produce what he describes as 'true oil of gold' or the primal element. He is a well-known medical practitioner and has studied occult science for more than 30 years. Chemists and physicists have examined this 'oil of gold' and admitted they don't know how it was made and they couldn't produce it themselves. This member of the Theosophical Society prefers to remain anonymous which is not surprising given that ridicule and public scorn are sometimes more threatening than the Spanish Inquisition itself. The primal element is closely related to the alkahest. It is one of alchemy's most important secrets. No Kabbalist will reveal it to the world because, as the saying goes: 'it would reveal the alchemists' power as spiritual 'eagles' and how to clip the eagles' wings.' It took the Welsh alchemist Thomas Vaughan (Eugenius Philalethes) 20 years to learn the secret of the primal element and its relationship to the alkahest.

As modern science has gained in importance it has eclipsed

the spiritual sciences leaving them neglected in its shadow. Now the greatest ancient thinkers are seen as nothing more than 'ignorant and superstitious ancestors.' They are dismissed as charlatans and tricksters. Modern science has been so effective that it is now common to say that the philosophers and scientists of ancient times were entirely unenlightened and blinded by superstition. But their detractors forget that today's science will seem primitive compared with scientific advances in the future. Contemporary thinkers always regard their predecessors as backward. In the same way future generations may look back and view current thinking as primitive. The world moves in cycles. Past generations will reappear as the generations of the future just as the present generation may be the recurrence of people who lived 100 centuries ago. A day of reckoning is approaching. There are people who discredit Hermetic thought in public but study it in private then claim the ideas as their own. The time is coming when they will get their comeuppance. The German mathematician Johann Pfaff asks, 'Has anyone ever taken a broader view of nature than Paracelsus? Paracelsus pioneered the development of medicines. He founded groundbreaking schools of thought. He was proven right whenever there was controversy. He is part of a school of innovators who have created new theories in the field of biology. He scattered through his work writings on the philosopher's stone, pygmies, spirits of the mines, omens, homunculi and the elixir of life. Critics use these writings to detract from his reputation. But nothing can lessen our admiration for his work, his freedom and boldness of thought and his exemplary intellectual life.'

Paracelsus' work has provided inspiration for many pathologists, chemists, homeopaths and experts in magnetism. Paracelsus inspired the German physician Frederick Hufeland's theories on infection in spite of being dismissed as a medieval 'quack' by the physician Kurt Sprengel. The Prussian surgeon Johann Hemmann tried to vindicate Paracelsus and restore his reputation by describing him as 'the greatest chemist of his time.' This view was shared by the philosopher Franz Molitor and the eminent German psychologist Joseph Ennemoser. In their analysis of his work they describe Paracelsus as the most 'wondrous intellect of his age' and 'a noble genius.' Paracelsus and his Rosicrucian followers held a number of ideas about elementary spirits, goblins and elves. But modern science believes it knows better and consigns these ideas to the obscurity of magic, treating them as fairy tales for young children.

It's possible that over half of all spiritual phenomena are the result of fraud. The recent exposure of many so-called 'materializing' mediums proves the fact all too well. Certainly, more fraud will be exposed until scientific tests are sufficiently accurate and impartial. Precise analysis will leave no room for charlatans and also ensure that no one is falsely accused of fraud.

There are angel guides who monopolize an unfortunate medium's life, perhaps for years, then suddenly abandon him when he needs their help most. What should serious spiritualists make of these angel guides? Only spirit entities without a soul or conscience would act in this way. Some people argue that perhaps conditions have changed and the spirit is forced to leave but this doesn't ring true. What sort of spirits wouldn't summon an army of spirit-friends to support the innocent medium in his hour of need? This kind of thing happened in the past, why shouldn't it happen now? Spiritual entities appeared long before modern spiritualism, and spiritualist phenomena have occurred throughout history. If modern spiritualist manifestations are genuine, the same must be true for the so-called miracles of antiquity. Or if the miracles of antiquity are simply the result of superstition, then this must also be the case for modern spiritualism because there is similar evidence for both.

Every day new occult phenomena occur around the world. Although two thirds of these cases are proven to be bogus, what about the ones proven to be genuine beyond doubt? In these cases sublime messages are communicated through both professional and non-professional mediums.

Often young children and uneducated people channel philosophical teachings and concepts, poetry and inspiring speeches, music and paintings. The quality of these messages is consistent with the skill and ability of the spirits supposedly being channeled. These spirits' predictions often come true and sometimes they give beneficial advice though this is less frequent. Who are these channeled spirits? What are these intelligences that are separate from the medium and entities in their own right? They definitely deserve the name 'intelligences.' They are entirely different from the majority of mischievous spirits that hover round the cabinet used in seances - they are as different as night and day.

The situation seems serious. Mischievous 'spirits' are controlling mediums more frequently. The harmful effects of apparent devil worship are multiplying. Consequently some of the best mediums are retiring from the field and the movement is coming under the influence of the Church. Spiritualists must study ancient philosophy to learn how to tell the difference between spirit types. Only this knowledge will enable them to protect themselves from the worst kind. Otherwise, within the next 25 years, they will have to turn to the Catholic church to escape from the malign spirits they have dabbled with unwittingly. The first signs of this catastrophe are already evident. At a recent convention in Philadelphia there was serious discussion about founding a sect of Christian Spiritualists! Without the Church and without knowledge of the ancient philosophy, they have no insight into the nature of their spirits. They are drifting on a sea of uncertainty like a ship without a compass or a rudder. They must choose between the ancient wisdom of the philosopher Porphyry or the Catholic doctrine of Pope Pius IX. There's no other way out.

Consider a roll call of scientists including Alfred Russel Wallace, William Crookes, Augustus de Morgan, Alexander Butlerov, C. F. Varley, Robert Hare, the German anatomist Rudolf Wagner, the American physician Joseph Buchanan, the German chemist Carl Reichenbach, the Swiss naturalist and physicist Marc Thury, the German naturalist Maximilian Perty, the Scottish chemist William Gregory, the German chemist August Hofmann, the French astronomer Camille Flammarion, the German astronomer Hermann Goldschmidt, and William Crookes' assistant Edward Cox. These and many others are convinced by the evidence that spiritualist phenomena occur but many reject the theory that the phenomena are caused by departed spirits. Katie King is the only materialized entity given credence by science. If it is not the spirit of an ex-mortal it must be a visible astral shadow of a Rosicrucian phantom or some other force of nature not yet understood. It doesn't matter whether it's benign or mischievous, if it is proven to be an organism without mass once and for all then it must be a 'spirit,' an apparition, a breath. It is an intelligence that acts outside the material plane and must belong to a hidden race of beings. But what is it? What is this being that thinks and even speaks but is not human? It is impossible to touch but it is not a disembodied spirit. It simulates affection, passion, remorse, fear, joy, but it feels none of these things. What is this cruel entity that deceives people at seances and makes fun of human feeling? William Crookes' Katie King might not have done these things but many similar entities have. Who can explain any of this?

Only the true psychologist. And the best place to begin his research is with the long-neglected works of Hermeticists and ancient miracle workers.

The cleric and scientist John Webster was skeptical about the existence of spiritualist phenomena. In response, the English Platonist Henry More referred to the Biblical story of Samuel's ghost, summoned by the Witch of Endor. More said, 'A large number of theologians hold the view that the Devil appeared in Samuel's shape. This idea is absurd. I am certain that many apparitions are caused by mischievous spirits, not the souls of the deceased. But in the case of Samuel's ghost, I am clear it is the kind of spirit described by Porphyry, the kind that can assume many different shapes, act the part of a demon or an angel or the soul of someone departed. I believe this kind of spirit impersonated Samuel regardless of Webster's arguments to the contrary which are weak and wooden.'

Henry More is a respected metaphysician and philosopher. When he expresses his view that spirit entities are genuine phenomena, this gives considerable weight to the argument. Psychic investigators are skeptical about spirits in general and 'departed human spirits' in particular. During the last 20 years they have gone to great lengths to invent new names for the same thing. William Crookes and Edward Cox call it 'psychic force.' Marc Thury calls it the 'psychode' or ectenic force. The Scottish physicist Balfour Stewart calls it 'electro-biological power.' Michael Faraday described it patronizingly as an 'unconscious muscular action,' an 'unconscious cerebration.' (He may have been the 'great master of experimental science in physics' but he was apparently a novice in psychology.) The Scottish metaphysician William Hamilton calls it a 'latent thought.' The English physician William Carpenter calls it the 'ideo-motor principle.' Etc., etc. So many scientists - so many names.

Years ago the German philosopher Arthur Schopenhauer debunked this force and the whole material universe with it. Since becoming an advocate of spiritualism, the great anthropologist Alfred Russel Wallace has evidently adopted Schopenhauer's ideas. Schopenhauer's philosophy suggests that the universe is nothing but the manifestation of will. Every force in nature is also the product of will, an instance of will made concrete. Plato taught that everything visible was created or evolved out of the invisible and eternal will. Our physical world is a reflection of the 'ideal or eternal world.' Its pattern is contained like everything else in the dodecahedron, the geometrical model used by God. According to Plato, the primal being emanates from the mind of God. From the beginning, the mind of God contains the idea of the world to be created. The will of God uses the idea as a template to bring the world into being. What we call the laws of nature are simply the relations between the idea in the mind of God and the physical forms of the created world. Schopenhauer described these forms as time, space and causality. He said that will expresses itself in infinite ways through time and space.

These ideas are not new. They were not original to Plato either. They are present in the earlier *Chaldean Oracles*. The *Oracles* describe nature as gaining its existence from the intellect or spiritual light of God. The soul gave life to the universe and did so in God's image.

Philo Judaeus says, 'Even before the world existed, it existed already in the mind of God.' Philo Judaeus is wrongly described as deriving his philosophy from Plato's.

In the cosmology of the early Phoenician philosopher Mochus, aether[8] is the first element to appear followed by the air. From these two elements, the visible universe is born.

The *Orphic Hymns*[9] are religious poems from the end of the Hellenic or beginning of the Roman period. They describe Phanes as the primeval god of procreation that hatches from a cosmic egg. In turn, the cosmic egg has been fertilized by the wind or the spirit of God. This wind is the divine idea which brings form to chaos. In the Hindu Katha Upanishad,[10] the divine spirit called Purusha[11] unites with primal matter giving rise to the great soul of the world. The Hindus call this Maha, Atma, Brahm, the spirit of life. These terms are synonymous with the universal soul or *anima mundi* (the 'world soul' according to several systems of thought) and the astral light - the term used by the ancient magicians and Kabbalists.

Pythagoras brought his philosophical ideas from the eastern mystery schools. Plato adopted these ideas and translated them from their original numerical symbolism into a form which was easier for the uninitiated to understand. Plato presented the cosmos as 'the son,' the father of the cosmos as 'divine thought' and the mother as 'matter.'

According to the American scholar Samuel Dunlap, 'Egyptian myths tell of an older and a younger Horus. The older Horus is the brother of Osiris. The younger Horus is the son of Osiris and Isis.' The older Horus is the idea of the world in the divine mind 'born in darkness before the creation of the world.' The younger Horus is the idea emerging from the divine mind, becoming concrete and assuming tangible existence.

In the *Chaldean Oracles*, the same idea appears in the following words: ' . . . the mundane God, eternal, boundless, young and old, of winding form.'

The term 'winding form' describes the vibration of astral light. The ancient priests were well acquainted with this light but would not have recognized or accepted the scientific theory of 'ether.' They believed that it was 'aether' that carried the divine idea pervading the universe. This divine idea, or will, becomes force and creates or organizes matter.

The chemist Jan Baptist van Helmont says, 'The will is the pre-eminent power because the will of God makes and animates everything. The will is the property of all beings and is more evident the more those beings are freed from matter.' Paracelsus adds, 'Faith is essential because faith supports the will . . . Determined will is the foundation of all magic . . . But because men have imperfect faith the magical arts produce imperfect results. With perfect faith the opposite would be true.'

Doubt and skepticism are powerful forces. If projected strongly enough they can counteract the forces of belief and faith and sometimes neutralize them entirely. Spiritualists shouldn't be surprised that the presence of skeptics hinders and often stops their manifestations. Unwitting skeptics may also be present, using their willpower unconsciously to oppose the seance. There is no conscious intention that isn't sometimes counteracted by conscious opposition. So why wonder when the unconscious intention of the medium is suddenly halted by the unconscious opposition of an unwitting skeptic? Michael Faraday and John Tyndall boasted that spiritualist manifestations stopped whenever they were present. This should have been enough to convince them that some force or other was at work. John Tyndall may have been an important scientist but that was irrelevant when he was at a seance. He could only see as well as the next person in the darkened room. If the medium could fool everyone else, she could certainly fool him and the manifestations needn't have stopped. No medium can perform miracles to rival Jesus or the Apostle Paul but even Jesus was disempowered by the doubt of others. The unconscious force of their resistance overpowered his will, 'And he did not many mighty works there because of their unbelief.'

All of these ideas are reflected in Schopenhauer's philosophy. Scientists would do well to read his work. In Schopenhauer they will find many strange hypotheses based on ancient ideas - theories about the 'new' phenomena of spiritualism. This will save them the trouble of having to invent their own. All their theories of psychic and ectenic forces, the 'ideo-motor' and 'electro-biological powers,' 'latent thought,' and even 'unconscious cerebration' are simply synonyms for the Kabbalists' astral light.

Schopenhauer's ideas are very different from the ideas of most orthodox scientists. Schopenhauer claims, 'There is neither matter nor spirit. A stone falling under the influence of gravity is as inexplicable as thought in the human brain. If matter can fall to the ground and no one knows why, then it can also think and no one knows why . . . Even in the field of mechanics, if we go beyond pure mathematics, we are confronted by a mystery. As soon as we reach the obscure forces of adhesion and gravitation, we are facing phenomena as mysterious as the will and thought in man. We are confronted by the incomprehensible because every natural force is exactly that. Where is matter in all this? You are so familiar with it that you base all your conclusions on it and attribute everything to it. But we can only really perceive the surface of phenomena. We can never see into the true inner substance of things. This was Kant's opinion. If you believe there is some sort of spirit in a human skull then you have to believe the same is true of a stone. If inert matter can fall under the influence of gravity or attract and repel or spark, as electricity does, then it can also think as well as any brain. In summary, every particle of so-called spirit can be replaced with an equal amount of matter and every particle of matter can be replaced with an equal amount of spirit . . . The division of everything into matter and spirit suggested by René

Descartes can never be proven philosophically. The only division that can be proven is the division of everything into will and manifestation. (This is not to be confused with the division of matter and spirit.) This division of everything into will and manifestation spiritualizes every thing. It transforms every real and objective thing - body and matter - into representation, and every manifestation into will.'

Schopenhauer supports the view that scientists are simply giving many different names to the same spiritual phenomena. It is only a battle of words. Call the phenomena force, energy, electricity or magnetism, willpower or spirit power, it doesn't really matter. Spiritual phenomena are the partial manifestation of the soul whether that soul is disembodied or encased in a body. They are the partial manifestation of the intelligent omnipotent will that pervades the universe and this will is known as 'God' for want of better words.

From a Kabbalist's point of view, modern scientific theories about matter are wrong in many ways. The German philosopher Karl von Hartmann suggests that scientists harbor 'an instinctual prejudice.' He demonstrates that scientists cannot work directly with matter itself. They can only work with the forces he identifies as the foundation of matter. The appearance of matter is only the action of force and he concludes that the sum of these forces is the phenomenon labeled as matter. Beyond that, 'matter' is a meaningless word for the purposes of science. For their part, scientists admit that they are not entirely sure what matter is but they continue to revere it. To ensure science remains unchallenged, any new phenomenon that science cannot explain is quietly put to one side.

No one has a clearer philosophical perspective than Schopenhauer. In his collection of essays *Appendices and Omissions*

(*Parerga und Paralipomena*) he discusses in detail animal magnetism, clairvoyance, sympathetic cures, seership, magic, omens, ghost-seeing and other spiritual fields. Schopenhauer says, 'All of these phenomena are branches of the same tree. They provide irrefutable proof of the existence of a chain of beings. The nature of these beings is entirely different from the natural world as we know it, which is founded on laws of space, time and natural selection. This other nature is more fundamental. It is the original and the primal nature. The common laws of nature are merely conventions which do not apply here. According to the laws of this other nature, time and space do not separate individuals. There are no barriers to prevent them from exchanging thoughts or exercising their will. In this way, changes can be created by a different method from the usual physical cause and effect. An atypical use of will, beyond the individual himself, can cause changes to take place. The supernatural manifestations described above all share a specific quality - vision and action take place at a distance without physical contact. Effects occur regardless of what we would think of as the barriers of time and space. This specific quality is the essence of what most people would describe as 'magical.' The immediate action of our will is magical because it is not dependent on the usual causal chain of physical action, it is not dependent on physical contact.'

Schopenhauer continues, 'These spiritualist manifestations contradict the philosophies of materialism and even naturalism. Both these philosophies present the order of things in nature as absolute. But in the light of spiritualist manifestations, this natural order appears purely phenomenal and artificial. The manifestations reveal that underpinning the natural order is a separate reality totally independent of natural laws. This is why the manifestations are so important both from a purely philosophical point of view and also compared with all the experimental data we have available. It follows that every scientist should be familiar with them.'

It is worth contrasting the philosophy of Schopenhauer with the ideas of some of the French academicians.[12] For example, compare Schopenhauer's thinking with the work of the astronomer Jacques Babinet and the chemist Jean-Baptiste Boussingault. In 1854-5 they presented to the Academy a detailed written study explaining the important spiritualistic phenomenon of table turning.[13] The purpose of their study was to corroborate and clarify the overly complex theory put forward by the French chemist Michel Chevreul who was a member of the commission set up to investigate spiritualism.

In the journal *Revue de Deux Mondes* they reported, 'The alleged movement of tables at seances is caused by invisible and involuntary muscular spasms. The extended contraction of the muscles creates a series of vibrations. These vibrations become a visible tremor causing the table to turn. It rotates with considerable energy getting quicker and quicker. Whenever someone tries to stop it, there is a strong force of resistance. This is a clear physical explanation of the phenomenon and requires no further investigation.'

As explanations go, this one is as clear as the stars on a foggy night.

It's also missing one important feature entirely - common sense. Karl von Hartmann maintains that the visible effects of matter are simply the effects of a force - to understand matter you must first understand the force that underlies it. It's uncertain whether or not Babinet agrees but several of the greatest German scientists certainly do. Schopenhauer calls an understanding of this underlying force the 'magical knowledge' and 'magical effect or action of will.' In Babinet's explanation of turning tables, it's important to understand whether the involuntary muscular spasm is caused by will acting within the individual or from outside. If the will acts within the individual then Babinet's theory makes that individual an unconscious epileptic. Babinet rejects the idea that the will is outside the individual altogether. He regards any apparent spirit communication (where intelligent answers are given by rapping or tipping tables) as 'unconscious ventriloquism.'

When will is exerted, it results in force. According to Hartmann and the German school, the action of will organizes atomic force. This causes atoms to assume the concrete image previously created by the will. The Greek philosopher Democritus (a pupil of Leucippus) taught that everything in the universe derived from atoms and a vacuum. In Kabbalistic tradition the word 'vacuum' means latent deity or latent force. This latent force first showed itself as will which then directed atoms to cluster and form matter. This vacuum was just another name for chaos - but not a particularly good one because 'nature abhors a vacuum,' according to Aristotle's Peripatetic school of philosophy.

Even before Democritus, the ancients were familiar with the idea of the indestructibility of matter. This is proven by the allegories in their writing and many other facts. In his book, *The Phoenicians (Die Phönizier)*, the German orientalist Franz Movers describes the Phoenician idea of 'ideal sunlight.' It is a spiritual power which issues from the original creator or god called IAO[14] in Greek. 'It is a light that can only be seen with the intellect. It is the physical and spiritual first principle of all things. The soul emanates from it.' It was the male essence or wisdom. The female essence was primitive matter or chaos. So the primitive Phoenicians already understood the two first principles as spirit and matter, both eternal and infinite. And this means the theory is as old as the world because Democritus was not the first philosopher to teach it and man was able to understand it intuitively even before he became rational. Science is powerless to explain occult phenomena. This is because it rejects the boundless and endless entity that exercises will - the thing called 'God' for want of a better word. Scientists reject out of hand everything that might force them to cross the line from modern science into the realm of psychological or metaphysical physiology. This is the real reason spiritualist manifestations make them uneasy and it accounts for the absurd theories they put forward to explain them away. The ancient philosophy maintained that the will brought everything visible and invisible into existence. Plato called this will the 'divine idea.' The divine idea brought objective forms into existence by directing its willpower toward a center of localized forces. A man can do the same because he is simply a microcosm of the greater whole or macrocosm. His power to manifest is in proportion to the development of his human willpower. Democritus was among the first to propose an atomic theory (later enthusiastically adopted by modern science). According to his theory, atoms are like automatons. The universal will permeates them and generates the force that sets them in motion. The plan of the structure to be created exists first of all in the divine architect's mind and reflects his will. At first it is abstract then it becomes concrete as the atoms follow every detail of the plan held in the divine architect's imagination.

Just as God creates, man can create by the same principle. With enough intensity of will the mind can create subjectively. We call these subjective creations hallucinations. But a hallucination is as real to the man hallucinating as a visible object is to everyone else. If a man learns to concentrate his will more intensely and intelligently he can produce a form that is concrete, visible and objective. He has learned the greatest secret. He is a magician.

Materialists should have no objection to this logic because they regard everything as matter including thought itself. If this is the case, then anything that can be imagined must also exist as matter. This includes the invention in the mind of the inventor, the romantic scenes imagined by a poet, the painting in the artist's mind's eye, the statue anticipated by the sculptor, the great buildings planned by the architect. All these are invisible and subjective but they must also exist since thought is matter. There may be some men whose will is powerful enough to transform images held in the mind into tangible substance.

The French academicians didn't get very far in their investigation of spiritualism. The same was true in England until William Crookes studied the subject impartially. About 20 years ago, Michael Faraday agreed to consider the question. This is the same Faraday who is often cited by anti-spiritualists as an authoritative debunker of spiritualism. The same Faraday who 'blushed' for having published research on such a trivial subject. But it is now proven that he never actually sat at a seance table. At the time, the famous Scottish medium Daniel Dunglas Home was in England but Faraday never took the opportunity to attend one of his seances. A quick look at a few old copies of the French newspaper the *Journal des Debats* brings the past back into sharp focus. For example, the French physicist Jean Foucault writes in defense of Faraday: 'Please don't think that a physicist as eminent as Faraday actually agreed to sit at a jumping table.' If Faraday never attended a seance, what does he have to blush about? To detect fraudulent mediums, Faraday invented his 'Indicator' or 'Medium-Catcher.' This complicated machine must haunt the dreams of dishonest mediums like a terrifying nightmare. The French author Comte de Mirville describes it in detail in his book

On the Question of Spirits (Question des Esprits).

Faraday created the Indicator to show participants at a seance that they were actually pushing the table unconsciously. He placed several cardboard discs on the table. The discs were stuck to the surface and each other using a tacky adhesive. This held the elements in place but meant they were able to move, if pushed. Once the table had turned the disks were examined. They were found to have slipped in the same direction as the table, proving without doubt that the attendees had pushed the table themselves.

Another so-called scientific test was devised though it's questionable how useful any scientific test can be for a phenomenon alleged to be psychic or spiritual. This test consisted of a small instrument to warn attendees if they were actively tensing their muscles. Or as Faraday put it, 'It warned them when they changed from the passive to the active state.' When the needle on the meter moved, it only proved one thing i.e. a force was acting which either originated from the people at the table, or controlled them. And no one has ever claimed that there is no such force. Everyone agrees that a force is acting whether it passes through the medium, as it generally appears, or acts independently of him as is so often the case. In *On the Question of Spirits*, Comte de Mirville says, 'The whole mystery of turning tables lay in the difference between the small force used by the participants (who pushed because they were forced to) and the effect produced - the dramatic racing rotation of the table. Faced with the strength of the phenomenon, how could anyone think that these measly scientific tests could have any value in the vast and newly discovered continent of spiritual possibility.'

The Swiss-American biologist Jean Louis Agassiz was almost as highly regarded in his own country as Faraday was in England. Agassiz's treatment of spiritualism was even more biased than

Faraday's. The anthropologist Joseph Buchanan has studied spiritualism more rigorously than anyone else in America. In a recent article he criticizes Agassiz and with good reason. Of all people, Agassiz ought to take spiritualist phenomena seriously since he is on record as having been successfully mesmerized. But both Faraday and Agassiz are now dead. There's more to be gained from questioning people who are still alive.

In essence then, modern science dismisses a force that was well known to ancient magicians. In ancient times, children played with this force, perhaps as if it were the 'vril' in Edward Bulwer-Lytton's novel *The Coming Race*. They called it the 'Water of Ptah,' (the ancient Egyptians' supreme god). Later the force was called *anima mundi*, the soul of the universe. Later still, medieval Hermeticists called it 'sidereal light' (the light of the stars), or the 'milk of the celestial virgin,' the *Magnes*, and many other names. But modern scientists will not accept its existence, whatever it's called, because it is related to magic, and magic is an unacceptable superstition in their view.

The philosophers Apollonius and Iamblichus maintained that it was not 'knowledge of the external world, but the perfection of the soul within that hastened the development of man as an ascendent being.' These philosophers had come to recognize their god-like souls. They used their soul power with wisdom gained from the esoteric study of Hermetic law and inherited from their forefathers. But modern thinkers, confining themselves to human experience, cannot see beyond the immediately comprehensible. For them, there is no future life. There are no godlike dreams. They reject them as unscientific. For them, the ancients are just 'ignorant ancestors.' And they are contemptuous of any author who believes human beings have an inherent desire for spiritual knowledge, and this desire must have been given to them for a reason.

According to a Persian proverb, 'The darker the sky, the brighter the stars will shine.' In the same way, the mysterious Brothers of the Rosie Cross began appearing like stars against the dark of the medieval sky. They founded no guilds or colleges. They were hunted like wild beasts by the Christian church and, when caught, they were unceremoniously roasted. As the French philosopher Pierre Bayle explains it, 'Religion forbids the spilling of blood so the church turned to burning!'

By following theories passed secretly from one generation to another, many of these mystics made discoveries that modern science would not dismiss. The English friar Roger Bacon was ridiculed as a quack and was one of a number of people who claimed to have knowledge of magic. But his discoveries were nevertheless accepted. They are now used by his greatest detractors. He never actually belonged to the Rosicrucian brotherhood but by his actions he earned the right to be a member. He lived in the 13th Century, a contemporary of the saints Albertus Magnus and Thomas Aquinas. His discoveries, such as gunpowder and optical lenses, were regarded as supernatural and he was accused of having made a pact with the Devil.

There is an anonymous 16th-century book called *The Famous History of Friar Bacon*. There is also a play that tells the same story, written by the Elizabethan dramatist Robert Greene. In these narratives, Friar Bacon was summoned to appear before the court. He was persuaded to demonstrate his skills to her majesty the Queen. He waved his hand (the text says 'his wand') and excellent music was heard. The people of the court said they had never heard anything like it before. Then even louder music was heard and four apparitions suddenly materialized and danced before dissolving into thin air. Bacon waved his wand again and suddenly a fragrance filled the air 'as if all the most exquisite perfumes in the whole world had been prepared according to the perfumer's art.' Then he promised to show to a gentlemen of the court that gentleman's sweetheart. He pulled aside a hanging in the King's apartment and everyone in the room saw a kitchen maid with a basting ladle in her hand. The kitchen maid vanished just as suddenly as she had appeared. The gentleman recognized her and was both humiliated and furious, threatening the friar with revenge. What does the magician do? He simply replies, 'Don't threaten me or I'll embarrass you even more; and think twice before you try to deceive someone as clever as me again.'

The English historian Thomas Wright comments on this story, saying, 'This kind of display of magic was probably the result of in-depth knowledge of the natural sciences.' Undoubtedly, magic was the result of this kind of knowledge and the Hermeticists, magicians, astrologers and alchemists never claimed anything else. It was certainly not their fault that the majority of people thought all magic was the work of the Devil. An unscrupulous and fanatical clergy encouraged the public in this belief. The Inquisition tortured anyone suspected of black or white magic. So it's not surprising then that the Hermeticists, magicians, astrologers and alchemists said nothing at all on the subject. In their own writings, they claimed that magic is simply the application of natural forces to passive objects or individuals. This produces effects which may be surprising but are entirely natural.

The mystical fragrance and music manifested by Roger Bacon are phenomena that are also seen today. Apart from the author's personal experience, people have written from England to the Theosophical Society describing their experiences. They have heard ravishing music coming from invisible instruments and smelled delightful fragrances produced by what they believed to be spirit-agency. One of these writers describes the most powerful perfume of sandalwood filling the house for weeks after a seance. In this case, the medium was a member of a private family and the seances all took place within the family home. Another writer describes what he calls a musical knocking. The forces producing these present-day phenomena must also have been at work in Roger Bacon's time. As for apparitions, they appear nowadays in spiritualist seances and are verified by scientists. This makes it more believable than ever that Roger Bacon was also able to manifest supernatural visions.

In 1558, the Italian philosopher Giambattista della Porta, known as Baptista Porta, published a book called *Natural Magic*. In it, he catalogues secret formulas for producing extraordinary effects by manipulating the occult powers of nature. Although 'magicians' believed as much in a world of invisible spirits as today's spiritualists, none of them claimed to produce their magic under the control of spirits or with their help alone. They knew only too well how difficult it is to keep away elementary spirit entities once the door has been opened to them. Even the magic of the Chaldeans was nothing more than a deep knowledge of the properties of medicinal herbs and minerals. A magician would only attempt to communicate directly with pure spiritual beings when he wanted divine help. Even when he tried to communicate through the use of religious rites, some spirits could only be evoked subjectively and only by someone who was spiritually pure and prayerful. This was especially true of spirits that remain invisible and communicate with the living through clairvoyance, clairaudience and trance. All physical phenomena were generated simply by applying an understanding of natural forces. They were certainly not produced by sleight of hand.

The ancient magicians worked patiently for something far

more important than passing fame. They did not pursue immortality but they became immortal nevertheless as anyone does who works selflessly for the good of humanity. These rich-poor alchemists were inspired by eternal truth. They turned their attention to matters beyond common knowledge. They believed every question had an answer with the exception of the ultimate mystery of God. They were daring in their investigations and faithful to the rule of remaining silent about what they had learned. Their instinct was to be benevolent, unselfish and unpretentious. They disregarded wealth, luxury and power and considered gaining knowledge to be the most important thing of all. They regarded poverty, hunger, hard work and loss of reputation as small prices to pay for the achievement of knowledge. These men could have lived in luxury. Instead they chose to die in poverty rather than betray their values and give in to worldly temptations. The lives of Paracelsus, the German polymath Cornelius Agrippa and the Welsh alchemist Eugenius Philalethes are all well-known examples of this kind of sacrifice.

If spiritualists want to hold on to their beliefs about the 'spirit world,' it's better not to invite scientists to run tests. Scientific experiment is bound to rediscover parts of the old magic practiced by Moses and Paracelsus. Scientists might see through the deceptive beauty of spiritualist apparitions and reveal the sylphs and fair undines of earlier Rosicrucian belief. They might discover these ancient spirits playing in the currents of modern spiritualism's psychic and odic force.[15]

William Crookes has already come to the conclusion that under the fair skin of the spirit Katie King, there is no soul. He believes she exists as some kind of entity but her apparent emotional warmth is just a reflection of the emotions of the medium and the other people at the seance. Meanwhile, Balfour

Stewart and Peter Guthrie Tait, authors of *The Unseen Universe*, have abandoned their 'electro-biological' theory. Instead they begin to perceive in the universal ether the possibility that the spirit world is a photographic album of the unmanifested, boundless God.

It's not accurate to classify all of the spirits that appear at seances as 'elemental'[16] or 'elementary.'[17] Many are human disembodied spirits. Especially those that control the medium subjectively to speak, write and behave in certain ways. Whether these spirits are good or bad largely depends on the morality of the medium, the circle of people present and their reasons for attending the seance. If they are there to satisfy their curiosity and to pass the time it is useless to expect anything serious. But, in any case, human spirits can never materialize themselves in human form. They never appear covered in warm solid flesh, with sweating hands and faces, and complete physical bodies. The most they can do is project a reflection of themselves into the seance. On rare occasions the touch of their hands and clothing can become perceptible to the senses. But it will not be felt as a human hand or solid material. It will be felt as a gentle passing breeze. 'Materialized spirits' that appear with beating hearts and loud voices (with or without the paraphernalia of an amplifying 'spirit trumpet'[18]) are not human spirits. Once heard, spirit voices are never forgotten. The term 'voice' doesn't begin to describe the extraordinary sound. The voice of a pure spirit is like the trembling murmur of an Aeolian harp echoing in the distance. The voice of a suffering, impure spirit sounds like a human voice echoing in an empty barrel.

This is the understanding of generations of magicians, based on their practical experience. The ancient wisdom is clear on this subject: the voices of spirits are inarticulate. The spirit-voice consists of a series of sounds like an ascending column of compressed air that surrounds the listener. Many eyewitnesses testified in the case of the prisoner Elizabeth Eslinger, who was under the care of a Dr Kerner. These witnesses were: Deputy Governor Mayer of Weinsberg Prison, magistrates Eckhart, Theurer, and Knorr (who gave sworn evidence), the engraver Duttenhofer, and Kapff, a mathematician. They testified that they saw the entity haunting Elizabeth Eslinger and it resembled a pillar of cloud. For eleven weeks Dr Kerner and his sons, several Lutheran ministers, Duttenhofer, the lawyer Fraas, the physicians Seifer and Sicherer, the judge Heyd, and the Baron von Hugel, and many others followed the entity each day. Whilst the entity was present, the prisoner Eslinger prayed constantly in a loud voice. The entity could also be heard at the same time and this ruled out ventriloquism. Its voice was described as having nothing human about it and no one could imitate its sound.

Further evidence on the nature of spirit voices appears in Chapter Seven. Suffice to say for now, there has never been enough evidence to support the spiritualists' claim that any materialized spirit was human. Disembodied spirits can make their presence felt and can communicate subjectively to people who are sufficiently sensitive. They can produce objective manifestations but they cannot manifest themselves other than in the way described above. They can control the body of a medium and express themselves in different ways that are familiar to spiritualists. But they do not materialize their own substanceless, purely spiritual divine essence.

This means that every genuine materialization in a seance is produced perhaps by the will of the spirit which seems to appear. But at best it is only an impersonation. Or the materialization is caused by mischievous sprites or goblins that are generally harmless and too stupid to warrant being called devils. Left to their own devices, they are always ready to act up. On rare occasions, a disembodied spirit is able to control one of these goblins. The mischievous goblin will appear to be a human spirit but it will be nothing more than a puppet. Everything it does or says will be controlled by the immortal soul. But this requires conditions that rarely occur even at the seances of the most experienced spiritualists. However much they want to, not everyone can attract human spirits. One of the most powerful attractions for departed spirits is their affection for the people they have left behind on earth. This affection draws them steadily and gradually into the astral light that vibrates between the loved one on earth and the universal soul. Other important conditions are that members of the seance are harmonious with each other and that each person is genuine in their desire to communicate with the other side.

But suppose this explanation is wrong. Suppose the 'materialized' spirits appearing in darkened rooms from even darker cabinets are, in fact, the spirits of deceased people. Why is there such a difference between these spirits and the ghosts that appear unexpectedly and spontaneously in the absence of any cabinet or medium? These ghosts, restless souls, may hover around the spots where they were murdered or come back for some other mysterious reasons of their own. But whoever heard of them coming back with warm hands, indistinguishable from living people apart from the fact that they are known to be dead and buried? There is clear evidence of ghosts appearing suddenly but nothing like a materialized spirit had ever been seen until the advent of spiritualism. On 8 September 1876, a letter was published in the weekly journal, *The Medium and Daybreak*.[19] It was written by a lady traveling on the Continent. She describes an incident in a haunted house. She says a strange sound came from a dark corner of the library . . . As she looked up she saw a cloud or column of luminous vapor. The earth-bound ghost was hovering above the scene of his crime. This ghost was doubtless a genuine elementary apparition. It made itself visible of its own free will. It was in short an umbra.[20] As every shadow should be, it was visible but imperceptible to the touch. Or if it could be touched at all, it would feel like a handful of water or cold steam. It was luminous and misty. And as far as anyone can tell, it might have been the shadow of a departed human, tortured and earth-bound by its own remorse and crimes, or by the crimes of another person or ghost. The after death state is full of mysteries and the materializations of spiritualism only cheapen the subject and make it ludicrous in the eyes of people who have no real interest in finding the truth.

That said, the author of this book has previously stated publicly that she has seen materialized spirits. This is true and I am happy to repeat the claim. I have seen materialized spirits with the outer appearance of acquaintances, friends, and even relatives. With many witnesses present, I have heard those friends and relatives speak in languages unknown to the medium and anyone else in the room apart from myself. In some cases the languages were unknown to almost every medium in America and Europe because they were dialects from the East. At the time, these examples were taken as proof of the genuine mediumship of the uneducated Vermont farmer who sat in the cabinet. But these figures were not the forms of the people they appeared to be. They were simply representations created and animated by the elementaries. I have not previously discussed this subject because the public was not ready to accept the idea that there are elemental and elementary spirits. Since then, this subject has been raised and discussed openly. There is less risk now in bringing the ancient wisdom to the public's attention. Public opinion is finally ready to consider the topic thoughtfully and without bias - two years of campaigning have changed things for the better.

According to the Greek geographer Pausanias, 400 years after the battle of Marathon (during the first Persian invasion of Greece in 490 BC), the battlefield still echoed with the neighing of horses and shouts of shadow-soldiers. If the ghosts of the slaughtered soldiers were their genuine spirits (after all, they looked like shadows, not materialized men), what produced the neighing of the horses? Was it horse spirits? It's impossible for any zoologist or spiritualist to prove whether or not horses have spirits. And if it turns out that horses don't have spirits, then do we assume that the neighing sounds at Marathon were made by the immortal souls of the soldiers? Were they simply trying to make the spectral battle appear more real? There are many stories of people having seen phantom dogs, cats and other animals. These are as reliable as the stories told about human ghosts. Who or what lies behind the appearance of the ghosts of departed animals? Is it human spirits once again? This is the crux of the matter. Either animals have surviving spirits and souls just like humans or Porphyry is right in claiming that there is an invisible world of tricky and malicious spirit beings. These are intermediary spirits between the physical and non-physical worlds who can take on any imaginable shape including the shapes of humans and animals.

Before deciding whether or not animal apparitions are the returning spirits of dead creatures, it should be considered how the spectral animals behave. Do they act like their living counterparts? Do the ghosts of predators stalk their prey? Are the ghosts of herd animals quick to flee? Or are they uncharacteristically aggressive? Famously, the Salem witches claimed that dogs, cats, pigs and other animals came into their rooms and trampled on them in their sleep, bit them and talked to them. Often these animals encouraged them to commit suicide or other crimes. In the well-documented case of Elizabeth Eslinger, the ghost of a Catholic priest was accompanied by a large black dog which the priest called his father. Many witnesses saw it jump on the beds of the prison inmates. At another time the same priest appeared with one or two lambs. Most of the people tried at Salem were accused of speaking to yellow birds and plotting evil with them. The birds would sit on their shoulders or on the beams overhead. Specter animals are genuine phenomena. Denying this would disregard the evidence of thousands of witnesses from all over the world and throughout history. It would also suggest that only modern mediums have the ability to communicate with the spirit world. Specter animals display all the worst characteristics of human nature without being human themselves. If they are not human what are they? The only explanation is that they are elemental spirits.

Descartes was one of few people bold enough to claim that occult medicine would lead to the advancement of science. The French psychiatrist Brière de Boismont shared Descartes' view and went further, openly expressing his belief in 'supernaturalism,' which he considered to be the 'universal belief system.' In his book *On Hallucinations (Des Hallucinations)*, he says, 'Along with the French Prime Minister Guizot, we believe that the existence of society is inextricably linked with supernaturalism. Modern reason, in spite of positivism, cannot explain the root cause of any phenomenon and yet it rejects the supernatural. The supernatural is universal and the source of all life. Often the cleverest minds are its most dedicated followers.'

Christopher Columbus discovered America but Amerigo Vespucci took the credit and the continent was named after him. The magnet - the bone of Horus[21] - had played an essential part in ancient magical nature rituals twelve centuries before Paracelsus. Paracelsus rediscovered the hidden properties of the magnet and became the rightful founder of the medieval school of magnetism and divine influence in human affairs. But it was Mesmer, nearly 300 years after Paracelsus' death, who demonstrated magnetism to the public and took the credit. This credit was really due to Paracelsus, who died in poverty. That's the way the world works. New discoveries evolve from old knowledge. New men appear but human nature remains the same.

Chapter Three

The mirror of the soul cannot reflect both earth and
heaven; and the one vanishes from its surface, as the other is
glassed upon its deep.

ZANONI, EDWARD BULWER-LYTTON

Qui, donc, t'a donné la mission d'annoncer au peuple que
la Divinité n'existe pas - quel avantage trouves-tu à
persuader l'homme qu'une force aveugle préside à ses
destinées et frappe au hasard le crime et la vertu?

*Who, then, gave you the mission to announce to the people that
there is no God? What advantage is there in persuading man
that nothing but blind force presides over his destiny
and randomly punishes both crime and virtue?*

DISCOURS, ROBESPIERRE 7 MAY 1794

Few genuine spiritualist phenomena are caused by disembodied human spirits. Some phenomena are produced by occult forces of nature acting through a few genuine mediums. These occult forces are also used consciously by the so-called 'jugglers' of India and Egypt. These cases deserve careful and serious scientific investigation especially now that several respected authorities have declared them genuine. No doubt there are 'conjurors' who can perform cleverer tricks than all the 'John Kings' in England and America put together. The French magician Jean-Eugène Robert-Houdin certainly could. But he still laughed out loud when the academicians wanted him to claim in the newspapers that he could rap answers to questions or make a table move without touching it. He said it was impossible unless he was allowed to prepare the table first. The Honorable Secretary of the National Association of Spiritualists, Algernon Joy, offered a notorious London conjuror £1,000 if he could produce the phenomena usually associated with mediums. The conjuror refused unless he was able to make the attempt without any interference from the committee. The fact that he refused proves that no exposé of occult phenomena is possible. Suppose he was challenged to reproduce even the simplest tricks of any common Indian conjurer under the same conditions. These would be: the place for the performance to be chosen by the investigators. The conjurer to be informed of the location only at the last moment. The experiment to be made in broad daylight without preparations, and with no accomplice other than a naked boy, and the conjurer to be semi-clothed. Suppose he was then asked to replicate three of the most common tricks performed by Indian conjurors. These tricks were recently performed for a group of gentlemen in the Prince of Wales' entourage. 1: Turn a rupee held in the hand of a skeptic into a live cobra with a venomous and fatal bite. 2: Take a seed chosen at random by the spectators, plant it in a flower pot provided by them, and make it mature and bear fruit in less than a quarter of an hour. 3: Lie out on the points of three swords which have their hilts buried in the ground and their sharp points facing upward. Then remove the swords one after the other until the conjuror is finally lying on nothing - lying on air, miraculously suspended about one yard from the ground. Suppose all of the above could be replicated by any illusionist - from the French magician Jean-Eugène Robert-Houdin to the latest charlatan famous for attacking spiritualism. On that day, we'll believe something equally impossible - that mankind evolved from the hind toe of Thomas Huxley's extinct mountain horse *Eocene Orohippus*.[1]

It's worth saying again that there is no professional conjuror in the North, South or West who can compete with the effects created by the untrained street conjurers of the East. They don't need a theatrical exhibition space like London's Egyptian Hall[2] and they don't need any special preparations or rehearsals. They are always ready at a moment's notice to summon the hidden powers of nature which are inaccessible to European conjurers and scientists. As the Biblical figure Elihu puts it in the Book of Job, 'It is not only the old who are wise, not only the aged who understand what is right.' In the words of the English philosopher Henry More, 'If there were any modesty left in mankind, the stories of the Bible would assure men of the existence of angels and spirits.' More goes on to say, 'I think it is fortunate that there are current examples of spiritualist phenomena to open our sluggish minds to the idea that there are other intelligent beings beyond the physical plane . . . If bad spirits exist, then by extension good spirits must also exist and ultimately there must be a God.' There is a moral to this story, not only for scientists but also for theologians. It seems our scientists and theologians take seriously any plausible fraudster who comes their way. By doing so they show how little they really know about psychology and make themselves ridiculous in the eyes of any serious thinker. Public opinion on the subject of spiritualism has been shaped by conjurors and self-appointed gurus who are not worthy of being taken seriously.

The ridicule of these people has done more to hold back the development of this area of science than the difficulties of the subject itself. Some people mock the subject just because it is fashionable to do so. Inexperienced scientists laugh at what they don't understand. This has done more to keep man in the dark about his psychic abilities than the complexities and challenges that surround the subject. This is especially true in the case of spiritualistic phenomena. In most cases these phenomena have been investigated by people without sufficient skill. This is because the scientists who might otherwise have studied the phenomena have been frightened off by sensational exposés of fraud, and by jokes and gossip that have caught the public imagination. Moral cowardice can strike even the most senior academics. Modern spiritualism is alive and well despite being ignored by the scientific community and despite the claims of self-appointed debunkers. Revered scientists Michael Faraday and David Brewster sneer contemptuously at the idea of spiritual manifestations. Mr X of London has made a career of debunking spiritual manifestations by replicating their effects. But none of these men can provide conclusive proof that spiritual manifestations do not occur. In his recent so-called exposé, Mr X says, 'My theory is that the medium Charles Williams dressed up and impersonated the spirits John King and Peter. Nobody can prove that this wasn't the case.' In spite of the emphatic tone of this statement, it appears that it is nothing more than a theory. Spiritualists could easily contradict

Mr X by saying it is up to him to prove that it is the case.

Fortunately there are very few sworn enemies of spiritualism. Although small in number, they shout all the louder and their zeal would be better spent on a worthier cause. They are pseudo-philosophers. They are young Americans proclaiming themselves to be men of science. Their academic credentials are sometimes based on little more than owning an electrical device or having delivered an immature lecture on insanity and 'mediomania' or the insanity of mediums. These men are profound thinkers and physiologists, if you believe their own publicity. There is no 'metaphysical nonsense' about them. They are positivists, unquestioningly devoted to the positivism of the French philosopher Auguste Comte. They are proud to be saving gullible humanity from the dangers of superstition and rebuilding humanity's perception of the cosmos on positivist principles. The fear of psychic phenomena drives them to distraction. The easiest way to offend them is to suggest that they may have immortal spirits. To hear them talk you would think that a man can have no soul other than a 'scientific' or an 'unscientific' soul, whatever that may mean.

Some 30 or 40 years ago in France, Auguste Comte woke up one fine morning with the very irrational idea of becoming a prophet. He had started out as a pupil of the École Polytechnique and gone on to work there for years as a répétiteur of transcendent analysis and rationalistic mechanics. In America there's a prophet on every street corner. In Europe they are as rare as black swans. But France is the land of novelties. Auguste Comte became a prophet and people are so easily influenced that even in England he was regarded for a while as the Isaac Newton of the 19th Century.

Enthusiasm for Auguste Comte spread like wildfire in

Germany, England and America. He gained well-informed followers in France but only for a time. The prophet needed money; the disciples didn't want to give it. Comte had created a religion without a god and the enthusiasm of his followers faded as quickly as it had appeared. Only one follower remained who was worthy of attention - the French language scholar Paul-Émile Littré. Littré was a member of the French Institute and hoped to become a member of the Académie Française but this was vetoed in a malicious intervention by the Archbishop of Orléans.

If positivism was the 'religion of the future,' Auguste Comte was its high priest. He taught his ideas just as modern prophets of positivism do today. He identified women as superior and separate from the rest of society. He put them on a pedestal and the price women paid was to be untouchable. The rationalists had laughed at the spirituality of the French philosopher Charles Fourier. They had laughed at the political movement Saint-Simonianism[3] for the same reason and their contempt for spiritualism was limitless. The same rationalists and materialists were snared by Comte's positivist rhetoric. Mankind has an inherent desire for some kind of divinity. He has an innate craving for 'the unknown.' These are desires that even the most committed atheist is not immune to. Comte's followers found themselves in an impossible position, seduced by the outward brilliance of his hyperbole.

The positivists of this country have disguised their bias as scholarship. They have organized themselves into clubs and committees to discredit spiritualism while pretending to investigate it impartially.

They are afraid to challenge the Church and Christian doctrine openly. So instead they try to undermine the basis of all religion - man's faith in God and his belief in his own immortality. Spiritualist phenomena offer an unorthodox foundation for faith and the positivists' strategy is to undermine that faith by ridiculing the foundation that spiritualism provides.

They attack spiritualism at its weakest point. They criticize it for lacking a scientific basis. They highlight the exaggerated claims made for it in the mystical theories of its promoters. They take advantage of its unpopularity. Like Don Quixote tilting at windmills, they claim to be benefitting society by freeing it from superstition.

How far is positivism superior to spiritualism? Are the followers of positivism less deluded than the mediums of spiritualism? Which of them needs psychiatric help most? Is it the mediums? Or the positivists who claim to be so concerned for them? Before answering these questions it's important to point out that three quarters of the scandalous revelations associated with modern spiritualism can be attributed to opportunistic fraud. Comte has depicted a sexless future where women are artificially inseminated for the purposes of procreation. This idea is simply an echo of the earlier ideal of free love personified by Aphrodite. Comte's followers offer an optimistic view of the future characterized by ever-increasing social progress. This has encouraged some pseudo spiritualists to organize themselves into communist groups. None of these groups has lasted very long. They were destined to fail because their main feature was a materialistic animalism dressed up in sham philosophy peppered with difficult Greek names.

In the fifth book of *The Republic*, Plato suggests a method for improving the human race. He suggests eliminating unhealthy or deformed individuals and allowing only the best specimens of men and women to breed. When Comte developed similar ideas, he was not suggesting anything new.

Comte was a mathematician. He combined several utopian

concepts, interpreted them in his own way, improved on Plato's original idea and formalized eugenics - the most monstrous ideology ever conceived by the human mind.

This is not a challenge to Comte as a philosopher but as a social reformer. His political, philosophical and religious views are irredeemably dark. But there are often isolated instances of profound logic and enlightened thought which are as brilliant as some commentators suggest. They are as dazzling as lightning but once the lightning has struck, the sky is darker than ever.

His works could be re-edited into a volume of highly original aphorisms. These would give a clear and clever definition of most social problems but no idea of how to remedy them. The same would be true of the six volumes of his dialogue parodying the priesthood, *The Catechism of the Religion of Positivism (Cors De Philosophie Positive)*. Comte's followers suggest his esoteric teachings were not intended for the general public. If the teachings of positivism are compared with the actions of its followers, it soon becomes apparent that a very poor belief system lies at the heart of it all.

Comte teaches that women must cease to be merely extensions of men. Positivist thinking on marriage and the family consists of making men and women equal by separating women from the idea of motherhood. Positivism anticipates a future where sex is replaced by artificial insemination. In the meantime Comte's rank and file followers openly recommend polygamy and others claim that their beliefs are the perfect example of spiritual enlightenment.

The Roman Catholic clergy are always ready to see the Devil in everything. In their view Comte's woman of the future is vulnerable to sexual possession by male demons. In the view of less fanciful people, the positivist woman must be regarded as a two-legged mare reserved for breeding. Even Paul-Émile Littré embraced positivism with some well-judged reservations. In 1859 he wrote:

'Comte thought he had established the founding principles of practical positivism and created the social and religious system of the future. We agree with the first part of the sentence but have reservations about the second.'

Littré goes on to say, 'In his book *System of Positive Philosophy (Système de Politique Positive)*, Comte established a philosophy which must ultimately replace all theology and metaphysics. Naturally, this philosophy can be applied practically to the organization of society as a whole. It has nothing arbitrary in it. It is a work of genuine social science. In following the principles of positivist philosophy, I accept its fundamental consequences.'

So saying, Littré shows himself to be a chip off the old block. Comte's entire system of thought seems to have been built on a play on words. For 'positivism' read 'nihilism.'[4] For 'celibacy' read 'permissiveness' and so on.

Positivism is a religion based on negation. It's almost impossible to follow without saying white when meaning black!

Littré continues, 'Positivist philosophy does not accept atheism. The atheist is not really free of belief but in his own way he is still religious. He gives his explanation about the origin of things. He knows how they began. Atheism is pantheism. Atheism as a system of thought is still theological and so it belongs to the ancient tradition of religious belief.'

Quoting any more of this paradoxical nonsense would be a waste of time. Comte reached the height of absurdity and inconsistency when he called his philosophy a religion. And as is usually the case, the followers have gone further in absurdity than their leader. There are American academies devoted to Comte's positivism where self-styled philosophers shine like glow worms next to the sun. They leave us in no doubt about their beliefs. They compare Comte's 'system of thought' with the 'idiocy' of spiritualism and naturally find positivism superior. Comte quotes the French revolutionary Marc Caussidière (without crediting him) exclaiming, 'To destroy you must replace.' And his followers take up the cause, promoting positivism as a replacement for Christianity, spiritualism and even science.

One of them lectures, 'Positivism is an integral doctrine. It rejects completely all forms of theological and metaphysical belief. It rejects all forms of supernaturalism including spiritualism. Instead of studying the fixed formulas of spiritualist phenomena, the true positivist focuses on the so-called causes of these phenomena, whether the immediate or the ultimate cause.' He goes on to plagiarize Littré, 'On this basis positivism also rejects atheism because the atheist is a theologian at heart. The atheist does not reject the question of whether or not there is a god. He only rejects religion's answer and so he is illogical. We positivists reject the same question on the basis that it is unanswerable by the intellect and it would be a waste of our efforts to search for immediate or ultimate causes. As you can see, positivism gives a complete explanation of the world, of man, his duty and destiny.'

Bravo! In contrast, here is what a leading scientist thinks about this system. The chemist Robert Hare says, 'It turns out that Comte's positivist philosophy is merely negative. Comte admits he doesn't know the sources or causes of nature's laws. He claims they are so perfectly unknowable that it's a waste of time investigating them. Of course this approach makes him a self-confessed dunce about the causes of natural laws or how they can be understood. His whole approach is based on negative argument and this forms the basis of his objection to the facts of spiritual creation.

Spiritualism concedes that the atheist has dominion over the material world. But over and above the material world spiritualism has a dominion of far greater importance, just as eternity is greater than the average human lifespan and the infinity of space is greater than the surface of planet earth.'

Positivism sets out to destroy theology, metaphysics, spiritualism, atheism, materialism, pantheism, and science, and in the end it must destroy itself. The writer Comte de Mirville attributes to positivism the idea that, 'The human mind will become more orderly only when psychology becomes a sort of cerebral physics and history a kind of social physics.' First, Auguste Comte does away with God and the immortal souls of men and women. He then unwittingly undermines his own belief system by introducing metaphysics (which all the time he thought he was avoiding). In doing so he says goodbye to the last traces of philosophical thought.

Paul Janet was a French philosopher and an elected member of the Academy of Moral and Political Sciences, one of the five academies of the Institut de France. In 1864, Janet gave a lecture on positivism including the following remarkable comments:

'Some people have been brought up on a diet of rational science. But in spite of this they feel an irresistible attraction to philosophy. They can only satisfy this interest with knowledge they already have. They have no real understanding of psychology. They have studied only the rudiments of metaphysics. Nevertheless they are determined to attack both metaphysics and psychology, knowing as little about the first as they do the second. Once they have defeated metaphysics and psychology they will imagine that they have founded a positive science. But in truth they have only created a new metaphysical theory that is deformed and incomplete. They claim to have the kind of authority that only really belongs to the true sciences, those that are based on experiment and rational evaluation. But they do not have this authority. Their flawed ideas belong to the same category as the ideas they attack. This explains the weakness of their position. Their ideas don't stand up to scrutiny and soon fall into obscurity.'

American positivists have joined forces to overthrow spiritualism. But to show that they are unbiased they ask questions such as: 'Could science find any rational basis for the religious beliefs of the Immaculate Conception, the Trinity and Transubstantiation?' In their own words, they also 'make a point of saying that spiritualism is no more absurd than traditional religious beliefs.' That's all well and good. But there is no religious absurdity or spiritualist fantasy as perverted and brutal as the positivists' artificial insemination. They ignore the full extent of a woman's nature. Instead they apply their insane theories to the creation of an impossible woman for future generations to worship. They would replace man's natural companion with the West Indian female fetish of the Obeah religion[5] - a wooden idol stuffed every day with serpents' eggs to be hatched by the heat of the sun!

Why should Christian mystics be criticized for being too ready to believe? Why should spiritualists be consigned to the insane asylum when a quasi-religion like positivism with its ideology of artificial insemination has followers even among academicians? Comte's followers lap up his insane expressions of feeling such as: 'My eyes are dazzled. Each day I see more clearly the increasing connection between the rise in society of idealized femininity and the mental and moral decline of the act of worshiping the Son of God. Already the Virgin has replaced God in the minds of southern Catholics! Positivism achieves the utopia dreamed of in the Middle Ages. It does so by presenting the Holy Family as the offspring of a virgin mother without a husband. . .' After describing the practicalities of artificial insemination, Comte continues, 'The development of the new process will create a class without heredity. This process will be better at producing spiritual and civic leaders than natural reproduction. The authority of these leaders will rest on their pure birth which will be unimpeachable.'

In response, it seems reasonable to ask if anything more ludicrous than this perfect 'future race' has ever been suggested by the 'vagaries of spiritualism' or the mysteries of Christianity? The course of positivism could well be altered by some of its followers who openly promote polygamy. But assuming this isn't the case, there will be a baby-boom of offspring from 'mothers without husbands.' Whether or not this baby-boom will produce a dynasty of spiritual leaders, it's impossible to say.

The philosophy of positivism has produced a circle of men quick to moralize. The positivist and prolific essayist Frederic Marvin wrote, 'These are sad, very sad times full of dead and dying faiths. They are full of pointless prayers searching fruitlessly for vanishing gods. But these are also great times full of golden light from the rising sun of science. But some people are abandoned by faith and intellectually bankrupt. They look for comfort in the illusion of spiritualism, the false hope of transcendentalism, or the will-o'-the-wisp of mesmerism. What should we do for them?'

Nowadays the will-o'-the-wisp is a familiar image in the popular imagination but this wasn't always the case. Not so long ago a correspondent of the *London Times* denied its existence. His views went unchallenged until the work of the British scientist Thomas Phipson. Supported by Giovanni Battista Beccaria, Friedrich Humboldt and other naturalists, Phipson was able to prove the *Times* correspondent wrong. Positivists like Marvin should choose their words more carefully. As far as mesmerism is concerned, this 'will-o'-the-wisp' has been adopted in many parts of Germany and is used successfully in more than one hospital. Its occult properties have been proven and many leading physicians are convinced of its value. That pompous lecturer on mediumship, the American physician Frederic Marvin, cannot compete with their expertise and hard-earned reputations.

Many positivists believe that Europe's greatest scientists were followers of Comte. It's difficult to say how far this is true but certainly Thomas Huxley refuses to be labeled a positivist even though he is widely regarded as one of Europe's greatest scientists. The London psychiatrist Henry Maudsley feels the same way. Thomas Huxley delivered a lecture in 1868 in Edinburgh called 'The Physical Basis of Life.' In this lecture he describes his surprise at being called a positivist by the Archbishop of York. 'As far as I am concerned, the Archbishop can rip Mr Comte to shreds with logic and I won't try to stop him. As far as I have studied positivist philosophy, I find little or nothing of any scientific value in it. A great deal of positivism is as hostile to science as Catholicism and its doctrine of absolute papal supremacy. In fact Comte's philosophy could be described as Catholicism minus Christianity.' Huxley goes on to accuse his audience of betraying their fellow Scot David Hume - they let the Archbishop get away with crediting Hume's philosophy to Comte. Huxley declares, 'It was enough to make David Hume turn in his grave. Almost within earshot of his house, a Scottish audience listened without a murmur as his most distinctive ideas were attributed to Comte - that Frenchman writing 50 years later - whose dull and overblown writings have none of Hume's vigorous thought and clarity of style.'

Poor Comte! In this country at least, it appears that the greatest exponents of his philosophy are now reduced to 'one physicist, one physician who specializes in nervous diseases, and one lawyer.' A very witty critic nicknamed this desperate trio 'an anomalistic triad, working hard in the name of positivism but never quite finding time to become properly acquainted with its own philosophy.'

In conclusion, the positivists take every opportunity to discredit spiritualism and advance their own religion. Positivists blow their trumpets incessantly but the blasts are never going to bring down the walls of any modern-day Jericho. Nevertheless they will try any tactic to bring about the fall of spiritualism. They make uniquely absurd and contradictory statements. Their 'logical' arguments against spiritualism are cast iron. For instance, in a recent lecture, it was claimed that: 'Too much religion leads to sexual immorality. Priests, monks, nuns, saints, mediums, mystics and zealots are famous for their incessant promiscuity.'

Positivism sets itself up as a religion while spiritualism has never pretended to be anything other than a science, an emerging philosophy. Spiritualism defines itself as an investigation into hidden and as yet unexplained forces of nature. More than one legitimate scientist has demonstrated various spiritualist phenomena to be objective. Meanwhile spiritualism's detractors have failed to discredit the phenomena.

Positivists who dismiss every metaphysical phenomenon are like Hudibras, the character created by the English satirist Samuel Butler. Hudibras was so skilled in rhetoric that every time he opened his mouth, out came a flowery metaphor:

> *For rhetorick, he could not ope*
> *His mouth, but out there flew a trope.*

Unfortunately, it's not just dilettantes and pseudo-scientists who need to be scrutinized carefully. When important scientists investigate new fields, their work is often accepted without being properly challenged. Experimental research is inherently cautious. Theoretical advances are always tentative. Authorities can be respected to such a degree that they become difficult to question. All of these things encourage narrow-mindedness which naturally turns into dogmatism. Scientific progress comes at a price. Too often someone with a new idea is ridiculed and rejected out of hand. An innovator must charge at the strongholds of scientific tradition and belief like a soldier with a bayonet. He can't rely on any inside help to open a door to the fortress. He can afford to ignore the objections of the dilettantes but he must face and overcome the opposition of the scientific establishment. Knowledge is increasing rapidly but it is not thanks to the majority of scientists. In every case they have done their best to discredit the new discovery and its pioneer. Individual courage, intuition and persistence should be recognized. Most discoveries were ridiculed at first and dismissed as absurd and unscientific. Some scientists had abilities that put other less skilled men to shame. The work of these pioneers went unrecognized until their discoveries could no longer be ignored. Unfortunately these same pioneers then went on to ignore the next generation of scientists in their field. So humanity progresses one step at a time within its limited circle of knowledge. Science has to correct its own mistakes constantly, each day revising the incorrect theories of the day before. This has been the case in areas of psychological research such as the study of the physical and spiritual phenomenon of mesmerism. But it has also been true of conventional scientific discoveries despite the fact that those discoveries are easier to analyze.

Where next? Is it better to look to the past, to the example of medieval scholars who conspired with the clergy? They set out to discredit the theory that the earth revolves around the sun simply to protect religious dogma. Or is it better to refer to the case of naturalists who maintained that fossils were not the remains of living creatures? These 18th-century naturalists, in their so-called facsimile theory, thought fossils were only replicas of animals. For more than a century, they fought amongst themselves over the true nature of the fossil record until the French naturalist Georges-Louis Buffon set them straight. There is nothing transcendental about an oyster shell. It ought to be a straightforward subject to study. If scientists could not agree about something so simple, how could they agree about the fleeting hands, faces and sometimes whole bodies manifested by a genuine medium?

Pierre Flourens, perpetual secretary of the French Academy of Sciences, wrote a book called *Buffon, the History of his Works and Ideas (Buffon, Histoire de ses Travaux et de ses Idées)*. This reviewed the contribution made by Georges-Louis Buffon to the field of naturalism. Skeptical scientists might benefit from reading this in their spare time. Flourens shows how Buffon finally overturned the facsimile theory and how its supporters went on to deny everything under the sun. At times the Academy would fall into a frenzy of denial. It rejected Benjamin Franklin and his theories of electricity. It laughed at the engineer Robert Fulton and his application of steam power. It implied the engineer Albert Auguste Perdormet and his scheme to build railways was insane. It belittled the theories of the English physician William Harvey and declared the Huguenot potter Bernard Palissy to be 'as stupid as one of his own pots!'

In his popular book *History of the Conflict Between Religion and Science*, John Draper claims that the clergy are the biggest obstacle to scientific progress. Many of the scientific discoveries listed above are referenced by Draper in his book. He condemns the clergy for resisting new discoveries but says nothing about the scientific community's resistance to new ideas. When it comes to science, he claims that 'knowledge is power' and he is absolutely right. But it is also true to say that the abuse of power is unforgivable. It makes no difference whether that abuse comes from a highly developed intellect or ignorance. The influence of the clergy has declined dramatically. Nowadays the scientific world takes no notice of them or their objections. With the clergy out of the way, the scientists have seized their power to endorse or reject ideas. They use it to isolate people from the spiritual realm and keep them confined to the material world.

On 13 August 1875, the physician James Gully wrote a letter to *The Spiritualist*, criticizing the physicist John Tyndall and his fire-mist theory. The editor replied by pointing out that all spiritualists would be burned at the stake if it weren't for the rise of science. Science has indirectly benefited public life - if nothing else by making it unacceptable to burn intellectuals. But scientists like Faraday, Tyndall, Huxley, and Agassiz are antagonistic toward spiritualism. Suppose these scientists and their followers had the unlimited power of the Inquisition. Wouldn't spiritualists have good reason to feel less safe than they do now? Even if they didn't burn spiritualists at the stake (it's against the law to cremate people alive) wouldn't they send every single spiritualist they could to the insane asylum? They call them names like 'incurable monomaniacs,' 'hallucinating fools' and 'fetish worshipers.' It's difficult to see why the editor of *The Spiritualist* should feel so grateful to science and scientists. The recent prosecution in London of the medium Henry Slade should make spiritualists pause for thought. Intransigent materialism is often more blindly bigoted than religious fanaticism.

In the December 1875 issue of *Popular Science Monthly*, John Tyndall published a caustic essay called 'Martineau and Materialism.' This essay is one of Tyndall's best works, although in future he'll probably to want to remove some of the strong language. That aside, it's worth considering what he has to say on the subject of consciousness. He starts by quoting the religious philosopher James Martineau. Martineau asks, 'A man can say *I feel, I think, I love* but how is consciousness a part of this?' Tyndall then answers, 'The link between the physical brain and the fact of consciousness is unfathomable. A thought and the corresponding biological action in the brain occur simultaneously. But we do not have the ability, or anything approaching it, to trace the link from one to the other. They occur simultaneously but we do not know why. Suppose our minds and senses were expanded so that we could observe the molecules of the brain directly. Suppose we were capable of following changes in their biological state. And suppose we were aware of the corresponding states of thought and feeling. We would still be unable to answer the question, *How are these physical processes connected with the facts of consciousness?* The chasm between the two classes of phenomena would still be intellectually impassable.'

Tyndall cannot cross the chasm between biological brain function and consciousness. Similarly, in his fire-mist theory, he cannot bridge the chasm between the fire-mist and its primal cause. But this chasm is only an obstacle to people with no spiritual sense. As far back as 1854, the physiologist Joseph Rodes Buchanan published a work called *Outlines of Lectures on the Neurological System of Anthropology*. This work suggests how this chasm can be bridged. It contains ideas that are likely to bear fruit in the future but have so far been marginalized by self-proclaimed experts with little real knowledge. The materialist establishment is built entirely on the foundation of reason. Even when materialists have stretched reason to its limits they can still only show us a universe of molecules brought to life by an unknown force. Tyndall wrote a text analyzing the mental state of clergy who believe in the supremacy of the

Pope. By changing a few words, the same text can be read as an analysis of the weaknesses of modern science. For 'spirit guides' read 'scientists.' For 'pre-scientific past' substitute 'materialistic present.' For 'spirit' read 'science.' Now the paragraph that follows gives a perfect picture of the modern scientist.

'. . . Their spiritual guides live entirely in the pre-scientific past. Even their cleverest minds are stunted when it comes to scientific truth. They have eyes but they do not see. They have ears but they do not hear. They are blinded and deafened by the preoccupations of another age. When it comes to science, the spiritual guide's brain is like the undeveloped brain of a child. He has childlike scientific knowledge but mature spiritual authority which he is able to wield over uneducated people. He is able to enforce practices that would make the more intelligent members of the spiritual community blush.' The above passage, interpreted as suggested, shows science for what it really is.

Ever since the first legal system was established, it has been necessary to have at least two or three reliable witnesses before a defendant could be found guilty and put to death. 'On the say-so of two or three witnesses shall the man who warrants it be put to death,' says Moses, the first law-maker in ancient history. 'The laws which put a man to death on the evidence of a single witness are fatal to freedom,' says the French lawyer and political philosopher Charles-Louis de Montesquieu. 'Common sense dictates that there should be two witnesses.'

The importance of reliable evidence has been accepted in every country. But even the evidence of a million people against one is not enough for scientists. Hundreds of thousands of people give evidence but it makes no difference. Scientists have eyes but they will not see! They are determined to remain blind and deaf. The evidence of millions of American and European spiritualists and 30 years of practical demonstration deserve serious consideration. The verdict of twelve spiritualists, based on the evidence of two witnesses, is enough to sentence even a scientist to hang. It makes no difference that his crime was prompted by 'the motion of cerebral molecules' unrestrained by morality or fear of future punishment.

Science in its totality should be respected as a way of approaching the divine. Only science can enable mankind to grasp the nature of God through a proper understanding of the cosmos. 'Science is the understanding of truth or facts,' says Webster's dictionary. 'It is an investigation of truth for its own sake and a pursuit of pure knowledge.' If this definition is correct, then the majority of scientists are not fulfilling their true purpose. 'Truth for its own sake!' Where best to search for that truth than in the unexplored mystery of the spiritual realm? Unfortunately, the majority of scientists are selective about the areas of nature they study. They choose only to investigate those areas that confirm their own biases.

Conventional medicine has no interest in studying the power of the mind. It's pointless to suggest that medicine is hardly an exact science and it could be beneficial for doctors to widen their horizons. They would do well to study psychism and mind power. Without a proper understanding of the mind, medical practice degenerates into mere guesswork. But of all the branches of medical knowledge, the mind is the one they almost totally ignore. The slightest challenge to established practice is seen as an outrage. An experimental treatment could save thousands of lives but the medical establishment confines itself to its tried and tested approaches. It rejects the new treatment and the person who discovered it until both have been officially endorsed. In the meantime thousands of unfortunate patients may die but that is of secondary importance as long as the medical establishment's reputation remains intact.

In theory, medicine should be the most benign of all scientific fields. But in practice no other discipline displays so many instances of petty prejudice, materialism, atheism, and damaging resistance to change. The work of leading physicians and the funding they receive hardly ever results in a useful discovery. Bloodletting (with leeches, suction cups or surgical knives) was overused and ultimately abandoned as a treatment. Patients with a fever are now given as much water as they like where previously they were not allowed any. They used to be given warm baths but now cold water is recommended. For a while, spa cures were all the rage. Peruvian bark was brought to Spain in 1632 but its potential as an anti-malarial drug went undiscovered for years. Unusually, the Church was one step ahead of science. Pope Innocent X highlighted the bark's medicinal properties on the recommendation of Cardinal Juan de Lugo. Later, the physicist and author Charles Bartlett Warring even attempted to identify the bark as originating from the Tree of Life in the Garden of Eden.

In his book *Demonologia,* the surgeon J.S. Forsyth describes many important remedies that were neglected at first and later came to attention by accident. He also shows that most of the new discoveries in medicine turn out to be no more than 'the revival and re-adoption of very ancient practices.' During the last century a female quack named Madame Nouffleur advertized and sold a secret cure-all for tapeworm. It was made from the root of the male fern. Louis XV bought the recipe for a large sum. The court physicians later discovered that the root had been recommended as early as the 2nd Century AD as a cure for tapeworm by the Greek physician and philosopher Galen. The gout powder, made famous by William Bentinck, the 2nd Duke of Portland, was known to the Roman physician Caelius Aurelianus as *daicentaureon*. Later it was discovered that it was also known to the earliest medical writers, who had found it in the works of ancient Greek philosophers. The same was true of Husson's eau medicinale, a medicinal water produced by the French army officer Nicolas Husson. This remedy for gout, made famous by Husson, was in fact a distillation of the *colchicum autumnale* or meadow saffron. The *colchicum* is identical to a plant called *hermodactylus* which was promoted as a cure for gout by the 4th and 5th-century Greek physicians Oribasius and Aëtius of Amida. Subsequently it went out of fashion and was no longer used. It was considered too old to be worthwhile by medical practitioners at the end of the last century.

Even the eminent French physiologist François Magendie rediscovered treatments that had already been used successfully by the earliest physicians. He proposed the use of prussic acid to treat tuberculosis. This treatment is described in the works of the 18th-century Swedish botanist Carl Linnaeus. In his *Amoenitates Academicae Volume IV*, Linnaeus describes the use of distilled laurel water to treat pulmonary tuberculosis successfully. The Roman philosopher and naturalist Pliny recommends the extract of almonds and cherry stones to cure persistent coughs. J.S. Forsyth writes in *Demonologia*, it is safe to assume that 'all of the opium derivatives thought to be modern discoveries can be found in the texts of ancient writers.' Those same writers nowadays go uncredited.

It is generally accepted that the East has been a center of advanced learning since the beginning of recorded history. Even the ancient Egyptians couldn't compete with the scholars of ancient Middle Asia in the study of botany and mineralogy. The German physician Kurt Sprengel, though biased in every other matter, acknowledges this point in *Toward a Pragmatic History of Medicine (Versuch einer Pragmatischen Geschichte der Arzneikunde)*. Despite this, whenever the subject of magic is raised, the magic of India is rarely discussed. This is because Indian magic is less well known than that of other ancient peoples. To Hindus magic is more esoteric than it was to the Egyptian priests, if that is possible. The existence of magic was regarded as so sacred that it was only ever half acknowledged, and it was only practiced in emergencies. It was seen as much more than mere symbolic ritual because it was thought to provide a direct connection to the divine. The Egyptian priests followed a strict moral code but this was nothing compared with the practices of the Hindu ascetics. They lived lives of greater spiritual purity. They developed miraculous powers by the supernatural command of everything earthly. People who knew them well held them in greater esteem than even the Zoroastrians of Chaldea. Hindu ascetics went without the basic comforts of life. They lived in woods as strict hermits. In comparison, the Egyptian priests gathered together in groups. Although history has maligned everyone who practiced magic and divination, it has recorded that the Hindu ascetics possessed great medical knowledge and unsurpassed skill in medical practice. There are many manuscripts preserved in Hindu temples providing written evidence of this. These ascetics may have been the founders of magic in India. Or they may have simply practiced what had been passed down to them by the seven primeval sages of India - the Rishis. Any attempt to verify this would be nothing more than speculation. A contemporary account describes them as follows: 'They took great care in the education of their young people, instilling the values of generosity and fairness. This did them credit. History records their debates and sayings proving they were experts in philosophy, metaphysics, astronomy, morality and religion.' They maintained their integrity under the rule of the most powerful princes. They would not lower themselves to visit the princes or ask for even a small favor. If the princes wanted the advice or intervention of the ascetics they would have to go themselves or send messengers. The ascetics had knowledge of the occult properties of every plant and mineral. They had gained a profound understanding of nature. They had expert knowledge of psychology and physiology, and the result was the science nowadays described condescendingly as magic.

Christians accept the miracles described in the Bible as fact. Not to believe in them would be sacrilege. However, they show contempt for the miraculous stories in the fourth Veda, the Atharva Veda, regarding them as evidence of devil worship. And yet there are many similarities between the Bible and the Atharva Veda, though this is an unpopular idea among certain Sanskrit scholars. In addition, it has now been proven that the Vedas were written thousands of years before the Bible. It is easy to see that if one book borrowed text from the other, it's not the authors of the Hindu sacred books that did the copying.

Many people in the West believe that the Hindus consider Brahma to be their supreme God. But the Hindu sacred books contain a story of the origin of the cosmos that shows this is not true. Brahma is a secondary deity. Like Jehovah he is 'a mover of the waters' - associated with the manipulation of water in the creation myth. Brahma is the creating god. Allegorical representations give him four heads corresponding to the four points of the compass. He is the maker of the physical universe, the architect of the world. In her book *Hindu Mythology* (*Mythologie des Indous*), the Swiss author Marie de Polier writes, 'In the beginning of creation the undeveloped universe was submerged in water, contained in the heart of the Eternal. The architect of the world, Brahma, sprang from this chaos and darkness. Balanced on a lotus leaf he floated on the waters unable to see anything but water and darkness.' This is almost identical to the Egyptian story of the origin of the cosmos. In the beginning, Athtor or Mother Night is the primeval element that fills the infinite void. Representing endless darkness, she exists alone in chaos brought to life by water and the universal spirit of the Eternal. Similarly, in Jewish scripture (when interpreted Kabbalistically) the story of creation opens with the spirit of God and his creative aspect - another deity. Seeing only chaos and darkness Brahma asks himself anxiously, 'Who am I? Where did I come from?' Then he hears a voice saying, 'Pray to Bhagavant - the Eternal, whose other name is Parabrahma.' Brahma rises out of the water and takes his place on the lotus. He contemplates the Eternal and the Eternal is pleased by his demonstration of piety. The Eternal lifts the primeval darkness, and opens Brahma's understanding. 'After this Brahma hatches as light from the universal egg which represents infinite chaos. His understanding is now opened and he begins work. He moves over the eternal waters inspired by the spirit of God inside him. As the mover of waters he is called Narayana.'

The lotus flower is sacred to both the Egyptians and the Hindus. It is the symbol of the Egyptian sky god Horus and of Brahma. It appears in every temple in Tibet or Nepal and is very rich in meaning. In pictures of the Annunciation, the archangel offers lilies to the Virgin Mary. The lilies have the same esoteric meaning as the lotus flower. (See *Dissertations Relating To Asia* by the linguistic scholar William Jones.) For Hindus, the lotus symbolizes the fertility of nature through the action of fire and water (spirit and matter). A verse in the *Bhagavad Gita* reads, 'I see Brahma the creator enthroned in thee above the lotus!' William Jones shows that the seeds of the lotus contain perfectly formed leaves even before they germinate. The seeds contain in miniature the plants they will become. In his book *The Heathen Religion in its Popular and Symbolical Development*, the American clergyman Joseph B. Gross described this phenomenon as 'nature giving us a complete miniature version of everything it produces.' Gross goes on to say that 'the seed of all flowering plants contains a preformed embryo plantlet.'

For Buddhists, the lotus also symbolizes fertility. The birth of Gautama Siddhartha was announced by Bhodisat, the spirit of Buddha. He appeared beside Gautama's mother, Maha-Maya, or Maha-Deva, holding a lotus flower. The Egyptians also depicted the gods Osiris and Horus with the lotus flower.

These examples demonstrate that the same idea is present in the three religious systems, Hindu, Egyptian and Judeo-Christian, suggesting a common source. Wherever the lotus appears it signifies the emergence of objective reality from obscurity or subjective thought. It signifies the eternal thought of the invisible deity passing from the abstract into concrete visible form. As soon as darkness was lifted and 'there was light,' Brahma's understanding was opened. The ideal world had previously been concealed in the divine mind. Now Brahma saw in it the quintessential forms of everything that would be called into existence in the future, and become visible. At this stage Brahma had not yet become the architect or the builder of the universe. First, like any architect, he had to familiarize himself with the plans. He had to understand the quintessential forms contained in the heart of the Eternal, just as the undeveloped lotus leaves are concealed in the seed of the lotus plant. In this story we can see the origins of the verse in Jewish scripture which reads, 'And God said, let the earth bring forth . . . the fruit tree yielding fruit after its kind, whose seed is in itself.' In all primitive religions, the 'Son of the Father' is the creative God i.e. God's thought made visible.

Before the Christian era there were trinities in Hinduism and Kabbalah. The trimurti of the Hindus is the trinity of Vishnu, Brahma and Shiva. In Kabbalistic Jewish scripture, the godhead is divided into three. The different trinities were fully explained and justified in the stories belonging to each faith tradition. In Christian belief we see symbols from the older faith traditions re-presented as Christian orthodoxy. For example, the lily held by the archangel in the Annunciation echoes the metaphysical significance of the lotus at the birth of Buddha.

The lotus is the product of fire (heat) and water. It is the dual symbol of spirit and matter. The god Brahma is the second person of the trinity. The same is true of Jehovah (Adam-Kadmon, the essence of the collective soul) in Kabbalah, and Osiris in the Egyptian tradition. A more accurate name for Osiris is Pimander, described by Hermes Trismegistus as 'the power of divine thought.' Pimander represents the root of all the Egyptian sun gods. The Eternal is the spirit of fire that gives concrete form to everything born out of water or the earth, everything evolved out of Brahma. But the universe is itself Brahma and Brahma is the universe. This is Spinoza's philosophy, derived from Pythagoras. The Dominican friar Giordano Bruno died a martyr for adopting it. The historical fact of Bruno's martyrdom shows how much Christian theology has deviated from its origins. Bruno was slaughtered for his interpretation of the symbol of the Cross, an interpretation which had been adopted by the earliest Christians and championed by the Apostles. The lotus flower held by the spirit of Buddha, Bhodisat, and later the lily held by the archangel Gabriel, both signify fire and water or the idea of creation and generation. This flower symbolism is worked into the earliest Christian dogma.

The beliefs of Bruno and Spinoza are almost identical, but

Bruno expresses his ideas much more explicitly. In his books *Concerning Cause, Principle and Unity (Causa, Principio et Uno)* and *On the Infinite Universe and Worlds (Infinito Universo e Mondi)*, Bruno's choice of words is far less cautious than Spinoza's. He is happy to acknowledge Pythagoras as the source of his information whereas Spinoza doesn't admit it as frankly. Both Spinoza and Bruno share the same view of the origin of the universe. For them, God is an entity complete in and of itself, an infinite spirit. God is the only being absolutely free and independent of any outside influence. God is the being who maintains the existence and order of the universe, exerting the same will that first brought material reality and the forces of the universe into being. The Hindu Svabhavikas believe that nothing exists but Svabhava (substance or essential nature) and this exists by itself without any creator. The Svabhavikas have been mistakenly described as atheists but they believe that everything is born out of Svabhava including men, gods and spirits. Similarly both Spinoza and Bruno came to the conclusion that the place to find God is within nature itself, not elsewhere. Creation is proportional to the power of the Creator. It follows then that the universe must be infinite and eternal if its Creator is infinite and eternal. One form emanates from its own essence and creates in turn another. Modern scholars claim that Bruno, 'unsustained by the hope of another and better world, still surrendered his life rather than his convictions.' From this it can be seen that Giordano Bruno had no belief in the continued existence of a person after death. John Draper says in no uncertain terms that Bruno did not believe in the immortality of the soul. He contrasts Bruno with the majority of Roman Catholic martyrs who did believe in an afterlife. In *History of the Conflict Between Religion and Science*, he writes, 'The transition from this life to the next, though hard, was the transition from temporary suffering to eternal happiness . . . On his way through the dark valley, the martyr believed that there was an invisible hand that would lead him . . . For Bruno there was no such comfort. He was prepared to die for a philosophical view that could give him no consolation.'

John Draper seems to have only a basic knowledge of Bruno and Spinoza's philosophical beliefs. Spinoza can be left out of the argument because it is extremely difficult to determine the full extent of his worldview. He wrote very cautiously and to grasp his exact meaning, it's necessary to read between the lines with a thorough understanding of Pythagorean metaphysics. (The idea that he was an atheist and materialist can even be left unchallenged for now.) But Giordano Bruno must have believed in an afterlife if he was a follower of Pythagoras. He could not have been an atheist with a philosophy that offered him no consolation. In his biography, *Life of Bruno (Vita di Giordano Bruno da Nola)*, the Italian academic Domenico Berti outlines the accusations against Bruno and his subsequent confession. Based on recently published documents, Berti's biography dispels any doubt about the actual nature of Bruno's philosophical and spiritual beliefs. The Alexandrian Platonists and the later Kabbalists believed Jesus practiced magic. Bruno also believed Jesus was a magician in the sense used by Porphyry and Cicero who called magic the *divina sapientia* (divine knowledge) and in the sense used by Philo Judaeus who described the Magi as the most wonderful inquirers into the hidden mysteries of nature. Bruno did not mean magic in the modern sense of the word which trivializes the original meaning. Bruno believed that the Magi were holy men who set themselves apart from everything else on earth and contemplated spiritual truth. As a consequence of their spiritual practice, they understood more deeply the divine nature of gods and spirits. They initiated other people into the same mysteries enabling them to hold an uninterrupted conversation with gods and spirits during life. Bruno's deepest philosophical convictions are illustrated clearly in the following fragments from the accusations made against him and his own confession.

Bruno was accused by the Venetian Zuane Mocenigo who stated the charges as follows:

'I Zuane Mocenigo, son of Marcantonio, denounce Giordano Bruno to your holiness as guided by my conscience and my priest. During discussions in my house, I have heard Giordano Bruno say several times that it is blasphemy for Catholics to maintain that the wafer used in Communion turns into the flesh of Christ. I have heard him say that he is opposed to the Mass and that no religion satisfies him. I have heard him say that Christ was a wretch (un tristo) who deliberately deceived people and should have expected to be punished. I have heard him say that there is no Holy Trinity and if there were, it would reveal an imperfection in God. I have heard him say that the world is eternal. There are infinite worlds and God makes them continually because he wants to create everything he can. I have heard him say that Christ only appeared to perform miracles. He was a magician and so were the Apostles. Christ intended to perform as much magic, or more, than they did. I have heard him say that Christ was reluctant to die and tried everything to avoid death. I have heard him say that there is no punishment of sin. I have heard him say that souls created by nature pass from one animal to another. Brutish animals are born out of decay, and so are men when they are born again after death.'

These accusations are unjustified but they reveal an important element of Bruno's philosophy. They plainly show that he believed in Pythagorean metempsychosis. This is a widely misunderstood concept but it indicates that Bruno believed a man can survive death in one form or another. Bruno's accuser,

Mocenigo, goes on to say:

'He has shown that he wants to make himself the founder of a new sect called 'New Philosophy.' He has said that the Virgin birth is impossible and our Catholic faith is full of blasphemy against God. He has said that monks should not be allowed to debate faith and their wages should be stopped because they corrupt the world. He has said the monks are all asses and the views of our church are the opinions of asses. He has said that we have no proof that Catholicism has the approval of God. He has said that following the maxim, 'Do unto others as you would have them do unto you' is all that is needed for a good life. He has said that he laughs at all other sins and wonders how God can tolerate so much heresy from the Catholic faith. He says that he is going to practice divination and make the whole world follow him. He says that Saint Thomas and all the other important saints knew nothing compared to him. He says that he could ask the world's first theologians questions that they could not answer.'

Bruno replied by stating his beliefs, which are shared by every disciple of the ancient masters:

'Put simply, I believe in an infinite universe created by infinite divine power. It would be unworthy of God, with all his divine goodness, to create just one world when he has the power to create an infinite number. So there are an infinite number of planet earths. Like Pythagoras, I understand the earth to be a celestial body similar to the moon, the other planets, and the other stars which are infinite in number. All of those celestial bodies are worlds and they are countless, making up an infinite universality in an infinite space and this is called the infinite universe. So there is a dual infinite greatness in the universe. This could be construed as contradicting the truth according to the Roman Catholic church.

'Additionally, I see a divine protective care operating in this universe. Everything lives, grows, moves and exists in all its perfection because of this care. I understand it in two ways. In the first way, all of God is present in the whole of the earth and in every part of it. This is nature - the shadow and footprint of the divine. In the second way, God is present in an indescribable manner where He is in everything but also above everything. He is not part of anything, not present as the soul, but present in another way that is inexplicable.

'Additionally, I believe that all the qualities of divinity are one and the same thing. Along with the theologians and great philosophers, I perceive three qualities: power, wisdom and goodness; or rather: mind, intellect and love. First, things have existence through the mind. Next they have ordered and separate existence through the intellect. And third, they have harmony and symmetry through love. This is how I conceive being as something in everything and over everything. Nothing exists without participating in being. Nothing exists without the essence of being, just as nothing can be beautiful without beauty being present. Therefore nothing exists independently of divine presence. This is how I understand the different qualities of divinity. I reach this conclusion not based on evidence but through pure reasoning.

'If the world was caused to come into being, by the very fact that it exists, it is dependent on the first cause. There is no denying that the world was created. I believe Aristotle expressed the same idea, saying, 'God is the thing that the world and all of nature depends on.' According to Saint Thomas, whether the world is eternal or finite, by the fact that it exists, it is dependent on the first cause. Nothing in it is independent.

'Take the Catholic doctrine of the Trinity, which implies the individuality of God the Father, and the Son. These can also be expressed as 'wisdom' and the 'son of the mind' which philosophers call intellect and theologians call the Word. The faithful are supposed to believe that the Word became flesh in the person of Jesus Christ. But, looking at it philosophically, I have not understood this doctrine. I have doubted it and found it difficult to believe. I don't remember expressing my doubt in writing or conversation. But it could be inferred from other things I have done by someone with enough ingenuity or scholarship. So, when it comes to the Holy Spirit as a third person, I haven't been able to understand the religious principle. But instead I have understood it as the soul of the universe or something next to the universe and joined to it. This is in line with the views of Pythagoras and Solomon. According to the wisdom of Solomon, 'The spirit of God filled all the earth, and that which contains all things.' This same idea can be found in Virgil's *Aeneid* where he explains the worldview of Pythagoras:

> *First, know that heaven and earth and the watery plains,*
> *The moon's bright sphere and Titan's star,*
> *A spirit within sustains;*
> *In all the limbs mind moves the mass*
> *And mingles with the mighty frame.*

Etc.

'This spirit is the life of the universe. In my philosophy, this spirit gives life and soul to everything that has life and soul. I understand this spirit to be immortal. I understand all bodies to be immortal in their substance because death is nothing more than deconstruction and reconstruction. It seems to me that this idea is expressed in Ecclesiastes in the line: *There is nothing new under the sun; that which is is that which was.*'

Bruno admits that he cannot understand the doctrine of the Trinity. He also doubts that God was incarnated as Jesus. But he clearly states that he believes in the miracles of Christ. As a Pythagorean philosopher, how could he dismiss them? Like Galileo, Bruno subsequently recanted at the hands of the Inquisition and threw himself on the mercy of his inquisitors. But it must be remembered that he was in an impossible position faced with either torture or burning at the stake. It is difficult for a man to be heroic when his body has been broken by torture and imprisonment.

If it hadn't been for Domenico Berti's biography, Bruno would still be regarded as a martyr to science. John Draper, himself, promoted Bruno's significance as a scientific martyr. Now it's clear that Bruno was not an atheist, materialist or positivist but simply a follower of Pythagoras. Bruno claimed to have the same powers as the ancient magicians who are so derided by scientists like Draper. This is an amusing case of mistaken identity. Nothing funnier has happened since archeologists discovered that the statue thought to be Saint Peter was none other than the Roman god Jupiter. Or when the legend of the Catholic saint Josaphat was proven to be nothing more than a retelling of the life of Buddha.

Every aspect of modern philosophy has its roots in oriental thought. This is true of Newtonian, Cartesian and Huxleyian philosophy, and all other schools. Even positivism and nihilism have their origins in the exoteric philosophy of the Indian sage Kapila. The German linguistic scholar Max Müller has emphasized this point. Enlightened Hindu sages unlocked the mysteries of perfect wisdom or Prajnaparamita.[6] These same sages nurtured the first ancestor of that weak but noisy child, modern science.

Chapter Four

I choose the nobler part of Emerson, when, after various disenchantments, he exclaimed, I covet Truth. The gladness of true heroism visits the heart of him who is really competent to say this.

JOHN TYNDALL

A testimony is sufficient when it rests on:
1st. A great number of very sensible witnesses who agree in having seen well.
2nd. Who are sane, bodily and mentally.
3rd. Who are impartial and disinterested.
4th. Who unanimously agree.
5th. Who solemnly certify to the fact.

DICTIONNAIRE PHILOSOPHIQUE, VOLTAIRE

The author Agénor de Gasparin was a dedicated Protestant. He argued fiercely with the journalist Roger des Mousseaux, the author Charles de Mirville and other Catholics who believed Satan was the cause of all spiritual manifestations. He set out his arguments in the 1500 pages of his two-volume work *A Treatise on Turning Tables (Des Tables Tournantes)*. He proved that spiritualist phenomena occur but denied that the Devil was the cause, putting forward instead every possible explanation other than the real one.

De Gasparin carefully described the spiritual manifestations he had seen. The *Journal des Debats* then had the audacity to suggest that anyone who believes in spiritual phenomena should be committed to an asylum. The journal claimed people must be mad if they continued to believe in spiritual manifestations after Faraday had explained them as 'spiritual hallucinations.' De Gasparin's comeback was read throughout Europe. 'Take care,' he wrote. 'Scientists are on their way to becoming Inquisitors . . . Facts are stronger than Academies. Even if they are rejected, denied and mocked, they are still facts, and they do exist.'

In *A Treatise on Turning Tables*, de Gasparin examines spiritualist manifestations in detail. He describes witnessing the following phenomena together with the physicist Marc Thury.

'People have often experienced phenomena involving the seance table itself. The legs appear to be stuck to the floor and however hard the table is pushed, it will not move. At other times the table has levitated dramatically. People have witnessed loud and soft rapping first hand. The rapping could be so violent, it threatened to shatter the table. The soft rapping was so quiet it was hardly perceptible . . . On the subject of levitations, we found a way to produce them easily without touching the table. We were able to do this more than once, repeating the levitation over 30 times . . . Sometimes the table will turn and its legs will lift up one after the other even with an 87kg man sitting on it. Sometimes the table refuses to move at all even though the person sitting on it weighs only 60kg . . . On one occasion, we willed it to turn upside down and it turned over with its legs in the air. This took place even though our fingers didn't touch it once.'

In his book *On the Question of Spirits*, Charles de Mirville remarks, 'Without doubt anyone who witnessed these phenomena repeatedly could not accept Faraday's explanation of them.'

Des Mousseaux and de Mirville are uncompromising Roman Catholics. Since 1850, they have published many books with titles designed to attract public attention. In these books, the authors reveal their fear that spiritualist phenomena are real - if the phenomena were easily debunked, the Roman Catholic church would not have gone to so much trouble to suppress them.

If skeptics are left out of the equation, people can be divided into one of two groups: those who believe in the agency of the Devil and those who believe in disembodied and other spirits.

Religious authorities are concerned about the revelations that spiritualism might produce. They are more concerned about these than the conflict between religion and science. This fact alone should make skeptics think again. The Catholic Church has never been easily fooled or afraid of a fight. This is clear from its Machiavellian politics. It has never bothered with conjurors, however convincing, because conjuring is nothing more than sleight of hand. The great theatrical magicians Jean-Eugène Robert-Houdin, Louis Comte, Hamilton (aka Pierre Chocat) and Bartolomeo Bosco could all rest easy in their beds. Meanwhile the Catholic Church persecuted men like Paracelsus, the occultist Alessandro Cagliostro, Franz Mesmer and the Hermetic philosophers and mystics. The Church put a stop to every genuine manifestation of the occult by killing the mediums.

Even someone who finds it hard to believe in Christianity has to admit that the clergy aren't fools. The Church is supposed to be infallible. No priest would risk its reputation by giving credence to manifestations that might someday be exposed as fraud.

But the best evidence for the authenticity of spiritualist phenomena was provided by Robert-Houdin. Being a great theatrical conjuror, he was invited to act as an expert witness at a series of seances. He observed compelling examples of clairvoyance as well as occasional mistakes in the meetings. In response he said, 'We conjurors never make mistakes and my second sight hasn't failed me yet.'

The astronomer Jacques Babinet enlisted the famous ventriloquist Louis Comte as an expert observer. Comte was expected to debunk the phenomena of spirit voices and table rappings. But if the people present are to be believed, Comte laughed at the very idea that the raps could be produced by 'unconscious ventriloquism.' This theory is the twin of 'unconscious cerebration' It embarrassed even the most skeptical academicians because its absurdity was all too obvious.

De Gasparin says, 'The supernatural as it was understood in the Middle Ages, and as we understand it now, is an idea that cannot be dismissed. No one can fail to grasp its scale and significance. Everything about it is deeply serious: both the evil in it and the good, the resurgence of superstition, and the facts that will halt that resurgence.'

De Gasparin expresses a clear opinion based on the various manifestations he witnessed. He says, 'Lately a large number of facts have come to light. They indicate that science must enlarge its field of study or the jurisdiction of the supernatural will become limitless.'

Both Catholic and Protestant authors have written a large

number of books against spiritualism. Charles de Mirville and Roger des Mousseaux have done the most damage. De Mirville wrote *On the Question of Spirits*. Des Mousseaux is the author of *Magic in the Nineteenth Century (La Magie au Dix-neuvième Siècle)*, *The Habits and Practices of Demons (Moeurs et Pratiques des Démons)*, *The Great Phenomena of Magic (Les Hauts Phénomènes de la Magie)* and *The Mediators and the Means of Magic (Les Mediateurs de la Magie)*. These four books add up to the most detailed biography of the Devil and his imps since the Middle Ages, offering gratification for good Catholics everywhere.

According to these authors, the Devil was 'a liar and murderer from the beginning' who was also the driving force behind spiritual phenomena. For thousands of years he had been at the center of Pagan mysticism. And he had reappeared in our century emboldened by increasing heresy, faithlessness and atheism. The French Academy of Sciences dismissed the whole thing while de Gasparin took it personally. In his book *A Treatise on Turning Tables*, he writes, 'This is war! Shields up! The work of Monsieur de Mirville is a real manifesto. I'd like to think it was simply one man's opinion, but that is impossible. So many things point to it being a collective endeavor: i.e the success of the book, its closeness to Catholic doctrine, the parroting of its ideas by Catholic writers and publications, the solid support established between these writers and the rest of Catholicism. I felt it was my duty to answer this challenge and champion the Protestant point of view.'

As expected, the medical profession supported the various arguments against de Mirville and des Mousseaux like a Greek chorus. The *Annales Médico-psychologiques*,[1] a medical journal of psychiatry edited by Alexandre Brière de Boismont and Laurent Cerise, had this to say, 'Apart from the current controversy, no

French writer has ever faced so much sarcasm with such determined composure. Nor has one faced the scorn of common sense. Des Mousseaux both defies and challenges ridicule. He strikes an attitude and has the audacity to present to the Academy what he modestly calls his memoir on the Devil.'

Without doubt that was an outrageous insult to the academicians. But ever since the rise of spiritualism, they've been forced to deal with more controversy than they can handle. Des Mousseaux had the audacity to present the Devil as the explanation for spiritualism to the 40 luminaries or 'immortals' of the Académie Française![2] The academicians got their revenge by clubbing together and proposing an even more far-fetched explanation. The physiologist Pierre-Francois Rayer and the surgeon Antoine Jobert de Lamballe were both celebrities in their own way. They teamed up and brought a German scholar to the Academy who claimed to have an explanation for all the knockings and rappings around the world. In his book *On the Question of Spirits*, Charles de Mirville says, 'It's embarrassing to admit that the whole phenomenon was caused simply by repeated twitching of the muscles of the legs. A demonstration of this was given to all members of the institute who expressed their thanks for this helpful explanation. A few days later a professor of the medical faculty assured the public that science had solved the mystery once and for all.'

But these scientific explanations did not stop the table rappings or de Mirville and des Mousseaux from spreading their theory that the Devil was behind it all.

Des Mousseaux denied that the church had any influence over his writing. In addition to his memoir, he presented to the Academy his philosophical ideas on the nature of Satan in his book *The Habits and Practices of Demons*:

'The Devil is the main cornerstone of faith. He is one of the great religious figures and his life is intimately connected with the life of the Church. If it weren't for his ideas communicated by his medium, the serpent, the Fall of Man would never have taken place. If it wasn't for the Devil, Christ would be redundant and the Cross would be meaningless.'

In truth, this writer is only a mouthpiece for the Church. And the Church condemns equally anyone who rejects God and anyone who doubts the existence of Satan.

But de Mirville takes the idea of God's partnership with the Devil even further. According to him it is a simple business arrangement. As the senior 'silent partner,' God allows the business to be run by Satan, his junior associate. God profits from Satan's audacity and hard work. This is the only reasonable interpretation of the following passage from de Mirville's *On the Question of Spirits*.

'No one paid much attention to the spiritual activity of 1853. But at the time, we spoke up about an impending disaster. Even though the world was at peace, we could see the signs that have accompanied calamities throughout history. We predicted the dire consequences of a law which the German theologian Johann von Görres has formulated as follows: *Mysterious apparitions of this kind have always been a sign of God's intention to punish us.*'

These arguments continued between supporters of the Church and the Academy of Science. They clearly show the Academy's lack of success in rooting out religious fanaticism in even well-educated people. Obviously science hasn't defeated theology or silenced it. Science will only replace theology when scientists investigate spiritual phenomena properly rather than simply dismissing them as hallucinations or fraud. What's needed is impartial examination of the facts. During a lecture in 1820, the Danish physicist Hans Ørsted noticed a compass needle was deflected by an electric current. This led to his discovery of electromagnetism. But suppose he had suffered from psychophobia (the fear of psychic phenomena). Suppose he saw the compass needle deflected but he had also heard of people using magnetized needles to communicate with invisible beings. Suppose he had heard that they received signals from these beings and even held conversations with them via the movements of the needle. Suppose as a result of this, the professor had had a psychophobic attack and refused to investigate the movement of the needle any further. What would have been the result? Electromagnetism might have remained undiscovered and science would have been the biggest loser.

Jacques Babinet, Pierre-Francois Rayer and Antoine Jobert de Lamballe were all members of the French Institute. In the conflict between science and the supernatural, they stood out, but for all the wrong reasons. Babinet had recklessly risked his reputation by investigating spiritualist phenomena. He had given a 'scientific explanation' for the manifestations. Like most scientists, he believed the spiritualist craze wouldn't bear close scrutiny or last more than a year. This prompted him to be even more reckless, publishing two articles on the subject. De Mirville cleverly remarks that if the articles had little impact in the scientific press, they had none at all in the popular press.

Babinet began by accepting that the rotation of tables took place, saying it was beyond doubt. In the magazine *Revue des Deux Mondes*,[3] he wrote, 'This rotation occurs with considerable force. It happens either with great speed or with powerful momentum which makes it difficult to stop.'

In the same journal, Babinet goes on to give this scientific explanation: 'At first the table begins to move slightly from right to left. This motion is produced by the hands of the attendees making similar small movements. After a while a nervous trembling takes hold of the hands and coordinates their movements so that the table starts to turn.'

Babinet finds it all very straightforward. He says, 'When a person uses muscular force to move an object, that movement is determined by the action of the person's arm which is a lever of the third order. In a lever of this type, the point where the force acts is very close to the lever's pivot. Consequently, the force has to move only a short distance to produce a large and rapid movement at the lever's end . . . Imagine a table moving under the intense influence of several ardent spiritualists. Some observers are astonished to see the table knock obstacles aside and even break its own legs when stopped forcibly. This is easily understood by taking into account the power of coordinated muscular movements. Given all of the above, it is not difficult to provide a physical explanation for this phenomenon.'

In this passage two things become clear: the phenomena are real and the scientific explanation is ridiculous. But it won't do Babinet any harm to be laughed at a little. As an astronomer, he knows that the occasional dim spot occurs even in the brilliance of the sun.

There is one thing, though, that Babinet has always vehemently denied. He refuses to believe that furniture can levitate without human contact. In *Revue des Deux Mondes*, de Mirville quotes him as saying that levitation is, 'simply impossible . . . as impossible as perpetual motion.'

After this, who in their right mind would still believe that scientists are invariably right when they say something is impossible?

After waltzing, rocking and turning, the tables began tipping and rapping. The raps were sometimes as explosive as gunshots. What is the explanation for this? 'The people at the seance are ventriloquists!'

De Mirville refers to an interesting dialogue published in the *Revue des Deux Mondes*. In this dialogue, Babinet speaks in a God-like way about himself to himself: 'What can we conclude from the facts before us? Are such raps produced? Yes. Do such raps answer questions? Yes. Who produces these sounds? The mediums. How do they do it? By ventriloquism. But we were led to believe that these sounds might be caused by the cracking of the toes and fingers? No; because if that were the case, the sound would always come from the same place and it doesn't.'

De Mirville asks, 'What about the thousands of American mediums who produce the same raps in front of millions of witnesses?' 'It's definitely ventriloquism,' answers Babinet. 'But there must be more to it than that?' Babinet has this to say: 'All it took to create the first manifestation in the first house in America was a street urchin knocking at the door of Michael Weekman (America's first believer). When Weekman opened the door no one was there. The knocking occurred a second time and again no one was there. Now Weekman held the door closed by hand so that the moment someone knocked he could open it immediately. But he still found no one there. Perhaps the urchin used a lead ball attached to a piece of string so he could knock on the door from a distance. The only reason Weekman didn't hear him sniggering in the street is because Americans are more reserved than us French when it comes to making mischief.'

De Mirville's reply to the attacks of de Gasparin, Babinet and other scientists, is famous. He said, 'And so according to Babinet, *1. the tables turn very quickly and very forcefully. 2. They have powerful momentum.* And according to de Gasparin, it's been proved that *3. they levitate without human contact.* Cardinal Richelieu once said he could take three lines from any author and interpret them in such a way as to have the author hanged for treason. In the same way, the three statements above could be interpreted as proof that the phenomena are supernatural in origin. This would throw the world's physicists into confusion and revolutionize the way the world thinks. If, like de Gasparin, Babinet had suggested the existence of a new type of force or law of physics - that would have neatly explained the phenomena on the scientists' own terms.'

De Mirville refers to Babinet extensively in the chapter 'Facts and Physical Theories' in his book *On the Question of Spirits*. He reveals Babinet's outstanding consistency and logic as an expert researcher in the field of spiritualism.

In the same book, de Mirville describes the uncanny manifestations at the Presbytère de Cideville. Even though they were authenticated in the magistrate's court, de Mirville wasn't bold enough to publish an account of them.

The events were as follows: 'A sorcerer promised revenge on the priest at the Presbytère de Cideville. At the precise moment he predicted, there was a violent clap of thunder above one of the chimneys of the presbytery. Spiritual fluid came down the chimney with an incredible noise. It knocked over both the sorcerer's believers and skeptics who were warming themselves by the fire. The fluidic force filled the room with a multitude of fantastical animals and then went back up the chimney with the same incredible noise.' De Mirville adds, 'We already had so many facts about the supernatural happenings at Cideville that this new drama was too much to take.'

But Babinet and his scientific peers had been keen to make fun of de Mirville and des Mousseaux. Consequently Babinet was determined to prove that all accounts of this kind were absurd. He set out to dismiss the Cideville phenomena by describing something even more incredible.

In *On the Question of Spirits*, de Mirville quotes a speech given by Babinet to the Academy of Sciences on 5 July 1852. This same text is included in the first volume of the works of the astronomer François Arago as a description of spherical lightning. Here it is in Babinet's own words.

'A tailor's apprentice who lived in the Rue St. Jacques was just finishing his dinner when there was a loud clap of thunder. A few moments later he saw the fire screen fall forwards from the fireplace, knocked over by what seemed like a small gust of wind. Next he saw a globe of fire as large as a child's head silently emerge from the grate. It moved softly and slowly around the room without touching the floor. The fire globe looked like a young cat. It was medium-sized and moved without using its paws. It was bright and luminous rather than hot or on fire and the apprentice felt no heat coming from it. The globe came closer, eager to rub itself against his legs just as a kitten would. But the apprentice moved his feet, careful to avoid contact with the fiery meteor. The meteor continued moving around his legs for several seconds while the apprentice examined it closely. It moved to and fro about the center of the room. Then it rose vertically until it was level with the man's head. The apprentice tilted backwards on his chair to avoid the globe touching his face. It stopped about a yard above the floor. It elongated slightly then took off diagonally toward a hole in the wall over the fireplace. The hole was at a height of a meter above the mantelpiece.' This hole had been made to take the pipe of a stove in winter. But according to the apprentice, 'The fire globe could not tell it was there because it was papered over to match the rest of the wall. The fire globe went straight to the hidden hole. It unglued the paper without damaging it and disappeared up the chimney . . . it traveled very slowly to the top of the chimney, at least 60 feet above ground, and produced a terrifying explosion partly destroying the chimney . . .' etc.

According to de Mirville, 'A clever woman once commented to the French historian Guillaume Raynal, 'If you are not a Christian it's not because you have a lack of faith.' The same comment could be applied to Babinet.'

Spiritualists were not the only ones who thought Babinet was mistaken when he called the manifestation a meteor. The army physician and anthropologist Jean-Christian Boudin was of the same opinion. In his article 'The Physical and Medical History of Lightning and its Effects,' Boudin writes, 'The details provided by Babinet and Arago seem to be accurate. If this is the case, it seems inappropriate to call it sphere-shaped lightning. But we'll leave it to someone else to explain the phenomenon properly if they can. How can a fire globe give out no heat, look like a cat, and walk slowly round a room? How can it escape back up the chimney through a hole in the wall that was covered in paper and that it unglued without causing any damage?'

De Mirville adds, 'We agree with Boudin on the difficulty of finding an exact definition. There's no reason why lightning in future shouldn't appear in the shape of a dog or a monkey etc. I dread to think of a whole meteorological menagerie coming down the chimney, powered by thunder, to walk around our rooms whenever they like.'

In *A Treatise on Turning Tables* de Gasparin writes, 'Evidence becomes unreliable as soon as we cross the line into the supernatural.' Given that this line is not fixed or clearly defined, who is best placed to give the most reliable evidence, spiritualists or scientists? Which of the two should be allowed to shape public opinion? Is it the spiritualists whose point of view is supported by thousands of witnesses? For nearly two years large crowds visited Cideville to see the miracles that took place there every day. And even these miracles have now been eclipsed by countless recent spiritual phenomena. Do we believe the spiritualists or do we turn to science as represented by Babinet? Babinet is ready to accept the fire globe or the meteor cat on the evidence of just one witness, the tailor's apprentice. And he classifies it as simply another natural phenomenon.

In the *Quarterly Journal of Science* of October 1871, William Crookes published an article called 'Further Experiments on Psychic Force.' In this article he referred to de Gasparin and *A Treatise on Turning Tables*. Crookes writes, 'De Gasparin concluded that all spiritualist phenomena are the result of natural forces. They do not require belief in miracles, the intervention of spirits or the work of the Devil! De Gasparin believes his experiments have proved the true cause of the phenomena: in certain states human will can influence matter remotely. Most of his work is focused on discovering the laws and conditions under which the will achieves this.'

This is true. De Gasparin's work was debated in print by many other commentators but his writing revealed his fervent Protestantism. His religious fanaticism made him just as unreliable as des Mousseaux and de Mirville. De Gasparin is a devout Calvinist. Des Mousseaux and de Mirville are fanatical Roman Catholics. De Gasparin reveals his bias in his own words: 'I feel I have a duty to perform . . . I promote the cause of Protestantism in opposition to Catholicism!' etc. When it comes to explaining so-called spiritual phenomena, the only reliable evidence can come from clear thinking, impartial witnesses and science. There is only one truth. But there are many different religious sects all claiming to have found the ultimate truth. In Catholicism the supernatural is central to the faith - 'the Devil is the main cornerstone of faith.' In de Gasparin's view there is no place at all for the supernatural when you become a follower of Calvinism.

But Crookes mentioned another prominent scholar, Marc Thury, Professor of Natural History at the University of Geneva. Thury was a co-researcher with de Gasparin into spiritualist phenomena at the Swiss village of Valeyres.[4] Thury would go on to contradict the findings of de Gasparin completely. De Gasparin writes, in *A Treatise on Turning Tables*, 'The first and vital pre-condition is that each participant wills the phenomenon to manifest. Without the will of the participants, nothing can be achieved. You can sit in a circle for a full 24 hours and the table will not move at all.'

This proves only that de Gasparin does not differentiate between purely magnetic phenomena and the so-called spiritual variety. Magnetic phenomena are produced by the concentrated will of the participants without the presence of a medium. They can be produced consciously by nearly anyone with a strong enough will, whereas spiritual phenomena often overpower the medium whether he likes it or not and they always act independently. The mesmerizer wills something to happen and if he is powerful enough, it happens. The medium may produce no manifestations at all even though he is honestly trying to. The less conscious effort he makes, the better the phenomena tend to be: the more anxious he is about the outcome, the less likely it is that anything will happen. You need a positive nature to be a mesmerizer, you need a perfectly passive nature to be a medium. This is simply how spiritualism works and every medium knows it.

Thury completely disagrees with de Gasparin's theories of willpower. He makes this clear in a letter to de Gasparin who had asked him for help in revising the final part of *A Treatise on Turning Tables*. Thury's suggested revision shocked the religious de Gasparin because it implied the existence and intervention 'of wills other than those of men and animals.' Here is a translation of his letter as quoted by de Mirville.

'I think you are right about the last pages of this book; they may be very damaging to my reputation in the scientific community. The thing I regret most is how much my position seems to upset you. But I feel I would be failing in my duty as a scientist if I didn't pursue this line of inquiry.

'Suppose there is some truth in spiritualism. I might inadvertently encourage people to experiment with the phenomena if I didn't express the opinion that it's only a matter of time before science disproves the existence of spirits. This is the main focus of the closing pages of the book. If people were tempted to experiment with spiritualism, they might be stepping into very uncertain territory.

'I will do my duty as a scientist, as I see it, regardless of the risks to my reputation. As you put it, a lot of scandal surrounds the subject of spiritualism. But I don't think it is necessarily a scandalous subject. In fact, I maintain that the subject can be studied as scientifically as anything else. Even if I wanted to support the theory that disembodied spirits can intervene in our world, it's just not possible. The facts are insufficient to prove that hypothesis. I believe the approach I've taken puts me in a strong position. Whether they like it or not, scientists must learn to reserve judgment about phenomena that they have not fully explored. The lesson you gave them on this topic cannot be ignored. Geneva, 21 December 1854.'

Analyzing this letter will show what Thury does and does not think of this new force. One thing is sure: this distinguished physicist and naturalist insists that various manifestations take place and he has proven this scientifically. Like William Crookes, he does not believe that phenomena are produced by the agency of spirits or disembodied men who have lived and died on earth. In his letter, he states that there is no evidence to support this theory. Nor does he believe that the phenomena are caused by Catholic devils or demons. De Mirville quotes Thury's letter as evidence against de Gasparin's naturalistic theory. But he adds a footnote giving his own interpretation: when Thury said the manifestations at Valeyres were not produced by demons, de Mirville implies that Valeyres was an exception and all other manifestations are demonic in origin.

Unfortunately de Gasparin has been caught up in numerous contradictions and absurdities. He vehemently criticizes the claims of Faraday's followers. But at the same time he contradicts himself, saying something magical can also be the result of perfectly natural causes. He says, 'If we confine ourselves to the phenomenon of table turning, as explained by Faraday, there would be nothing further to add. But we have moved beyond that single phenomenon. Now, how useful is Faraday's apparatus that supposedly proves tables turn as a result of 'unconscious pressure'? Despite Faraday, the table still resists pressure and control! It still moves on its own in the direction indicated by someone's pointed finger. It still levitates even though no one is touching it and turns itself upside down!'

De Gasparin then offers his own explanation for the phenomena.

'People will think everything is a miracle or magic, you say! Every new law seems miraculous to them. Don't get carried away. Let me reassure you, there's nothing supernatural about these phenomena - they can be explained by the laws of nature.'

But can scientists explain the laws of nature? De Gasparin thinks they can.

'I won't risk explaining anything. It's not my responsibility.

But I will confirm some simple facts and defend a truth that science tries to suppress. I'd like to point out to anyone, who might label us illuminati or sorcerers, that tables turning etc can be explained using the ordinary laws of science.

'Imagine a magnetic fluid flowing from each of the participants at a seance. It flows from some of them more strongly than others. Suppose the combined willpower around the table dictated the direction of the fluid. If that combined will directs an excess of fluid toward one of the table's legs then it is easy to understand the resulting rotation and levitation. If a glass tumbler is placed on the table, the table stops turning. It's easy to understand why, if we assume that the glass dispels the magnetic fluid. If the tumbler is placed on its side, it funnels the magnetic fluid to the opposite side of the table causing that side to levitate!'

This explanation, give or take a few details, would only be acceptable if every one of the attendees was a skilled mesmerist. So much for de Gasparin's explanation of the power of human will over inanimate matter. But what about the intelligent responses given by the table in answer to questions? One of de Gasparin's favorite theories is that these answers are 'reflections of the brains' of the people present. But how does he explain the liberal answers given by the table when the sitters are extremely conservative? He is silent on this topic. He attributes the table's intelligence to anything other than spirits, whether human, Satanic or elemental.

So the theories of 'simultaneous concentration of thought' and 'accumulation of fluid' are no more helpful than the ideas suggested by other scientists like 'unconscious cerebration' and 'psychic force.' Science can come up with a thousand and one theories but none of them will be successful until scientists approach the subject differently. They must accept that the force behind spiritualist phenomena is not a projection of the collective will of the sitters. On the contrary it is paranormal, unknown to science and ultra intelligent.

Marc Thury rejects the idea that spiritualist phenomena are caused by departed human spirits. He also rejects the Christian view that they are the Devil's work. He doesn't support William Crookes' theory of a parallel spirit world, an idea shared by the Hermeticists and ancient theurgists. And he is just as skeptical of de Gasparin's hypothesis of 'unconscious willpower.' Instead he adopts a theory which he says is the most prudent, and puts him in a strong position. In his pamphlet *The Physics of Turning Tables (Les Tables Tournantes Considérés au Point de Vue de la Question de Physique Générale)*, Thury says:

'Phenomena have been described such as tables levitating without human contact and furniture propelled by invisible forces. Deductive reasoning cannot prove that these phenomena are impossible. So no one has the authority to discredit the serious evidence suggesting these phenomena occur.'

Thury is a harsh critic of de Gasparin's theory. He seems to accept that in the table turning experiments at Valeyres, the origin of the force might have been in the individual. He also seems to accept that the will of the participants is required in most cases. Nevertheless, he still dismisses de Gasparin with these words, 'De Gasparin lays out the facts and gives us his explanations for what they are worth. Blow on them and, like a house of cards, almost all of them will fall down. Very few will stand up to scrutiny. But the fact remains that the tables turned.'

In his book *Psychic Force and Modern Spiritualism*, William Crookes states that Thury 'considers spiritual phenomena to be produced by a singular substance, fluid or agent which he calls 'psychode.' Scientists theorize the existence of a medium for transmitting light called luminiferous ether. Like this ether, Thury believes psychode infuses all matter whether neurological, organic or inorganic. He gives a full description of the properties of psychode, coining the term ectenic force to describe the power of the mind when it acts remotely through the medium of psychode.'

Crookes goes on to say that what Thury describes as 'ectenic force' is the same as his own 'psychic force.'

It could very easily be demonstrated that the two forces are identical. And that they are the astral or sidereal light identified by the alchemists and the French occult author Eliphas Levi in his book *Dogma and Ritual of High Magic (Dogme et Rituel de la Haute Magie)*. In addition, under the name of akasha or life principle, this force was understood thousands of years ago by Hindu ascetics and magicians, and adepts across the world. This force is still understood and used in the present day by Tibetan lamas, fakirs, miracle workers of all nationalities and even by many Hindu conjurors.

Many instances of trance are artificially induced by mesmerization. In these cases, it's probable that the medium's spirit acts under the direction of the spirit operator's[5] will. But what if the medium remains conscious and manifestations still occur that suggest the presence of another directing intelligence? Unless the medium is a magician who can project his double, then his physical exhaustion can only be due to the stress caused by a separate controlling entity. It seems conclusive that he is a passive instrument directed by as yet unknown powers. Thury's ectenic force and Crookes' psychic force may well be substantially the same. But the two scientists seem to have different views about the characteristics and strength of this force. Thury suggests that the phenomena are often caused by 'wills not human' and so supports Crookes' Sixth Theory. Crookes admits that the phenomena are genuine but he hasn't yet come up with a definitive cause.

Thury investigated spirit manifestations with de Gasparin in 1854. Crookes accepted that manifestations were genuine in 1874. But none of them has provided a conclusive explanation. Both Thury and Crookes are highly qualified men and have given serious thought to the question. Many other scientists have come to share the same opinions on the subject and been equally unable to explain the cause. In 20 years, no scientist has been able to unravel the mystery. It is still as impenetrable as the walls of some enchanted castle.

Scientists have got caught up in a vicious circle, hamstrung by their reliance on materialism. What they call 'the exact sciences' are unable to demonstrate the existence of a spiritual universe more densely populated than the visible one. Their reliance on materialism means they are doomed forever to go round and round within the vicious circle. They are unwilling rather than unable to escape the circle and explore the spiritual universe in its entirety. It is only prejudice that stops them from looking beyond material science and choosing to collaborate with expert magnetists and mesmerists such as Jules du Potet and Antonio Regazzoni.

In Plato's dialogue *Phaedo*, Socrates asks his student Cebes, 'What then is produced from death?' 'Life,' was Cebes' reply. Socrates goes on to say, 'Can the soul, since it is immortal, be anything else than imperishable?' In *Popular Science Monthly* 1873, the American geologist Joseph Le Conte wrote that the 'seed cannot develop unless it is in part consumed.' In Corinthians, Saint Paul writes, 'What you sow does not come to life unless it dies.'

A flower blooms, then it fades and dies. It leaves traces of its perfume on the air long after its petals have turned to dust. We may not be able to detect these vestiges of its fragrance, but they exist all the same. A note played on an instrument, however softly, produces an eternal echo. A ripple is created on the invisible waves of the shoreless ocean of space, and the vibration is never wholly lost. Once its energy is transmitted from the material to the immaterial world, it will continue forever. Yet when it comes to mankind, we are asked to believe that the living, thinking, reasoning entity will simply die. Man, the god present inside a masterpiece of nature, will leave his body and cease to exist. The principle of continuity is applied to inorganic matter, e.g. a vibrating atom, but the same principle is not applied to the spirit of mankind which experiences consciousness, memory, mind and love! This seems incredible. The more the subject is considered, the more difficult it is to explain why so many scientists are atheists. It's easy to understand how an ignorant man, unfamiliar with the laws of nature, can be drawn to materialism. Materialism is so attractive to him because he has no understanding of the philosophy of science: he doesn't know how to observe the visible world and draw conclusions about the invisible world. Similarly, a man who dreams vividly and often may wake up suddenly and say to himself, 'I know dreamed this but I have no concrete proof that any of it happened. It's all just an illusion.' etc. But a scientist, familiar with the principle of continuity and the nature of universal energy, has no excuse. If he argues that life is only a phenomenon of matter, he is simply admitting he doesn't understand the fundamental energetic nature of matter itself.

Skepticism about the immortality of the soul has always existed, like illness or mental disorder. Just as some babies are born with part of the amniotic membrane still covering their heads, some men never throw off the 'materialist membrane' that limits their spiritual development. But they have a different reason for rejecting the possibility of spiritual and magical phenomena. That reason is vanity. If a scientist cannot replicate an effect or explain its cause then he will argue that it doesn't exist and could never have existed. About 30 years ago, the French occult author, Eusèbe Salverte, startled the so-called 'gullible' public with his book *The Occult Sciences*. His book claimed to reveal the truth about Biblical and Pagan miracles. In summary, the book describes how a golden age of observation produced a great body of knowledge about the natural sciences and philosophy. Over time, this body of knowledge was lost and replaced by misrepresentation, sleight of hand, optical illusions, elaborate slide shows and exaggeration. The final and logical conclusion of the book is that the power of miracle workers was lost in a line of descent from prophets and magicians to rascals and knaves. And the rest of the world turned into fools.

Salverte gives convincing evidence of this. In the same book, he says, 'Followers of the Neoplatonist philosopher Iamblichus maintained he rose ten cubits above the ground whenever he prayed. Later Christians, impressed by this image, have been naive enough to attribute a similar miracle to Saint Francis of Assisi and his follower Saint Clare.'

Hundreds of visitors to India claim to have witnessed ascetics levitate in a similar way and all of those visitors were thought to be lying or hallucinating. But only yesterday, the same phenomenon was observed and validated by the well-known scientist, William Crookes. Under test conditions, he confirmed that levitation was genuine and ruled out the possibility of illusion or trickery. Levitation has occurred throughout the ages. It has been corroborated by numerous witnesses but these witnesses are now invariably disbelieved. Eusèbe Salverte may be dismissed as a credulous occultist but Crookes has now corroborated his belief in levitation. Soon perhaps a new proverb will be needed: 'As incredibly credulous as a scientist.'

When the spirit is separated from the body, it may have the power to take on a temporary form. This form is created by the 'psychic,' 'ectenic' or 'ethereal' force with the help of the elementaries who provide the refined substance of their own bodies. Why should this seem so impossible? The essential thing to realize is that the space around us is not an empty void. It is a reservoir filled with the templates of all things that ever were, that are and that will be. It is alive with infinite varieties of beings different from us. Many scientists acknowledge supposedly supernatural phenomena that contradict the laws of gravitation, like the instance of levitation described above. Every scientist, bold enough to research these phenomena thoroughly, has been forced to admit they are true. It is impossible to explain the phenomena using the laws of forces already known to science. When some of the most respected scientists have tried it, they have got themselves into extreme difficulties!

In the summary at the end of *On the Question of Spirits*, de Mirville addresses the scientific opponents of spiritualism. According to de Mirville, their objections consist of five paradoxes, which he calls distractions.

First distraction: Faraday's explanation of turning tables. Faraday explains the phenomenon by claiming that participants at a seance push the table unconsciously.

Second distraction: Babinet's explanation of rapping. Babinet says the messages conveyed by rapping are created in good faith with meticulous attention to detail - but by ventriloquism. The use of ventriloquism necessarily implies bad faith.

Third distraction: Chevreul's explanation of moving furniture without contact - people are able to move furniture remotely because they have previously acquired the ability.

Fourth distraction: the French Institute's paradoxical acceptance of supernatural phenomena. The Institute and its members agree to accept miracles, provided they do not contradict in any way the laws of science.

Fifth distraction: de Gasparin's explanation of spiritualist phenomena. He introduces the very simple, elementary idea that human will can influence matter remotely. This idea is rejected by everyone because no one has ever seen it happen.

These are some of the many imaginative theories proposed by leading scientists. Meanwhile some less well-known neurologists suggest an abnormal discharge produced by epilepsy is the cause of all occult phenomena. In his lecture on the pathology and treatment of mediomania, the physician Frederic Marvin recommends treating mediums with a tincture of asafetida and ammonia. (He would probably treat poets in the same way.) Marvin declares that all believers in spiritualist phenomena are lunatics or hallucinating mystics.

Marvin should take the advice of the New Testament: 'Physician, heal thyself.' No one in their right mind would make the sweeping statement that 446 million people across the world are insane because they believe in spirit communication!

How did scientists become so self-important? They want to be respected as high priests of science because of their expertise. But then they have the arrogance to attempt to classify a phenomenon they know nothing about. Surely, if several million people are deluded, their situation warrants as much serious attention as the study of potato bugs or grasshoppers. In fact the reverse is true. Members of the American Association for the Advancement of Science urged Congress to establish and fund the United States Entomological Commission. Chemists are now occupied boiling frogs and bugs. Geologists pass their time studying the bone structure of armor plated primitive fish and discussing the teeth of various extinct species of giant fish. Carried away by their enthusiasm, entomologists are dining on boiled or fried grasshoppers and grasshopper soup. Meanwhile millions of Americans are victims of what some of these leading scientists would call 'crazy delusions.' Or they are deteriorating physically from 'nervous disorders' brought about by their susceptibility to mediomania.

At one time it looked like Russian scientists were going to conduct a detailed study of the phenomena. The Imperial University of St. Petersburg set up a commission led by the prominent physicist Dmitri Mendeleev. The commission's investigation included a series of 40 seances. Mediums were invited to the Russian capital to be examined under test conditions. The majority of them refused to go. Most likely they had a premonition that they were being set up. Only eight seances took place. Just when the manifestations were becoming interesting, the commission made a snap judgment and published its findings. It concluded that mediumship was nothing more than trickery. Instead of using serious scientific methods, the commission effectively used spies to peep through keyholes. In a public lecture, Mendeleev announced that spiritualism and any belief in the soul's immortality was a mixture of superstition, delusion and fraud. He commented on manifestations including mind-reading, trance and any number of other psychological phenomena. He stated that every one of these was produced using ingenious apparatus concealed under the medium's clothing.

Alexander Butlerov, professor of chemistry at the University of St. Petersburg, and Alexandr Aksakov, St. Petersburg Councilor of State, were both members of the commission. They resigned in protest at the uninformed and biased content of Mendeleev's lecture. They published their objections in the Russian newspapers. They were supported by the majority of the press who were openly sarcastic toward Mendeleev and his high-handed committee. The public also gave their support. 130 influential citizens of St. Petersburg signed a petition. Many of them were not even spiritualists but simply people who wanted to know the truth.

Consequently, global attention was drawn to the subject of spiritualism. Private spiritualist circles were organized throughout Russia. Some of the most liberal journals began to cover the subject. And at the time of writing, a new commission is being set up to complete the unfinished investigation into mediumship.

But none of this will make any difference - the job still won't be done properly. The British zoologist Ray Lankester handed skeptics the perfect excuse when he supposedly exposed the medium Henry Slade. Slade was accused on the evidence of just one scientist, Lankester, together with his friend Bryan Donkin. The case against Slade contradicted the previous findings of Wallace, Crookes and a host of other scientists. The weight of their scientific opinion invalidates any accusation based purely on circumstantial evidence and prejudice.

The London Spectator reported the case as follows:

'Because we think we know so much about how the world works, we tend to reject anything that doesn't tally with our preconceptions. Lankester appears to assume that fraud and gullibility must explain the reports of accurate and unbiased observers simply because fraud is so commonly connected with mediumship. This is like sawing through the branch on the tree of knowledge that science, itself, is sitting on. The whole structure will eventually come crashing down.'

But does any of this matter to scientists? According to them, a torrent of superstition engulfs millions of otherwise reasonable minds. But it doesn't affect the scientists themselves. The tidal wave of spiritualism cannot overwhelm their superior intellects. The muddy waves of the spiritualist flood crash at their feet but their boots don't even get wet. God's miracles have very little chance of impressing scientists nowadays. It's just old-fashioned stubbornness on God's part that stops Him from admitting it. By now even God should be aware that scientists had this motto inscribed long ago on the porticos of their universities and colleges:

Science commands that God shall not
Do miracles upon this spot!

This year materialism seems to be under siege from spiritualists and Roman Catholics alike. A rise in skepticism has been matched by a rise in gullibility. Champions of the Bible's 'divine' miracles compete with fans of spiritualist phenomena. It's as if the Middle Ages have returned in the 19th Century. Once again the Virgin Mary communicates with the faithful. While spirits scribble messages through mediums, the Mother of God drops letters from heaven to earth. The shrine of Notre Dame de Lourdes is like a spiritualist cabinet complete with 'materializations.' Meanwhile the cabinets of popular American mediums are like sacred shrines, where Leonidas Polk (the Bishop of Louisiana), Mohammed, Joan of Arc and other notable spirits cross over from the other side to 'materialize' in full view. And if the Virgin Mary is seen in human form walking in the woods around Lourdes, why shouldn't the same be true of Mohammed or Bishop Polk? Either both these kinds of 'miracles' are possible or both 'divine' and 'spiritualist' manifestations are total frauds. Only time will tell. Meanwhile science refuses to shed any light on these mysteries, so ordinary people are none the wiser, whether they are interested in the subject or not.

The recent 'miracles' at Lourdes caused some controversy in the London papers. In response, the Irish clergyman Thomas

Capel wrote to *The Times* outlining the views of the Roman Catholic church:

'On the subject of the miraculous cures that have occurred, I suggest your readers look at *The Grotto of Lourdes (La Grotte de Lourdes)*. This is an impartial and thoughtful book written by Pierre Dozous. He is a respected local doctor at Lourdes, inspector of epidemic diseases for the district and medical adviser to the Court of Justice. He has studied in depth a number of cases of miraculous cures. In his preface to these cases he writes: 'The cures at Lourdes are produced by the water of the fountain and people of faith accept them as supernatural. I myself am rarely convinced by any explanation that gives the supernatural as the cause. I have to admit that if it wasn't for the evidence of the cures, I would have found it very difficult to accept the remarkable idea that the Virgin Mary had appeared at Lourdes. But being an eyewitness to the cures has opened my mind to the importance of Saint Bernadette's visits to the grotto and the apparitions of the Virgin Mary she saw there.' This is the evidence of a respected physician. He has observed Bernadette and the miraculous cures at the grotto from the beginning. His evidence should at least be given serious consideration. I can add that most of the people who come to Lourdes want to confess their sins and increase their religious feeling. They come to pray for the reconstruction of their countries and to demonstrate publicly their belief in Jesus and Mary. Many come to be cured of illnesses and, according to eyewitnesses, several do return home healed. Your article criticizes other users of the waters for lack of faith. This is like accusing magistrates of lack of faith whenever they prosecute the Peculiar People[6] for refusing vital medical treatment on religious grounds. For health reasons I spent the winters of 1860 to 1867 at the Pyrenean resort of Pau. This gave me the opportunity for detailed research into the appearance of the Virgin Mary at Lourdes. I examined the case of Bernadette thoroughly, including some of the miracles that occurred. I am convinced that, *if people are to be believed, the appearances at Lourdes are undeniable facts*. However, these appearances are not part of Catholic orthodoxy and Catholics can accept or reject them as they please.'

Note the sentence in italics. This makes it clear that the Catholic church accepts people's word as proof of divine miracles. This is despite the fact that the Church is supposed to be infallible and have direct lines of communication with heaven. In his recent New York lectures on evolution, Thomas Huxley says, 'A large part of our knowledge about the past is based on what people have told us throughout history.' In a lecture on biology he has said, 'Anyone who genuinely wants to get to the truth must agree that every valid criticism that can be made should be made. But the critic must know what he is talking about.' Huxley should bear this in mind himself when commenting on psychic phenomena. This truism, added to his views on the value of personal historical accounts, would make a good starting point for discussion.

So a conventional scientist and a Catholic priest both agree that anecdotal evidence is enough to prove the things they each want to believe. For a long time spiritualists and occultists have argued that spiritualist phenomena should be accepted as facts simply because they are supported by so many eyewitness accounts. If anecdotal evidence is good enough for the Church and the scientific community, then it is good enough for everyone else. Some good came out of the Lankester/Slade controversy. The secular press voiced some remarkably liberal views. In 1876, *The London Daily News* reported, 'We are ready to accept spiritualism as a mainstream belief and leave it at that. Many of its followers are as intelligent as the next person. If spiritualism was nothing more than trickery, they would have discovered it by now. Some of the world's wisest men have believed in ghosts and would have continued to believe even if a succession of frauds had been convicted of frightening people with parlor tricks.'

This is not the first time in human history that spirituality has been opposed by materialist skepticism. The soul-blind Sadducees[7] of the Bible refused to believe in the Resurrection and Plato condemned materialist unbelief on more than one occasion in his works.

Every age has had its Doubting Thomases. Long before Christ, the Hindu philosopher Kapila doubted mystic yogis who claimed that a man in an ecstatic trance can see God face-to-face and communicate with the 'highest' beings. In the 18th Century, the followers of the French satirist Voltaire laughed at everything people held sacred. None of these Doubting Thomases ever stopped the progress of truth any more than Galileo's critics could stop the earth's rotation around the sun. No subsequent revelation can undermine a belief handed down to humanity from the first races of mankind. If man evolves spiritually as well as physically, then these first races received the great truth from their ancestors, the gods of their fathers who lived before the Flood. At some point in the future, it will become clear that the Bible contains the same legends as the Hindu sacred books and the creation myths of other nations. It will become apparent that people in ages past used myths to understand themselves and their place in the cosmos. In time it will be understood that these myths were simply representations of geological and anthropological facts. It's to these fantastical myths that science will have to look for the 'missing links' in the ancestry of man.

This explains the strangely similar events in the histories of far flung nations. This accounts for the similarity of the early stories, now regarded as fables, even though they contain a grain of historical truth. That truth may have been obscured as the story was told and added to over the ages, but it is still a truth. Compare Genesis VI with its counterpart in the Hindu Vedas. Genesis reads, 'When human beings began to increase in number on the earth and daughters were born to them, the sons of God saw that the daughters of humans were beautiful, and they married any of them they chose. . . The Nephilim, or giants, were on the earth in those days.' Compare this with the descent of the Brahmans[8] described in the Vedas. The first Brahman complains that he is alone and has no wife. The Eternal tells him simply to devote himself to study of the sacred knowledge. But the first Brahman, the first-born of mankind, insists he doesn't want to be alone. The Eternal became angry at his ingratitude and gave him a wife who was a giant from the race of Daints. She became the maternal ancestor of all the Brahmans. The entire Hindu priesthood is descended from superior spirits (the sons of God) and from Daintany, the daughter of giant primitive men. This is echoed in Genesis VI: 'The sons of God went to the daughters of humans and had children by them. They were mighty men, the heroes of old, men of renown.'

Echoes of the same story are found in the Scandinavian Prose Edda.[9] The Prose Edda is a work of Medieval Icelandic literature and the source of Norse mythology. King Gylfi of Sweden disguises himself as a commoner, calling himself Gangleri. He meets Harr, one of the Scandinavian Holy Trinity.[10] (The others are Jafnharr and Thridhi.) Harr tells Gangleri about the first man who was called Búri. He describes Búri as 'the father of Borr, who married Bestla, a daughter of the giant Bölþorn, one of the primitive frost giants.' The complete text can be found in sections four to eight of the Prose Edda, in the book *Northern Antiquities* by Paul Mallett.

The same narrative underpins the Hellenic myths about the Titans,[11] the first Greek gods. Elements of it are found in the Popol Vuh, the sacred book of Guatemala's K'iche' Indians, that tells the story of four progenitors of human beings. This repeating theme is one of many common threads running through the spiritual narrative of humanity. Its existence supports the belief in an underlying supernaturalism. It would be absurd to claim that this common narrative is the arbitrary result of random make-believe. To say that it occurred spontaneously, with no cause or firm basis, is as ludicrous as the theological doctrine that the universe was created from nothing.

It's too late now to reject evidence which is plain for all to see. Liberal and Christian papers as well as scientific journals begin to stand collectively against ill-informed dogmatism and prejudice. *The Christian World*,[12] a religious newspaper, adds its own voice to the opinions of the secular London press. *The Christian World* shows its common sense in the following extract:

'Even if a medium is proven to be a fraud, that still doesn't justify the attitude of some scientists who ridicule any serious study of spiritualism. The English physicist William Barrett came up against this attitude in 1876 when he was prevented from presenting his paper on spiritualism to the British Association for the Advancement of Science.[13] Spiritualists have accepted many ideas that have subsequently been shown to be absurd. But that's no reason to regard all spiritualist phenomena as not worth examining. Scientists should investigate examples of mesmerism or clairvoyance etc rather than avoiding the whole subject in the way some adults dismiss children with the phrase, *Children should be seen and not heard.*'

Scientists can no longer be described in John Milton's words, 'O thou who, for the testimony of truth, hast borne universal reproach!' Science has taken a backward step like the 'doctor of physic' described 180 years ago by the English philosopher, Henry More. When this doctor heard the supernatural story of the Drummer of Tedworth and an account of the ghost of Anne Walker, he exclaimed, 'If this is true, I've been barking up the wrong tree all along and must start again from scratch.'

Nowadays, even though Thomas Huxley stresses the significance of eyewitness accounts, an eminent philosopher like Henry More is still regarded as 'an enthusiast and a visionary, both of which, united in the same person, constitute a canting madman.'

It's not a lack of facts that makes the mysterious laws governing psychic phenomena so difficult to understand.

There are plenty of facts already. What's needed is for those facts to be recorded and classified by trained observers and competent analysts. Science should have provided these people.

Misconceptions and superstitions have proliferated in the western world for centuries to the detriment of ordinary people and the shame of science.

Generations have come and gone. Each generation has produced people of conscience and moral courage who have been martyred for their beliefs. Psychic phenomena are understood only a little better in modern times than in the past when the Vatican was all-powerful and the Church put brave men and women to death denouncing them as heretics and sorcerers.

Chapter Five

Ich bin der Geist der stets verneint.
I am the spirit which still denies.
MEPHISTO IN *FAUST*, GOETHE

The spirit of truth, whom the world cannot receive
because it seeth Him not; neither knoweth Him.
JOHN 14:17

Millions of spiritual creatures walk the earth
Unseen, both when we wake and we sleep.
JOHN MILTON

Mere intellectual enlightenment cannot recognize the
spiritual. As the sun puts out a fire, so spirit puts out the eyes
of mere intellect.
WILLIAM HOWITT

An infinite variety of names exists to express one and the same thing.

The chaos of the ancients / the sacred fire[1] of the Zoroastrian religion or the antus-byrum,[2] the sacred fire carried by the Parsis[3] in India / Hermes' invention of fire / the Elmes-fire[4] or eternal life-force of the ancient Germans / the lightning that demonstrated the power of the goddess Cybele[5] / the burning torch of the sun god Apollo / the perpetual fire at the altars of the nature god Pan / the inextinguishable fire in the temple on the Acropolis, and the fire at the temple of Vesta, the virgin goddess of the hearth / the hell fires of the god Pluto / the brilliant sparks of the stars Castor and Pollux (the Dioscuri)[6] in the constellation of Gemini, the Algol[7] star associated with Medusa, the Gorgon, the asteroid Pallas[8] and the southern constellation of the Caduceus[9] or staff of Mercury / the Egyptian god Ptah, who thought the world into being and invented fire, or the sun god, Ra / the Greek god Zeus who, according to Pausanias, descends as lightning (Zeus Cataibates) / the Holy Spirit descending at Pentecost upon the Apostles as tongues of fire[10] / the burning bush through which God speaks to Moses / God's presence as a pillar of fire in Exodus, and the 'burning lamp' which appeared to Abram in Genesis representing God / the eternal fire of the 'bottomless pit'[11] where God keeps demons captive / the vapors inducing trance in the Oracle at Delphi / the record of everything that has ever happened called the sidereal light[12] by the Rosicrucians[13] and the astral light by the great Kabbalist Eliphas Levi / the akasha[14] or universal aether of the Hindu adepts / the magnetic force, nerve aura or emanation of nervous fluid of the magnetists / the vital energy of life called the odic force by Carl Reichenbach / the phenomenon of the cat-like fire-globe described by Babinet to the Academy of Sciences / the link between soul and body called psychode and the force that energizes it called ectenic force by Marc Thury / the psychic force generated by mediums described by Edward Cox and William Crookes / the magnetic qualities of oxygen studied by some scientists / the animal magnetism or galvanism discovered by Luigi Galvini, and finally, electricity: - these are only different names for the same omnipresent causal force. The Greeks called it archeus, the vital force at the margin between matter and spirit.

In his 1871 novel *The Coming Race*, Edward Bulwer-Lytton called this force the 'vril.' He described its use by subterranean peoples and let his readers believe it was all a fiction. In the novel he writes, 'These people consider that in the vril they have arrived at the unity in natural energetic agencies.' He goes on to say that Faraday hinted at this unity using the more cautious term 'correlation':

'Like many other scientists, I have long believed that the various forms of force have one common origin. In other words, the various forms are so closely related that they can convert into one another and are equivalent in power.'

It may seem far-fetched to compare Bulwer-Lytton's fictitious vril and Faraday's primal force with the Kabbalistic astral light. But this is the true definition of that force. Discoveries are constantly being made to support this bold statement. Several newspapers have recently reported the alleged discovery of a new force by the inventor Thomas Edison. Like electricity and galvanism, this force will travel through a conductor but there the similarity ends. If this new force is proven to exist, its true identity may be obscured for a long time under a scientific name. But it will in fact be only one of a large family of forces originating from the astral light since the beginning of time. Edison says the force is as distinct as heat, magnetism or electricity and has similarly consistent laws. The first journal to report the discovery adds, 'Mr Edison thinks the force exists in connection with heat, and can also be generated independently in a way that hasn't yet been discovered.'

Alexander Graham Bell's telephone or 'distance-sounder' is another exciting recent discovery. It allows people to speak to each other across long distances. This idea was first explored in the tin can phone or 'lovers' telephone.' Two small tin cups with a length of taut string between them made it possible to speak to each other at a distance of 200 feet. This principle has been developed into the modern telephone which will become the wonder of the age. A long telephone conversation has taken place between Boston and Cambridgeport. According to the official report, 'Every word was clearly heard and perfectly understood, and the modulations of the voices were easily audible.' The sound is transmitted by electricity fluctuating in accordance with a magnet. Success depends on the perfect unison between the magnet and the electrical current. The official report continues, 'The telephone can be roughly described as a trumpet. Inside the mouth of the trumpet there is a thin membrane. When a voice speaks into the phone, the membrane vibrates in proportion to the sound wave. A piece of metal on the outer side of the membrane connects with a magnet creating an electrical current as the membrane vibrates. This electric current transmits the sound wave as it is spoken into the trumpet (though how this happens is not yet completely understood). The person at the other end of the line listens to the receiver, a replica of the trumpet, and hears every word clearly as well as the modulations of the voice.'

The age we live in is full of similar discoveries. And there may be further incredible inventions to come currently hidden within the world's limitless potential. It's highly likely that Edison's etheric force and Bell's telephone will turn our understanding of subtle energies upside down. Given these points, it might be a good idea for skeptics to reserve judgment on these theories until they are proven or disproven by further discoveries.

Perhaps these are only so-called 'discoveries.' During the celebrations of the Mysteries, Egyptian priests could communicate instantly between temples even though one may be at Thebes and the other at the opposite end of the country. In legend this was attributed to the actions of the 'invisible tribes' of the air who carry messages for mortals. In *The Pre-Adamite Man*, the African American occultist Paschal Beverly Randolph describes another example of instant communication. He seems uncertain about the source of the story saying it may come from Macrinius or another writer, so it has to be taken for what it's worth. During his stay in Egypt, Randolph says he found good evidence that 'one of the queens of Egypt sent news by telegraph to all the cities on the Upper Nile from Heliopolis to Elephantine.'[15]

Not so long ago John Tyndall astonished the world by making vapor of different types assume beautiful shapes.

He says, 'The shapes are produced by concentrating sunlight or electric light onto the vapor given off by volatile liquids.' Light is focused on the vapors of certain nitrites, iodides and acids in a test tube. The test tube is lying on its side with the beam of light running parallel to it. The vapors turn into beautifully colored clouds suggesting the shapes of vases, bottles and cones (sometimes there are six or more inside each other). They take on the appearance of shells, tulips, roses, sunflowers, leaves and intricate scrolls. Tyndall adds, 'Once a small cloud expanded rapidly into the shape of a snake's head. A mouth appeared and a thread of cloud came out of the mouth looking like a tongue.' Finally, to cap it all, Tyndall reports, 'At one time, the cloud took on the appearance of a fish complete with eyes, gills and feelers. The symmetry of its markings were perfect. There was no pattern on one side that wasn't repeated on the other.'

These phenomena could be partly explained by referring to William Crookes' recent investigations into the mechanical action of light. For example, it's possible that the molecules of the vapors gathered around a horizontal axis created by the light beam. As they gathered at this axis, they turned into the shapes of globes and spindles. But how do you account for the fish or the snake's head, the vases and the different varieties of flowers, and the shells? This seems to be as difficult for science to explain as Babinet's cat-like fire-globe. Babinet's explanation was complex and absurd. It's unclear whether Tyndall ever offered a similarly bizarre explanation for his vapor shapes.

There is an all-pervading, subtle principle known nowadays as the universal ether. It may come as a surprise that a great deal was known about it in previous ages.

Before going any further it is worth looking at two distinct arguments. These arguments were self-evident truths to the magicians of the ancient wisdom.

1. Consider the so-called miracles from the time of Moses to the 18th-century Italian occultist, Alessandro Cagliostro. When genuine, they occurred 'in accordance with natural law' as de Gasparin writes in his book on the subject. Therefore they were not in fact miracles. Electricity and magnetism were undoubtedly used to create some of these effects. Nowadays, as in the past, psychically sensitive people channel the forces of electricity and magnetism, using them unconsciously. A particular characteristic of the sensitive person's nature conducts these fluids which are not yet fully understood by science. The forces involved are the cause of limitless phenomena, the majority of which physics can't yet explain.

2. Consider the examples of natural magic found in Siam,

India, Egypt and other eastern countries. These examples are nothing like sleight of hand. Natural magic produces tangible physical effects as a result of occult natural forces. Whereas sleight of hand is nothing more than deception by manual dexterity often with the help of an accomplice.

Miracle workers of all kinds produced miraculous phenomena through their familiarity with the nature of the astral light. They understood that it produced mysterious effects but was itself composed of entirely tangible waves. They controlled those waves using the power of their minds. The results were both physical and psychical. Physical effects were produced on material objects. Psychical effects included phenomena like mesmerism, hypnosis and trance states. Two of today's greatest mesmerists are Jules du Potet and Antonio Regazzoni. Their extraordinary abilities have been endorsed in France and other countries. Mesmerism is the most important form of magic. The phenomena of mesmerism are produced by an underlying universal agent. This same agent produces all magic and all of history's so-called miracles.

The ancients called it chaos; Plato and the followers of Pythagoras called it the soul of the world. The Hindus believe that God, in the form of aether, pervades everything. As previously stated, it is an invisible but entirely tangible fluid. De Mirville mocked the idea of this universal agent, calling it 'the nebulous Almighty.' The ancient magicians called it by several names, including 'the living fire,' the 'spirit of light,' and Magnes. Magnes was the first king of Magnesia, a city or district in Thessaly with large deposits of the magnetic ore, magnetite. Therefore many people believe the name Magnes refers to the magnetic properties of the universal agent and accounts for its magical nature. As one skeptic put it, with unwitting accuracy, Magus (magician) and Magnes (magnetism) are two branches of the same tree producing the same net effects.

It's necessary to look to an incredibly early era for the origin of the word 'magnetism.' Many people believe the magnet got its name from Magnesia but it is the Hermeticists who know the name's true origin. The word 'Magh'/'Magus' comes from the Sanskrit word 'Mahaji' meaning the great or the wise, those anointed by the divine wisdom. In his book, *Sōd: The Mysteries of Adoni*, Samuel Dunlap cites the example of the priests called Eumolpidae[16] who traced the origin of their wisdom back to divine wisdom itself. Different creation stories describe divine wisdom or universal soul in different ways. People of different nations viewed it as the 'mind' of the Universal Architect or the Sophia of the Gnostics (embodying wisdom, the human soul and the feminine aspects of God) or the Holy Ghost (regarded by the early Syrian Orthodox Church as female). The Magi derived their name from the Sanskrit for 'divine wisdom' and magnets were named after them because they were the first people to understand the extraordinary properties of magnetism. The Magi had many temples spread all over the country and some of them were dedicated to Hercules. It became common knowledge that the Magi used magnetic stones for healing and magic. Consequently the magnets were given the name Magnesian or Heraclean stones. Socrates remarks on the subject, 'Euripides calls it the Magnesian stone, but the majority of people call it the Heraclean stone.' It was the country 'Magnesia' and the stone 'magnet' that were named after the Magi and not vice versa. The Roman author Pliny tells us it was the Roman custom to have the wedding ring magnetized by the priest before the ceremony. The old Pagan historians are careful to keep certain mysteries of the Magi hidden. Pausanias says he was warned in a dream not to reveal the holy rites of the temple of Demeter and Persephone[17] at Athens.

For a period of time, modern science rejected the phenomenon of animal magnetism. But now it accepts it as fact. It is now a recognized property of human and animal physiology. When it comes to the psychical and occult effects of magnetism, scientific institutions struggle with it now more than ever. It is regrettable and surprising that scientists are unable to explain something as simple as a magnet. They cannot even offer anything like a reasonable hypothesis for the undeniable but obscure power of magnetism. There is mounting evidence that this power lies behind the mysteries of ritualistic magic. It might also explain the occult powers of ancient and modern miracle workers and many of their greatest miracles. This was the gift Jesus passed on to some of his disciples. As he cured people he felt a power coming out of him. In the dialogue *Theages*,[18] attributed to Plato, Socrates describes his familiar or daemon to Theages. This daemon has the power to determine whether Socrates' wisdom will be passed on to his followers or not. Socrates gives an example to prove his point by quoting the Athenian statesman Aristides, 'I will tell you, Socrates, something incredible but true. I learned a good deal simply by being near you even if it was only in the same house, not the same room. I learned more when I was in the same room with you . . . and even more when I looked at you . . . but I learned by far the most when I sat near you and touched you.'

This is the same as the modern mesmerism practiced by du Potet and other experts. They bring a person under their magnetic influence and then they can transmit their thoughts to them even at a distance. With irresistible power they force the person to succumb to their mental influence. But the ancient philosophers had far better knowledge of this psychic force! Greater understanding can be gained by referring to the earliest sources. Pythagoras taught his followers that God is the universal mind diffused through all things. He taught that this mind is omnipresent and uniform. Because of these qualities, it can pass from one object to another and man's will can direct it to create all things. In ancient Greek, the word 'kurios' means god-mind ('nous' or higher mind). In Plato's dialogue *Cratylus*, Socrates says, 'Now koros (kurios) stands for the pure and whole nature of intellect - wisdom.' Kurios is also known as Mercury, the divine wisdom, and according to the early Christian apologist Arnobius, Mercury is the sun. Hermes Trismegistus received divine wisdom from the sun and shared it with the world in his books. Hercules is also the sun - the cosmic source of universal magnetism. The sun was not considered by the ancients as the origin of light and heat. It was a portal through which light passes to bring everything into creation (the Egyptians called it the eye of the god Osiris). Hercules is the magnetic light that passes through the 'opened eye of heaven' and becomes the architect of our planet. In Greek mythology Hercules completes twelve labors as described in the epic poem *The Heracleia* by Peisander. In the *Hymns of Orpheus* he is called 'father of all' and 'self-born' or 'autophues'. Hercules, the sun, is killed by the giant serpent Typhon. Osiris, the father and brother of Horus, was also killed by Typhon, known to the ancient Egyptians as Set. It's worth remembering that magnets were also called the 'bone of Horus' and iron was known as the 'bone of Typhon.' Hercules is called Hercules Invictus (the undefeated) when he enters the mythological garden of the Hesperides.[19] He steals 'golden apples' that grant eternal life and kills the hundred-headed dragon, Ladon, that guards them. Driven up by the immense raw power of every sun god, unconscious matter clashes with the divine magnetic spirit which tries to harmonize everything in nature.

The sun gods and their symbol, the sun, create physical nature only. The spiritual domain is created by the highest God and his demiurge or architect. The highest God is also known as the concealed, the central, spiritual sun. The architect is divine mind according to Plato and divine wisdom according to Hermes Trismegistus. This wisdom emanates from Oulom, the Phoenician word for eternity, or Kronos, described as 'great wisdom' in Plato's *Cratylus*.

According to the classical scholar Charles Anthon in his *Dictionary of Greek and Roman Antiquities*, 'After the distribution of pure fire, in the Samothracian Mysteries,[20] a new life began'. This is the new birth alluded to by Christ in his conversation with the Pharisee Nicodemus. In Plato's dialogue *Phaedrus*, Socrates says to Phaedrus, 'Initiated into the most blessed of all Mysteries, being ourselves pure . . . we become just and holy with wisdom.' John 20:22 describes Jesus appearing to his disciples with the words, 'He breathed on them and said, *Receive the Holy Spirit*.' And this simple act of willpower was enough to convey prophecy in its higher and perfect form if both the initiator and the initiated were worthy. In his book *Heathen Religion in its Popular and Symbolical Development*, the clergyman Joseph B. Gross tells us that it is a mistake to condemn the gift of prophecy as a corrupt legacy of an ignorant and superstitious age. Deciding it is not worth proper investigation is unreasonable and wrong. He goes on to say, 'Throughout history, attempts have been made to see the future. Therefore it is with God's blessing that we should regard prophecy as one of the faculties of the human mind. Huldrych Zwingli, leader of the Reformation in Switzerland, had complete faith in the benevolence of the supreme being. This was evident in his belief that the blessings of the Holy Ghost were not denied to worthy non-believers. If this is true, there's no reason why a non-believer shouldn't have the gift of prophecy.'

What is the first mystical substance from which everything

originates? In the first chapter of the book of Genesis, the spirit of God is described as moving over the 'face of the waters.' In the book of Job, 26:5, Job states that 'dead things are formed from under the waters and the inhabitants of the waters.' In the original Hebrew, 'dead things' is written as 'dead Rephaim,' the Hebrew for 'giant' or 'mighty primitive man.' Evolutionary science may one day trace the origin of modern humans to these giants. In Egyptian mythology, Kneph is the eternal unrevealed God. He is represented by a snake which is a symbol of eternity. The snake is coiled around a water urn and the snake's head hovers over the water vivifying it with its breath. In this case the snake represents the agathodaemon[21] or good spirit. But in its inverse form it represents the cacodaemon[22] or evil spirit. The Scandinavian books of mythology, the Eddas, describe the Yggdrasil[23] or tree of life. Dew falls from the tree during the night when the atmosphere is humid. The dew is the food of the gods and feeds all bees, and men call it honey-dew. In the northern mythologies honey-dew is the passive element of creation. It represents the creation of the universe out of water. The dew is a form of the astral light and has both creative and destructive powers. The Babylonian writer Berossus describes the legend of Oannes, a mythical man-fish also called Dagon in the Bible. Oannes declares that the world was created out of water and all beings originate from this primal source. Moses teaches that only earth and water can bring a living soul into being. The Bible recounts that plants could not grow until God made rain fall on the earth. In the Mayan book of cosmology, the Popol Vuh, man is made out of mud or clay found underwater. Brahma called spirits into being before man existed. Then, seated on his lotus, he creates Lomus, the great Muni or first man out of water, air and earth. Alchemists aim to reduce materials to their first matter or universal essence. They believe there are seven stages of transformation. The first stage is calcination. The second stage is dissolution. When primordial earth is reduced to its first matter it is, in its second stage of transformation, like clear water. In its first stage of transformation it is the alkahest or universal solvent. This first matter contains the essence of everything required to create man. It contains all the elements of his physical being as well as the 'breath of life' ready to be awakened. It is awakened by the spirit of God moving upon the face of the waters - chaos. In fact, first matter is chaos itself. The alchemist Paracelsus claimed to be able to create a homunculus or small man from this chaos. The Greek philosopher and father of naturalism, Thales of Miletus, believed that everything in nature was the product of endless modifications of the single material substance, water.

What is the primordial chaos but the ancient material known as aether that fills the region of the universe above the earth? This is the ether familiar today, but not as it is understood by science. It is the ether known to ancient philosophers since before the time of Moses. It is the mysterious and occult ether containing the seeds of universal creation. It is the ether also regarded as the celestial virgin or spiritual mother of every form and being. Matter, life, force and action spring into existence from her once incubated by the divine spirit. Even now our knowledge of electricity, magnetism, heat, light, and chemistry is limited. New discoveries are constantly improving our understanding. Ether is like a protean giant. Who knows how far its power extends or where it originates? Who would deny its ability to generate all visible forms?

Several branches of modern science support the theory of evolution. The ancients' working knowledge of scientific principles formed the basis of the world's origin myths. Further research may show that the ancients had a better knowledge of the physical and spiritual aspects of evolution than we do now. Ancient philosophers regarded evolution as a universal theory. For them it embraced the whole of existence including the spiritual as well as the physical and it was an accepted truth. By contrast modern evolutionary theory is speculative and only looks at part of the picture. Modern science can't claim that the Biblical account of evolution has been discredited simply because its phraseology is obscure and clashes with scientific dogma.

One thing is for certain. Creation stories in every culture include the allegory of water animated by spirit. This demonstrates that none of these stories' authors believed the universe to have sprung into existence out of nothing. This is in line with the position of modern physicists. All creation legends begin with primordial vapor and darkness over a liquid mass ready to be prompted into life by the breath of the originating god or first cause. The writers of these creation stories intuited the existence of the originating god even though they couldn't see him. Their spiritual intuition was not as confused as ours is now by rarified and deliberately complex arguments. They may not have written much about the transition from one geological period to another (from the Silurian[24] to the Mammalian or Cenozoic Period[25]) but this doesn't prove that they knew any less about it.

In Democritus and Aristotle's time, the cycle of human understanding had already begun on its downward path. The two philosophers understood atomic theory sufficiently well to argue about the physical structure of the atom. Their ancestors may have been able to trace the atom's origins back to the first cause or beyond that incomprehensible limit where scientists like John Tyndall are afraid to go. Enough is known about these lost arts to prove that the ancients' practical knowledge in phytochemistry and mineralogy far exceeded our own. Their achievements in physical geography are only doubted because of the incomplete records left by their physicists and naturalists. In addition they may have had comprehensive knowledge of the physical evolution of the earth. But they might not have published their findings because it was customary to confine knowledge to the sanctuaries and withhold it from the general public.

Therefore it's necessary to look further than the texts of the Old Testament to support these arguments. In their early history the Jewish people gained their religious and secular knowledge from their interactions with many different cultures. The Jewish Kabbalistic 'secret doctrine' is the oldest of all the sciences. It can be traced to its original source in Upper India or Turkistan long before the Indo-Iranian and Semitic nations became distinct from one another. In his work, *Antiquities of the Jews (Antiquitates Judaicae)*, the Roman historian Titus Flavius Josephus describes King Solomon as famous for his skill in magic. Solomon learned the secrets of Indian magic from Hiram, his master mason, also from the King of Ophir[26] and perhaps from the Queen of Sheba. The ring worn by King Solomon, commonly known as 'Solomon's seal,' is also of Hindu origin. The seal is famous for its power over genii and demons. The English clergyman Samuel Mateer of the London Missionary Society served in India for 33 years. In his book *The Land of Charity*, he describes demon worship in the kingdom of Travancore.[27] He describes an old manuscript in the local Malayalam language giving

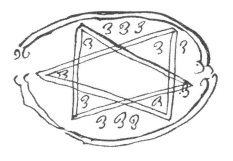

magical incantations and spells for a variety of different purposes. 'Many of these are fearful in their viciousness and obscenity,' he writes. His book contains facsimiles of amulets with magical symbols and designs. One of the designs is accompanied by the following instructions: 'To remove trembling arising from demonic possession, draw this symbol on a plant that has milky juice and drive a nail through it. The trembling will cease.' The symbol has the same design as the seal of Solomon - the double triangle used by the Kabbalists. Did the Hindu get it from the Jewish Kabbalist or did the Jewish Kabbalist get it from India via King Solomon? In the end it makes little difference. Of greater interest is the astral light and its hidden properties.

If the astral light is the same substance as ether, it makes sense to examine how much is known about ether by the scientific establishment.

In his book, *Researches on Light in its Chemical Relations*, the British scientist Robert Hunt observes the properties of light of different colors. He explains that, 'Those rays which give the most light - the yellow and the orange rays - will not change the color of silver chloride.' He goes on to say, 'Those rays which have the least illuminating power - the blue and violet - produce the biggest change very quickly . . . the yellow filters obstruct scarcely any light; the blue filters may be so dark that they allow hardly any light to pass through them.'

Both plant and animal life respond definitively and rapidly to the blue light whilst under yellow light very little happens. The only way to account for this is to regard both animal and plant life as differentiated electro-magnetic phenomena. But the basic nature of these phenomena is not yet fully understood.

According to Robert Hunt, the wave theory of light does not explain the results of his experiments. In his book, *A Treatise on Optics*, the Scottish physicist David Brewster shows that 'the colors of a plant are caused by the particles of that plant attracting differently colored rays of light.' He goes on to demonstrate that, 'the light of the sun determines the color of a plant's sap and also determines the different colors of plants themselves.' He then remarks that 'it is not easy to accept that these effects can be produced by nothing more than the vibration of an ethereal medium.' He says he is forced 'by these facts to approach the subject as if light was material.' In *The New Chemistry*, the Harvard scientist Josiah Cooke says he 'cannot agree with those people who consider the wave theory of light to be a proven scientific fact.' According to the British astronomer Frederick Herschel, 'The intensity of light (in effect the intensity of each light wave) is inversely proportional to the square of the distance from the light source.' If this is correct, it significantly undermines the wave theory even if it doesn't disprove it entirely. Experiments with photometers have repeatedly proven that Herschel is right and confidence in the wave theory has been dented though the theory still persists.

In *The Influence of the Blue Ray of the Sunlight and of the Blue Color of the Sky*, General Augustus Pleasonton argues against the wave theory of light. His book is well worth reading for its comprehensive counter arguments. The wave theory was presented to the Royal Society in 1800 by the English physicist Thomas Young. According to John Tyndall, Young's paper 'made the wave theory of light indisputable.' It will be interesting to see if Young's theory can stand up against the arguments of General Pleasonton.

The French occult author Eliphas Levi explains how to influence the astral light through the action of willpower. 'To acquire magical power, two things are necessary: to free the will from all outside influences and to exercise control over it.

'Free will is represented in the symbolic language of the occult by a woman crushing a serpent's head and by a radiant angel overpowering a dragon with his foot and spear. In the ancient stories of the gods, the dual current of light, the living and astral fire of the earth, has been represented by a serpent with the head of a bull, a ram or a dog. It is the double serpent seen in the caduceus,[28] the staff carried by Hermes in Greek mythology. It is the snake in the Garden of Eden. But it is also Moses' brazen serpent wrapped around the 'taw', the last letter of the Hebrew alphabet symbolizing the revelation of truth. It is the fertile lingam, phallic symbol of divine procreative power. It is also the goatish devil present at the Witches' Sabbath, and the Baphomet or horned devil worshiped by the Knights Templar. It is the Gnostics' hyle or generative proto-matter. It is the two serpents that form the legs of the Gnostics' Abraxas, a figure with the head of a cock, emblematic of the sun. Finally, it is the Devil described by the Comte de Mirville. But in actual fact it is a blind force. Souls must overcome this force to free themselves from earthly ties. If they fail to free themselves from this fatal attraction, they will be absorbed into the current of light by the power that made them, they will return to the central and eternal fire.'

This last sentence is a Kabbalistic figure of speech. In spite of its strange wording, this is exactly the phrase used by Jesus. In his mind it can only have had the meaning given to it by the Gnostics and the Kabbalists. It simply means what it says - that the astral light is both the generator and destroyer of all forms. (Christian theologians later interpreted it differently as the doctrine of Hell.)

Eliphas Levi continues, 'All magical powers depend on freeing oneself from the temptation of the ancient serpent. Conquer it and lead it according to your will. In Matthew 4, the Serpent says, 'I will give you all the kingdoms of the earth if you will bow down and worship me.' The initiate should reply to him, 'I will not bow down. Instead you will crouch at my feet. You will give me nothing but I will use you and take whatever I want because I am your master!' This is the real meaning of Jesus' ambiguous reply to the Devil. This shows that the Devil is not an entity but a deviant force as its name suggests. A chain of perverse wills creates an odic or magnetic current. This current constitutes the evil spirit called Legion in the Bible. Legion is exorcised by Jesus and then possesses a herd of pigs causing them to drown themselves. This allegory shows how the lives of the weak-willed can be controlled by blind forces created by error and evil intent.'

In his book, *Mystical Manifestations of Human Nature (Die Mystischen Erscheinungen in der Menschlichen Natur)*, the German naturalist and philosopher, Maximilian Perty devotes a whole chapter to modern forms of magic. In his preface he writes, 'Magic partially exists on a different plane. It is beyond our own plane and our experience of time, space and causality. Magic cannot be experimented with to any great extent. But it can be carefully observed whenever it occurs spontaneously. Different magical phenomena can only be loosely categorized and only general principles and laws can be deduced from observation.' Maximilian Perty obviously belonged to the school of Schopenhauer. According to Perty, the phenomena associated with the Indian fakir Covindasamy occurred in line with Schopenhauer's theory of will. Covindasamy's abilities are described by the French author Louis Jacolliot in his book *Occult Science in India and Among the Ancients (Les Sciences Occultes dans l'Inde et Chez Tous les Peuples de l'Antiquité)*. Covindasamy had made his body subject to the absolute control of his will. In this way he had reached a state of spiritual purity. His spirit was almost free from its corporeal prison and could produce wonders. Not just his will but even a simple desire had become a creative force. He could control the elements and forces of nature. He was no longer limited by his physical body. He could communicate 'spirit to spirit, breath to breath'. Louis Jacolliot describes choosing a seed at random and planting it in a flower pot. Under Covindasamy's outstretched palms, the seed germinates instantly and pushes its way through the soil. In less than two hours it grows to a size and height that under ordinary circumstances would take several days or weeks. It grows miraculously before Jacolliot's eyes undermining every accepted botanical principle. Is this a miracle? No it isn't. Perhaps it could be taken as one according to Webster's dictionary definition: 'an extremely outstanding or unusual event, thing, or accomplishment; an event that cannot be explained by the known laws of nature.' But are naturalists prepared to claim that every law, derived from observation, is infallible? Are they bold enough to claim that they know every law of nature? In this case of instant germination the 'miracle' is only a exaggerated example of the well-known experiments conducted by General Augustus Pleasonton of Philadelphia. In his experiments, Pleasonton passed light through blue filters and rapidly increased the growth of his vines. Meanwhile, Covindasamy produced magnetic fluid from his hands that brought about even more intense and rapid changes in his Indian plants. It attracted and focused the akasha or life-principle on the seed. Akasha is the Sanskrit word for 'sky'. It also suggests the unfathomable and formless life-principle. This life-principle is the astral and celestial lights combined together. The astral light is the lower aspect of akasha. It is particular to the earth and close to the material plane. The celestial light is akasha's higher universal aspect. Together they form the world soul or *anima mundi* and make up the soul and spirit of man. The celestial light forms man's divine spirit. The astral light forms his soul or astral spirit. Akasha is equivalent to 'the all-pervading ether' described by modern science. Akasha is essential to all natural magic. It produces mesmeric, magnetic and spiritual phenomena. When Covindasamy's hands produced magnetic fluid, they drew a concentrated current of akasha up through the plant toward them. Covindasamy sustained an uninterrupted flow of akasha for the right period of time so that the plant's life-force accelerated the production of layer after layer of cells and the plant was instantaneously mature. The life-force is only acting under the influence of Covindasamy's control. Ordinarily it would have been concentrated and directed by the plant's protoplasm at the expected rate. This rate would have been dependent on the prevailing weather. The plant's growth would have been fast or slow in proportion to the season's light, heat and rainfall. But Covindasamy assists nature using his powerful will and his spirit, uncontaminated by contact with matter. He condenses the essence of the plant's life into its seed and forces it to full growth prematurely. The blind life-force obeys his will absolutely. If he chose to imagine the plant in a monstrous form, it would assume that form just as surely as it usually grows into its natural shape. The physical form reflects the image held in Covindasamy's imagination. It follows the original image precisely just as the painter's hand and brush follow the image held in the mind's eye of the artist. Covindasamy's will creates an invisible but objective matrix. His will causes the plant's cells to populate the matrix, taking its shape. The will creates. Will in motion is force and force produces matter.

Someone could object to this explanation on the basis that Covindasamy had no idea what kind of seed Jacolliot had picked out for the experiment. How then, could he create an image of the full grown plant in his imagination? This objection can be overcome by considering the essential nature of the spirit of man. Like God's, it is omniscient. In his waking state, it's true that Covindasamy couldn't know what kind of seed it was. But once in a trance state, his spirit could realize its omniscient nature. While Covindasamy's body appeared lifeless, his spirit had no difficulty in perceiving that the seed was a melon seed. To the spirit there is no distance, no material obstacles, no time. The melon seed was apparent to his spirit whether it was buried in the flower pot or held as an image in Jacolliot's mind. Visions, omens and other naturally occurring psychical phenomena operate on a similar basis and corroborate the above example.

Someone could also object that Indian conjurors are able to produce similar effects to Covindasamy. This is undoubtedly true. But it is important to understand that these itinerant conjurors do not live a spiritual life and they are not considered holy by anyone, visitors or locals. They are generally feared and rejected by local people because they are sorcerers, men who practice the black art.

A holy man like Covindasamy needs only his divine soul united with the astral light, and the help of a few ancestor spirits or pitris.[29] Pure ethereal beings, the pitris choose living counterparts to support and serve. A sorcerer, on the other hand, can only rely on help from the spirits known as elementals. Like attracts like. Qualities such as greed, corruption and selfishness cannot attract anything other than impure spirits. Examples of these spirits are the Kabbalists' qlippoth,[30] inhabitants of Assiah,[31] the fourth world. Or the afrits,[32] as they are known to the eastern magicians, powerful, evil demons. Or the devs,[33] Zoroastrian spirits of darkness.

An English newspaper describes how an Indian conjuror appeared to replicate Covindasamy's feat of accelerated plant growth:

'An empty flower pot was placed on the floor by the conjuror. He asked if his companion could fetch some garden mold from a small plot of ground. Permission was given and the man returned two minutes later with a small quantity of fresh earth tied up in the corner of his robe. The earth was put into the flower pot and lightly pressed down. The conjuror took a dry mango stone from a basket and handed it round so everyone could examine it. Once they had confirmed that it really was a mango stone, the conjuror scooped out a little earth from the center of the flower pot. He then put the stone in the earth and covered it over. He poured a little water over the surface and then hid the flower pot from view behind a cloth on a triangular frame. To chanting from the crowd and an accompanying drum roll, the stone appeared to germinate. The cloth was partially pulled aside to show the tender shoot - two long leaves of a blackish-brown color. The cloth was then put back in position and the chanting started again. Shortly afterwards the cloth was pulled aside a second time to show that the first two leaves had been replaced by several green ones and the plant was now nine or ten inches tall. The cloth was opened a third time to show much thicker foliage and the sapling about 13 to 14 inches tall. The fourth time the cloth was opened, the miniature tree was about 18 inches tall with ten or twelve walnut-sized mangoes hanging from its branches. Finally after three or four minutes the cloth was removed altogether. The fruit had reached full size but were not fully ripe. They were picked and handed to the spectators to taste. They were sweet but still acidic.

The author has also seen the same feat performed in India and Tibet. On more than one occasion I provided the flower pot myself by emptying out an old tin of beef extract. I filled it with earth with my own hands and planted a small root that the conjuror handed to me. The pot was put in my own room and I didn't take my eyes off it until the experiment was over. The result was invariably the same as described above. Do you believe a western illusionist could produce the same effect under the same conditions?

The Italian physicist Francesco Orioli was an honorary member of the French Institute. He describes a number of incredible effects produced by willpower acting on the universal, vital or magnetic fluid identified by the mesmerists. He writes, 'I have seen people halt charging bulls and horses simply by saying certain words. And I have seen someone suspend an arrow in mid-air.' The Danish physician Thomas Bartholin endorses Orioli's experiences, describing similar effects.

In *Magic Unveiled (La Magie Dévoilée)*, Jules du Potet writes, 'When I draw this sign on the floor with chalk or charcoal, a fire or light illuminates it. Anyone who comes near is attracted to it. It holds and fascinates them and it is impossible for them to cross the line. A magic power compels them to stand still. After a few moments, they give up, sobbing . . . I am not personally the cause of this, it is caused by the Kabbalistic sign drawn on the floor - restraining me would not make it stop.'

In Paris in 1856, Antonio Regazzoni made a series of remarkable experiments observed by several well-known French physicians. On the evening of 18 May, he traced with his finger an imaginary Kabbalistic line on the floor and made a few rapid gestures over it. The test subjects were selected by the French physicians and were all strangers to Regazzoni. They were brought into the room blindfolded and guided to walk toward the line without being told what to expect. The test subjects walked toward the invisible barrier. What happened next is described by occult author Alcide Morin in his book *Magic in the Nineteenth Century (Magie au Dix-neuvième Siècle)*, 'Their feet stuck to the ground as if they had been screwed down and the test subjects fell onto the floor, toppled by their own momentum. Their limbs were suddenly rigid like the limbs of a frozen corpse. And their feet were stuck to the ground exactly where the line was drawn.'

Another experiment involved a blindfolded girl, stood some distance away from Regazzoni. One of the physicians agreed to begin the experiment by signaling silently to Regazzoni with a glance of his eye. Magnetic fluid emitted by Regazzoni would then make the girl fall to the ground as if struck by lightning. The signal was given and, though no one in the room spoke or gestured, she fell to the ground instantly. Without thinking, one of the spectators reached out to catch her. Regazzoni shouted, 'Do not touch her! Let her fall; a magnetized subject is never hurt by falling.' Quoted in *Magic in the Nineteenth Century*, des Mousseaux observed that, 'Her body was as stiff as marble. Her head did not touch the ground. One of her arms was stretched up in the air. One of her legs was lifted up and the other was horizontal. It's impossible to say how long she stayed in this unnatural position, rigid like a bronze statue.'

During public lectures, Regazzoni successfully demonstrated a range of mesmeric effects without a word being spoken to the test subjects. He even produced effects on total strangers through the force of willpower. The effects on their bodies were profound and astonishing. The committee of physicians would whisper directions to Regazzoni. These were obeyed immediately by the test subjects even though they had cotton wool in their ears and their eyes were bandaged. In some cases the physicians didn't even need to tell Regazzoni what they wanted the test subjects to do. Their own thoughts were enough to influence the subjects so that they complied with their mental instructions.

Regazzoni conducted similar experiments in England. In these instances he was over 300 feet away from the test subject. This demonstrated the extent of his ability to exert influence remotely. The evil eye, or jettatura as it is known in Italian, is simply a particular use of the magnetic fluid. The invisible fluid is charged with hostility and hatred and projected from one person to another with the intention of causing harm. The magnetic fluid can be used for good or evil. When it is used for good, it is magic. When it is used for evil, it is sorcery.

What is the essence of will? Can modern science explain it? What is the nature of that intelligent, intangible and powerful something that exerts its supreme will over all inert matter? The cosmos sprang into existence because the great universal idea exerted its will. I exert my will and my limbs respond. I exert my will and my thought crosses space. Existing beyond space, my thought takes control of another entirely separate person. If their will is weaker than mine then my thoughts will dominate them, forcing them to carry out any action I choose. My will acts like the fluid in a galvanic or wet battery. The battery terminals in contact with a corpse make its limbs contract. This strange phenomenon of attraction and repulsion is the unconscious agent of the will. One animal can exert a fascination over another, for example when a predatory snake transfixes a bird. This fascination is the conscious action of the will directed by thought. A latent heat exists in every substance. When sealing wax, glass or amber are rubbed, that latent heat is awakened and attracts lightweight objects like small pieces of leaves and dust. The wax, glass and amber exert will unconsciously. Inorganic as well as organic matter contains a fragment of the divine essence, however infinitesimally small. And how could it be any other way? During its evolution inorganic matter may have passed through millions of different forms. Even so, it must retain its fragment of pre-existent matter - the first sign of God and the first gift. So what is this power of attraction in essence? It is that minute fragment of the life-principle recognized by both scientists and Kabbalists. It is the akasha. Bodies of inorganic matter exert blind or unconscious attraction. But in the case of organic beings, the life-principle within them becomes more marked and determined as they become more highly developed. Man is the most highly evolved being on earth. In him matter and spirit (i.e. will) are the most highly developed and powerful. Only man can consciously direct the life-principle within him. Only man can direct the magnetic fluid at will and without limitation. As Jules du Potet puts it, 'Man exerts his will and living matter obeys. It has no choice.'

In his book, *On Hallucinations*, the French physician Brière de Boismont describes a variety of visions, apparitions and ecstasies. He writes, 'Undeniably certain diseases cause an increase in the acuity of the senses. This explains how some people can tell someone is approaching from a considerable distance even though no one else present can hear or see them coming.'

A lucid patient lying in his bed announces the imminent arrival of a visitor. The only way he could know this is if he could see through walls. And yet Brière de Boismont describes this as a hallucination. Surely, to be accurately described as a hallucination, a vision must be subjective. It must exist only in the patient's delusional mind. But suppose the patient predicts the arrival of someone miles away. And suppose the person arrives at the exact moment predicted. Then the patient's vision wasn't subjective. On the contrary it was entirely objective because he perceived the objective fact of the person approaching. And how could the patient see someone hidden from view? Could it be that he was seeing spiritually? Or was it merely coincidence?

The French physiologist Pierre Cabanis describes particular nervous disorders in which vision becomes extremely acute. Unaided, patients can see microorganisms that are usually only visible through a microscope. In his book, *On The Relations Between The Physical And Moral Aspects Of Man (Rapports du Physique et du*

Moral de l'Homme), Cabanis writes, 'I have met subjects who could see as well in absolute darkness as in a brightly lit room . . . I have met others who, like dogs, could track people by smell. They could also identify objects that belonged to them or had only been touched by them. All of this was done with an accuracy previously seen only in animals.'

With an increase in reason comes a decline in natural instinct, as Pierre Cabanis says. Reason becomes like the Great Wall of China, shutting out man's spiritual perceptions and one of the most important of these is instinct. In certain states of physical exhaustion the mind becomes too weak to reason. Then instinct - the spiritual unity of the five senses - sees, hears, feels, tastes, and smells unlimited by either time or space. How much is really known about the true extent of the power of the mind? How can a doctor tell the difference between imaginary and actual sense perception in a patient living a spiritual life and whose body is so exhausted that it lacks the strength to prevent the soul from escaping?

Through the divine light, the soul sees things past, present and to come, unencumbered by matter. It is as if the rays of past, present and future were focused in a mirror. In a moment of extreme anger or as a result of intense hatred, a deadly energy may be directed from one person to another. A blessing may be given in gratitude or kindness or a curse may be pronounced in vengeance or spite. All these things - divine light, deadly energy, blessing or curse - have to pass through the universal agent. Directed one way, the universal agent acts for good. Directed another, it is the agent of evil. The universal agent was supposedly discovered by the German chemist Carl Reichenbach. He called it 'Odic force' or 'Od'. It's impossible to say if he chose that name deliberately but it seems remarkable that the same name appears in the most ancient books of the Kabbalah.

What is this universal agent? Why hasn't modern science discovered its particular properties? Scientists may be unfamiliar with it, but that doesn't mean it's not as the ancients described. Science often rejects a hypothesis which it is later forced to accept. Less than a century ago scientists rejected the idea that lightning was electricity. But nowadays almost every house has one of Franklin's lightning conductors on its roof. Shooting at the barn door, science often misses the barn itself. With their usual skepticism and partial knowledge, modern scientists do this time and again.

In Egyptian cosmogony, Emeph is the supreme first principle. Emeph produced an egg and fertilized it. This led to the birth of Ptah, the god of creation, who then began his work. Ptah breathed - or willed - a boundless expanse of cosmic matter into existence. This cosmic matter has been called by many different names - astral light, aether, fire-mist, life-principle. What it's called makes no difference. Ptah, or evolution, released the potential in the cosmic matter forming suns, stars and satellites. Ptah positioned them in the universe according to the fixed law of harmony and populated them with every kind of life. In ancient eastern mythology, the origin myth says there was only water (the father) and primordial mud (the mother). This mud was also called 'ilus'[34] by the Greeks or 'hyle' by the Gnostics. The combination of water and mud produced the primordial snake. This was the Greek god of procreation, Phanes, the revealed one, the Word, or Logos. This myth was readily accepted even by the Christians who compiled the New Testament. This is easy to deduce by their adoption of the snake symbol. In this symbol, Phanes, the revealed god, is represented as the primeval deity of procreation. He is depicted with the heads of a man, a hawk or eagle, a bull and a lion, and with wings on either side. Each of the heads relates to a sign of the zodiac. Each one also represents the four seasons of the year because the primordial serpent represents the terrestrial year. The serpent also represents Kneph, the hidden or unrevealed deity - God the Father. Time flies and so the serpent is represented with wings. Traditionally each of the Four Evangelists is represented in association with one of the four animals described above. They can be found grouped together in the figure of Solomon's triangle in the pentacle of Ezekiel. Suggestions of them appear in the four cherubs or sphinxes on the sacred Ark of the Covenant. These elements point to the serpent symbol's secret meaning and explain why the early Christians adopted it. The Evangelists are still depicted with these animals in illustrated Roman Catholic and Greek Orthodox editions of the Gospels. In the third volume of his work *Against Heresies (Adversus Haereses)*, Irenaeus, the Bishop of Lyon, underlined the importance of there being four gospels. He said this was because there were four zones in the world and four winds associated with the four points of the compass.

In one Egyptian myth, the island of Chemmis[35] was hatched from an egg by the sun god Horus. The mythological isle floats on waves of ether in the celestial sphere.

The Icelandic text of the Gylfaginning describes the origin of the cosmos. It also refers to the Völuspá, the first poem of the Poetic Edda, narrated by a female shaman. The mythological seed of the universe is contained in the Ginnungagap - the cup of illusion, a gaping abyss or yawning void. A ray of cold light came from the formerly dark and desolate region of Nebelheim, the mist-world. This light (or aether) overwhelmed the cup of Ginnungagap and caused it to freeze. Then the creator caused a fiery wind that melted the ice and dispelled the mist. The meltwaters were the Elivagar, rivers that existed in the Ginnungagap at the beginning of the world. These rivers were distilled into life-giving drops which fell like rain and created the earth and the giant Ymir. Ymir embodied the male principle. At the same time, Audhumla, the cow, was created and she embodied the female principle. From her udders, four streams of milk flowed, spreading throughout space. (They were the astral light in its purest form.) Audhumla licks stones covered with salt and so gives rise to Búri, the handsome and powerful first Norse god.

The ancient philosophers regarded salt as one of the main building blocks of organic life. The alchemists regarded it as the universal menstruum or solvent obtained from water. It is regarded by everyone else, including scientists and the general public, as an essential nutrient for humans and animals. When all of this is taken into consideration, the wisdom hidden in the Norse creation myth is revealed. In *Archidoxis Volume X* Paracelsus calls salt 'the center of the water, in which the metals ought to lose their body.' And the Flemish chemist Jan Baptist van Helmont describes the alkahest as the most potent of all salts.

In Matthew 5:13, Jesus says, 'You are the salt of the earth. But if salt loses its saltiness, how will it become salty again?' And in 5:14, he adds, 'You are the light of the world.' This is more than an allegory. These words have a direct and categoric meaning regarding the dual nature of man. They indicate he has both a spiritual and a physical body. And in addition they reveal a knowledge of the 'secret doctrine'. Traces of this doctrine are found in both ancient and modern belief systems, in the Old and New Testaments and in writing attributed to ancient and medieval mystics and philosophers.

In the Edda myth, Ymir, the giant, falls asleep and sweats profusely. This sweating creates a man and a woman from his left arm pit. His foot produces their son. While Audhumla, the cow, gives life to a race of superior spiritual men, Ymir creates a race of evil depraved men, the Hrimthursen or Frost Giants. The same creation story appears in the Hindu Vedas with slight variations. This story is described in *The Heathen Religion in its Popular and Symbolical Development* by Joseph B. Gross. The Supreme God, Bhagavanta, endows Brahma with the power of creation. Brahma creates generations of beings consisting of Dejotas or Daints. The Dejotas are inhabitants of the Surges or celestial spheres. The Daints or giants inhabit the Patals or lower spheres or regions of space. Therefore neither the Dejotas nor the Daints can populate Mirtlok, the earth. To set this right, Brahma produces the first Brahmin priest from his mouth, who becomes the father of humanity. Brahma then produces Raettris, the warrior from his right arm. From his left arm he produces Raettris' wife, Shaterany. Then their son Bais springs from Brahma's right foot and his wife Basany springs from Brahma's left foot. In the Scandinavian legend, the cow, Audhumla, gives birth to Búri, the first god. Búri's son Borr marries Bestla, a daughter of the depraved race of giants. Similarly in the Hindu tradition, the first Brahmin marries Daintany who is also a daughter of giants. Likewise, in Genesis, the sons of God marry the daughters of men and their offspring are giants, the Nephilim. These three examples establish without doubt that the Bible and the Scandinavian and Indian legends have a common origin. A close look at the legends of most other cultures would reveal a similar commonality.

The Egyptians compressed a whole world of meaning into the simple symbol of a serpent in the shape of a circle. It's hard to imagine that any modern cosmogonist could do the same. The whole philosophy of the universe is represented by the snake; the way matter was brought to life by spirit and how the two together created everything out of chaos (or force - the vital force at the margin between matter and spirit). All of the elements are tightly woven into the cosmic matter represented by the snake. To signify this the Egyptians depicted the snake's tail tied into a knot.

There is one more important symbol to examine which has so far been overlooked by modern anthropologists. This symbol is based on the image of the snake shedding its skin. When a snake goes through this transformation, it leaves behind the material constricting its body and can go on to thrive and grow. Similarly, when a man casts off his material body, he can move on to the next stage of existence with greater powers and newly awakened vitality. According to the Chaldean Kabbalists, primeval man was finer, wiser and far more spiritual than first thought. This idea is contrary to Darwinian theory but it is supported by the myths of the Scandinavian god Búri, the Hindu Dejotas and the Biblical 'sons of God.' In essence, primeval man was spiritually far superior to modern man. But his spiritual nature became polluted with matter and, for the first time, he was given a body made of flesh. This idea is expressed in Genesis 3:21: 'The Lord God made garments of skin for Adam and his wife and clothed them.' Either God is a celestial tailor or these apparently absurd words must have a symbolic meaning. Spirit descended into matter in a process called involution. As involution progressed, matter so dominated spirit that it transformed spiritual man into the physical man of the second chapter of Genesis.

This Kabbalistic concept is described more fully in the Hebrew text, Book of Jashar.[36] The text describes how Noah inherits these garments of skin from Methuselah and Enoch who had inherited them in turn from Adam and his wife. Noah takes the skins into the Ark where his son, Ham, steals them. Ham gives them 'in secret' to Cush who conceals them from his sons and brothers and passes them to Nimrod.

Some Kabbalists and certain archeologists maintain that 'while Adam, Enoch, and Noah might appear to be different men on the surface, they were really one divine person.' Others claim that Adam and Noah were separated by aeons of time. In other words, Adam, Enoch and Noah each represented a race of people and these races appeared in successive cycles with each race being less spiritual than the last. So Noah, though a good man, could not compare with his ancestor Enoch, who 'walked with God and did not die.' In the allegorical interpretation of the story, Noah inherits the coat of skin from Adam and Enoch but doesn't wear it himself - if he had been wearing it, how could Ham have stolen it? This interpretation suggests that Noah belonged to the old and still spiritual antediluvian generation (he was, after all, chosen by God over all mankind because of his spiritual purity). His children, on the other hand, were post-diluvian. Cush wore the coat of skin 'in secret' as his spiritual nature became increasingly polluted by the material. The coat of skin was then placed on Nimrod, the most powerful physical man to exist after the Flood and the last in the line of antediluvian giants.

In the Edda, the giant Ymir is killed by Búri's sons. So much blood flows from his wounds that it drowns the entire race of ice and frost giants except Ymir's grandson, Bergelmir, and his wife. Búri's sons also escaped the flood. Bergelmir, and his wife survived by taking refuge in a boat which meant Bergelmir could father a new generation of giants from the original bloodline.

When the symbolism of this legend is examined, the real meaning becomes clear. The giant Ymir represents crude organic matter and unconscious cosmic forces in a state of chaos. The intelligence of the divine spirit later took control of these unconscious forces causing them to behave in predictable ways governed by fixed laws. The offspring of Búri are the 'sons of God', or the minor gods mentioned by Plato in the *Timaeus*. As Plato put it, they were entrusted with the creation of men. So Búri's sons take the remains of Ymir to the Ginnungagap, the chaotic abyss, and use them to create the world. Ymir's blood forms oceans and rivers. His bones form mountains. His teeth become rocks and cliffs. His hair forms trees. His skull becomes the dome of the sky supported by four pillars representing the four points of the compass. Ymir's eyebrows form man's future home - Midgard or the earth. According to the Edda, the earth should be conceived as a ring or a disc floating in the middle of the celestial ocean or the ether. The earth is encircled by Yormungand, a gigantic serpent holding its tail in its mouth. It is both matter and spirit, the combined product of Ymir's gross matter and the spirit of the 'sons of God', who created all forms. This product is the Kabbalists' astral light or physicists' ether, the hypothetical elastic agent thought to fill all space.

The ancients were certain that man's physical and spiritual nature was threefold. This can be seen in the same Scandinavian creation myth. According to the Völuspá, Odin, Hœnir and Lóðurr were the fathers of humanity. Walking by the sea, they found two branches floating in the waves 'powerless and without destiny.' Odin breathed life into them, Hœnir animated them with a soul and Lóðurr gave them beauty, speech, sight and hearing. One of the branches became the first man and they called him Askr - the ash tree. The other branch became the first woman, Embla - the alder tree. The first man and woman found themselves in Midgard (mid-garden or Eden). From their creators they had inherited three things - matter or inert life, mind or soul, and pure spirit. They had inherited matter or inert life from the remains of Ymir; mind or soul from the Aesir,[37] the gods descended from Búri; and pure spirit from the god Vanr.[38]

In another version of the Edda, the universe comes into existence among the branches of the Yggdrasil, the great ash tree with three roots. The well of Udr runs under the first root. The well of Mimir runs under the second root and contains wit and wisdom in its depths. Odin is the Alfadir - the All-father or father of the gods. In search of wisdom, he asks for a drink of water from the well of Mimir and sacrifices one of his eyes in return. In this account, the eye has a particular meaning. Odin leaves it at the bottom of the well of wisdom, so symbolizing the act of God manifesting in the wisdom of his own creation. The Yggdrasil is looked after by three women (the Norns in old Norse) who rule the destiny of gods and men. They are called Urdr, Verdandi, and Skuld (or the Present, the Past, and the Future) and they plan the fates of newborn children. Every morning they water the roots of the Yggdrasil with water drawn from the Udr well. Drops fall from the Yggdrasil onto the earth and create all forms of matter. This tree is the symbol of 'universal life', both organic and inorganic. It represents the spirit that gives life to every form of creation. The first of its three roots extends to heaven. The second extends to the cradle of wisdom where giants inhabit lofty mountains. The third lies over the spring of Hvergelmir where the dragon Níðhöggr gnaws at the root and constantly tempts mankind into evil. The Tibetans call the tree of life Zampun and the legend is immensely old. The first of the tree's three roots also extends to heaven, to the top of the highest mountains. The second extends down into the lower region or hell. The third remains on the earth, stretching to the east. The Hindus call the tree of life the Ashvattha, the Sacred Fig. Its branches are the components of the visible world. Its leaves are the mantras of the Vedas, symbolizing the intellectual or moral character of the universe.

Careful study of ancient religious and creation myths reveals a striking similarity between them. This similarity of exterior form and esoteric spirit is obviously more than mere coincidence. It shows that different creation myths were designed concurrently. What happened in the distant past is now obscured by different religious traditions. But in that distant past, human religious thought developed uniformly in every part of the world. Christians use the term pantheism to describe a belief system that looks to nature for inner truth. Pantheism reveals God in his only possible objective form - in nature. It reminds humanity continually of the presence of God, the creator. But a theologically dogmatic religion only abstracts and then obscures God from lived experience. Which of the two approaches best serves mankind's needs?

The theory of evolution is supported by modern science, rational thought and esoteric teachings. It is corroborated by ancient legends and myths and even by the Bible when read esoterically. A flower develops slowly from a bud. The bud develops from its seed. But what is the origin of the seed with its genetic programing and spiritual life force that produces its shape, color and scent? The word evolution speaks for itself. The seed of the present human race must have existed within its ancestors. In the same way, the seed that will produce next summer's flower was produced in the seed-pod of its parent flower. The parent may be only slightly different but it is still different from its future offspring. The ancestors of the elephant and the lizard were perhaps the mammoth and the plesiosaurus. If this is the case, why couldn't the ancestors of modern humanity have been the giants described in the Vedas, the Völuspá and Genesis? It is completely absurd to believe that different species have evolved in the way described by dogmatic evolutionists. It's only reasonable to think that each genus, from the mollusc to the primate, evolved from its own primordial and distinctive form. Suppose we accept that 'animals have descended from at most only four or five ancestors' as Darwin claims in the *Origin of Species*. Suppose we go as far as to accept that 'all organic beings which have ever lived on this earth have descended from a single primordial form.' It is still difficult to believe that man's mental ability evolves solely in response to his environment and that the human psyche will be studied on this basis in future. No one but a stone-blind materialist, with no intuitive power whatsoever, could seriously believe this.

Science can explain the physical origins of humanity and the evolutionary development of the human body. But it is incapable of explaining mankind's psychical and spiritual evolution. The highest faculties of mankind cannot be proven to be 'as much products of evolution as the humblest plant or the lowest worm' as Thomas Huxley put it in his article 'Darwin and Haeckel' (*Popular Science Monthly Volume VI*, March 1875).

Contrast this with the theory of evolution according to the ancient Brahmans. They represent their theory using the allegory of the mythical tree Ashvattha. They conceptualize it very differently from the way the Scandinavians represented Yggdrasil. They picture it upside down. The branches extend downwards and the roots grow upwards. The branches represent the external world of the senses - the physical universe. The roots represent the invisible world of spirit because they are literally rooted in heaven - the place that humanity has always imagined God to inhabit. The religious symbols of every culture illustrate essentially the same metaphysical hypothesis - that the originating creative force came from a single primordial point. This is supported by Pythagoras, Plato and many other philosophers. In his work *On the Migration of Abraham*, Philo Judaeus writes, 'The Chaldeans imagined that this visible universe was the only thing in existence, either being itself God or containing God in itself as the soul of the whole.'

The Egyptian Pyramid also represents the mythical tree. Its apex is the mystical link between heaven and earth and represents the root. The base of the pyramid represents the tree's branches spreading out to the four compass points of the material world. It conveys the idea that everything has its origin in spirit. Evolution originally began in a higher state and progressed into lower states rather than the opposite as claimed by Darwinian theory. In other words spiritual forms have gradually evolved into material forms until the densest state has been reached. It's here that modern evolutionary theory operates. Here, it's easier to understand the naturalist Ernst Haeckel's theory of anthropogeny. According to Thomas Huxley in his article, 'Darwin and Haeckel,' Haeckel traces the lineage of man 'from its protoplasmic origins, sodden in the mud of seas which existed before the oldest fossil-bearing rocks were deposited.' The idea that man evolved 'by the gradual modification of an ape-like mammal' is easier to believe when we remember that the same theory was taught thousands of years earlier. In *Babyloniaca*, Berossus says evolution was taught by Oannes, the man-fish of Babylonian mythology (also called Dagon in the Bible). He used fewer words and the theory was less elegantly phrased but it was just as understandable. As a matter of interest, this ancient theory of evolution is not only preserved in allegory and legend. It is also depicted on the walls of temples in India. Fragments of it have also been found in Egyptian temples and in the ruins of the Mesopotamian cities, Nimrud and Nineveh, excavated by the English archeologist Austen Henry Layard.

But what preceded Darwinian evolution? As far as Darwin is concerned, nothing but conjecture. As he puts it in the *Origin of Species*, all beings are the descendants of a few beings living long before the Silurian geological period. He makes no attempt to describe what these few beings were. But simply by admitting their existence, he supports the idea of referring to the ancients for further explanation of the idea. The earth has gone through many changes of temperature, climate, soil and, controversially, its magnetic field. But nevertheless, nothing in present science disproves the ancient hypothesis that man existed before the Silurian period. The French archaeologist Boucher de Perthes was the first to discover flint axes in the valley of the Somme, proving man must have existed an incalculably long time ago. If Ludwig Büchner's *Man in the Past, Present and Future (Die Stellung des Menschen in der Natur)* is to be believed, man must have lived during and before the last Ice Age. But who can tell what the next scientific discovery will reveal?

If man has existed this long - and there is undeniable proof - his physiology must have evolved in response to changes in his environment. The earliest ancestors of the 'frost giants' may have evolved at the same time as the fish of the Devonian and the molluscs of the Silurian periods. They may have left behind no flint axes, bones or cave paintings but if the ancients are correct, the earth at that time was populated not only by giants or 'mighty men of renown' but also by 'sons of God.' There are people who believe in spiritual evolution as much as physical evolution. They could be criticized for believing in unprovable theories and they could just as easily reply that physical evolution is itself an unproven, if not unprovable, theory. At least spiritual evolutionists can infer proof for their beliefs from the world's mythologies. Both language scholars and archeologists estimate these mythologies to be immensely old. Meanwhile the Darwinian evolutionists have nothing similar to support their theories. Their only option would be to refer to some of the ancient hieroglyphics provided they suppressed any that didn't support their position.

The work of some leading scientists might contradict theosophical hypotheses. But fortunately, other equally prominent scientists have conducted studies that endorse theosophical ideas completely. In his recent work, *The Geographical Distribution of Animals*, the British naturalist Alfred Russel Wallace examines the evolution of species. He strongly supports the idea that present species developed slowly from their predecessors. He suggests this process extends back in time over an innumerable series of cycles. And if this is true of animals, why shouldn't the same apply to man? Why shouldn't man's earliest ancestor be a entirely spiritual one - a 'son of God?'

Returning to ancient nature-religion myths, it can be demonstrated how closely they correlate with many of the latest findings in modern physics and the natural sciences. Evidence of scientific knowledge lies hidden in the symbolism and distinctive language of the ancient priesthood. This scientific knowledge has not yet been rediscovered during the present cycle of human development. A scholar may be familiar with the writing of Egyptian priests and their use of hieroglyphics. But first of all, he has to learn how to access their records. As he examines a sample of hieroglyphics, he has to check that the hieroglyphs conform to certain fixed geometrical shapes by measuring them with a compass and a ruler. These geometrical shapes are the hidden keys to the records and he must identify them before he can make an accurate interpretation of the text.

But there are myths that speak for themselves. For example, every creation myth includes male and female gods who are the first creators of the universe. The Greek god Zeus is identified with aether. He is paired with his wives, Chthonia[39] (the primordial chaos that became the earth) and Metis (a water nymph). The Egyptian god Osiris also represents aether - the first creation of the supreme Egyptian deity, Amun, the primeval source of light. Osiris is paired with his wife Isis (Latona in Greek) who also represents earth and water. The Roman god Mithras was born from rock. He is the symbol of male earthly fire or primordial light personified. His mother and wife is the Zoroastrian goddess Mithra. She is associated with water and fertility. The pure element of fire (the active or male principle) is united with earth and water (the female or passive elements of creation). The father of Mythras is Bordj, the earthly volcano, from which Mythras appears in flashes of radiant light. Brahma the fire-god and his prolific consort, Saraswati, are paired with the brightly shining Hindu deity Agni. A thousand streams of glory and seven tongues of flame stream from Agni's body and in his honor, the Sagnika Brahmins burn a perpetual fire. The god Shiva is represented by the Himalayan mountain, the Meru. Legend describes how Shiva descended from heaven in a pillar of fire, like the Jewish Jehovah. This mighty fire-god and a dozen other ancient double-sexed deities, all strongly indicate a hidden meaning. These dual myths point to the biochemistry of creation. They point to the first appearance of the supreme cause which manifests as spirit, force and matter. They point to the beginning of cosmic evolution where divine forces correlate. This divine correlation is presented allegorically as the combination of fire and water, energized by spirit. The union of the male active principle with the female passive element, gives birth to their earthly child, cosmic matter. This cosmic matter is the *prima materia* or first matter, the aether or astral light!

The allegorical mountains, eggs, trees, snakes and pillars can be seen to represent proven facts of the natural sciences. With slight variations, all of the mountain myths describe the first origins of the cosmos. The trees describe allegorically the subsequent evolution of spirit and matter. The snakes and pillars symbolize the processes of this evolution involving the infinite interrelation of cosmic forces. The mountain represents the matrix of the universe. Within the mountain the gods or cosmic forces prepare the seeds of organic life and at the same time the life-drink. When this life-drink is tasted, it awakens the spirit in material man. This life-drink is the soma, the sacrificial drink of the Hindus. At the point of creation, the densest elements of the *prima materia* were used to produce the physical world while its ethereal, divine aspects spread throughout the universe, enveloping the newborn world and bringing it to life as it evolved out of chaos.

Gradually, these poetic and abstract ideas were translated into concrete cosmic symbols. It is these symbols that are now discovered by archeologists. The snake plays a prominent part in the imagery of the ancients. It was devalued by its interpretation in Genesis as a synonym for Satan, the Prince of Darkness. In fact, the snake is the most ingenious of all mythical symbols because of its suggestive power. As the Greek spirit of the vineyards and grain fields, or agathodaemon, it represents healing and man's immortality. It encircles the images of most of the gods associated with health. For example, in the Egyptian Mysteries, the cup of health was entwined by snakes. Evil arises where there is a super-abundance of goodness. (In the Old Testament, Lucifer was originally God's most perfect creation and favorite of all the angels. But Lucifer's pride caused his fall into hell and his transformation into Satan.) Similarly, the snake sometimes represents matter which is more prone to evil the further it is removed from its original spiritual source. The snake appears in the oldest Egyptian imagery, for example in the creation myth of Kneph. Representing matter, it is usually shown contained within a circle. It lies straight across the circle's equator, indicating that the universe of astral light, which produced the physical world, also encircles the world. It also indicates that the universe of astral light is itself encircled by Emeph, the supreme first cause. The ancient Egyptians' supreme god, Ptah created Ra and all subsequent forms of life. Life is depicted as emerging from an egg because the egg is the most familiar form associated with the development of life. When the snake represents eternity and immortality, it encircles the world, biting its own tail, evoking infinity. It then becomes the astral light. The followers of the Greek writer and philosopher, Pherecydes, taught that ether (Zeus or Zen) is the highest part of heaven. It encloses the celestial world beneath it and its light is the astral light, the *prima materia*.

This is the origin of the snake which Christian teachings later associated with Satan. It is the great agency of life called the Od, the Ob, and the Aour[40] by Moses and the Kabbalists. When the astral light is in its passive state, it draws people under its influence and it is called the Ob, symbolized by the Python. Moses was determined to eradicate anyone sensitive enough to fall under the control of the vicious beings who move in the astral waves like fish in water. These beings surround us like 'dwellers on the threshold' as Bulwer-Lytton calls them in his novel *Zanoni*. The astral light becomes the Od when it is directed by the consciousness of an immortal soul. The astral currents are guided either by an adept - a pure spirit - or by a mesmerizer (an able mesmerizer is pure themselves and knows how to direct the astral currents). In cases like these, even an entity as high as a planetary spirit occasionally descends to our realm. A planetary spirit is a being that has never been physically embodied (though many have existed on our earth). This planetary spirit cleanses the surrounding atmosphere, enabling seership and opening the way to true divine prophecy. The term Aour is used to describe certain hidden properties of the ether. It is directly relevant to the work of alchemists and of no interest to the general public.

The pre-Socratic Greek philosopher, Anaxagoras of Clazomenae, believed that the ether contained the spiritual prototypes of all things and the elements needed to create them. Everything was generated within the ether, evolved out of it, and eventually returned to it from earth. The Hindus personified akasha (sky or ether) as a god. The ancient Greeks and Romans worshipped Zeus/Jupiter calling him *Magnus Aether*, the Great God Ether. And in *The Georgics*, Virgil describes him as *Pater, omnipotens Aether*.

When Edward Bulwer-Lytton wrote about the 'dwellers on the threshold,' he was referring to the elemental spirits first described by the Kabbalists. The same spirits were denounced by the Christian clergy as 'devils,' the enemies of mankind. 'Already Tertullian has formally discovered the secret of their cunning,' remarks des Mousseaux gravely in chapter three of his book *Magic in the Nineteenth Century*.

A priceless discovery! Now it's clear how much the holy fathers have achieved in understanding the astral nature of man! They've been so busy looking at the spiritual world, they've failed to understand their own planet, claiming at times that it doesn't move at all or it isn't round.

John Langhorne, an English clergyman, translated the works of the Greek biographer Plutarch known as *Plutarch's Lives (Bioi Parallēloi)*. These works included the biography of the historian Dionysius of Halicarnassus. Dionysius believed that the king of Rome, Numa Pompilius, built the temple of the virgin goddess Vesta. He had it built with a circular footprint to represent the earth. In addition, the Greek philosopher Philolaus believed that fire existed at the center of the universe, a belief shared by all Pythagoreans. According to Plutarch, the Pythagoreans believed the earth 'not to be without motion, nor situated in the center of the world, but to make its revolution round the sphere of fire, being neither one of the most valuable, nor principal parts of the great machine.' Plato is said to have held the same view. So it seems that the Pythagoreans had discovered heliocentricity long before Galileo.

The geophysicist Balfour Stewart and the mathematician Peter Guthrie Tait proposed the existence of an invisible universe that interpenetrates the material plane. They described this theory in their book, *The Unseen Universe*. If accepted, the theory makes many previously inexplicable phenomena clear. This invisible universe acts on the organism of mediums when they are in a trance. It penetrates and saturates them, either directed by the powerful will of a mesmerizer or by invisible beings. Either way, the result is the same. Under the influence of the invisible universe, the astral or star body of the mesmerized subject leaves its transfixed earthly form. It roams in infinite space and eventually arrives at the threshold of a mysterious 'boundary.' It finds the gates to the 'silent land' only slightly ajar. The gates will only open fully when the soul of the entranced medium leaves his body on death and is reunited with its higher immortal essence. Until then, he is only able to look through a chink. How much he can see is dependent on the acuity of his spiritual sight.

The idea of the trinity is common to all ancient nations. The three Dejotas - Brahma, Vishnu, and Shiva - make up the Hindu Trimurti. There are Three Heads in the Jewish Kabbalah. The Kabbalistic text, the Idra Zuta, says, 'Three heads are hewn in one another and over one another.' Both the trinity of the Egyptians and the trinity of the ancient Greeks represent the original tri-part emanation from the first cause consisting of two male principles and one female principle. It is the union of the male Logos (wisdom or God revealed) with the female Aura (the goddess of the air) or *anima mundi* (the world soul) that produced all things. It is 'the holy pneuma' or breath. It is the Kabbalists' sefirot[41] or ten emanations of God. It is the Gnostics' Sophia or human soul. The true metaphysical interpretation of this universal principle was kept within the sanctuaries. But the Greeks used poetry to personify it in many charming myths. The Greek poet Nonnus of Panopolis, described the life of the god Bacchus in his work the *Dionysiaca*. Bacchus falls in love with the breeze (or the holy pneuma[42]) who goes by the name of Aura Placida (literally gentle gale). In *Anacalypsis*, the religious historian Godfrey Higgins says, 'When the ignorant church fathers were constructing the Roman Catholic calendar, they made out of this gentle gale two saints!' Saint Aura and Saint Placida. They even went as far as to turn the Greek god Bacchus into the Catholic Saint Bacchus and showed his supposed coffin and relics in Rome. The festival of the two 'blessed saints,' Aura and Placida, takes place on 5 October close to the festival of Saint Bacchus.

By comparison, the 'heathen' Norse creation legends are far more poetic with much greater religious feeling. In the Ginnungagap or boundless abyss, cosmic matter and primordial forces rage in conflict with each other. Then suddenly a thawing wind blows. It is the breath of the 'unrevealed God' blowing from Muspellheim, the realm of heavenly fire. In this realm the unrevealed God exists beyond the world of matter. The animus of the unseen is a spirit brooding over the dark water of the abyss. It creates order out of chaos. Once the first cause has ignited the spark of creation, it retires and then remains hidden forever.

The Scandinavian legends have both scientific and religious aspects. The scientific aspect is clear in the story of Thor, the son of Odin. Whenever he takes hold of his thunderbolt or hammer, he has to wear iron gauntlets. He also wears a belt described as the 'belt of strength.' Whenever he wears it, his divine powers are greatly increased. He rides in a chariot drawn by two rams with silver bridles. His mighty brow is circled by a wreath of stars. His chariot has a pointed iron pole and the wheels scatter sparks as they roll continually over rumbling thunderclouds. With irresistible force he hurls his hammer at the rebellious frost giants, dissolving and annihilating them. He returns to the Udr well where the gods meet in private to decide the fate of humanity. He is the only Norse god to travel there on foot. The rest of the gods travel on horseback. He doesn't travel in his chariot of thunder for fear of engulfing the rainbow bridge or Bifrost in fire and causing the Udr well to boil.

It can be inferred from this myth that the creators of the Norse legends were familiar with electricity. Thor personifies electricity. He handles electrical current only when wearing protective gloves made of iron, which is a natural conductor. His belt of strength is a closed circuit. Isolated current travels around the circuit instead of being diffused through space. When he speeds through the clouds in his chariot, he represents active electricity. This is suggested by the rumbling of thunder and the sparks showering from the chariot's wheels. The chariot's pointed iron pole is like a lightning rod. The two rams that pull his chariot are the well-known ancient symbols for male, or generative, power. Their silver bridles symbolize the female essence, silver being the metal associated with the Roman moon goddess Luna, the Middle Eastern fertility goddess Astarte and Diana, the Roman goddess of the hunt, the moon and nature. The ram and his bridle symbolize the active and passive principles of nature in opposition. The active rushes forward. The passive holds back. Both are controlled by the electricity that charges the world and gives them life. The evolution of visible nature is the result of the male and female principles endlessly combining and recombining, energized by electricity. The crowning glory of this evolution is the planetary system symbolized by the crown of glittering orbs worn by the mythical figure of Thor.

When Thor is proactive, his impressive thunderbolts destroy everything, including less powerful divine forces. He crosses the rainbow bridge on foot, i.e. in his latent state, so that he can mix with less powerful gods without destroying them. If he were to cross the bridge in his chariot, he would annihilate everything with fire. Thor is afraid of causing the Udr spring to boil. The allegorical meaning of his reluctance will only become clear when physicists understand more about planetary systems. They need to determine the electromagnetic relationships between the universe's innumerable planetary bodies. But at present, science is only just beginning to consider their existence. Glimpses of the truth can be found in recent scientific essays by two American professors: the physicist Alfred Marshall Mayer and the chemist and geologist Thomas Sterry Hunt. The ancient philosophers believed that both volcanoes and hot springs were caused by concentrated electric currents underground. They also believed that this electricity produced the various mineral deposits that gave the springs their healing properties. It could be argued that the ancient authors didn't state this theory directly. It could also be argued that the ancients were unfamiliar with electricity. But the simple fact is this - not all records of ancient knowledge are still in existence. The clear and cool waters of the Udr spring were needed every day to irrigate the mystical tree of life. If they had been disturbed by Thor, i.e. by an electric current, they would have been turned into mineral springs. These springs would have been unsuitable for watering the tree. Examples like these support the ancient philosophers' claim that there is a logos in every mythos, or a fundamental truth in every fiction.

Chapter Six

Hermes, who is of my ordinances ever the bearer
Then taking his staff, with which he the eyelids of mortals
Closes at will, and the sleeper, at will, reawakens.

THE ODYSSEY, BOOK V, HOMER

I saw the Samothracian rings
Leap, and steel-filings boil in a brass dish
So soon as underneath it there was placed
The magnet-stone; and with wild terror seemed
The iron to flee from it in stern hate

ON THE NATURE OF THINGS, BOOK VI, LUCRETIUS

But that which especially distinguishes the Brotherhood is
their marvelous knowledge of the resources of the medical
art. They work not by charms but by simples.

MS. *ACCOUNT OF THE ORIGIN AND ATTRIBUTES OF THE TRUE ROSICRUCIANS*,

QUOTED IN *ZANONI* BOOK III BY EDWARD BULWER-LYTTON

ATTRIBUTED TO J. VON D.

In *The New Chemistry*, the American chemist Josiah Cooke writes, 'The history of science shows that the ground must first be prepared before any scientific discovery will be accepted. Where a new scientific discovery fails to make an impact, it is usually because the groundwork hasn't been done. When the time is right the same idea is adopted and advances scientific thought . . . Every student is surprised to learn how small a contribution even the greatest genius makes to the sum total of human knowledge.'

Recently there has been a revolution in the field of chemistry, proving that the time must be right before a new scientific idea can take hold. It may not be long before the ideas of the alchemists are reassessed and subject to proper scientific study. To make the leap from old alchemy to new chemistry may be no more difficult than the leap from the idea that all molecules are salts composed of basic and acidic oxides (electrochemical dualism[1]) to the idea that equal volumes of all gases, at the same temperature and pressure, have the same number of molecules (Avogadro's law[2]).

Avogadro's law was supported by the French physicist, André-Marie Ampère, who lobbied the establishment to accept Amedeo Avogadro's theory. Perhaps one day, Carl Reichenbach and his theory of Odic force will be recognized as having paved the way for a proper appreciation of Paracelsus. It was more than 50 years before the molecule was accepted as a unit of measurement in chemistry. It may take less than half that time for the full significance of Paracelsus to be acknowledged. In *History of Magic (Geschichte der Magie)*, Joseph Ennemoser repeats Paracelsus' warning about the risks of consulting a healing medium. 'The spirit of life is a magnet at the centre of every human being, attracting chaos to itself. The infected person is drawn to the magnetism of others. And so the healthy are infected by the unhealthy through magnetic attraction.'

In his extensive works Paracelsus describes and accounts for the root causes of human diseases. He examines the relationship between physiology and psychology which modern scientists have so far wrestled with unsuccessfully. He describes the precise nature and treatment of every physical disorder. He was using electromagnetism three centuries before the Danish physicist Hans Ørsted supposedly discovered it. His achievements in chemistry are indisputable. He has been described as one of the greatest chemists of his time by astute writers like Johann Hemmann in his *Medico-Surgical Essays (Medicinisch-Chirurgische Aufsätze)*. The French physician Brière de Boismont calls him a 'genius,' agreeing with the French naturalist Joseph Deleuze that Paracelsus opened a new chapter in the history of medicine.

His cures were often described as magical. He was successful because he took no notice of the so-called medical establishment. Paracelsus wrote, 'I thought to myself, if there were no medical teachers in the world, how would I go about learning medicine? The only way was to look at nature - the great open book written by the hand of God . . . I am criticized and dismissed because I am not part of the medical establishment. But which medical establishment? The school of the Greek physician Galen, the Persian physician Avicenna, the Christian physician Mesue, the Persian polymath Rāzī or simply nature itself? I believe we have to look to nature! I am guided by nature not by medical conventions.'

Paracelsus' small-minded contemporaries despised him because he turned his back on the establishment so completely. Instead, he studied nature closely to gain insights into the truth. It's no wonder they tried to discredit him. They accused him of being a charlatan and a drunk. In his *Medico-Surgical Essays*, Johann Hemmann, exonerates Paracelsus of the charge of drunkenness and proves that the accusation came from a former assistant,

'Oporinus who lived with him for a while, hoping to learn his methods. When he failed in his studies, he set about discrediting Paracelsus among his followers and pharmacists.' Paracelsus pioneered the field of animal magnetism and discovered the hidden properties of the magnet. He was labeled as a sorcerer by his contemporaries because his cures seemed miraculous. Three centuries later Baron du Potet was also accused of sorcery and Devil worship by the Catholic Church. And he was accused of being a charlatan by the European scientific establishment. As the alchemists say, you won't find a chemist who will look at the elements differently from his peers. The Paracelsian physician Robert Fludd wrote, 'You have forgotten what the ancients taught you or you have never known it - it is too much for you to take!'

Paracelsus astonished academics in the latter half of the 16th Century with his studies in animal magnetism. No book about the philosophy of magic and spirituality, and occult science would be complete without special reference to the history of this phenomenon.

Mesmerism was brought to Paris from Germany by Anton Mesmer. Careful examination of papers at the Academy of Sciences in Paris reveals that the academicians rejected every scientific discovery made since Galileo, finally outdoing themselves by rejecting magnetism and mesmerism. They voluntarily closed the doors that led to an understanding of nature's greatest mysteries. These mysteries lie hidden in the dark regions of the psychical as well as the physical world. The alkahest, the universal solvent, was within their reach but they chose not to pursue it. Now, nearly a hundred years later, Josiah Cooke writes in *The New Chemistry*:

'Beyond that which can be confirmed through direct observation, chemistry is an imprecise science. Although many theories contain a grain of truth, they have to be modified frequently as new observations are made and often they have to be completely revised.'

Scientists have dismissed mesmerism and animal magnetism as nothing more than hallucinations. But where is their proof? Shouldn't proof be the only deciding factor in science? The academicians have been given thousands of chances to discover the truth but they have refused every time. Mesmerists and healers cite the evidence of deaf, disabled, ill or dying people who were cured by simple bodily manipulation and the 'laying on of hands.' When the evidence makes it impossible to deny that these people have been cured, skeptics will put it down to 'coincidence.' Other favorite explanations include 'it's just an illusion,' 'exaggeration' and 'fraud.' The well-known American healer James Newton has cured more people than many a famous New York doctor. The healer Auguste Jacob, know as 'Le Zouave' has been similarly successful in France. Is the accumulated evidence of the last 40 years merely an illusion? Is it simply the result of a conspiracy of clever frauds and madness? You would have to be mad yourself to believe nonsense like this.

The editor of the *Revue Spirite*, Pierre-Gaëtan Leymarie was found guilty of fraud in connection with spiritualism and sentenced to one year in prison. The vast majority of physicians and scientists derided spiritualism as a hoax. The whole subject was deeply unpopular. On their part, the Roman Catholic clergy were relentless in their condemnation of mesmerism as witchcraft. But in spite of this, the French Court of Appeal was forced to admit the truth of mesmerism in the case of Madame Roger. The famous French clairvoyant was charged with obtaining money under false pretenses while working with her mesmerist Dr Fortin. On 18 May 1876, she was summoned to the Tribunal Correctionnel of the

Seine. Her chief witness was Baron du Potet, the leading mesmerist in France for the last 50 years. Her lawyer was Jules Favre, the famous barrister and French statesman. For once the truth triumphed and the accusation was dropped. Was it Jules Favre's extraordinary eloquence or the quality of the evidence that won the day? Bear in mind that Leymarie also had evidence in his favor and the testimony of over a hundred witnesses including some of the most respected figures in Europe. The only possible conclusion is that the magistrates were happy to question spiritualism but dared not question the fact of mesmerism. The majority of spiritualist phenomena can be simulated: spirit photography, rapping, writing, telekinesis, spirit voices and even materializations. A clever conjuror with the right equipment can reproduce almost all the physical phenomena of spiritualism occurring now in Europe and America. Only the effects of mesmerism and its subjective phenomena are beyond the reach of tricksters, skepticism, modern science and fraudulent mediums. It is impossible to fake a cataleptic state. Spiritualists who want science to accept spiritualism turn to mesmerism. Take a subject in a deep mesmeric trance. Place her on the stage of a theatrical exhibition space like the Egyptian Hall in London. Watch as her mesmerist sends her disembodied spirit to places suggested by the public. See him test her clairvoyance and clairaudience. Stick pins into any part of her body that the mesmerist has passed his hands over. Stick needles in the skin below her eyelids. Burn her skin and cut it with a knife. 'Do not fear! A mesmerized subject is never hurt!' This is what the leading lights of mesmerism will claim - the Italian mesmerist Antonio Regazzoni, the French mesmerists Jules du Potet, Alphonse Teste and the Marquis de Puységur, Zéphyr-Joseph Piérart (founder of *La Revue Spiritualiste*), and the Russian mesmerist Prince Alexei Dolgorukov. And when these feats of mesmerism are performed, invite any popular illusionist to submit his own body to the same tests! Especially if he is keen for publicity and is clever at mimicking spiritualist phenomena, or thinks he is.

During the trial of Madame Roger, her lawyer Jules Favre is reported to have spoken for an hour and a half. His eloquence held the attention of both the judges and the public. This is easy to believe for anyone who has ever heard him speak. Only his final statement was premature and inaccurate: 'Mesmerism is a phenomenon that science accepts without attempting to explain. The public might find it amusing but the most respected doctors take it seriously. Justice cannot dismiss a phenomenon acknowledged by science!'

The public would have no reason to laugh at mesmerism if Favre's sweeping statement had been based on fact. It would have been better if mesmerism had been investigated impartially by a large number of scientists rather than a dedicated few who genuinely wanted to understand nature. The public is like a child that does everything the teacher tells it to. Its attention is caught by the latest craze. But then it turns and looks to see if the teacher, Mrs Public Opinion, approves.

The early Christian author Lactantius was advisor to the Roman emperor, Constantine I. He is reputed to have commented that no skeptic would dare say to a Magus that the human soul died with the body. According to the physician Alexander Wilder, writing in the *American Phrenological Journal*, this is because, 'The Magus would disprove this idea by conjuring up the souls of the dead, making them visible and having them predict the future.' The same was true in Madame Roger's trial. Baron du Potet was present and the judges were afraid that he would mesmerize her forcing them to believe in mesmerism and, even worse, forcing them to acknowledge it publicly.

Paracelsus expresses his ideas in an incomprehensible but lively style. Like the double-sided scroll given by God to Ezekiel, his ideas have to be read 'within and without.' In his time the risks of putting forward alternative theories were very great. The Church was powerful and dozens of people were burned at the stake. This explains why Paracelsus, the German theologian Heinrich Agrippa and the Welsh alchemist Eugenius Philalethes were all known for their declarations of faith. They were as famous for their apparent faith as they were for their achievements in alchemy. Paracelsus gives his full views on the occult properties of the magnet in a deliberately fragmented form across a number of his writings. In his famous book *Archidoxis*, he describes a medicine called *magisterium magnetis*, extracted from the magnet. The remainder of his views appear in *On God (De Ente Dei)* and *On Stars (De Ente Astrorum)*. But his explanations are written in a style that is impossible for the uninitiated to follow. Paracelsus writes, 'Anyone can see that a magnet attracts iron. But a wise man must look past the obvious. I have discovered that, beyond the property of attracting iron, the magnet possesses another hidden power.'

Paracelsus goes on to demonstrate that a 'sidereal force' lies hidden in man. This sidereal force originated in the stars and is the material that makes up man's spiritual form or astral spirit. The astral spirit and the sidereal force are essentially identical. They share what could be called the spirit of stellar matter. This spirit is always aligned with the stars it originated from. There is a mutual attraction between the two because both are magnetic. The earth is identical in composition to all other planets and to man's terrestrial body. This was a fundamental idea in Paracelsus' philosophy. 'Man's body comes from material elements. His (astral) spirit comes from the stars. Man nourishes himself by consuming the elements. From the stars intellect and thought are kindled in his spirit.' Spectroscopy has proven Paracelsus correct in his hypothesis that man and stars are identical in composition. Physicists now lecture on the magnetic forces that act between the sun and the planets.

Hydrogen, sodium, calcium, magnesium and iron are all substances found in the human body. It has already been discovered that these substances are also present in the stars. Hundreds of stars have been observed. Hydrogen was found in all but two. Paracelsus was ridiculed for his theory that the human body and stars are composed of the same materials. Astronomers and physicists disapproved of his ideas about the attraction between man and the stars and about chemical affinity - the way dissimilar chemicals combine to form a new chemical compound. Now that spectroscopy has proven at least one of his theories to be true, is it ridiculous to predict that the rest of his theories will be validated in the future?

All of this begs the question, how did Paracelsus know what the stars were made of? Until very recently, modern academics knew nothing about the subject. Accurate observation only became possible with the invention of spectroscopy.

Academics have successfully identified a few elements and hypothesized the existence of a chromosphere around the sun. But despite important improvements in spectroscopy, the composition of the stars is still largely a mystery. How could Paracelsus have known what the stars are made of unless he had an approach unknown to modern science? In spite of this gap in scientific knowledge, scientists refuse to listen to the truth about his methods founded on Hermetic philosophy and alchemy.

It's important to bear in mind that it was Paracelsus who discovered hydrogen. He was familiar with its composition and its properties long before any orthodox scientist. He had studied astrology and astronomy as all alchemists did. When he claimed that the substance of the human body and the stars were alike, he knew what he was talking about.

The next theory for physiologists to verify is Paracelsus' belief that the human body is not fed solely through the stomach. He suggests the human body is also nourished 'imperceptibly by the magnetic field present everywhere. Each individual draws from the field what it needs.' He goes on to say that the human body derives health from the surrounding elements when they are in balance and disease when they are unbalanced. Science maintains that all organic bodies are subject to the laws of attraction and chemical affinity. According to physiologists, absorption is the most remarkable physical property of organic tissue as when a seed absorbs water rapidly to facilitate its growth. It follows that nothing seems more natural than Paracelsus' theory that our bodies absorb energy from the stars. 'There is a mutual attraction between the sun and the stars and ourselves.' What evidence does science have to disprove this? Carl Reichenbach discovered the nature of this life force emanating from the human body. He found that this same Odic force is radiated by crystals, magnets and all living things.

Paracelsus identified the unity of the universe, saying, 'The human body is composed of primeval (or cosmic) matter.' Spectroscopy supports this view, demonstrating that the same chemical elements found in the earth and the sun are also present in the stars. Spectroscopy has also revealed that all stars are similar in composition to our sun. In his lecture, 'The Earth A Great Magnet,' Alfred Mayer explains that the earth's magnetic field fluctuates in response to changes on the sun's surface. He says the earth's magnetism is 'influenced by solar activity.' Given that the stars are suns, they must also affect the earth to a degree.

Paracelsus says, 'When we are dreaming we are like the

plants that have a physical body but no spirit. When we are asleep the astral body becomes free. It has inherent elasticity. It can hover close to the sleeping physical body or it can soar higher to commune with the stars. It can even communicate over great distances with other astral bodies. The astral spirit has the ability to dream prophecies of the future and visualize answers to present-day problems. The material body does not have this ability because it returns to the physical earth when it dies while mankind's spirit-bodies return to the stars. The animals also have intuitive feelings about the future because they too have an astral body.'

The chemist Jan Baptist van Helmont, a follower of Paracelsus, says much the same thing but his theories about magnetism are more comprehensive and better explained. He created the term *magnale magnum* to describe how magnetism enables one person to affect another and vice versa. The basis of the *magnale magnum* according to van Helmont is the *anima mundi* or the universal soul that connects everything in nature. The cause produces the effect and the effect has an influence back on the cause. They are reciprocal. In his book, *On the Magnetic Cure of Wounds (De Magnetica Vulnerum Curatione)*, van Helmont writes, 'Magnetism is a mysterious force, celestial in origin. Like the stars it is not limited by space or time . . . Every living being has its own celestial power and is intimately connected to the cosmos. This power lies hidden in the inner essence of each person. It is dormant until made active by the power of suggestion. It becomes more vital the more the outer worldly person is subdued and spiritual awareness is developed. The practice of Kabbalah gives back to the soul its natural mystical strength which the soul had previously lost, like someone losing sleep when startled awake.'

Both van Helmont and Paracelsus agree that the will is most powerful when in an ecstatic state. They say that 'the spirit permeates everywhere and it is magnetism's medium.' They say that pure essential magic is not to be found in superstitious rituals and empty ceremonies. It is to be found in the independent will of the individual. 'Physical nature is not ruled over by good and evil spirits. It is governed by the soul and spirit hidden inside every one of us just as potential fire is concealed in every flint.'

All medieval philosophers supported the theory that the stars have an influence on mankind. According to Cornelius Agrippa, 'The stars and the earth and everything on it are made up of the same elements. Therefore they attract each other. This influence is only possible through the medium of spirit but this spirit permeates the whole universe and is in harmony with the human spirit. Any magician who wants supernatural powers must have faith, love and hope . . . There is a secret power hidden in all things and all potent and transformative magic derives from it.'

In his book *The Influence of the Blue Ray*, General Pleasonton puts forward a modern theory that mirrors the alchemists' views. He regards men and women as electrically charged negatively and positively. His idea that everything in nature is either mutually attracted or repelled seems to be copied from Robert Fludd, the Grand Master of the English Rosicrucians. According to Fludd, 'When two men approach each other, their magnetism is either passive or active, positive or negative. If the magnetic waves they emit are disrupted or returned, the result is repulsion. But when the waves pass from one man to the other, and through each other, the result is positive magnetism as the waves travel from the center to the circumference. In this case the waves promote healing and a heightened moral sense. Examples of this positive magnetism are found not only in animals but also in plants and minerals.'

Anton Mesmer arrived in Paris in 1778. To meet the growing demand for his mesmeric treatments, he invented an apparatus called a 'baquet.' It was a large tub filled with water charged by his own animal magnetism. The magnetism was then transferred to as many as 20 patients at a time sitting around the baquet and holding on to its conducting rods. Mesmer's methods were based entirely on the ideas of Paracelsus. It's important to note how this great psychical and physiological discovery was treated by the medical establishment. It demonstrates how a scientific body can succumb to ignorance, superficiality and prejudice when a new finding contradicts established theory. In 1784 the French Academy of Sciences failed to examine Mesmer's ideas properly and this was significant because it led to a shift in public opinion toward a more materialistic worldview. It also explains the gaps in current atomic theory. The committee of 1784 (later known as the Franklin committee) was made up of prominent scientists such as the physicians Jean-François Borie and Jean-Charles-Henri Sallin, the chemist Jean d'Arcet, and the famous physician Joseph-Ignace Guillotin. Further members were added to the committee: Benjamin Franklin, the physicist Jean-Baptiste Le Roy, the astronomer Jean Sylvain Bailly, the chemist Antoine Lavoisier and the physicist Gabriel de Bory. Shortly after joining the committee Jean-François Borie died and was replaced by Michel-Joseph Majault. Two things are certain. Firstly, members of the committee lacked objectivity and only started work because the king ordered them to. And secondly, they showed poor judgment as well as bias in their observations of mesmerism's subtle effects. The committee's report was drawn up by Jean Sylvain Bailly and was supposed to deal a deadly blow to the new science. It was widely distributed, causing consternation among the aristocracy and successful businessmen who had supported Mesmer and seen his cures firsthand. The botanist Antoine Laurent de Jussieu was a highly respected academician. Together with the eminent physician

Charles Deslon he published a meticulously compiled counter-report. He called on the Academy of Medicine to investigate the magnetic fluid's therapeutic effects and publish their findings immediately. This resulted in the publication of many works on mesmerism, revealing new aspects of the subject. With his work *Researching and Questioning Animal Magnetism* (*Recherches et Doutes Sur le Magnétisme Animal*), the physician Auguste Thouret inspired further research into the history of magnetism. In this way it became public knowledge that magnetic phenomena had occurred in ancient civilizations.

Mesmer's ideas were simply a restatement of the ideas of Paracelsus, Jan Baptist van Helmont, the author Ferdinand Santanelli, and the Scottish physician William Maxwell. He was even guilty of appropriating the work of the French mathematician Louis Bertrand Castel and presenting it as his own. In *The Conservation of Energy*, Balfour Stewart describes the universe as a machine composed of atoms with some kind of medium between them. He says the laws that govern this machine are the laws of energy. The American scientific writer Edward Youmans calls this 'a modern theory.' But one century earlier, in his *Letter to a Foreign Physician* (1775) Mesmer put forward 27 propositions about the nature of the universe. They included the following:

1. The heavenly bodies, the earth, and living bodies exert a mutual influence on each other.

2. This influence is transmitted through a medium - an all-pervasive and uniform fluid. The fluid excludes any vacuum and is incomparably complex. It responds to, amplifies and transmits all the forces of motion.

This suggests that the theory is not so modern after all.

Stewart says, 'We can regard the universe as a vast physical machine.' And Mesmer says much the same thing in his third proposition:

3. This reciprocal influence is governed by mechanical laws that are not presently understood.

In 1600, the English astronomer William Gilbert theorized that the earth is an immense magnet. Alfred Mayer corroborates this theory, adding that the fluctuations in the earth's magnetic field are influenced by solar activity. He describes the magnetic field as 'changing in concert with the apparent daily and yearly motion of the sun. It fluctuates in response to the appearance of solar flares on its surface.' He describes 'the constant fluctuation, the ebb and flow of the sun's influence on the earth.' Mesmer says something very similar in his fourth and sixth propositions:

4. The alternate effects produced by this influence can be described as flux and reflux.

6. The operation of these laws applies universally and governs the way the heavenly bodies, the earth and its constituent parts influence each other.

Two more of Mesmer's propositions make interesting reading in the context of modern science.

7. The operation of these laws also dictates the nature of matter and of organic bodies.

8. The alternate effects of this fluid affect the physical body. The fluid acts on the nerves immediately by penetrating the nervous system.

A number of important publications appeared between 1798 and 1826, which was the year the French Academy of Medicine convened a second commission to investigate mesmerism. Among these was the informative monthly journal *Archives du Magnétisme Animal*[3] published by Baron Étienne Félix d'Hénin de Cuvillers. Hénin de Cuvillers was a lieutenant general, awarded the medal of the Chevalier of St. Louis, a member of the Academy of Sciences, and a regular correspondent with many European academic institutions. In 1820, at the request of the Prussian government, the Academy of Berlin offered a prize of 300 gold ducats for the best thesis on mesmerism. Under the presidency of Louis Antoine of France, the Duke of Angoulême, the Royal Scientific Society of Paris offered a gold medal for the same thing. Pierre-Simon, Marquis de Laplace, was one of the 40 Immortals of the Académie Française, and an honorary member of almost all the Academies of Europe. In his work, *A Philosophical Essay on Probabilities (Essai Philosophique sur les Probabilités)*, this respected scientist writes, 'The nerves are the most sensitive tool we have for appreciating the subtle forces at work in nature. This is especially true when nervous sensitivity is heightened in exceptional circumstances. The extreme sensitivity of certain individuals produces unique phenomena. These phenomena have caused speculation about the existence of a new force which has been described as animal magnetism . . . We are a long way from understanding all the forces of nature and how they work. It would be unreasonable to dismiss these phenomena just because we currently have no explanation for them. However difficult it seems to accept them, it is simply our duty to examine them with as much accuracy as we can.'

The Marquis de Puységur improved on Mesmer's experiments. He abandoned the use of apparatus entirely and on his estate at Busancy cured many of his tenants' illnesses. His methods were made public and many other men were able to experiment with similar success. In 1825, the young French doctor Pierre Foissac lobbied the Academy of Medicine to set up a new inquiry. This proposal was supported by a special committee consisting of the physiologist Nicolas-Philibert Adelon, the psychiatrists Étienne Pariset and Charles Chrétien Henri Marc, and the physicians Jean Burdin Sr. and Henri-Marie Husson. The members of this special committee boldly declared, 'No decision is final or irreversible in science.' This opened the way to reevaluate the significance of the 1784 Franklin Committee's conclusions. The special committee members found that 'the Franklin results were based on experiments that were not properly carried out. Not all of the Franklin commissioners were present at the same time to witness each experiment. The commissioners were biased and according to the principles of mesmerism itself this bias must cause the experiments to fail.'

The special committee's recommendations echo what has been said many times before by respected writers on spiritualism. The committee reports, 'It is the duty of the Academy to study magnetism and subject it to scientific tests. This will prevent amateurs and charlatans from exploiting magnetism for money and personal gain.'

This report caused a great deal of debate. In May 1826, the Academy appointed a new commission (later known as the Husson commission) consisting of the following leading scientists: the medical professor Jean-Jacques Leroux, the physician Edme-Joachim Bourdois de la Motte, the founder of the Académie Nationale de Médecine François-Joseph Double, the physiologist

François Magendie, the doctor and botanist Louis Benoît Guersant, Henri-Marie Husson, the pharmacist Antoine Thillaye-Platel, the psychiatrist Charles Chrétien Henri Marc, the physicians Jean Marc Gaspard Itard, Pierre Eloy Fouquier, and François Guéneau de Mussy. They began work immediately and continued for five years. Their findings were reported to the Academy by Henri-Marie Husson. The report covers magnetic phenomena classified under 34 different headings. The summary that follows is not exhaustive. The Husson commission found that it was not essential for the magnetizer to touch, use friction or pass his hands over the subject. Several times force of will and a fixed stare were enough to produce magnetic phenomena. On these occasions the subject was not even necessarily aware of being magnetized. 'Well-evidenced healing phenomena' are entirely dependent on magnetism and cannot be produced without it. The magnetized or trance state is a verifiable fact. 'New abilities arise in the trance state which have been described as clairvoyance, intuition and psychic prevision.' The trance state has 'been induced where the subject has not been able to see the magnetizer and has been entirely unaware of how the trance was brought about.' Once a subject has come under the influence of a magnetizer, the magnetizer can 'put him into a complete trance and take him out of it again. All this can happen without the subject knowing that the magnetizer is the cause. He can be out of sight, a certain distance away and behind closed doors.' In the trance state, the subject's senses seem to be completely paralyzed. It is as if a second set of senses has been put in their place. 'Most of the time trance subjects are oblivious to sudden or unexpected sounds. For example, the sound made by someone striking a metal pan or dropping a heavy object close to the subject. They can be made to inhale the fumes of hydrochloric acid or ammonia without any ill effects or even realizing they are doing so.' The committee could 'tickle subjects' feet, nostrils and the corners of their eyes with a feather. They could pinch subjects' skin, causing bruising. They could stick pins a long way into the skin under the subjects' nails without causing any pain or the subjects giving any sign that they were in any way aware of it.' The committee underlined this point by saying, 'We have seen an entranced subject show no reaction while undergoing major surgery. Their pulse and breathing remained unaffected.'

That sums up the Husson committee's findings about the physical and sensory perceptions of mesmerized subjects. The committee went on to examine subjects' subjective experiences. These internal experiences, part of the inner life of every human being, are arguably what differentiates mankind from simple single-celled organisms. The committee reports, 'The entranced subjects we have studied retain the same physical and mental capabilities as someone who is awake. If anything, they can remember more and remember it more accurately . . . We have observed two subjects with their eyes tightly closed. They were able to name objects put in front of them. They could discern the color and value of playing cards. They were able to read words traced in the air in front of them and lines of text from books opened at random. They could do all this even with fingers pressing their eyelids tightly shut. Two subjects were able to predict the onset of seizures. One of them predicted several months in advance the precise moment an epileptic fit would occur. The other was able to pinpoint the precise moment the seizures would end. The accuracy of their predictions was remarkable.'

The commission goes on to report that 'it has established and shared a number of important facts. These facts prompt it to recommend that the Academy encourages continued research into magnetism. The subject of magnetism can be viewed as a highly intriguing branch of psychism and natural history.' The committee concludes its report by admitting that the facts are so extraordinary that they doubt the Academy will believe them. But they insist they have been guided by the highest principles and a love of science. They have endeavored to meet the Academy's expectations of their dedication and commitment.

They were right to expect dissent. One of the committee members, who had not attended the experiments, 'didn't think it was right to sign the report,' according to Henri-Marie Husson, when preparing the final draft.

The abstaining member was the physiologist François Magendie. The official report stated that he had not 'been present at the experiments.' But this did not stop him from devoting four pages to mesmerism in his book *An Elementary Treatise on Human Physiology (Précis Élémentaire de Physiologie)*. He outlined the magnetic phenomena that had supposedly taken place during the committee's investigations. But unlike the other committee members, he did not verify these phenomena as scientific facts. He reserved judgment despite the enthusiasm of his knowledgeable and expert colleagues. In his book, Magendie writes, 'These points must be judged carefully by any serious member of the profession. Any physician knows how easily unverified phenomena can be exploited by fraudsters. In the eyes of legitimate practitioners, the reputation of the profession can be damaged by even a hint of deception.' Nothing in his text reveals that he was a member of the Academy's 1826 commission. He says nothing about being absent from the committee's sessions. Nothing in the text explains that he had failed to ascertain the truth about mesmerism and was now making judgments as a self-interested outsider. When Magendie wrote 'these points must be judged carefully by any serious member of the profession' he probably sentenced himself to silence!

Thirty-eight years later, the English scientist John Tyndall did something similar. Tyndall was even more respected as a scientist than Magendie. He was invited to investigate spiritualist phenomena which would ensure the investigation was taken out of the hands of amateur or untrustworthy researchers. Tyndall declined. However in his book *Fragments of Science*, he dismissed spiritualism out of hand, as quoted previously in Chapter Two.

To say he declined entirely would be wrong. He made one attempt to examine the phenomenon and that was enough for him. In *Fragments of Science* he describes how he got under a table to see how the raps were made. Having assured himself that no sound could be produced without its origin being obvious, he requested that the seance continue. But now the spirits refused to communicate. He stayed under the table for at least a quarter of an hour then returned to his chair full of despair for the credulity of humanity! It must have taken courage to go groping in the dark for the ugly truth about spiritualism. Just as the American general Israel Putnam must have needed courage to kill Connecticut's last wolf in her den. The difference is that General Putnam killed his wolf whereas Tyndall's wolf outwitted him. Perhaps the motto on his shield should be: *sub mensa desperatio,* under the table I despair.

The distinguished French physician and mesmerist Alphonse Teste, referred to the 1826 Husson committee's report, saying it had a powerful impact on the Academy but it failed to convince the academicians:

'No one could question the truthfulness of the commissioners. Their integrity was undeniable and their knowledge was extensive but it was suspected that they had been duped. In truth, there are certain facts that would undermine anyone's belief in the commission's findings. These same facts would put anyone who publicly supported the commission in a difficult position.' This is true, as history has shown time and time again. When the American chemist Robert Hare announced the preliminary findings of his investigations into spiritualism, he was regarded as a victim of deception. This is despite the fact that he was one of the world's most prominent scientists. When he proved that he had not been deceived, he was simply dismissed as an old fool and ridiculed by Harvard professors for 'his insane belief in a gigantic hoax.'

He began his investigations in 1853 saying he felt it was his duty 'to counter the mania leading the public to believe in the delusion called spiritualism.' By his own admission, he began his study agreeing 'entirely with Faraday's explanation of table turning.' But like any fair-minded scientist, he conducted a thorough and impartial investigation and reported his findings truthfully. He summed up the reaction of his fellow scientists in a speech given in New York in September 1854. He said that he 'had been a scientist for over 50 years. In all that time his competency had never been disputed, until he became a spiritualist. His integrity had never been questioned until the Harvard professors attacked spiritualism even though he knew it to be true and they had no evidence that it was false.'

What a sorry state of affairs these words describe! A man of 76, after 50 years of scientific work, is ostracized for telling the truth! Similarly, the once prominent naturalist Alfred Russel Wallace is now looked on with pity having admitted his belief in spiritualism and mesmerism. In St. Petersburg, the highly regarded zoologist Nikolai Wagner met the same fate, being treated appallingly by his fellow Russian scientists for admitting his belief in spiritualism!

There are conventional scientists and there are occult scientists. When it comes to modern spiritualism, the occult sciences are subjected to the negative bias of conventional science. That said, the occult sciences have had their supporters throughout history - men notable for furthering the cause of science itself. The most prominent of these men is Isaac Newton, 'the light of science.' He was a committed supporter of the theory of magnetism formulated by Paracelsus, van Helmont and other alchemists. It is widely accepted that Newton's theory of universal space and attraction has its origins in the theory of magnetism. In *The Principia: Mathematical Principles of Natural Philosophy* Newton's own words suggest that he based his theories on the idea that space constitutes the divine sensorium, the collective senses of God. He referred to space as the 'soul of the world' and the great universal magnetic agent. He goes on to say, 'The divine sensorium can be thought of as a very subtle spirit which penetrates everything including the densest objects. It forms an elusive but inherent part of their makeup. It is the power and action of this spirit that causes material bodies to attract each other and bind together when brought into contact. The power and action of this spirit causes electrically charged objects to attract or repel each other whether close together or far apart. It is by the power and action of this spirit that light is emitted, refracted, reflected and warms objects. The power and action of this spirit creates all sensation including stimulation of the nerves which enables animals to move their limbs. But these things cannot be explained in just a few words. And we don't yet fully understand the laws that govern this universal spirit.'

There are two kinds of magnetism. The first is purely physical - e.g. animal magnetism where the prey is transfixed by the hunter. The second kind is beyond the physical - a metaphysical phenomenon dependent on the abilities of the magnetizer and the subject. This form of magnetism depends on the strength of will and the expertise of the magnetizer. It depends on how spiritually developed the subject is and on the subject's receptivity to the impressions of the astral light. Successful clairvoyance depends primarily on the expertise of the magnetizer rather than the quality of the subject. Even the most resistant subject will have to yield to the influence of an expert mesmerist like du Potet. The astral light will reveal its secret records when the subject's sight is effectively directed by the mesmerizer, magician or spirit. Picture these secret records as a book. This book remains closed to anyone who can only see the surface and not perceive the depth. On the other hand the same book is open to anyone who focuses their will sufficiently to see it opened. It constitutes a complete record of all that was, is, or will be. The minutest details of our lives are recorded in it and even our thoughts are captured for eternity. Revelation describes this same book, opened by an angel on the Day of Judgment. It is the book of life. The dead are judged according to what they have done as recorded in the book. In short it is the memory of God!

Fragments of the *Chaldean Oracles*, attributed to Zoroaster, say, 'The oracles assert that the impression of thoughts, characters, men, and other divine visions, appear in the aether . . . In this way things without form are recorded.'

Evidently then, ancient and modern wisdom, prophesy and science all corroborate the Kabbalists' claims. The impression of every thought we think and every act we perform is preserved in the indestructible records of the astral light. Future events produced by unseen causes are already clearly represented in the records and accessible to the seer or prophet. Materialism cannot explain the phenomenon of memory. To the psychologist memory is an enigma and to science it is a mystery. But to the student of the old philosophies, 'memory' describes an unconscious power available to mankind. In common with many animals, man is able to intuit in the astral light the records of past sensations and occurrences. Students of the old philosophies did not go looking at the brain through a microscope. As the scientist John Draper put it in the *History of the Conflict Between Religion and Science*, they did not go 'searching for traces of the living and the dead and of scenes that we have visited, of incidents in which we have played a part.' Instead they referred to the vast repository of records in the astral light where every man's life is documented and every beat in the rhythm of the cosmos is stored for eternity.

A drowning man is supposed to see his whole life flash before him in much the same way as lightning shows the overnight traveler intermittent flashes of the landscape around him. The drowning man's soul sees into the akashic records where his history is indelibly written and it is this vision he experiences as a flash of memory.

The same process produces déjà vu - the well-known phenomenon experienced by nine out of ten people. For example, landscapes, conversations and even countries can all seem startlingly familiar even though they are seen and heard for the first time. Believers in reincarnation claim this as evidence of our previous existence in other bodies. They regard déjà vu as flashes of soul memory revealing previous incarnations. But the ancients, like the medieval philosophers, firmly believed the opposite.

They maintained that déjà vu is not proof of reincarnation even though it is one of the strongest arguments in favor of immortality, the soul's pre-existence and the soul having an individual memory independent of the physical brain. As the French occult author Eliphas Levi puts it beautifully 'nature closes the door behind everything that passes through and propels life onward' to greater perfection. The chrysalis becomes a butterfly but the butterfly can never become a caterpillar again. At night our senses are suspended by sleep. As the physical body rests the astral body is set free. It escapes from its physical prison and, as Paracelsus puts it, 'interacts with the outside world.' It travels on the visible and invisible planes. Paracelsus goes on to say, 'When we are asleep, the soul or astral body is lighter and freer. Then it can rise above the earth and commune with its parents, the stars.' We experience the impressions left by the astral spirit as dreams, omens and intuitions about the future. The vividness of these impressions is dependent on the amount of blood supplied to the brain during sleep. The more tired the physical body, the freer the astral body becomes and the more able to leave stronger impressions in memory.

If someone sleeps very heavily, when they wake up they may have no conscious recollection of the astral body's travels. But the impressions of everything the astral body has seen are still there lying latent and buried under the coarser material of the physical world. These impressions can leap into consciousness at any moment. During these flashes of inner memory, energies flow between the visible and the invisible universes. A current is established between the physical brain and the three-dimensional record held in the astral light. Consequently a person can claim to know an individual or a place even though they have never encountered them before in the physical world. This is because they have encountered them previously in 'spirit.' Biologists might object, saying that in deep sleep 'half of our nature which is volitional is in the condition of inertia' and so unable to travel anywhere. This is how the British physician Benjamin Richardson put it in *Popular Science Monthly* in August 1872. The astral body or soul is especially unable to travel given that biologists regard its existence as a romantic myth. The German physician Johann

Blumenbach states that all communication between mind and body is suspended during sleep. In the same *Popular Science Monthly* article, Richardson contradicts this view. He cautions Blumenbach that this is an overstatement, 'the precise limits and connections of mind and body being unknown.' The French physiologist Germain Fournié admitted much the same. Even more recently the prominent London physician William Allchin conceded to his students that 'of all the human sciences, medicine is the one with the most uncertain and insecure foundation.' Since modern science itself recognizes its own limits, it seems only reasonable to draw on the ideas of ancient science to supplement modern theories.

However grounded in the material world somebody may appear, they are really leading a double existence. They have one existence in the visible universe and one in the invisible. The life-principle that animates someone's physical body is found primarily in their astral body. While someone's physical being is at rest, their spiritual being faces no limits or obstacles. Many people will object to this theory of the life principle's location. They would prefer to remain in the dark rather than consider what to them is an old and discredited theory. They would be happy to go on believing that no one knows where the life principle comes from and where it goes to. Some people may raise the objection that animals have no immortal souls and therefore no astral spirits. This is the argument put forward by theology. But both theologians and laymen wrongly believe that soul and spirit are one and the same thing.

Careful study of Plato and other ancient philosophers soon reveals the difference between the irrational soul and the divine spirit. Plato used the words 'the irrational soul' to describe our astral body or the more ethereal representation of ourselves. The irrational soul can endure for a short time after death but it is the divine spirit (wrongly called the soul by the Church) that is inherently immortal. The difference between the two will be easily grasped by any Hebrew scholar who understands the difference between the words 'nephesh' (meaning sentience, soul, astral self) and 'ruah' (meaning breath, the eternal divine spirit). If the life principle is located primarily in the physical body rather than the astral, why does the intensity of clairvoyant powers increase when the physical body is at rest? The physical body shows fewer signs of life as it enters into a deeper trance. Spiritual perception becomes proportionately clearer and the soul experiences powerful visions. When the soul is undistracted by the physical senses it becomes capable of greater activity. It becomes even more powerful than when it is in a strong physical body. The work of Brière de Boismont has proved this point repeatedly. The five senses become heightened in a mesmerized subject. Even though the subject is unable to use the senses physically, they are even more acute than in the waking state.

These proven facts should be enough to show that an individual's life continues after death, at least for a while. It makes no difference whether death is due to a sudden accident or natural causes. Our soul is like a light hidden under a bushel during its brief time on earth. Nevertheless it is still a light that attracts to itself the energies of kindred spirits. A good or evil thought attracts good or evil energies in the same way as a magnet attracts iron filings. The force of the attraction is in proportion to the intensity of the thought in the ether. The impression someone makes is determined by the exchange of energy between the visible and invisible worlds. In this way someone can make such a strong impression on the world that it is felt by many generations to come.

It's difficult to say how much Balfour Stewart and Peter Guthrie Tait would have agreed with this train of thought. On reading their work, it's reasonable to conclude that they are not telling the whole story:

'Whichever way you look at it, there's no doubt that the properties of ether are far superior to those of physical matter. Even the greatest scientists still struggle to explain the fundamental nature of matter. At best they understand a large number of small and unrelated details. And so it's probably wise not to speculate further. From what we currently know about the ether, it is safe to say that it is capable of much more than anyone has dared to suggest so far.'

One of the most interesting recent discoveries is the phenomenon of psychometry. A person with psychometric abilities is able to receive impressions from an object held in the hand or against the forehead. These impressions may reveal the character or the appearance of an individual who has been in contact with that object. Or they may show further objects that have been in contact with the original. A person with psychometric ability will receive clear impressions from a manuscript, painting, article of clothing or jewelery however old those objects may be. These impressions will reveal the manuscript's writer, the painter of the picture or the wearer of the clothes or jewelery even though they may have lived as long ago as Enoch or the pharaoh Ptolemy. A fragment of an ancient building will reveal its history and events that took place in and around it. A piece of ore will provide a vision of the time when it was formed. Psychometry was discovered by the American professor of physiology Joseph Rodes Buchanan and the world owes him a great debt for his work in the field of psychical science. Once the skeptics have been silenced by the weight of evidence in support of psychometry, perhaps a statue will be erected in his honor. When he announced the discovery of psychometry to the public, he focused on its power to reveal impressions of human personality. In his book *Outlines of Lectures on the Neurological System of Anthropology*, he says, 'The psychometric impressions attached to samples of writing appear to be permanent. When I have investigated older pieces of writing they have given clear and powerful impressions unaffected by time. Some old manuscripts have such unusual calligraphy that it takes an expert to decipher them. These same manuscripts were easily interpreted by psychometry. The effect is not limited to writing. Drawings and paintings also retain psychometric impressions. In fact, any object that comes into physical contact with a person can become linked to that person and later transmit impressions to the psychometrist.'

Perhaps Buchanan did not realize just how significant his words were when he said, 'Psychometry applied to history and the arts will open up a mine of interesting knowledge.'

Psychometry was first demonstrated under test conditions in 1841. Since then the results have been repeated by a thousand psychometers around the world. The phenomenon proves that everything that happens in nature leaves an impression on the physical world. It doesn't matter how small or insignificant the event happens to be. But the impression doesn't change the object physically in any way. The physical world is unaffected at a molecular level and so the only reasonable conclusion is that psychometric images are produced by the invisible universal force of the ether or astral light.

In his book *The Soul of Things*, the American geologist William Denton discusses psychometry at length. He gives many examples of the advanced psychometric abilities demonstrated by his wife Elizabeth Denton. For example, Cicero once owned a house in the ancient Roman city of Tusculum. A fragment from this building was placed against Elizabeth Denton's forehead. Even though she was given no prior information about the object, she was able to describe Cicero's home. She was also able to identify the building's previous owner, the Roman general Cornelius Sulla Felix or Sulla the Dictator. A marble fragment from the Christian church in the ancient Greek city of Smyrna[4] gave her impressions of the congregation and priests. Objects from Nineveh,[5] China, Jerusalem, Greece, Ararat and other far flung places were equally effective. Elizabeth was able to describe scenes from the lives of various people who had lived and died in those places thousands of years ago. Often Denton was able to verify his wife's statements using historical records. More incredibly, a fragment of bone or tooth from a prehistoric animal brought that animal to life again for Elizabeth. She even experienced its sensations for a few brief moments, seeing the world through its eyes. Psychometry reveals information otherwise hidden in the natural world. Events from ancient history can be seen as clearly as if they happened yesterday.

In the same book William Denton writes, 'Nothing moves - no leaf, insect or wave - without being recorded meticulously in a perfect and permanent record. This has been true for all time. From the earth's beginning to the present moment nature has been busy photographing everything. What a comprehensive photographic record the natural world is!'

It seems improbable that scenes from ancient Thebes or a prehistoric temple would only be captured on the surface of certain materials. The images are embedded eternally in a universal medium called the 'soul of the world' by philosophers and 'the soul of things' by William Denton. When a psychometrist places an object against his forehead, he brings his inner self into contact with the object's inner soul. It is now an accepted fact that a universal agent called the aether permeates everything in nature, even the most solid materials. It is also beginning to be accepted that this agent records the images of everything that happens.

When a psychometrist touches an object, he comes into contact with the current of astral light connected to that object. It's this current that holds images and impressions of the object's history. According to William Denton these images appear to the psychometrist at the speed of light. Images appear so rapidly that it takes a supreme effort of will to keep any one image in the mind's eye long enough to describe it.

The psychometrist is clairvoyant. In other words, he sees with his inner eye. His visions of people, places and events are bound to be very confused unless he is strong willed. He must have trained thoroughly in psychometry and he must have a deep understanding of the powers of his clairvoyance. Clairvoyance is also an inherent part of mesmerization. But the mesmerizer uses his will to control the mesmerized subject. In this way, he can compel the subject to concentrate on a particular image long enough to observe it in great detail. When guided by an experienced mesmerist, a mesmerized subject has a clearer picture of future events than any psychometrist. If someone is skeptical about the possibility of perceiving future events, the question could be asked: why is it more impossible to see into the future than it is to resurrect the past? According to Kabbalistic belief, the future exists in embryo in the astral light, just as the present existed in embryo in the past. A man is free to do as he likes. But the knowledge of each choice he will make has existed since the beginning of time. This is not fatalism or destiny. It is simply the principle of universal unchangeable harmony. When a musical note is played, the knowledge already exists that its vibrations won't and can't turn into a different note. Apart from anything else, eternity cannot have a past or a future, it only consists of the present. In the same way, infinite space cannot have distant or nearby places if it is taken literally. Our understanding is limited to the narrow field of human experience.

Instinctively we try to explain the beginning or the end of time and space. But in reality the beginning and the end don't exist. If they did, time would not be eternal and space would not be infinite. The past and the future do not exist. Only our memories survive and they are merely glimpses of the reflections of the past held in the astral light. Similarly, when a psychometrist holds an object, he perceives impressions of its past from the astral plane.

In 1851, the American geologist Edward Hitchcock published *The Religion of Geology and its Connected Sciences*. In this book, he considers how light affects matter and records pictures within it. He writes, 'This photographic effect seems to occur throughout nature and its full extent is impossible to estimate. For all we know it may record pictures of the emotions written on our faces, filling nature with high definition pictures of all our actions . . . It may also be the case that nature is more skilful than any photographer and has ways of developing these portraits so that they can be perceived by beings with sharper senses than our own. These beings may see them as an immense canvas spread over the material universe. Perhaps these images never fade but become permanent exhibits in the gallery of eternity.'

The success of psychometry demonstrates that there is no 'perhaps' about it. Anyone who understands clairvoyant ability will disagree with Hitchcock's view that sharper senses than our own are needed to perceive the pictures on his universal canvas. They will argue that it is only the physical senses of the human body that are limited. Whereas the human spirit, being part of the divine immortal spirit, is able to see everything as if it were in the present moment. It doesn't perceive past or future. The high definition pictures referred to by Hitchcock are held in the astral light. According to early Hermetic ideas (which are now proven by modern science) it's here that the record is kept of everything that is, was or ever will be.

Recently some scholars have turned their attention to a field usually regarded as little more than 'superstition.' They have begun speculating on the possibility of invisible worlds. The authors of *The Unseen Universe*, Balfour Stewart and Peter Guthrie Tait, were the first to lead the way. They already have a follower in the form of Professor John Fiske who outlined his own ideas in his book *The Unseen World*. It seems that scientists are starting to question the value of materialism and exploring alternative fields in case materialism is ultimately discredited. Both the English logician William Stanley Jevons and the English polymath Charles Babbage agree that there doesn't have to be a conflict between science and religion. Both believe that every thought creates a wave in the particles of the brain and this wave travels throughout the universe. According to *Principles of Science* by Jevons, 'each particle of extant matter must contain a record of everything that has happened.' In *A Course of Lectures on Natural Philosophy and the Mechanical Arts Volume I* the English physician Thomas Young asks the reader to 'speculate freely on the possibility of parallel worlds. Some of these may exist in different parts of the universe. Others may exist in the same space and interpenetrate even though they are unknown and invisible to one another. There may be others that do not need space at all in order to exist.'

When scientists speculate on the existence of parallel worlds, they consider scientific theories like the transfer of energy into other universes and the continuity principle. This principle, developed by the physicist William Thomson, suggests that everything is connected, cohesive and unending. If scientists are free to speculate in this way, why shouldn't occultists and spiritualists do the same? In *History of the Conflict Between Religion and Science* William Draper describes how a surface of polished metal will register the impression of an object and preserve it for an indefinite amount of time. It is as if the metal has captured a nerve-like impression. Draper continues in a poetic vein: 'Whenever a shadow is cast against a wall it leaves a permanent trace. This trace can be made visible again with the right methods. Pictures of friends or landscapes are hidden from view on the light-sensitive surface of a photographic plate. But as soon as the plate is developed, the images will appear. It is as if a specter is hidden on the plate's surface until the photographer brings it to light and makes it visible again. When someone is in the privacy of their own home, they assume no one is watching and their privacy is complete. But the walls themselves hold impressions of everything that has taken place inside.'

Objects and events leave a permanent impression on inorganic matter. Equally nothing in the universe is ever lost or ceases to exist completely. Why then is there so much hostility from the scientific community toward Balfour Stewart and Peter Guthrie Tait? Why does science reject the hypothesis that: 'Thought in this universe also affects the fabric of a parallel invisible universe. This may explain how consciousness can pass from this universe but continue to exist in an immaterial future state.'

Psychometry offers powerful proof that matter is indestructible, retaining impressions of people and events eternally. The ability to perceive those eternal impressions is even more powerful proof that man's individual spirit is immortal. Man's inner sight is capable of discerning events that took place hundreds of thousands of years ago. Why can't his inner sight use the same ability to perceive the future? When inner sight is directed at eternity it sees the future contained in a boundless present where past and future co-exist.

Scientists are the first to admit that there are significant gaps in scientific knowledge. But they still refuse to accept the existence of an esoteric spiritual force beyond the laws of physics. They want to take the laws that govern the inanimate world and apply them to living beings. They're lucky to have discovered that light, heat, electricity and motion are the main constituents of ether (described by the Kabbalists as its 'gross purgations'). They have found that different wavelengths produce the colors of the spectrum. Satisfied with their achievements, they avoid looking any further. Several scientists have investigated the nature of ether. As they have not been able to measure it with photometry, they have described it as 'a hypothetical medium.' They define it as 'rarified, extremely flexible and thought to suffuse everything, including solid objects.' According to the dictionary definition it is 'the medium of transmission of light and heat.' Others who could be described as pseudo-scientists have also investigated ether, claiming to have examined it 'through powerful lenses.' Even so, they failed to find anything supernatural or to discover anything of scientific value about its elusive nature. Consequently, they went on to dismiss everyone who believes in immortality in general and spiritualism in particular. Out of spite, they called them all 'insane fools' and 'visionary lunatics' in the words of the US physician Frederic Marvin in his lecture, 'Mediomania.'

In *The Unseen Universe* Stewart and Tait write:

'Scientists like Thomas Huxley have chosen to regard the mystery of life or will as something separate from the objective, scientifically observable universe. Their mistake is to think that consequently the mystery disappears from the universe altogether. It does no such thing. It only disappears from that small circle of light - the universe as studied by science. There are three great mysteries (a trinity of mysteries): the mystery of matter, the mystery of life, and the mystery of God - and these three are one.'

Stewart and Tait observe that 'the energy in the visible universe must come to an end and probably the matter in it as well.' At the same time they acknowledge that 'the principle of continuity requires that the universe continues.' Therefore they are forced to believe 'that there is something beyond the visible universe and that the visible universe may be only a small part of the whole.' They go on to consider the origin of the visible universe, reasoning that 'if the visible universe is all that exists then its beginning, as much as its end, would amount to a break in continuity.' Because a break of this kind is in conflict with the accepted law of continuity, Stewart and Tait come to the following conclusion:

'We have reason to believe that an invisible universe of this kind exists and is connected to the visible universe by energetic ties. It seems reasonable to theorize that this invisible universe must also be capable of receiving energy from the visible. Ether or the universal medium can be regarded as more than simply a bridge between realms. It can also be thought of as a kind of cement that holds the different aspects of the universe together and makes them into one. To sum up, what has been described as ether may be more than just a medium. It may be a medium encoded with the laws that govern the invisible universe. When events in the visible universe are transmitted into the ether, it is as if some part of them crosses by a bridge into the invisible universe to be used and stored. It may even be possible to dispense with the idea of a bridge entirely. Perhaps it can be put more directly: when energy travels from matter into ether, it travels from the visible into the invisible universe. When it travels from ether to matter, it travels from the invisible into the visible.'

The physicist John Tyndall described the physical processes of the brain and consciousness as being divided by an impassable chasm. If science investigated the 'hypothetical medium' of ether more seriously, it might be possible to cross that chasm successfully, at least in theory.

As early as 1856, the French inventor Marcellin Jobard had the same ideas about ether as Stewart and Tait. In his time, Jobard was considered an authority in the field of innovation. He astonished the press and the scientific establishment when the following letter was published in the Parisian newspaper *L'Ami des Sciences*:[6] 'I have made a frightening discovery. There are two forms of electricity. The first is a form of brute force produced when metals and acids come into contact with each other. The second form is intelligent and clairvoyant! . . . In the work of Luigi Galvani, Leopoldo Nobili, and Carlo Matteucci, these two forms of electricity became evident. Moritz von Jacobi, Gaetano Bonelli and Théodose du Moncel have all worked with the first brute form of electricity. Louis-Joseph Lavallée, Marquis de Bois-Robert, Adrien Thilorier and the Marquis du Planty have concentrated on the second intelligent form. Globe lightning shows an apparent intelligence that defies the laws of gravity described by Isaac Newton and the French physicist Edme Mariotte . . . The French Academy of Sciences holds thousands of pieces of evidence for the intelligence of electricity. But I'm aware that I am in danger of saying too much. If I continue I risk disclosing the key to the universal spirit.'

Jobard's letter, science's acknowledgment of its own limits, and the extract quoted above from *The Unseen Universe* - these all add even greater weight to the wisdom of past ages. In 1826, the British antiquarian Isaac Preston Cory published *Ancient Fragments*, a compendium of texts from ancient writers. He includes a passage from the *Chaldean Oracles* that appears to express the same idea about ether as Stewart and Tait and in remarkably similar language. This passage states that everything has come from the aether and everything will return to it. It states that the image of everything is permanently recorded in it. Aether stores the first essence and the final remnants of every visible form and even of ideas. This example seems to support the truism that there is nothing new under the sun: whatever discoveries are made today, will turn out to have been discovered many thousands of years earlier by our so-called 'primitive ancestors.'

By now the materialists' attitude to psychic phenomena is perfectly clear. It's safe to say that if the key to the universe were lying on the floor, no modern scientist would pick it up.

Certain Kabbalists would find these attempts to solve the mystery of the universal ether unbelievably timid. The speculations in *The Unseen Universe* are more advanced than anything described by contemporary philosophy. But to the ancient Hermetic philosophers these concepts were simply basic science: ether was not simply a theoretical bridge that connects the seen and the unseen realms of the universe. It was a bridge they could cross, leading them through the mysterious portal that modern scientists will not or cannot open.

Anyone carrying out advanced research eventually uncovers truths already known to the ancients. What happens when the French geologist Élie de Beaumont theorizes that convection currents circulate under the earth's crust? He finds his theory has already been described by the ancient philosophers. What happens when a metallurgist like the American Thomas Sterry Hunt is asked how metal ore deposits are laid down? He replies by describing water as the universal solvent. And in doing so, he is simply repeating the theory taught by the Greek philosopher Thales of Miletus. More than two thousand years ago Thales described water as the fundamental basis of everything. Hunt refers to de Beaumont's theory of convection currents in the earth's mantle, describing the planet's chemical and physical processes. He explains his theories with the welcome caveat that 'chemical and physical processes alone cannot account for the whole phenomenon of organic life.' He continues: 'In many ways we regard the organic and the mineral worlds as similar. We come to understand that they are connected and dependent on each other. We begin to see the truth behind the ancient philosophers' thinking when they extended the idea of life force to include the mineral world. This led them to consider the earth itself as a living organism. They viewed changes in its atmosphere, its waters, mantle and crust as the life processes of the planet.'

Everything in the world must have a beginning. Given how intractable scientists have become, it's surprising they're prepared to credit ancient philosophy with even this much knowledge. Modern science has long discounted the ancient doctrine that there are four primordial elements: earth, air, fire, and water. Meanwhile scientists compete with each other to discover another elementary chemical substance to add to the growing list of 63 or more in the periodic table. Modern chemistry will not classify earth, air, fire and water as 'chemical elements' because they are not 'primordial principles or self-existing essences.' They are not, as the American chemist Josiah Cooke writes in *The New Chemistry*, 'the building blocks of the universe,' but they were good enough for the old Greek philosophers. Nevertheless modern science rejects them. Josiah Cooke goes on to write, 'These are inappropriate terms.' Science will not deal 'with any kind of essences unless they can be seen, smelt or tasted.' Science will only deal with 'essences' that can be put in the eye, up the nose, or in the mouth! It relegates all other kinds to metaphysics.

According to Jan Baptist van Helmont, it's possible to 'convert elementary earth into water artificially.' 'This doesn't happen in nature because no naturally occurring agent can transmute one element into another.' Van Helmont says in nature the elements always remain the same. When he makes these claims, it's easy to see him as little more than a primitive follower of moldy 'old Greek philosophy,' if not a total fool. What could he, or his old master Paracelsus, possibly have achieved, given that they died long before the 63 elements on the periodic table had been identified? Nothing of course, except crazy metaphysical speculations, expressed in the meaningless jargon used by every medieval and ancient alchemist. That said, it's revealing to compare notes with the latest thinking in Josiah Cooke's *The New Chemistry*: 'Modern chemistry has discovered a remarkable class of substances. No chemical process applied to any of these substances has ever produced a second substance weighing less than the first. For example, no process has ever produced a substance from iron weighing less than the original iron sample. In short, nothing can be derived from iron except iron.' According to Cooke, '75 years ago no one knew there was any difference' between elementary and compound substances. In the distant past, alchemists did not understand 'that weight is the key measure of any material.' They were unaware that 'measured by weight no amount of material is ever lost because the total weight stays the same. Instead alchemists believed that substances underwent a mysterious transformation in experiments like these.' Put simply, 'centuries were wasted in vain attempts to transform the baser metals into gold.'

Josiah Cooke may be a leading chemist but is he equally knowledgeable about what the ancient alchemists did or didn't know? Does he fully understand the meaning of the terms used by alchemists? Maybe not. Compare his ideas quoted above with the straightforward writings of van Helmont and Paracelsus below. According to them the alkahest or universal solvent produces the following changes:

'1. The alkahest never destroys the essential qualities of the substances it dissolves. For instance, the alkahest turns gold into a salt of gold. It turns the chemical element antimony into a salt of antimony and so on. The salts have the same essential qualities or characteristics as the original substances. 2. Any substance exposed to the alkahest is converted into its three constituent parts - salt, sulfur and mercury. Subsequently it turns into salt only, which then becomes volatile. Eventually it is turned completely into clear water. 3. Any substance dissolved in the alkahest can be made volatile by heating the solution using a sand bath. If the vapor is then distilled, the result is pure water weighing the same as the original substance.' In addition, van Helmont says this salt will dissolve the most resistant materials into substances that have the same essential qualities. The substances produced are always 'equal in weight to the original material that was dissolved.' Van Helmont adds, 'When this salt is distilled again several times with the alkahest (named *sal circulatum* by Paracelsus) it loses all density. Eventually it becomes plain water. The quantity of this water is equal to the quantity of the salt it was made from.'

As a modern chemist, Josiah Cooke could criticize these Hermetic texts. This criticism would equally apply to the writings of the ancient Egyptian priesthood. In both cases the meaning of certain passages is deliberately concealed. If Cooke wants to benefit from the knowledge of the ancients, he must decode their texts, not make fun of them. Following Hermetic tradition, Paracelsus ingeniously coded his work by transposing letters and making abbreviations of words and sentences. For example, he used the word 'sutratur' to indicate potassium hydrogen tartrate and he disguised niter as 'mutrin' and so on. There was an endless number of theories about the nature of the alkahest. Some people believed it was an alkaline of potassium carbonate that had been treated with salt. Others thought it referred to the German word 'algeist' meaning 'all spirit' or 'full of spirit.' Paracelsus often described salt as 'the center of water where metals ought to die'. This gave rise to a host of absurd speculations. Some people like the German alchemist Johann Glauber thought the alkahest was the spirit of salt. It would be arrogant to suggest that Paracelsus and his peers didn't know about elementary and compound substances. He may not have referred to these substances using modern terms, but the results of his experiments prove that he knew of their existence. It doesn't matter what name Paracelsus gave to the gas he produced by dissolving iron in sulfuric acid. He is still acknowledged by modern science as the discoverer of hydrogen. Van Helmont used the term 'essential qualities' to conceal his knowledge that elementary substances have immutable properties. He knew that when elementary substances formed compounds their immutable properties were only temporarily modified - never destroyed. Even though he hid his understanding from the world, he was nonetheless the greatest chemist of his age and just as expert as any modern chemist. He described how *aurum potabile* or drinkable gold could be produced using the alkahest. Gold is converted completely into salt. It retains its essential qualities and is soluble in water. Modern chemists must first understand precisely what Paracelsus meant by the terms *aurum potabile*, 'alkahest,' 'salt,' and 'essential qualities.' They need to understand fully his esoteric meaning rather than what he said he meant or what other people thought he meant. That's the only way they can criticize the work of the alchemists and their ancient teachers with any authority. One thing is clear though. In its literal sense, the language used by van Helmont shows he understood that metallic substances could be made soluble in water. Thomas Sterry Hunt draws on the same principle in his theory of how metal deposits are laid down. Now try this thought experiment: picture a torture chamber in the basement of the new Court House or the cathedral on Fifth Avenue. Suppose a judge or cardinal had the power to send modern scientists there for their blasphemous suggestion that man's 'only God is the gray matter of his brain.' What clever terms would scientists invent to conceal but also to convey their view that this is a godless universe?

In his lecture *Origin of Metalliferous Deposits,* Hunt says: 'The alchemists never did find a universal solvent. But now we know that in certain cases water can dissolve even the most insoluble materials. Its power as a solvent is increased by heat, pressure and the addition of common substances such as carbonic acid and alkaline carbonates and sulphides. So in some ways water itself can be regarded as the alkahest or universal menstruum that alchemists pursued for so long.'

It's as if Hunt is simply paraphrasing van Helmont or Paracelsus! Both were as familiar as any modern chemist with water's solvent action but had they thought it was the alkahest, they would have hidden everything they knew about it. Many commentaries and criticisms of their works still exist. Almost any book on the subject of alchemy contains observations about the nature of water as a solvent. But the authors haven't made these references obscure or veiled them in mystery. The following passage is found in the *Demonologia,* an exposé of ancient and modern superstitions by J.S. Forsyth. It was written at the beginning of the 19th Century when the properties of water as a chemical agent were already well understood.

'It may be helpful to know that van Helmont and Paracelsus regarded water as the principal agent in both chemistry and physics. They saw the earth as the unchangeable foundation of everything. They regarded fire as a force sufficient to cause everything. They believed that potential was seeded in the structure of the earth and that water gives rise to everything by dissolving the earth and fermenting it, aided by fire. For them, this explained the origin of the animal, vegetable, and mineral kingdoms.'

The alchemists understood full well the universal power of water. They were clear that 'the main characteristic of the alkahest' is to 'dissolve and change all material with the sole exception of water.' This was explicitly stated in the works of Paracelsus, van Helmont, Eugenius Philalethes, the obscure alchemist author Pantatem, the German pharmacist Otto Tachenius and even the chemist Robert Boyle. Consider that van Helmont's character was spotless and his expertise was widely acknowledged - is it possible that it was only empty boasting when he claimed to know the secret of the alkahest?

In a recent talk in Nashville, Tennessee, Thomas Huxley put forward a rule for judging whether or not an eyewitness account was trustworthy. His rule helps to decide which accounts make reliable contributions to an understanding of history and science. It is equally applicable to the records of alchemists' work. Huxley says, 'What someone believes about past history inevitably influences their daily life. Eyewitness accounts can give valuable insight into past events whether spoken or written down for posterity . . . In his *Commentaries (Commentarii)*,[7] Caesar describes his battles with the Gauls. When you read his descriptions you take them on trust. You feel that Caesar would not have made these statements if he hadn't believed them to be true.'

If this rule can be applied to Caesar's military career, logically it can also be applied to the rest of his experiences. He was either a generally honest man or a pathological liar. Huxley has decided that Caesar is telling the truth about military history. If this is the case, Caesar must also be a reliable witness when it comes to things like prophecy, divination and psychic phenomena. The same can be said about Herodotus and others like him. Unless they were generally honest men, their accounts of civil or military affairs shouldn't be believed. False in one thing, false in everything. Equally, if they can be believed about the material world, they can be believed about the spiritual world. This holds true because, as Huxley says, human nature does not change. Brilliant and honest men did not lie simply for the fun of confusing or disillusioning generations to come. Given this is the view of a leading scientist like Thomas Huxley, there seems no need to question the integrity of Paracelsus or his follower van Helmont. The French naturalist Joseph Deleuze describes van Helmont's work as containing many 'mythic, illusory ideas.' Perhaps this is only because he could not understand them. Nevertheless he recognizes that van Helmont has vast knowledge, 'acute judgment' and has brought to light 'great truths.' He adds, 'He was the first to coin the term 'gas' to describe fluid substances that expand freely to fill the available space around them. Without him it's likely the chemistry of steel would have remained unknown to science.' It's common knowledge that early researchers were capable of separating and recombining chemical elements. What are the chances that they knew nothing about the properties of elementary chemical substances? Is it possible that they were unaware of the energy released when those substances were combined? And were they unaware of the solvents required to dissolve them? If these early scientists had only worked theoretically, the argument that they understood elementary chemical substances would be much weaker. But even their detractors acknowledge their achievements in applied chemistry. Their expertise could be underlined even more forcefully but it's more important to maintain an unbiased tone. This book is based on the idea that man has a higher nature. A psychological judgment should be made of his moral intent and his intellectual capability. Van Helmont claimed 'most solemnly' that he knew the secret of the alkahest. Therefore no modern commentator can describe him as either a liar or a visionary until more is known about the alkahest or universal menstruum.

'Facts are stubborn things,' writes the British naturalist Alfred Russel Wallace in *Miracles and Modern Spiritualism*. Facts are the strongest allies of truth and many compelling facts are provided by the miracles of both the ancient and modern eras. In *The Unseen Universe* Stewart and Tait have demonstrated the theoretical possibility that energy and information can be transmitted between parallel universes. They theorize that the medium of transmission is the universal ether. Wallace has shown that the arguments against this theory do not stand up to logical scrutiny (any more than the skepticism of a philosopher like David Hume). For more than three years, William Crookes conducted a rigorous scientific investigation into the phenomenon of spiritualism. He was ultimately convinced by his own direct experience that mediums can produce genuine paranormal phenomena. A long list could be made of scientists who have been similarly persuaded by their own subjective experience. The French astronomer Camille Flammarion is the author of many works that skeptics could label as 'deluded,' along with those of Wallace, Crookes, and Robert Hare. In the following lines, he corroborates the idea that direct experience is a strong indicator of truth:

'Any scientist who simply dismisses magnetism, somnambulism and mediumship etc as impossible doesn't know what he is talking about. Anyone used to making accurate scientific observations will want to ascertain the exact nature of these phenomena one way or another. His investigations will be impartial. He won't be misled by the idea that science understands the laws of nature entirely and anything beyond the limits of our current understanding is impossible.'

In his article 'Notes of an Inquiry into the Phenomena Called Spiritual During the Years 1870 - 1873' (*Quarterly Journal of Science* 1874), William Crookes quotes his assistant Edward Cox. Cox used the word 'psychic' to describe spiritual force. He explains it as follows: 'The individual being we call 'a man' is an organism moved and directed by a force inside it. This force is either the soul, spirit, or mind or it is controlled by them. It's reasonable to assume that the force that causes effects beyond the limits of the body is the same force that produces effects within the body. The external force is often seen to be directed by intelligence, so it seems reasonable to assume that the intelligence directing the external force is the same intelligence that directs the force inside the body.'

Cox's ideas are easier to understand when presented as four key points:

1. The force that produces physical phenomena is generated inside the medium.

2. The intelligence directing the force that produces phenomena may sometimes be different from the intelligence of the medium. But this is impossible to prove. Therefore the directing intelligence is probably the intelligence of the medium himself. Cox calls this 'a reasonable conclusion.'

3. He assumes the force that moves the table in a seance is the same as the force that moves the medium's body.

4. He strongly disagrees with the spiritualists' view that 'spirits of the dead are the sole agents producing all spiritualistic phenomena.'

Before analyzing these key points it's important to remember that there are two opposing sides in this debate - people who believe in the power of human spirits and people who don't. Neither side is capable of answering the question put forward by Cox (i.e. is the medium the source of spiritualistic phenomena rather than spirits of the dead?) The spiritualists are so completely credulous that they believe every sound and movement at a seance is produced by human spirits. Meanwhile the non-believers argue that nothing can be produced by spirits because they simply don't exist. Neither group can tackle the question in an unbiased way.

The force that 'produces motion within the body' may well be essentially the same as the force that 'causes effects beyond the limits of the body.' But the similarity between the two ends there. The force that animates Edward Cox is essentially the same as the force that animates a psychic medium but Cox is not a medium and the medium is not Cox.

This force (labeled 'psychic' by Cox and Crookes) comes through the medium. It does not come from the medium. If the force did come from the medium it would have to be generated internally. This is never the case. It makes no difference if the phenomenon in question is levitation, telekinesis or if the force shows apparent logic or intelligence. Mediums and spiritualists know that the more passive the medium, the better the results. And they are also aware that phenomena like levitation and telekinesis require the action of a conscious will. Suppose the psychic force was generated inside the medium. In cases of levitation you would have to believe that this force could lift an object off the ground, transport it through the air and lower it back onto the ground, avoiding obstacles. Consequently, it would be displaying intelligence but it would also be acting independently while the medium remained in a passive trance state. If this were the case, the medium would clearly be a conscious magician and it would be a waste of time pretending to be a passive instrument directed by an invisible intelligence. It would be like saying that filling a boiler with enough steam would raise it off the ground. Or that a Leyden jar[8] full of electricity could move itself. These are physical impossibilities. These analogies suggest that the force operating in the presence of a medium comes from somewhere beyond the medium himself. It would be better to compare it with the hydrogen used in a hydrogen balloon. The right amount of gas is carefully calculated to fill the balloon and counteract the force of gravity. By the same principle psychic force moves pieces of furniture etc and creates other manifestations. Whilst it is essentially the same as the astral spirit of the medium, it cannot be his spirit alone because the medium is immobilized in a deep trance state throughout any genuine seance. Therefore Edward Cox's first key point doesn't hold up. It is based on a physically impossible principle. Of course, all this is assuming that levitation is something that does actually take place. Any complete theory of psychic force must explain all 'visible motions . . . in solid substances' and levitation is one of these.

In his second key point Cox says that the force producing psychic phenomena may sometimes be directed by intelligences beyond the medium's mind. But he claims this is impossible to prove. This view cannot go unchallenged. There is a great deal of evidence that the mind of the medium has nothing to do with the phenomena in the majority of cases.

Cox's third key point is equally illogical. For argument's sake, suppose the medium's body is not the generator of the force but simply channels it to produce psychic phenomena. (Cox's research throws no light on this idea whatsoever.) Just because the medium's 'soul, spirit, or mind' directs his body, it does not follow that his 'soul, spirit, or mind' also directs levitation or raps on a table.

Cox's fourth key point rejects the idea that 'only spirits of the dead produce psychic phenomena.' This subject doesn't need further discussion here as it is dealt with in detail in Chapter Two.

Philosophers, especially those initiated into the Mysteries, maintained that the astral soul is the non-physical duplicate of the physical body. The French writer Allan Kardec called it the 'perispirit'[9] and spiritualists know it as the 'spirit-form.' The divine spirit lies above and illuminates the astral soul, just as the sun illuminates the earth, fertilizing the seed and awakening the spiritual potential inside it. The astral soul is contained and confined within the physical body in much the same way as ether is contained in a bottle or magnetic force in a magnet. The astral soul is both a center and an engine of force. It is part of a universal force and subject to the same laws that govern nature and all cosmic phenomena. The action of the astral soul keeps the physical body alive, wearing it out eventually and escaping from it on death. It is not the willing tenant of the body. It is a prisoner. It is powerfully attracted to the universal force and reunites with it once the body is worn out. The stronger and more robust a person's physical body, the longer the astral soul will be imprisoned inside it. A door prevents most people from communicating with the world of the astral light. But some people are born with such special abilities that they can easily open this door. Their souls can see or even travel into that world and return again. People who can do this consciously and deliberately are called magicians, high priests, seers and adepts. People who are compelled to do this under the influence of a mesmerist or of 'spirits' are called 'mediums.' The astral soul is powerfully attracted to the universal force whenever the door is open. Sometimes this attraction is so strong that the soul lifts the body with it, suspending it in mid air. The body descends when gravity takes hold again.

Two conditions are necessary before any objective phenomenon can occur (whether it's the motion of a person's arm or the movement of an inanimate object). There must be will and force, and both of these must act on matter. According to the scientific principle called 'the correlation of forces,' will, force and matter are convertible and interchangeable. In their turn they are directed or overseen by divine intelligence. Scientists omit divine intelligence from their theories but without it even the smallest creature would be unable to move. One of the most common of all natural phenomena is leaves rustling in the breeze. Even this simple action requires divine intelligence if it is to take place. Scientists may prefer to regard it as the result of mechanical laws but it is important to discern the intelligent cause that created these laws in the first place and informed them with its own consciousness. Regardless of whether this is referred to as the first cause, the universal will or God, it must always have intelligence.

This leads to the question, how can will express itself intelligently and unconsciously at the same time? It is difficult or impossible to imagine an intellect operating independently of consciousness. But consciousness is not necessarily physical or embodied. Consciousness is a quality of sentience or the soul and the soul is often active even when the body is asleep or paralyzed. When someone casually raises their arm, it may appear to be an unconscious act because human senses cannot perceive the split second delay between the decision and the action. It might seem as if no thought was involved but nevertheless the person's will caused the muscles of the arm to move. Edward Cox theorizes that the force behind spiritualist phenomena is generated by the medium. But nothing about even the simplest spiritual phenomena supports his theory. The intelligence shown by this psychic force does not prove that it belongs to a disembodied spirit. There is even less evidence that it is produced by the medium unconsciously. In his book *Researches in the Phenomena of Spiritualism*, William Crookes describes cases where the intelligence could not possibly have been produced by anyone at the seance. He gives the example where the word 'however' was hidden from everyone in the room including himself. But it was accurately written out by the planchette[10] in automatic writing. There is absolutely no explanation to account for this. If the presence of spirits is excluded, clairvoyance seems the most reasonable alternative hypothesis. But scientists reject this idea out of hand. The only reason they might accept it is to avoid having to consider spirits as a possible cause. In that case they must accept the Kabbalists' theory that clairvoyance is possible because the future exists in embryo in the astral light. Alternatively they must come up with a new theory that fits the facts but so far this has proven impossible.

Suppose, for the sake of argument, the word 'however' really was read clairvoyantly. What are the implications when it comes to clairvoyant knowledge of future events? Is there a theory of clairvoyance that accounts for the ability to predict the future beyond the knowledge of those involved? Edward Cox will have to go back to the drawing board.

Whether terrestrial or celestial, the modern psychic force and the energies of the ancient oracles are essentially identical. They are simply a neutral medium. As is air. In a conversation between two people, the sound waves produced by each speaker cause one and the same volume of air to vibrate. But there is no doubt that there are two people speaking. Similarly, when a clairvoyant and a 'spirit' use one and the same medium to communicate, is it reasonable to assume that there is only one intelligence present? Air is necessary for sounds to be communicated between two people. In the same way, certain currents of astral light are necessary to produce spiritualist phenomena (where the astral light, or ether, is directed by an intelligence). Place two people in a vacuum. If they could survive, they would be unable to speak to each other because there would be no air to carry the vibration of their voices. Place the most adept medium in an inhibiting atmosphere created by a powerful mesmerizer and no phenomena will occur. To interrupt this psychic inertia, it needs an opposing intelligence strong enough to overcome the mesmerizer's negative influence.

The ancients were able to tell the difference between a force acting blindly and the same force directed by an intelligence.

The Oracle of Delphi was famous for its intoxicating vapors, a subterranean gas with magnetic properties. Plutarch, a priest of Apollo at Delphi, shows the Oracle's nature to be dual when he speaks to it in these words: 'And who are you without a God to create and nurture you? Without a spirit, directed by God to guide and oversee you, you can do nothing. You are nothing but an empty breath.' By the same token, 'psychic force' would also be nothing but an 'empty breath' in the absence of an inner soul or intelligence.

Aristotle believes this subterranean gas to be the sole sufficient cause of life on earth. It is an astral emanation that rises from inside the planet giving life to every living being and plant on the surface. Cicero answered the skeptics of his time with justified irritation. In his treatise *Concerning Divination (De Divinatione)* he writes: 'What could be more divine than the earth's breath that intoxicates the High Priestess and enables her to predict the future? Do you think time could weaken this miraculous power? It's not perishable like wine or cured meat.' Modern scientists must think they're cleverer than Cicero when they claim the power of prophecy has been lost.

The ancient prophets were inspired sensitives, said to make their predictions by similar means. They were informed directly by the astral emanation or by a sort of damp mist rising from the earth. It is this damp astral mist that temporarily wraps the souls that form in the astral light. The German occultist Heinrich Cornelius Agrippa expresses the same view about the nature of these spirits. In his book *On Occult Philosophy (De Occulta Philosophia)*, he describes them as moist or humid: *In spirito turbido humidoque.*

Prophecies are made in two ways. They are conceived consciously by seers who are able to look into the astral light and unconsciously by prophets acting under what is known as inspiration. Biblical prophets fall into this second category and so do present-day clairvoyants. Plato was familiar with this fact. In the *Timaeus* he writes, 'No man in his right mind can make a prophecy . . . he must first be unbalanced or possessed . . . ' (by a demon or spirit). Plato adds, 'People like this are sometimes called prophets but they are only repeaters . . . they should not to be called prophets at all. They are only transmitters of vision and prophecy.'

Edward Cox continues Plato's argument, saying, 'Spiritualists practically admit the existence of psychic force, misusing the term 'magnetism' and claiming that the spirits of the dead can only act through the magnetism (i.e psychic force) of the medium.'

Misunderstandings are inevitable when different names are used to describe what may ultimately be the same thing. Electricity wasn't the subject of serious scientific study until the 18th Century. But no one would be fool enough to suggest that electricity hasn't always existed. It can even be proven that the ancient Hebrews were familiar with it. It wasn't until 1819 that scientists discovered the connection between magnetism and electricity. Just because this discovery was made so late, it doesn't mean the two forces haven't always been interchangeable. A bar of iron will become magnetic when electricity is passed through a conductor close to it. In theory, could a medium at a seance also be a conductor and nothing more? Could the theory be developed further as follows? The 'psychic force' draws electricity from the ether using the medium as a conductor. It activates the latent magnetism that fills the atmosphere of the seance room and this is how it produces spiritualist phenomena. The word 'magnetism' is as appropriate as any, until science can provide a more concrete theory.

'The difference between the supporters of the theory of psychic force and the spiritualists is this,' says Edward Cox, 'We contend that there is not enough evidence to prove that any other force is at work apart from the medium's intelligence and there's no proof at all that the 'spirits' of the dead are involved.'

It is undeniable that there is a lack of evidence for the involvement of spirits. But Cox's conclusion that only the medium's intelligence is at work is surprising given the 'wealth of facts' described by William Crookes. Crookes says, 'Looking at my notes, I find . . . such an overwhelming amount of evidence, such a vast number of eyewitness accounts . . . that I could fill several issues of the *Quarterly Journal of Science*.'

Some of this 'overwhelming evidence' is as follows: 1. Heavy objects move easily when touched lightly. 2. Knocking and other sounds are heard. 3. Objects become lighter or heavier. 4. Heavy objects move at a distance from the medium. 5. Tables and chairs rise up from the ground without anyone touching them. 6. Human beings levitate. 7. Ghostly lights appear. Crookes writes, 'Under controlled conditions, I have observed a solid glowing object about the size and shape of a turkey's egg. It floated silently around the room, rose higher than anyone could reach on tiptoe, then descended gently to the floor. It was visible for more than ten minutes and before it faded away, it hit the table three times and sounded solid.' (It seems likely that the egg was similar to Jacques Babinet's meteor-cat described by François Arago in his book *Meteorological Essays*.) 8. Hands appear, either glowing or visible by the ambient light. 9. These same glowing hands produce spontaneous writing clearly directed by an intelligence (psychic force?). 10. 'Phantom forms and faces' appear. Psychic force comes from the corner of the room in the form of a phantom. It takes an accordion in its hands and glides around the room playing it. Throughout this spectacle, the medium Daniel Dunglas Home is in plain sight. Crookes observed and investigated these ten phenomena in his own home. He verified the authenticity of each one to his own satisfaction then reported to the Royal Society. The reception given to his discoveries is described in his book, *Researches in the Phenomena of Spiritualism*.

In addition to these tricks played on human credulity by 'psychic force,' Crookes identifies another class of phenomena which he calls 'special instances.' These seem to suggest that a separate intelligence is at work.

Crookes writes, 'I have seen the medium Kate Fox write a message automatically to one person present in the room. At the same time, another message was being spelled out to someone else in a series of 'raps.' While all this was going on, Kate Fox was also speaking to a third person on another subject entirely . . . During a seance in a well-lit room, conducted by Daniel Dunglas Home, a small piece of wood moved across the table toward me and delivered a message by tapping my hand. I recited the alphabet and the piece of wood tapped me when I came to the right letters. All this took place so far away from the medium Home that he couldn't have been the cause of it.' At Crookes' request, the same piece of wood tapped a message in Morse code against his hand. (No other person in the room knew Morse code and Crookes was only vaguely familiar with it himself.) Crookes adds, 'It convinced me that there was a good Morse operator at the other end of the line, wherever that might be.' Perhaps Edward Cox should look for the Morse operator in his own little kingdom - Psychic Land. The small piece of wood goes on to do even more extraordinary things. In the same well-lit room, Crookes asks it to produce a written message. '. . . A pencil and some sheets of paper were lying in the middle of the table. The pencil rose on its point, moved jerkily toward the paper and then fell down. It rose and fell three more times without getting any further. The small piece of wood, that had tapped out Morse code, slid across the table toward the pencil and rose up a few inches. The pencil rose again and propped itself against the piece of wood and the two then tried to write on the paper together. After the third attempt, the piece of wood gave up and returned to its original position. The pencil lay on the paper where it had fallen and a message read: *We have tried to do what you asked us to but our power is exhausted.*' The use of the word 'our' suggests two psychic forces were present.

But is there any evidence that 'the intelligence of the medium' was the force that moved the pencil and the piece of wood? On the contrary, the evidence suggests that the movement was caused by so-called spirits 'of the dead' or other invisible intelligent entities.

When it comes to explaining what's happening in this example, the word 'magnetism' is no more helpful than the term 'psychic force.' Nevertheless, it is better to use the word 'magnetism' because transcendent magnetism - or mesmerism - produces effects that are identical to spiritualism. Jules du Potet and Antonio Regazzoni are both able to mesmerize subjects so they are physically unable to move. This is a phenomenon that conventional physiology cannot explain. In a seance, a table can rise from the floor without anyone touching it. This is something conventional physics is equally unable to explain. A group of adults has been unable to lift a small table weighing only a few pounds and broken it in the attempt. On another occasion, a dozen people (including some scientists) were unable to step across a line chalked on the floor by du Potet. A skeptical Russian general tried repeatedly to cross the line, eventually collapsing in violent convulsions. The magnetic fluid resisting his movement was the psychic force described by Cox - the same force that makes seance tables extraordinarily and supernaturally heavy. If magnetism and psychic force produce the same psychical and physiological effects, it's reasonable to assume they are more or less identical. This seems a perfectly sound conclusion. Besides if someone objected to the idea, that wouldn't make it untrue. Once upon a time the scientific establishment maintained there were no mountains whatsoever on the moon. There was also a time when someone claiming that life existed in the upper atmosphere or the deep ocean would have been considered a fool.

The Abbé Almignana, a parish priest in Paris, investigated the phenomena of mediumship and table turning. He used to say, 'If the Devil says it's true, it must be a lie!' Very soon it may well make sense to paraphrase the sentence so that it reads, 'If scientists say it's a lie, it must be true!'

Chapter Seven

Thou great First Cause, least understood.

THE UNIVERSAL PRAYER, ALEXANDER POPE

Whence this pleasing hope, this fond desire,
This longing after immortality?
Or whence this secret dread, and inward horror
Of falling into naught? Why shrinks the soul
Back on herself, and startles at destruction?
Tis the divinity that stirs within us;
Tis heaven itself that points out our hereafter
And intimates eternity to man.

Eternity! Thou pleasing, dreadful thought!

CATO, A TRAGEDY, ACT V, SCENE I, JOSEPH ADDISON

There is another and better world.

THE STRANGER, AUGUST VON KOTZEBUE

Previous chapters have analyzed contrasting scientific opinions about modern occult phenomena. Now it's time to focus on the ideas of medieval alchemists and other notable figures. Almost all ancient and medieval scholars believed in the secret wisdom tradition. This tradition included alchemy and the Chaldeo-Jewish Kabbalah. It also included the hidden schools of thought attributed to Pythagoras, the old Magi, the later Platonic philosophers and the ancient magicians. This chapter will also discuss the subjects of Hindu asceticism and Chaldean astrology. It is important to reveal the great truths that underlie the disregarded religions of the past. The four elements were once known to the ancients as earth, air, water, and fire. Anyone studying alchemy and ancient psychology (or magic as it's now called) can learn a lot from these traditions. They contain truths that Western philosophy has never decoded. Summoning the spirits of the dead has been practiced the world over from the earliest times. The Church calls it necromancy, modern believers call it spiritualism.

Henry More was not an alchemist, magician or astrologer but simply one of Cambridge University's greatest philosophers. He can be described as a shrewd logician, scientist and metaphysician. Throughout his life, he believed in both witchcraft and man's immortality. He used the work of Pythagoras to support his view that man's spirit survives after death. Pythagoras' belief system also underpinned the work of Jan Baptist van Helmont, the Italian philosopher Gerolamo Cardano and other mystics. God is an infinite and uncreated spirit. It is pure and perfect. Everything emanates from this first cause. God is the primary substance. Everything else is secondary. If we accept that God created matter with the power to move, then He is the ultimate cause of both the matter and the movement. Yet it's also true to say that the matter moves by itself. In *An Antidote Against Atheism* Henry More writes,

'We may define this infinite and uncreated spirit as an imperceptible substance, that can move itself, that can penetrate, contract, and dilate itself, and can also penetrate, move and alter matter,' which is the third emanation (according to Plotinus' theory of emanation). Henry More believed in ghosts and supported the theory that every human soul is individual - a 'personality, memory, and conscience that continues in a future state beyond death.' He believed that a man's astral spirit divided into two types after it had left the body. These were the 'aerial' and the 'ethereal' forms. In the aerial form the spirit is controlled by fate - evil and temptation exploit its previous mortal self-interest. In this form the spirit is not completely pure. It must evolve beyond the first spheres of astral existence[1] and become ethereal for its immortality to be assured. 'In its ethereal form, the soul is pure transparent light with no darkness or evil in it whatsoever. In this form the soul's destiny is fulfilled and it exists beyond the reach of fate and mortality.' More concludes that this transcendent and pure state was the Pythagoreans' sole aim.

More was also a theologian and wrote scathingly about non-believers. On 25 May 1678, he wrote to the English philosopher Joseph Glanvill referring sarcastically to the politician Reginald Scot, the physician Thomas Ady, and the cleric John Webster as 'our new inspired saints . . .' He continues his attack on them, quoting the Biblical tale of the Witch of Endor: King Saul commands the witch to summon the spirit of the prophet Samuel. More calls Webster, Ady and Scot 'the supporters of witches, who ignore common sense, history and the Bible itself insisting that the spirit of Samuel never appeared and the witch was nothing more than a conjuror working with an unscrupulous accomplice!' He goes on to say, 'Is the Bible to be believed or these self-important fools, puffed up with stupidity, vanity, and lack of faith? The answer should be obvious to anyone.'

Imagine the language this great man would have used to put present-day skeptics in their place.

Descartes was an enthusiastic teacher on the subject of magnetism even though he was essentially a rationalist. He could even be said to be a teacher of alchemy if his lessons are interpreted in a certain way. His theories about physics were similar to those of other notable philosophers. The infinity of space is filled with an elementary fluid-like matter. It is the primary source of all life. It encloses all celestial bodies and keeps them in perpetual motion. Descartes hypothesizes that the movement of planets is driven by ether particles in a vortex. In Mesmer's theory it is the flow of magnetic fluid. Both draw on the same principle. In *History of Magic* Joseph Ennemoser asserts that both have more in common 'than people suppose, who have not examined the subject carefully.'

The French philosopher Pierre Poiret Naudé was a strong supporter of occult magnetism and the people who first popularized the practice. His works support and vindicate magico-theosophical philosophy.

In his book *On Sympathy (Über Sympathie)*, the well-known physician Friedrich Hufeland proposes there is a universal magnetic resonance between animals, plants, and even minerals. He confirms the evidence collected by the Italian philosopher Tommaso Campanella, Jan Baptist van Helmont and the Italian professor of medicine Petrus Servius. This evidence points to a connection between different parts of the body as well as a connection between all organic and even inorganic bodies.

The German professor Tenzel Wirdig put forward the same theory of magnetic resonance. He explained it more clearly, logically and emphatically than other occult authors who have written on the same subject. In his famous paper 'The New

Spiritual Medicine' (*Nova Medicina Spirituum Curiosa*), he demonstrates that the whole of nature has a soul. He bases his theory on the idea of universal attraction and repulsion, an idea later accepted as fact and renamed 'gravitation.' Wirdig calls magnetic resonance 'the agreement of spirits.' Like attracts like. All things join with what is compatible. This attraction and repulsion creates the constant movement of the world and everything in it. It creates an uninterrupted connection between heaven and earth producing universal harmony. Everything lives and dies through magnetism. One thing affects another even at great distances. One thing may influence another by the power of the magnetic resonance between them. One thing may promote health or disease at any time, regardless of how far away from the other it may be. In *History of Magic* Ennemoser writes, 'Hufeland refers to the case of a nose cut from the back of a porter. When the porter died, the nose died as well, detaching itself from its artificial position. Hufeland also describes the instance of a piece of scalp removed from a person's head. When the person's hair turned gray so did the hair on the separated piece of scalp.'

In many ways, the German mathematician Johannes Kepler was the forerunner of Newton. He accurately attributed the force of gravity to magnetic attraction. Despite describing astrology as the 'insane daughter' of astronomy's 'wise mother,' he still shares the Kabbalists' belief that the spirits of the stars are 'intelligences.' He believes that each planet houses an intelligent principle and all planets are inhabited by spiritual beings. These beings influence other beings inhabiting denser material planes, particularly the earth. Kepler's theory of 'celestial' influence was superseded by Descartes' more materialist theory of magnetic vortices. But the materialist Descartes was also prepared to believe that a mysterious diet could prolong his life for 500 years or more. By the same token, someone may one day discover that Descartes' materialist vortices are really intelligent magnetic streams directed by the 'celestial' *anima mundi*.

The Italian philosopher Giambattista della Porta worked hard to prove to the world that magic is more than superstition and sorcery. Despite his efforts, later critics treated him with the same unfairness as his peers. In *Natural Magic (Magia Naturalis)*, he explains all the occult phenomena that man is capable of, attributing them to the world soul which connects everything. He shows that the astral light acts in harmony and sympathy with the whole of nature. He reveals that our spirits are formed from its essence. He explains that our astral bodies become capable of magic when they act in unison with their source, the astral light. The key to natural magic lies in understanding how elements are related. He believed in the philosopher's stone, 'regarded highly all over the world, talked about enthusiastically by many and obtained by some.' He shares many valuable insights into the deeper 'spiritual meaning' of the philosopher's stone. In 1641, the German Jesuit scholar Athanasius Kircher published a treatise on magnetism called *Magnets and the Magnetic Art (Magnes Sive De Arte Magnetica)*. He covered many subjects that Paracelsus only touched on. He contradicted the theory proposed by the English astronomer William Gilbert that the earth was a giant magnet. This made his definition of magnetism highly original. According to Kircher, all matter and even the invisible 'forces' of nature were magnetic but they did not themselves constitute a magnet. There is only one magnet in the universe and it magnetizes everything in existence. The Kabbalists call it the central spiritual sun or God. Kircher confirmed that the sun, moon, planets, and stars are highly magnetic but their magnetism is derived by induction from the universal magnetic fluid - the spiritual light. He proves the mysterious connection that exists between the animal, vegetable and mineral kingdoms and he strengthens his argument by providing an exhaustive catalogue of examples. Naturalists have confirmed many of these examples but a great deal are still unsubstantiated. Consequently these examples are dismissed by scientists who follow usual scientific practice and some very doubtful logic. For instance, Kircher demonstrates that there is a difference between mineral magnetism and animal magnetism (also called 'zoomagnetism'). With the exception of magnetite, all minerals are magnetized by the stronger magnetic force of animal magnetism. Whereas animal magnetism itself emanates directly from the first cause - the Creator. A strong-willed man can magnetize a needle simply by holding it in his hand. Rubbing amber makes it magnetic and the human hand is better than any other object for producing this effect. To a certain degree, it appears man can transmit his own life force and animate inorganic objects. This, 'in the eye of the foolish, is sorcery,' writes Kircher and he anticipates General Pleasonton's work by more than two centuries when he writes, 'The sun is the most magnetic of all bodies.' He continues his train of thought, saying, 'The ancient philosophers never denied this. They have always understood that the sun's magnetism binds everything to it and equally the sun magnetizes everything it illuminates.'

To prove his point, he gives the example of plants that are particularly responsive to the sun, following its movement across the sky. He also gives the example of plants that are similarly responsive to the moon. Tithymal, a plant in the Euphorbia family, follows the sun even when the sun is hidden by fog. The flowers of the acacia open at sunrise and close at sunset as does the Egyptian lotus and the common sunflower. The nightshade behaves in the same way toward the moon.

He gives examples of plants that have an affinity or an aversion to each other. Grapevines don't thrive next to cabbages but do well with olive trees. *Ranunculus* is a good companion for water lilies. The herb rue grows well with fig trees. But the shoots of the Mexican pomegranate repel each other violently when cut into pieces. This demonstrates the powerful aversion that can exist even between parts of the same organism.

Kircher attributes every human emotion to changes in a person's magnetic condition. Anger, jealousy, friendship, love, and hate, all result from fluctuations in the magnetic field generated inside human beings and constantly flowing from them. Love is one of the most volatile feelings and as a result it has many aspects. These include spiritual love, the love a mother feels for her child, the love an artist feels for a particular art form, and love as pure friendship. These aspects of love are seen when the magnetic fields of compatible people interact. The magnetism of pure love creates everything. Ordinary sexual love is electricity and Kircher calls it *amor febris species* or the fever of species. There are two forms of magnetic attraction: affection and fixation. Affection is wholesome and natural. Fixation is unwholesome and unnatural. The poisonous toad induces fixation in its prey just by opening its mouth. A passing reptile or insect will rush into the toad's mouth to its death. The boa constrictor uses its breath to fixate deer and other smaller animals compelling them to come within reach. The electric ray or torpedo fish can repel a man's arm with an electric shock causing temporary numbness. For a man to use this kind of power to do good, he needs three things: 1) a selfless soul, 2) strong will and fertile imagination, 3) a subject less forceful than himself, otherwise the subject will be able to resist. Free from worldly desires, a man can cure the most 'incurable' diseases and may even develop clairvoyance.

As described above, a universal attraction binds all planetary bodies and everything associated with them (organic and inorganic). An interesting example of this force of attraction is described in a book called *A New Historical Relation of the Kingdom of Siam (Du Royaume de Siam)*. The book was written in the 17th Century by the French ambassador to Siam, Simon de la Loubère. It contains a description of his travels and an official report to the King of France about his impressions of the country. De la Loubère writes, 'In Siam there are two species of freshwater fish called the Pal-out and Pla-cadi fish. First they are salted and then put whole in a pot to pickle. The pot's contents appear to follow the ebb and flow of the tide exactly. The level rises at high tide and sinks when the tide is low.' De la Loubère experimented at length with this fish, helped by M. Vincent, a provincial doctor.[2] Vincent confirms that this phenomenon is true even though it was originally dismissed as nothing more than a myth. This universal attraction is so powerful that it affected the fish even when they were rotten and disintegrating.

Developing countries are especially helpful in understanding what ancient philosophers called the 'world's soul.' They are the best places to explore its nature and observe the effects of its subtle power.

Anyone interested in psychic phenomena will find plenty to satisfy their curiosity in the East or on the vast plains of Africa. It's only here that so much psychic activity freely occurs. The reason is obvious. In industrialized regions the atmosphere is badly polluted by smoke and fumes from factories, steam engines, railroads, and steam boats. And it is particularly marred by the environmental impact of overpopulation. Just like a human being, nature must have the right conditions to function normally. Nature can be easily disrupted and the interaction of natural forces obstructed in any affected region. This is not only true of climate. Daily occult influences also have an effect. They alter man's physical and psychic nature. They even change the makeup of what is usually regarded as inorganic matter to an extent not fully realized by European science. *The London Medical and Surgical Journal* advises surgeons not to carry surgical knives to Calcutta because 'English steel could not tolerate the Indian climate.' After 24 hours in Egypt, English or American keys will be completely covered with rust. Meanwhile objects made from local steel remain unoxidized. A Siberian shaman from the Chukchi peninsula[3] can demonstrate incredible occult powers among his own people but if he comes to smoky, foggy London, often he loses some of those powers completely. A human being is bound to be more sensitive to changes in climate than a piece of steel. The shaman may not be able to do as much in London or Paris but it makes no sense to dismiss eyewitness accounts of the powers he has shown in his own country. And it would be rash to dismiss shamanism entirely. In his lecture *The Lost Arts* the American abolitionist Wendell Phillips acknowledges that the quality of human psychic ability is affected by changes of climate. He goes on to prove that people from the Far East have heightened physical senses compared with Europeans. He refers to the fabric dyers from the French city of Lyon who are acknowledged as the most skilful in the world. He says they 'have a theory that there is a certain shade of blue so delicate that Europeans cannot see it . . . In Kashmir there are young women who make shawls worth $30,000 each. They can show 300 different colors to a fabric dyer from Lyon. Not only will he be unable to manufacture any of them, he won't even be able to discern the difference between them.' If the physical senses of two races can be so vastly different then their psychic abilities could be equally dissimilar. A young Kashmiri woman is able to see a color that a

European can't. Because the color is imperceptible to the European, it is effectively non-existent to him. It seems logical to suggest that someone with second sight might see their visions as clearly as the young Kashmiri woman is able to see different colors. The images associated with second sight may not be hallucinations or the products of imagination. They may be reflections of real things and real people recorded in the astral ether. This is the explanation given in the *Chaldean Oracles* and the conclusion reached by contemporary thinkers like the English scientist Charles Babbage, the English logician William Jevons, and Peter Guthrie Tait and Balfour Stewart.

Paracelsus teaches that 'human beings are driven by three inner spirits. The influence of these spirits emanates from three different realms, different aspects of a single unified source of creation. The first spirit is the spirit of the elements (the physical body and brute life force). The second is the spirit of the stars (the astral body - the soul). The third is the divine spirit (or the Augoeides as it was called by the Neo-Platonists).' The human body is made of 'primeval earth-stuff' (as Paracelsus puts it) so it's reasonable to accept the modern scientific view that 'the processes of life are purely physical and chemical.' Science corroborates the beliefs of the ancient philosophers and the Bible that man is made of dust and will return to dust. But it's important to remember as Longfellow writes in his poem 'A Psalm of Life':

> *Dust thou art, to dust returnest,*
> *Was not spoken of the soul.*

A human being is a little world - a microcosm inside the vastness of the universe. The three inner spirits suspend the human being like a fetus in the matrix of the macrocosmos. The physical body exists in harmony with the earth and the astral soul exists in unison with the non-physical *anima mundi*. The human being is in the *anima mundi* and the *anima mundi* is in the human being. The *anima mundi* permeates the world. It fills all space and is space itself. It is shoreless and infinite. The divine in the human being - the third spirit - is a ray originating from the infinite. It is one of countless rays emanating directly from the highest cause - the spiritual light of the world. This is the trinity of organic and inorganic nature - the spiritual and the physical, which are three in one. The Greek philosopher Proclus describes this trinity, saying, 'The first monad, or discrete consciousness, is the eternal God. The second is eternity. The third is the paradigm or pattern of the universe.' The three monads together make up the intelligible triad. Everything in the observable universe is the product of this triad and is itself a microcosm of the triad. The elements of the triad move eternally around the spiritual sun just as planets orbit their stars. Pythagoras described the monad as living 'in solitude and darkness.' It may exist on earth as something intangible and undetected by experimental science. But the whole universe will still be gravitating around it as it did from the 'beginning of time.' Every second, humanity approaches a singular moment in eternity when its spiritual sight will be able to detect the invisible presence. The organic atom began as intangible spirit. It became material through the process of involution and will return to intangibility through the same process. Evolution drives matter onwards for millions of years and through many different stages before producing its final creation - the last link in the chain of involution and evolution. This final creation will free itself of matter entirely reassuming the same spiritual form as God. When this happens, the organic atom will have completed its journey and the sons of God will once more 'shout for joy' at the return of the pilgrim.

Van Helmont says, 'Man is the mirror of the universe and his triple nature stands in relationship to all things.' The Creator's spiritual power brought everything into existence and set it in motion. This power is shared by all living things. Because man is more spiritual than other animals, he has the largest share of the Creator's power. He will be able to use this power with more or less success depending on the degree of his spiritual awareness. The power is also in every inorganic atom. Man uses it throughout his whole life whether consciously or not. When he uses the full force of his power consciously he will be in control. He will be able to influence and guide the *magnale magnum* or universal soul. This is not the case with animals, plants, minerals and even the average person. In these instances, the *magnale magnum* is undirected and influences them independently. Every being on earth is made from the *magnale magnum* and connected to it. But man has a dual spiritual power and is bound to heaven. In *Works (Opera Omnia)*, van Helmont writes that this power is 'not just in the physical man but is also found in animals to a degree. Perhaps it exists in everything since everything in the universe is interrelated. The ancients were absolutely right when they observed that at the very least God is in all things. The spiritual force in the inner man must be awakened and brought into consciousness in the outer man . . . And if this spiritual force is described as magic power, it will only terrify simple folk. But it can also be described as true spiritual strength. And it is this that exists in the inner man. Because the inner and outer man are connected, this spiritual strength must be spread throughout the whole man.'

In *A New Historical Relation of the Kingdom of Siam* Simon de la Loubère gives an account of the religious rites, monastic life and superstitions of the Siamese people. He describes the Talapoin[4] or Buddhist monks and their remarkable power over wild animals.

He writes, 'The Talapoin spend weeks in the woods under a small awning of branches and palm leaves, and never make a fire in the night to scare away the wild animals, as all other people do who travel through the woods in this country.' People think it's a miracle that no Talapoin is ever attacked. The area is inhabited by large numbers of tigers, elephants and rhinoceroses but these seem docile around the Talapoin. Travelers hidden at a safe distance have often seen these animals lick the hands and feet of a sleeping monk. De la Loubère says of the monks, 'They all use magic and believe everything in nature has a soul. They believe in protective spirits.' But de la Loubère is most startled by the Siamese people's belief 'that the physical body continues in spiritual form after death.' He continues, 'During the Mongol rule of China, the Chinese would be forced to shave their heads. Many chose to die rather than go into the next world to meet their ancestors without hair. They imagined that shaving their heads in this life meant the heads of their souls would be shaved in the next!' De la Loubère considers this to be 'the most outrageous thing about this absurd belief. People in the Far East think the soul is shaped like the human body rather than anything else.' De la Loubère says nothing about what shape these people should think the soul takes. He simply vents his anger on the 'savages.' Finally, he attacks the memory of the King of Siam's father. He criticizes him for foolishly spending over two million pounds looking for the philosopher's stone. 'People think the Chinese are so wise but for three or four thousand years they have believed in the existence of the philosopher's stone and searched for it. They regard it as a magic bullet that will enable them to escape death itself. Their ideas are based on naive tradition - legend has it that a small number of people have made gold and lived for a very long time. Many people in South-East Asia believe these stories to be true. The stories describe some individuals who can make themselves absolutely immortal and others who can only die as a result of violence or accident. Because of this tradition some people who live simply as hermits are given the name 'immortals.' These so-called immortals are credited with exceptional knowledge.'

Descartes firmly believed that the philosopher's stone existed. If he could obtain it, he thought he could live for at least 500 years. If Descartes could hold this belief in a nation as advanced as France, it seems reasonable that the people of South-East Asia should be allowed to believe the same thing. The great mysteries of life and death have still not been solved by western scientists. They hold many different opinions about the cause of something even as simple as sleep. How then are they in any position to define the limits of the possible or determine what is impossible?

Throughout history, thinkers have claimed that music has a beneficial effect on certain diseases, especially mental health disorders. Kircher recommends the use of music based on direct personal experience of its effectiveness. He gives a detailed description of the musical instrument used in his own treatment. It was a harmonica consisting of five thin glass tumblers in a row. Two of them contained two different kinds of wine, the third contained brandy, the fourth contained oil and the fifth, water. He produced five different tones by rubbing his finger on the edge of each tumbler. Sound has an attractive property. The musical wave draws disease to it. The disease and the wave blend together and dissipate in space. The Greek physician Asclepiades employed music in the same way 2,000 years ago, using a trumpet to treat sciatica. The trumpet's sustained sound made the nerve fibers palpitate and this caused the pain to subside. Similarly, the Greek philosopher Democritus maintained that many diseases could be cured using a flute. Mesmer used the harmonica described by

Kircher for his own magnetic cures. Many medical schools regarded certain diseases as incurable including epilepsy, impotence, insanity, leg injuries, swelling and very high temperatures. The Scottish physician William Maxwell offered to prove to a number of these schools that he could cure those conditions using magnetism.

These examples are likely to remind most people of the exorcism in the first book of Samuel. An evil spirit sent from God possesses the Hebrew king Saul. 'Whenever the spirit from God came on Saul, David would take up his lyre and play. Then relief would come to Saul; he would feel better, and the evil spirit would leave him.'

In his book *On Magnetic Medicine*, Maxwell puts forward the following propositions which are identical to the ideas of the alchemists and Kabbalists:

'What's known as the 'world soul' is a living thing like fire. It is spiritual, fleeting, substanceless and as other-worldly as light itself. It is a life-spirit which is everywhere and uniform . . . Everything is dead matter until this spirit brings it to life. It gives everything its particular character. It is found freely in nature and anyone who understands how to align their body to it has a priceless treasure.'

'This spirit links every part of the world and lives through and in everything.'

'Anyone who knows how to direct this universal life-spirit becomes invincible.'

'If you can take advantage of this spirit and focus it on a particular object you will be able to perform magic.'

'Anyone who knows how to affect a person with this universal spirit knows how to heal. This healing can take place at any distance.'

'Anyone who can use the universal life-spirit to energize their own individual spirit can live forever.'

'Spirits flow and blend together even when they are far apart. In this blending the rays of one body stream eternally and constantly into another.'

Maxwell concludes, 'For now, it's safer not to talk about these things because they can all too easily be horribly abused.'

For example, here are some of the ways mediums abuse mesmeric and magnetic powers in so-called healing.

In healing, either the patient must have faith or the healer must be in excellent health and strong willed. If people expect to get well and believe it strongly enough they can cure themselves of almost any condition. People use different means to focus their belief: a saint's tomb, a holy relic, a lucky charm, a piece of paper or cloth touched by a healer, a potion, a confession or ritual, the laying on of hands or chanting. What really matters is the person's character and imagination. In thousands of cases a doctor, priest or holy relic has been credited with healing when it was actually the patient's own will that produced the cure. The Bible describes a woman who had been bleeding for twelve years. She pushed through the crowd to touch Jesus' robe believing it would cure her. Jesus told her that her faith had made her well. The power of mind over body has produced miracles throughout history.

In *The Occult Sciences* Eusèbe Salverte writes, 'Many surprising, sudden, and uncanny cures have been produced by imagination. Medical history is full of examples that could easily be taken for miracles.'

But what if the patient has no faith? Suppose he is physically weak but mentally receptive and the healer is strong, healthy, positive and determined. Then the healer can use his will to eradicate the disease completely. Consciously or unconsciously, the healer's will reinforces itself by drawing on the universal spirit of nature. The healer is then able to restore balance to the patient's aura. He may use a crucifix to enhance the effect - like Johann Gassner, the Catholic priest and exorcist from Klösterle. He may lay on hands and project his 'will' - like the French soldier Auguste Jacob known as 'Le Zouave,' or the celebrated American healer James Rogers Newton (who healed thousands of sufferers), and many others. Or he may heal using the power of words - like Jesus and some of the Apostles. In each case the process is the same.

In all of these examples the healing is genuine and dramatic without any side effects. But if healing is attempted by someone who is ill, it will fail and often the illness will be transferred to the patient. What's left of the patient's strength will also disappear. In the first Book of Kings, the Bible tells the story of King David who drew strength in old age from the energy of a young woman called Abishag. Medical journals describe the case of an old woman from Bath, England who rejuvenated herself by consuming the youthful energy of two young women, one after the other. Like some ancient healers, Paracelsus cured diseases by applying a mineral or vegetable medicine with appropriate energetic properties. Paracelsus outlines this theory explicitly in his writings. A healer in anything less than perfect health will not be able to cure a disease, only displace it. This holds true whether the healer is a medium or not. The patient will think he has been cured but the disease will soon reappear somewhere else.

But what happens if the healer is corrupt? The consequences may be even more unpredictable because a physical disease is easier to cure than moral corruption. In the 18th and 19th Centuries, French children and religious pilgrims experienced religious fervor, convulsions and prophecy. The convulsions spread among children in the French towns of Cevennes and Morzine[5] and among members of the Jansenist religious sect[6] in Paris. To this day, the phenomenon is still a mystery to physiologists and psychologists alike. If the power of prophecy, hysteria and convulsions can spread like an infection, what else might be contagious? A corrupt healer transfers elements of his corrupt nature to the patient, who now becomes a victim. The healer's energetic touch is destructive. His presence is damaging. The patient is completely vulnerable because of his receptiveness. The healer transfixes him just as a snake transfixes a helpless bird. A 'healing medium' of this kind can cause untold harm - and there are hundreds of them.

That said, there are genuine spiritual healers who have become world famous despite the attacks of biased critics. These include the parish priest of Ars, Jean-Baptiste-Marie Vianney, (known as the Curé d'Ars), Auguste Jacob, and James Rogers Newton. Further genuine healers include Johann Gassner and the Irish healer Valentine Greatrakes. Several of Greatrakes' cases were authenticated in 1670 by Robert Boyle, the President of the Royal Society of London. Two centuries later a different president of the Royal Society would probably have sent Greatrakes to a mental hospital along with all other healers or someone like the British zoologist Ray Lankester might have 'summoned him' under the Vagrancy Act for 'practicing palmistry on the public.'

A list of cases of genuine healing could go on forever. The important point is this: everyone, from Pythagoras to Eliphas Levi, is of the same opinion - magical power is never held by people who are inherently corrupt. Only someone spiritually pure can 'see God' or possess spiritual abilities. Only they can heal and connect with spiritual forces safely. Only they can provide spiritual peace to others. The power of healing does not come from an evil place, just as grapes don't grow on brambles and figs don't grow on thistles. Ultimately 'there is nothing supernatural about magic.' It is a science. Even exorcism was simply a branch of that science studied closely by the initiates. In *Antiquities of the Jews* the Roman historian Titus Flavius Josephus writes, 'Exorcism is a healing science, beneficial to mankind.'

These examples show that the ancient wisdom is preferable to more recent theories about communication between worlds and man's occult powers. Spiritual phenomena that manifest physically prompt scientific investigation and this may be their real value. They also help to support the belief in the soul's survival after death. That said, it is difficult to tell whether these phenomena are doing more harm than good in the current climate. Many people are anxious for proof of immortality and will believe anything. As the American author Harriet Beecher Stowe put it, 'Fanatics are ruled by imagination rather than judgment.'

Modern spiritualists claim a variety of psychic abilities. Apparently, telling the difference between true and false spirits isn't one of them. In his pamphlet *The Diakka and their Earthly Victims*, the famous American spiritualist Andrew Jackson Davis describes deceitful spirits called the Diakka[7] who inhabit a spiritual realm in space called Summerland. He writes, 'A Diakka is crazy about role-playing, trickery and pretending to be what he is not. To a Diakka, prayer and blasphemy are the same. He is crazy about telling wild stories and lies. He has no morality, no sense of justice, philanthropy or kindness. He has never felt gratitude. Love and hate are the same to him. His motto is often terrifying to other people: *Life is nothing more than self-interest and its aim is delicious destruction.* Only yesterday, a Diakka deceived a medium into thinking he was the Swedish mystic Emanuel Swedenborg. He said to her, 'I am the god of whatever is, has been, will be or may be. An individual life is only the sum total of the ghosts of fragments of thought rushing headlong into the heart of eternal death!'

The works of the philosopher Porphyry have been dismissed

by one particularly hostile materialist as 'moldering like all other antiquated trash in the closets of oblivion.' Nevertheless, Porphyry gives a striking account of the spirits, later referred to as Diakka by Andrew Jackson Davis. Porphyry says, 'Every kind of sorcery is made possible with the help of these bad demons. They are responsible for it. People who practice black magic venerate these demons, especially their leader. These spirits spend their time deceiving people with cheap tricks and illusions. They want to be mistaken for gods and their leader wants to be seen as the supreme god.'

The Diakka, who impersonated Swedenborg and claimed to be God, bears a striking resemblance to Porphyry's demon king.

The Syrian philosopher Iamblichus was an exponent of theurgy or ancient magical practice. He said no one should attempt to produce spiritualist phenomena without a long period of moral and physical preparation. And he maintains that this preparation should be overseen by experienced theurgists. It's no wonder then that some mediums denounce theurgy violently. Iamblichus makes matters worse when he writes, for a person 'to appear elongated or thicker, or be borne aloft in the air,' is almost invariably a sign of demonic possession.

Timing is everything. However self-evident a truth may be, it won't be accepted unless the timing is right. The American scientist Josiah Cooke said, 'The age must be prepared.' 30 years ago, the book you are reading now would never have seen the light of day. Despite daily exposés and ridicule, the evidence for modern spiritualist phenomena continues to grow stronger. Prominent scientists now acknowledge these phenomena and what would have seemed unbelievable 20 years ago may be accepted today as fact.

Epes Sargent, the author from Boston, Massachusetts, is perhaps the most highly regarded of all present-day spiritualist writers. He is widely admired for his honesty and expertise. His book *The Proof Palpable of Immortality* is considered to be one of the best works on the subject. He is sympathetic to mediums and their work. However, he still feels the need to ask, 'If spirits can reproduce likenesses of the dead, it begs the question - how can we be sure of any spirit's identity, whatever tests we use? We don't yet understand enough to answer this question properly . . . The way these materialized spirits behave and communicate is still a mystery.' Sargent is a reliable judge of the intelligence of spirits that produce spiritualist phenomena. He says, 'The majority are not that clever.' Why are they are so lacking in intelligence if they are, in fact, human spirits? Either intelligent human spirits cannot materialize or the spirits that do materialize don't have human intelligence. Therefore, according to Sargent, they must be 'elementary' spirits that are no longer human or, alternatively, demons described by the Persian Magi and Plato as halfway between gods and disembodied men.

There is plenty of evidence from William Crookes and other researchers that many 'materialized' spirits have a clearly audible voice. On the other hand, evidence from the ancients indicates that human spirits do not have voices in the usual sense. According to Swedenborg, the spirit voice is like 'a rushing breath.' Is it better to believe the ancients or modern spiritualists? The ancients had the experience of many ages of magical practice whereas modern spiritualists have had none at all. Spiritualists rely on information communicated to them by 'spirits' but they have no way of proving who these spirits really are. Many mediums have produced hundreds of manifestations in 'human' form. But none of them has ever expressed anything out of the ordinary. This ought to make even the most ardent spiritualist suspicious. For sake of argument, suppose spirits really can speak and it is just as easy for intelligent and unintelligent ones to make themselves heard. Surely what is sometimes said should be as clever as the messages received through 'direct writing?' In *The Proof Palpable of Immortality* Epes Sargent asks this important question, 'Does the process of manifestation limit a spirit's intellectual capabilities and memories or is the determining factor the intellectual ability of the medium?' The same kind of spirits communicate through a medium in two different ways - either by materializing or through direct writing. Why does the first way produce nonsense while the second produces sublime philosophical prose? If the medium's intellectual ability limits the intellectual capabilities of the spirit, why is it more true in the case of manifestation than direct writing? As far as it's possible to tell, materializing mediums are no more uneducated than many spiritually gifted peasants and mechanics. Under the influence of the supernatural, many uneducated people have communicated profound and sublime ideas. The history of psychism is full of examples that illustrate this point. Jakob Boehme, a simple German shoemaker, shared his vision of the spiritual structure of the world in his book *Aurora*. Andrew Jackson Davis, an uneducated American from Poughkeepsie, dictated his book of cosmology *A Voice to Mankind* while in a trance. There are also many examples of people with learning difficulties (sometimes described as 'idiots savants') expressing spiritual wisdom. These include the convulsive religious fervor experienced by the children of Cevennes, and the poets and seers described in previous chapters. Once spirits have the power of speech, they ought to be able to talk with the same intelligence as the people they are assumed to be. Instead they drone on using nothing but banal clichés. Epes Sargent remarks hopefully that 'the science of spiritualism is still in its infancy and we can hope that more light will be shed on this question.' But it is doubtful that the answers he is looking for will ever come from spiritualism's 'spirit cabinets.'

It's ridiculous to expect everyone investigating the phenomena of spiritualism to have a master's degree. The past 40 years have shown that the most 'scientifically trained' minds are not always the best at using common sense or grasping the truth. Dogma and bias blind people to the truth. Take the example of oriental magic or ancient and modern spiritualism. Thousands of reliable witnesses have returned from living or traveling in the East. They confirm that fakirs, sheiks, dervishes, and lamas produced miracles without any accomplice or apparatus. They claim that these miracles contradict the known laws of science, proving the existence of hidden natural powers that are seemingly directed by a superhuman intelligence. What is the attitude of the scientific establishment toward this subject? How far has scientific evidence changed the establishment's view? Has its skepticism been shaken by the investigations of Hare and de Morgan, Crookes and Wallace, de Gasparin and Thury, Wagner and Butlerov etc? How did the establishment judge the personal experiences of Louis Jacolliot with the fakirs of India or the psychical explanations of Maximilian Perty, Professor of Zoology at Bern? Mankind craves evidence of a God, an individual soul and eternal life. How does this affect the establishment and what is its response? They discount spirituality but don't offer anything in its place. They say, 'We can't find God with retorts and flasks, so God must be a delusion!' In the scientific age, even the Church has to look to science for help. Beliefs based on shaky evidence collapse under scrutiny and discredit genuine religious truths in the process. But nevertheless human beings still hope for evidence of a God and an afterlife. Scientific argument simply can't stop human beings wanting to believe in God. Science itself has poisoned the pure waters of simple faith. Now humanity sees itself reflected in water clouded by mud churned up from the bottom of the once pure spring. An anthropomorphic God is replaced by anthropomorphic monsters. Worse still, God is replaced by the reflection of humanity itself in waters that send back distorted images of truth and facts. The English Unitarian minister Brooke Herford writes, 'We don't want a miracle, we want to find concrete evidence of the spiritual and the divine. People look to scientists for this evidence rather than prophets. They feel that exhaustive scientific investigation should reveal the deep underlying facts of all things. Science should be able to produce some unmistakable signs of God.' The signs are there, and the scientists too - what more can we expect of them, now that they have done their job so well? They have dragged God down from His hiding place, and given us a protoplasm instead.

At a meeting of the British Association in Edinburgh in 1871, the Scottish physicist William Thomson said, 'Science is honor-bound to confront every reasonable problem put before it.' On the same subject, Thomas Huxley says, 'Regarding the question of miracles, it's my opinion that every mystery must have a scientific explanation.' The great Prussian naturalist Friedrich Humboldt remarks that 'dogmatic skepticism is, in some ways, worse than simple credulity.'

None of these men practices what he preaches. Not one of them took up the opportunity to investigate phenomena that travelers claim to have witnessed in the East. This is despite the fact that it is now easier to travel to the East than ever before. None of them took the opportunity to settle the fundamental question of whether or not miracles actually occur. Europe and America's academicians were never going to travel to Tibet and India together and investigate the mystery of the fakirs! And if one of them had gone alone and seen countless miracles, none of his colleagues would have believed him on his return.

According to Alfred Russel Wallace and William Howitt, the French and English Academies have made a huge number of errors because of their dogmatic skepticism. Why would anyone believe that science is infallible when there are so many examples to the contrary? In 1828, the French geologist Ami Boué excavated a fossil from the banks of the Rhine. His colleague Georges Cuvier questioned its authenticity, refusing to believe that human skeletons could be found 80 feet deep in the mud of the river. In 1846, the French archeologist Jacques de Perthes discovered flint implements in the gravels of the Somme valley. In his opinion they had been worked by early humans, proving the existence of man in pre-history. The French Academy of Sciences dismissed de Perthes' ideas until 1860 when he was vindicated by the discovery of large numbers of flint weapons in the same region. In 1825, the Irish priest John MacEnery said he had discovered worked flints in Kent's Cavern together with the remains of extinct animals. He was laughed at. 15 years later, the English geologist Robert Godwin-Austen claimed to have made a similar discovery in south-east Devonshire and was ridiculed even more. In 1865, the scientific establishment's skepticism and ridicule were shown to be completely misplaced. Alfred Russel Wallace summed up the situation saying, 'The hypotheses of the previous 40 years were confirmed and the reality of the findings was even more sensational than predicted.' Given these examples, why would anyone be surprised by the short-sightedness of scientists and the inflexibility of modern science?

Over and over again, what was once thought to be the truth has had to be revised. Scientists are constantly frustrated by their own lack of knowledge. 'Hardly anything is known about psychism,' concedes one Fellow of the Royal Society. 'We have to accept how little we really know about physiology,' says another.

'Of all the sciences, medicine still has the most unanswered questions,' reluctantly admits a third. 'We know nothing as yet about nervous fluids - they are still only hypothetical,' adds a fourth. It's the same story in every branch of science. Meanwhile there are phenomena that are more interesting than anything occurring naturally. But to understand them requires knowledge of physiology, psychism, and the 'hypothetical' nervous fluids. These phenomena are either dismissed as fantasy or, if they are accepted, they simply 'do not interest' serious scientists. But this is not the worst of it. For example, when someone with powerful, natural occult abilities (like the British medium Francis Ward Monck) agrees to take part in a study, he is tricked by a so-called scientist and ends up serving three months in prison. This is not exactly promising.

The *Dictionarium Britannicum*, compiled by Nathan Bailey in 1731, describes a perpetual lamp found burning in a tomb during the reign of the 16th-century pope, Paul III. Legend has it that the Romans used liquid gold to keep lights burning endlessly in their tombs. According to the dictionary, this was the case in the tomb of Cicero's daughter Tulliola, or Tullia, even though it had been sealed for 1,550 years. Someone today would struggle to believe this 140-year-old story, which was derived from an even older source. As for scientists, they have every right to discount such stories, ignoring the evidence of all the ancient and medieval philosophers, until they have proven the possibility of perpetual combustion for themselves. The same is true when it comes to stories of fakirs buried alive but still living when exhumed 30 days later, or reports of lamas fatally wounding themselves, displaying their innards to the people present, then healing themselves almost instantaneously.

Some people refuse to believe the evidence of their own eyes, even when phenomena occur in their own country and in front of many witnesses. References in classical literature and even the eyewitness accounts of travelers seem ridiculous to them. What is harder to understand is the attitude of the scientific academies and their flat refusal to engage with these accounts. History shows that the academies are often mistaken in thinking these accounts 'confuse things by the use of words in the absence of knowledge.' Like God speaking to Job 'out of the storm,' magic can say to modern science: 'Where were you when I laid the earth's foundation? Tell me, if you understand! Who are you to dare to say to nature, *This far you may come and no farther; here is where your proud waves halt?*'

It doesn't matter if the academies accept paranormal phenomena or not. However skeptical academicians may be, they can't prevent them from happening all over the world. Fakirs will still be buried alive and survive the experience to the amazement of European travelers. Lamas and Hindu ascetics will still wound, mutilate and even disembowel themselves without harm. The cynicism of the whole world will not be enough to snuff out the lamps burning perpetually in certain subterranean crypts in India, Tibet and Japan. The clergyman Samuel Mateer of the London Mission mentions one of these lamps in his book *The Land of Charity*. He writes about Travancore's temple of Trevandrum in southern India as follows: 'Year after year immense riches are thrown into a deep well inside the temple, and in another place, in a hollow covered by a stone, a great golden lamp, lit over 120 years ago, still continues burning.' Catholic missionaries describe these lamps as the work of the Devil. More cautiously, Protestant ministers mention their existence but offer no explanations. The French Catholic missionary Abbé Huc has seen and examined one of these lamps. So have other people who were lucky enough to win the trust of eastern lamas and holy men. Now the existence of phenomena like these can't be denied - for example, the British orientalist William Lane has described wonders of Egyptian magic, astrology and alchemy. The French author Louis Jacolliot and the British Major General Charles Napier have both encountered the supernatural in Benares. Multiple witnesses have seen human beings levitate in broad daylight. Levitations like these have been verified by both William Crookes and Maximilian Perty. Perty describes them taking place in the open air and sometimes lasting as long as 20 minutes. All of these phenomena and many more occur in every country of the world. They will continue to occur in spite of all the skeptics and scientists who have ever evolved out of the Silurian mud.

Many people find the ideas in alchemy hard to accept, the perpetual lamp being no exception. But the author of this book has seen one. It's fair to ask: how can you tell that the lamp is perpetual if you have only observed it for a limited period of time? The author could reply: 'I know the materials used, how the lamps are constructed and the physics of how they work. I am confident that if you look in the right place, there's plenty of evidence that supports my claim to have seen one. My critics will have to work out for themselves where to look and who to ask, just as I did. In the meantime, I'll quote some of the 173 reliable sources on the subject. As far as I can remember, none of these sources has ever claimed that the lamps burn perpetually. They've only said that they burn for countless years and there are records of lamps that have remained alight for many centuries. If a lamp can be made to burn unattended for ten years, there's no reason why it can't be made to burn for a hundred or a thousand years.'

According to many well-respected people, there are lamps that would have burned forever had they not been inadvertently put out or accidentally broken. These reliable authorities include: the Christian theologian Clement of Alexandria, the Italian scholars Ermolao Barbaro and Giambattista della Porta, the Greek historian Appian of Alexandria, the Italian Egyptologist Tito Burattini, the French physician François Citois, the Roman historian Lucius Coelius Antipater, the writers Sebastián Fox Morcillo and Jacobonus, the Italian physician Giovanni Costeo, the Italian historian Joannes Casalius, the Byzantine historian George Kedrenos, the Jesuit theologian Martin Delrio, the Roman consul Aulus Hirtius, the Swiss naturalist Konrad von Gesner, the Bishop of Seville Leander, the German alchemist Andreas Libavius, the Austrian humanist Wolfgang Lazius, the Italian philosophers Pico della Mirandola and Fortunio Liceti, the Italian authors Simone Majoli and Bernadinus Scardeonius, the Italian philologist Francesco Maturanzio, the Spanish humanist Juan Luis Vives, the Italian historians Guido Panciroli and Raffaello Maffei, the Italian polymath Girolamo Ruscelli, Paracelsus, several Arabian alchemists, and finally, the Latin compiler Gaius Julius Solinus, Athanasius Kircher, Pliny, and the German bishop Albertus Magnus.

The perpetual lamp is thought to have been discovered in ancient Egypt where chemistry was already a highly developed science. The use of these lamps was more widespread here than anywhere else because of the Egyptians' religious beliefs. During the 3,000 year-long cycle of reincarnation, the astral soul of the mummy was thought to remain close to the physical body. It was attached by a magnetic thread which only it could break. The Egyptians regarded the ever-burning lamp as a symbol of the incorruptible and immortal spirit. They hoped it would encourage the soul to abandon the body and unite forever with its divine self. This is why the rich had perpetual lamps placed in their crypts.

The lamps are also often found in catacombs. Fortunio Liceti wrote extensively on the subject in *On the Mystery of Ancient Lamps* (*De Lucernis Antiquorum Reconditis*). According to Liceti, whenever a burial vault was opened, a burning lamp was found inside but went out instantly because the tomb had been disturbed. Burattini and the Egyptian lexicographer Michael Schatta wrote letters to Athanasius Kircher confirming that they found many lamps in the subterranean caves of Memphis, the ancient Egyptian capital. The Greek geographer Pausanias describes the golden lamp in the temple of Minerva at Athens. He says it was made by the sculptor Callimachus and burned for a whole year. Plutarch reports that he saw one in the Temple of Jupiter Amun[8] in ancient Libya. He says the priests assured him that it had burned continually for years in spite of being stood out in the open, exposed to the elements. Saint Augustine describes a perpetual lamp in a Temple of Venus[9] unaffected by the strongest winds or even water. George Kedrenos says a lamp was found at Edessa in Upper Mesopotamia 'hidden at the top of a certain gate and burning for 500 years.' But perhaps the most miraculous lamp of all is the one associated with Olybius, a wealthy citizen of Padua. It was found near Ateste, and Bernadinus Scardeonius gives a vivid description of it: 'A burning lamp was discovered inside an earthenware urn, contained inside an even larger urn. The lamp had continued to burn for 1500 years, fueled by liquids contained in two bottles. One of the bottles contained liquid gold, the other liquid silver. These are currently the prized possessions of Francesco Maturanzio.'

If perpetual lamps really did exist in the past, were the lamps that burned in Christian shrines different from the lamps on the altars of Jupiter, Minerva and other Pagan gods? According to certain theologians, the lamps in Christian shrines were fueled by divine power whereas the lamps dedicated to Pagan gods were fueled by the work of the Devil. Kircher and Liceti agree that all lamps fall into one of these two categories. The lamp at Antioch burned for 1500 years over the door of a church. It was sustained by the 'power of God' and it is God who 'has made an infinite number of stars burn with perpetual light.' But according to Saint Augustine, Pagan lamps were the work of the Devil 'who deceives us in a thousand ways'. Christians during the papacy of Paul III believed it was Satan who produced a flash of light or a bright flame when a burial chamber was opened. They believed this was the case with a certain tomb in the Appian Way in Rome. Inside was the body of a young girl immersed in a bright liquid. The liquid had preserved her body so well that the face was still beautiful and lifelike. A lamp burned at her feet but went out as soon as the tomb was opened. Engravings in the tomb suggested that the girl was indeed Tullia, Cicero's daughter.

According to modern chemistry and physics, a lamp cannot burn perpetually. The lamp's fuel is used up as it turns into vapor and smoke. The flame cannot be perpetual because it must eventually run out of fuel. On the other hand, alchemists reject the idea that all of the lamp's fuel must inevitably turn into vapor. They claim there are certain elements in nature that are resistant to fire. They are not consumed by it and cannot be extinguished by wind or water. In *The Art of Embalming* the English surgeon Thomas Greenhill dismisses the claims of various alchemists. He refuses to accept that any fire can burn forever but is half-inclined to believe that a lamp could burn for several centuries. Alchemists devoted years to experimenting with perpetual fire. They came to the conclusion that a perpetual flame is possible and left behind a wealth of evidence to support their claim.

There are particular preparations of gold, silver, mercury, naphtha, petroleum, and other bituminous oils that alchemists list for use in perpetual lamps. They also list oil of camphor and amber, several forms of asbestos and the related mineral asbestine. They recommend a preparation of molten gold or silver, indicating that gold is preferable because it is the most stable when heated or melted. In addition, gold will reabsorb its own vapor as soon as it's produced, continuing to feed the flame. According to the Kabbalists, Moses learned the secret from the Egyptians and the lamp ordered by God to burn on the tabernacle was perpetual. The Book of Exodus 27:20 includes the lines: 'Command the people of Israel to bring you pure oil of pressed olives for the light, to keep the lamps burning always.'

Liceti suggests these lamps were not made of metal but on page 44 of *On the Mystery of Ancient Lamps*, he describes lamps made of quicksilver filtered seven times through white sand. Both Francesco Maturanzio and Franciscus Citesius believe that the same degree of purification can be achieved through a chemical process alone. Alchemists knew this preparation of quicksilver by a variety of names, including Aqua Mercurialis, Materia Metallorum, Perpetua Dispositio, Materia Prima Artis, and Oleum Vitri. The Germans Johannes Trithemius (abbot and occultist) and Bartholomäus Korndörffer (alchemist) also made fuel for perpetual lamps and published their formulas.

The word 'asbestos' comes from the ancient Greek ἄσβεστος, meaning 'unquenchable' or 'inextinguishable.' Pliny and Solinus describe it as a kind of stone that cannot be put out once set alight. The German saint Albertus Magnus describes it as an iron-colored stone found mostly in Arabia. It is usually covered in an almost invisible film of oil which will catch fire immediately if it comes into contact with a naked flame. In the past, chemists made many attempts to isolate this oil without success. But is it beyond the reach of modern chemistry? If this oil could be obtained, there's no doubt it would provide a viable perpetual fuel. The ancients claimed to be able to extract it and this is not unreasonable since present-day researchers have achieved the same. In previous unsuccessful attempts, chemists extracted a fluid that was more like water than oil and was so contaminated that it would not burn. Others found that the oil became thick and viscous on exposure to air. When it was lit, it produced no flame, only copious dark smoke. By comparison, the lamps made by the ancients are said to have burned with a pure bright flame and produced no smoke at all. Kircher demonstrates that it is possible to purify the oil but it is so difficult that only alchemy's greatest experts are capable of it.

Saint Augustine claims all of this is the work of that Christian scapegoat, the Devil. Juan Luis Vives disagrees. In his commentary on Saint Augustine's *City of God (De Civitate Dei)*, he maintains that what may seem magical and miraculous is really man-made, based on a deep understanding of the laws of nature. The Italian scholar Tommaso Porcacchi describes seeing both flax and linen made out of asbestos. He was shown these materials at the house of Podocattarus, a Cypriot knight. Pliny calls this flax *linum vinum* and 'Indian flax,' and says it is made out of *asbeston* or *asbestinum*. He says this kind of flax was used to make cloth which was then cleaned by setting it alight. He adds that it was as precious as pearls and diamonds because it was very rare and difficult to weave as the threads were so short. First it is beaten flat with a hammer, then it is soaked in warm water. When dry, its filaments can be easily divided into threads and, like flax, woven into cloth. Pliny says he has seen towels made of it and helped in the process of purifying them by fire. Giambattista della Porta says he was shown similar towels in Venice by a Cypriot woman. He calls this material one of the supreme secrets of alchemy.

In 1681, the English botanist Nehemiah Grew catalogued the Royal Society's collection of human, animal and mineral specimens held at Gresham College in London. On the subject of asbestos, he wrote that the ancients were able to make fireproof sheets from it but the technique was now thought lost. It seems this is not quite the case. The museum in Milan founded by the Italian collector Manfredo Settala held thread, ropes, paper and netting made of asbestos as late as 1726. According to Greenhill's *The Art of Embalming*, some of these items were made by Settala himself. Greenhill goes on to write, 'Grew doesn't distinguish between different types of asbestos, calling them all thrum-stone.' He says thrum-stone grows in short threads or thrums from about a quarter of an inch to an inch in length. The fibers grow parallel and glossy and as fine as a single thread of silk. They are very flexible like flax or tow (flax fibers prepared for spinning). The technique cannot have been lost entirely given that the cloth is still in use in some Buddhist convents in China and Tibet. The author has seen a Buddhist nun's yellow gown thrown into a large pit of glowing coals. It's impossible to say for sure if it was made of asbestos but when it was taken out of the fire pit two hours later, it was as clean as if it had been washed with soap and water.

In present-day Europe and America, asbestos has been rigorously assessed as a fire-proof material. Its industrial applications include roofing, fire-proof clothing and safes. A particularly valuable deposit is found on Staten Island in New York. There it occurs in bundles like dry wood with fibers several feet in length. The finest asbestos was given the name αμόλυντος (undefiled) by the ancients because it was white and lustrous like satin.

The ancients made wicks for perpetual lamps using asbestos from the city of Carystus.[10] The citizens of Carystus made no secret of the craft of working with asbestos. In his commentary on the Roman poet Martial, the Jesuit historian Matthew Rader wrote that the citizens 'combed, spun, and wove this fibrous stone into cloaks, table linen and similar things. When these items needed washing, they were cleaned with fire instead of water.' In his description of Athens, Pausanias confirms that the wicks of perpetual lamps were made from Carystian asbestos. Plutarch agrees in his essay *On the Failure of Oracles (De Defectu Oraculorum)* but adds that the technique had been lost by the time of writing. Liceti believes the perpetual lamps in ancient tombs had no wicks at all since so few have been found. Vives disagrees, saying he has seen a number of them.

In addition, Liceti believes a 'fuel exists with such a finely balanced composition that it lasts for aeons of time. This fuel does not combust in the usual way but resists the destructive force of the fire. Equally the fire is unable to consume the fuel but is held in check by the fuel as if chained down and unable to break free.' In his book *Vulgar Errors*, the English polymath Thomas Browne describes even small lamps that have burned for hundreds of years. He writes that the perpetual flame 'depends on the purity of the oil which ensures the lamps never soot up. If the flame needed air to burn, it wouldn't have lasted more than a few minutes.' But he adds, 'The method for preparing this inexhaustible oil is lost.'

This is not quite true, as time will tell. But the world isn't ready yet to accept this idea and others like it.

The scientific method is based exclusively on observation and experiment. And humanity has 3,000 years of recorded observation demonstrating man's occult powers. More recently, modern spiritualist phenomena have provided ample opportunity for scientific scrutiny. In 1869, the London Dialectical Society invited various scientists to investigate spiritualism. The society's

Report on Spiritualism noted how they responded. Thomas Huxley wrote, 'I don't have time for an inquiry like this. It'll be a lot of trouble and, unless it's very different from previous inquiries, it'll also cause a lot of grief . . . I have no interest in the subject . . . Even supposing the phenomena are real, they still don't interest me.' The English philosopher George H. Lewes offers this insight: 'When any man says that phenomena are produced by no known physical laws, he is implying that he knows of other laws capable of producing the phenomena.' John Tyndall suggested any seance he attended was unlikely to be successful. Tyndall's presence, according to the engineer C. F. Varley, was enough to throw everything into confusion. William Carpenter writes, 'I have proved to my own satisfaction that a great number of so-called spiritual manifestations are examples of deliberate fraud or self-deception. But there are some phenomena which are quite genuine and are legitimate subjects for scientific study . . . these phenomena are not the result of communication with another spiritual realm but depend on the suggestibility of the individual. This is determined by the individual's physiology in ways that are now well understood . . . I have called this 'unconscious cerebration' (or group hallucination) and it plays a large part in spiritualist phenomena.'

So, 'unconscious cerebration' is how modern science explains guitars flying in the air and furniture performing tricks!

Science in America hasn't done much better. In 1857, a Harvard University committee warned members of the public against investigating spiritualism, saying it 'corrupts the morals and degrades the intellect.' In addition, they called it, 'a contaminating influence, which lessens the truth of man and the purity of woman.' Despite the reluctance of his peers, the chemist Robert Hare went on to investigate spiritualism. When he started taking it seriously, he was labeled delusional. In 1874, one of the New York daily papers published an open letter to American scientists inviting them to investigate spiritualism and offering to pay their expenses. Like the guests in the Parable of the Great Banquet, 'they all began to make excuses.'

Nevertheless, many leading scientists have investigated the topic and been convinced by the overwhelming evidence. All this regardless of Huxley's indifference, Tyndall's jokes and Carpenter's 'unconscious cerebration.' And John Draper, a noted scientist and author but not a spiritualist, has this to say in *History of the Conflict Between Religion and Science*: 'Throughout history and in every European country, people have believed that the spirits of the dead sometimes revisit the living or haunt their former homes. This is a belief shared by both intellectuals and ordinary country folk. If eyewitness accounts are accepted as reliable evidence, then extensive and reliable proof has existed since earliest memory.'

Unfortunately, a hardened skeptic won't change his mind whatever the evidence. And like Thomas Huxley, scientists only believe what suits them. As John Milton writes in Paradise Lost:

> *O shame to men! Devil with Devil damn'd*
> *Firm concord holds; men only disagree*
> *Of creatures rational . . .*

Why do men who have had similar educations hold such different views? No two men see the same thing in exactly the same way, as the saying goes. The English homeopath J.J. Garth Wilkinson summed it up well in a letter written to the London Dialectical Society.

'I have extensive experience of working with unconventional ideas that are now becoming accepted. This experience convinces me that nearly all truth is subjective. Discussion and investigation do little more than support a person's subjective position.'

Wilkinson could also have quoted the English philosopher Francis Bacon who said, ' . . . a man who knows a little philosophy is likely to be an atheist but a man with a deeper knowledge of philosophy is more likely to lean toward religion.'

The modern scientific method will accept even the most outlandish theory if there is conclusive evidence to support it. The English physician William Carpenter accepts the importance of a man like Faraday but would be the first to ignore evidence, just as valid, proving the ancients had advanced philosophical and scientific knowledge. The names of Benjamin Franklin and Samuel Morse dominate the study of electricity and electromagnetism today. But as long ago as 600 BC, the Greek philosopher Thales is said to have discovered static electricity, and recent research by the German physicist Johann Schweigger shows that all ancient mythologies were based on a deep understanding of the natural sciences. Schweigger's research indicates that the hidden properties of electricity and magnetism were known to the ancient seers of Samothrace who presided over the earliest Mysteries in recorded history. The Greeks Diodorus Siculus and Herodotus and the Phoenician Sanchuniathon described these Mysteries as originating in the night of time, centuries, probably thousands of years before historical records began. In *Figurative Art from Antiquity, Greek, Etruscan and Roman (Monuments Inédits d'Antiquité Figurée, Grecque, Étrusque et Romaine)*, the French archeologist Désiré Raoul-Rochette reproduces an image of figures with hair streaming out in every direction. This remarkable picture, thought to be a scene from the Cabeirian Mysteries,[11] is one of the best proofs that the ancients knew about electricity and magnetism. The power issues from the central figure of Demeter, the goddess of the harvest. She is one of only two figures who are unaffected - the other is a kneeling man. According to Schweigger, the picture shows part of an ancient initiation ceremony. But it is only recently that modern physics text books have been illustrated with similar images - heads with hair standing on end due to static electricity. Schweigger shows that the most important religious ceremonies drew on an ancient understanding of physics which is now lost. He demonstrates that magic played a part in the Mysteries of prehistory. He shows that the so-called miracles of Pagan, Jewish and Christian tradition were in fact the product of secrets known only to the ancient priesthood - knowledge of physics and alchemy.

Classical literature reveals that the priests in the sanctuaries were well acquainted with electricity and even lightning conductors long before the siege of Troy.

Schweigger and Ennemoser were able to learn a great deal from the ancient magicians' knowledge of magnetism even without understanding its occult aspects. They have been able to equate the mythological twins of Castor and Pollux (the Dioscuri) with the twin poles of electricity and magnetism. The Dioscuri were previously regarded as nothing more than myths but are now recognized as revealing important scientific truths. As Ennemoser puts it in *History of Magic Volume II*, these myths are now seen to be 'the cleverest and deepest expressions of scientific fact.'

Physicists are quick to congratulate each other on their achievements. With a few minor changes, their lectures could be turned into poetry. They are the modern equivalents of Petrarch, Dante and Torquato Tasso. They could give Medieval troubadours a run for their money. Regarding matter as the be-all and end-all, they sing the praises of atoms and protoplasms as they merge and combine. They moan about the unpredictability of forces in the great drama of life they call 'the correlation of forces.' They declare matter to be the one and only queen of the infinite universe. They insist on divorcing her from her consort, spirit, and place her alone on the great throne of nature. Now they try to build her up, burning incense and worshiping at the shrine they've made for her. But without spirit this throne is nothing but a tomb. Everything inside is rotten and corrupt. Matter without spirit is nothing but a soulless corpse. It is nothing more than the physical residue of spirit or, to use the Hermetic phrase, its 'gross purgation.' The limbs of a soulless corpse can only move if there is an intelligence operating the great galvanic battery called life!

In what way is modern knowledge superior to the knowledge held by the ancients? The word 'knowledge' is used here to mean the deepest possible understanding of life itself - not the complex, convoluted explanations of science - not merely labeling everything as in modern education. Knowledge is more than learning a term for every nerve and artery in the body or simply remembering the name of every component in plant structure.

Even the greatest ancient philosophers are now regarded as limited. This is because they had only a superficial understanding of topics that modern science has explored in detail. Plato is criticized for his ignorance of human anatomy and the function of the nervous system, and for basing his understanding of human physiology on little more than guesswork. He simply generalized about the different parts of the human body, describing nothing resembling anatomical facts. He believed that the structure of the body reflected the structure of the universe, that the microcosm reflected the macrocosm. His ideas are too transcendental to be taken seriously by modern scientists. According to Plato, the human form, like the form of the universe, is made up of triangles. This idea seems ridiculous to many of his translators with the exception of the English theologian Benjamin Jowett. In his introduction to Plato's *Timaeus*, Jowett points out that the modern physicist 'won't admit his modern theories rest on the shoulders of long-dead predecessors.' Physicists forget how much the metaphysics of the past has contributed to the physics of the present. Instead of criticizing the lack of scientific terms in Plato's work, it's better to analyze it closely. For example, the *Timaeus* alone contains traces of important scientific discoveries to come. It contains references to the circulation of the blood and the force of gravity, though the circulation is not described clearly enough to satisfy modern science. According to Jowett, Plato did not know that the blood flows out of the heart through the arteries and returns through the veins. But he did understand 'that blood is a fluid in constant motion.'

He began with universal truths and, like the method used by the geometers, he worked backwards to gain insight into particular examples. While modern science focuses its search for a first cause on the molecular level, Plato looked outwards to the planets. To grasp the overall scheme of creation was enough for him. It was enough to be able to follow the movement of worlds. The ancient philosophers paid little attention to the details classified so painstakingly by modern scientists. A school boy can talk more knowledgeably about trivial scientific facts than Plato himself. But Plato's least able student could say more about the interrelation between the great cosmic laws than any university professor. Plato's student would also understand the occult forces behind cosmic laws and how to control them.

None of Plato's translators grasped this idea about him, which explains how modern thinkers are able to feel so superior. Allegedly the ancient philosophers made mistakes in anatomy and physiology. These mistakes are exaggerated to suit modern man's sense of self-importance. In convincing ourselves that our own knowledge is superior, we lose sight of the intellectual splendor of past ages, much like magnifying sunspots until they eclipse the sun itself.

Science has labeled minerals, plants, animals, and human beings in minute detail but even the best teachers are unable to explain the forces that drive evolution. This illustrates the limitations of modern scientific research. To corroborate this idea, it's necessary to look no further than orthodox science itself.

It takes moral courage for a leading scientist to recognize the scientific knowledge of the ancient world. This is particularly true when public opinion prefers to regard the ancients as primitive. When a scientist speaks up, it's something to be admired. Take, for example, Benjamin Jowett, Master of Balliol College and Regius Professor of Greek, Oxford. In his introduction to the *Timaeus*, he writes, 'To do justice to the subject we should consider the physical philosophy of the ancients as a whole. We should remember, 1. The early physicists adopted the nebular theory that the stars and planets were formed from interstellar dust.' (John Draper suggests this theory was based on Frederick Herschel's astronomical observations but this clearly can't have been the case.) '2. As early as the 6th Century BC, the Greek philosopher Anaximenes of Miletus maintained animal life on land evolved from amphibians, and man evolved from animals.' Jowett could have added that this theory probably predated Anaximenes by several thousand years and was also accepted by the Chaldeans. He might also have added that the origin of Darwin's evolutionary theory predates the Flood. '3. Philolaus and the early Pythagoreans believed the earth was a celestial body like the other stars spinning in space.' According to the German scholar Johann Reuchlin, Galileo could have had sight of fragments of Pythagoras' work. In addition, Galileo was familiar with the ideas of the ancient philosophers. Consequently, when he suggested that the earth orbits the sun, he was simply restating an astronomical theory that had existed long before in India. '4. The ancients theorized that there were different sexes in plants as well as animals.' Modern naturalists only needed to look to the past for this insight. '5. The ancient philosophers understood that musical notes depended on the relative length or tension of the vibrating strings. They knew that different notes were related to each other mathematically. 6. They believed the world was governed by the laws of mathematics and even qualitative differences were numerical in origin. 7. They believed that matter could not be destroyed, only transformed.' Jowett concludes, 'One of these discoveries might have been a lucky guess, but they can't all be put down to coincidence.'

In conclusion, Plato's philosophy was about order, method and proportion. It dealt with the evolution of worlds and species, and the principle that matter and energy are interchangeable and cannot be created or destroyed. It accounted for the transmutation of one material into another (like the transmutation of base metal into gold). Its explanation of the indestructible nature of matter and spirit was more advanced than any theory offered by modern science. The concept of indestructibility firmly underpinned Plato's entire philosophical system. Modern science has supposedly made great advances. If we understand the laws of nature so much better than the ancients, why is it we still don't have answers about the nature of life and its origins? If modern research is so effective, why are advances only made in directions that were already well explored before the time of Christ? How come modern knowledge only extends as far as the achievements of much earlier researchers?

If modern thinking is so advanced, why can't it match the lost knowledge of the ancients? Why can't it replicate the colorfast pigments used in the Luxor Temple?[12] Its walls were decorated with Tyrian purple, bright vermilion and dazzling blue and remained as bright as the day they were painted. Why can't modern science reproduce the indestructible cement used in the pyramids and ancient aqueducts or a blade made of Damascus steel[13] which can be twisted without snapping? Why can't it match the gorgeous, unparalleled colors of stained glass found in ancient cathedrals or recover the secret of malleable glass? Chemists in the early Middle Ages had certain skills that modern chemistry cannot match. Why do modern chemists claim to have discovered things that were probably first discovered thousands of years before? Mounting evidence from archeology and the study of language suggests that the ancients were highly advanced. Previously they had been regarded as blinkered by ignorance and superstition simply, perhaps, because they lived so long ago.

It should be remembered that long before Christopher Columbus, Phoenician vessels had circumnavigated the globe and spread civilization across the world. Who can say for certain that the same people who created the pyramids in Egypt, the Karnak temples,[14] and thousands of ruins along the Nile, didn't also create Angkor Wat[15] in Cambodia? Who's to say they didn't also write the hieroglyphics in the ancient settlement in British Columbia discovered by the Marquess of Dufferin? Or even those on the Mayan ruins of Palenque[16] and Uxmal?[17] Museums are full of exhibits that evoke ancient civilizations and the lost skills of their craftsmen. These exhibits prove that scientific knowledge disappears when nations and continents are lost. From medieval alchemists to modern scientists, no one has been able to rediscover that lost knowledge and probably no one will - in this century at least.

John Draper admits that the ancients 'had some knowledge of optics and lenses.' Other scientists are less generous and won't even admit that much. In *History of the Conflict Between Religion and*

Science Draper writes, 'The convex lens found in the Assyrian city, Nimrud,[18] shows that the ancients were familiar with magnifying instruments.' If this weren't the case, it would make liars of many classical authors. It would mean Cicero is being wildly deceitful when he claims to have seen the entire *Iliad* written on a piece of vellum so small it could fit inside a nutshell. It would mean Pliny is deliberately misleading when he describes Nero using a ring that held a magnifying glass to watch distant gladiators. In his lecture 'The Lost Arts' Wendell Phillips describes a Sicilian pirate called Mauritius. From Sicily, Mauritius could see all the way to the coast of Africa using an instrument called a 'nauscopite.' Either all of the above witnesses were lying or the ancients must have been very well acquainted with optics and magnifying glasses.

In the same lecture, Wendell Phillips describes an extraordinary ring belonging to a friend. The ring is 'perhaps three quarters of an inch in diameter, and on it is the naked figure of the god Hercules. With a magnifying glass, it's possible to see the interlacing muscles and every hair of the eyebrows . . . The English orientalist Henry Rawlinson brought home a stone about 20 inches long and ten wide, containing an entire mathematical thesis. It would be totally illegible without a magnifying glass . . . In Henry Abbott's Egyptian museum, there is a ring of Cheops dated 500 BC by the German scholar Christian von Bunsen. The signet of the ring is about a quarter of the size of a dollar coin and the engraving is invisible to the naked eye . . . In Parma, there is a ring that once belonged to Michelangelo. On it is a 2,000 year-old engraving of seven women. Without a powerful magnifying glass it's impossible to make out anything at all . . .' Wendell Phillips adds, 'Rather than being a modern invention, the microscope's earliest prototypes date from Biblical times.'

These examples show that the ancients had much more than

merely 'some knowledge of optics and lenses.' Although the American historian John Fiske is critical of Draper, really Draper's only fault is emphasizing aspects of history according to his personal bias. For example, Draper stresses the atheism of Bruno while minimizing the knowledge of the ancients.

It's admirable how theologians and scientists attempt to separate fact from fiction in ancient writings. But it means nothing is accepted without an accompanying note of caution. They believe the Greek geographer Strabo when he estimates the circumference of the ancient city of Nineveh at 47 miles. But it's a different story when he vouches for the accuracy of the Sibylline Oracles.[19] Although Herodotus is known as the 'Father of History,' his eyewitness accounts of miraculous events are dismissed. Perhaps this caution is justified more than ever now that the 19th Century has been called the Century of Discovery. The actual truth may prove extremely difficult for Europe to accept. The English philosopher Roger Bacon and the German alchemist Berthold Schwarz have long been credited with the invention of gunpowder. But now, every schoolchild knows that the Chinese used it for leveling hills and blasting rock, centuries before Bacon and Schwarz. According to Draper: 'In the Musaeum of Alexandria there was a machine invented circa 100 BC by the Greek mathematician Hero. It was steam driven and resembled what would now be called a reaction steam turbine . . . The modern steam engine wasn't an original invention.' Europe is proud of the discoveries made by Copernicus and Galileo. But now it's clear that the Chaldeans had far more comprehensive astronomical records stretching back to within a hundred years of the Flood, and the Flood occurred at least 10,000 years ago according to Christian von Bunsen. In addition, more than 2,000 BC (long before Moses), a Chinese emperor executed his two chief astronomers for failing to predict an eclipse of the sun.

Matter and energy are interchangeable and cannot be created or destroyed. The discovery of this principle is regarded as one of the greatest achievements of modern science. William Armstrong, president of the British Association for the Advancement of Science, described it as 'the most important discovery of the present century.' But this is a misconception - this 'important discovery' is really no discovery after all. Traces of it are evident in the work of the ancient philosophers. But its true origins are lost in the dense shadows of prehistory. The first traces of it can be found in Vedic theology. The idea is expressed in the doctrine of emanation and absorption otherwise known as nirvana. The principle is outlined by the Irish theologian John Eriugena in *The Division of Nature (De Divisione Naturae)*, published in the 8th Century. Anyone looking for the truth should read this book. The Greek philosopher Democritus was the first person to suggest that atoms are indestructible. When the theory was discovered by modern science, it was extended to include force. Just as no atom can be destroyed, no force simply vanishes into thin air. Force, just like matter, was shown to be indestructible. Different forces were shown to be transmutable and the difference between forces was shown to be a difference in the way atoms move. Consequently, the principle of the correlation of forces was rediscovered. As early as 1842, the Welsh scientist William Grove theorized that forces like heat, electricity, magnetism, and light could convert into one another. They were capable of being at one moment a cause and the next moment an effect. But where do these forces come from and where do they go when they disappear from view? Science offers no answers.

Many people regard the correlation of forces as 'the greatest modern scientific discovery' but the theory still doesn't explain how forces arise or what causes them to come into being in the first place. Forces may convert into one another but science is still unable to explain the phenomenon in its entirety. In what way is modern thought more advanced than Plato? In the *Timaeus*, Plato discusses the subjective and objective characteristics of matter and the limits of human intellect. His message is: 'Only God knows for certain the essential nature of things. The most man can hope for is to know what things probably are.' Any of Thomas Huxley's or John Tyndall's pamphlets say much the same thing. Huxley and Tyndall then go one step further than Plato, excluding the idea of a god who knows more than they do. And perhaps it's on this basis that they claim to be superior. The ancient Hindu belief system of emanation and absorption is clearly based on the correlation of forces. The To Ov ('the supreme being' or God in Greek) is the primordial point in the boundless circle 'whose circumference is nowhere, and the center is everywhere.' Everything emanates from it, and manifests in the visible universe in many different forms. Those forms interact and mix together. Gradually they transform from pure spirit ('pure nothing' or 'non-existence' in Buddhism) into physical matter. Then they begin to withdraw and gradually re-enter into their primitive state. This primitive state is the absorption into Nirvana. What else is all of this but the correlation of forces?

Science has shown that heat can be used to generate electricity, electricity can be used to create heat, and magnetism will produce electricity and vice versa. According to science, once something is in motion, it will go on forever until stopped by a counteracting motion. These are also the fundamentals of occultism and the earliest alchemy. Now that the indestructibility of matter and force has been discovered and proved, the great problem of eternity is finally solved. Why do we need to worry about spirit anymore now that it's been scientifically proven to be useless!

Modern scientists are no more advanced than the priests of Samothrace, the Hindus, and even the Christian Gnostics. This is wonderfully illustrated by the German physicist Johann Schweigger and his interpretation of the classical myth of the Dioscuri or 'the sons of heaven.' Schweigger sees the twin brothers Castor and Pollux as symbols of the electric poles, 'who constantly die and return to life together' and 'it is absolutely necessary that one should die so that the other may live.' Like Schweigger, the ancient priests knew full well that when a force seems to have disappeared it has simply been converted into a different one. Archeologists have not discovered any ancient apparatus for converting forces - nevertheless it's perfectly reasonable to make the following deductions: nearly all ancient religions were based on the indestructibility of matter and force. Nearly all of them referred to the emanation of everything from a single ethereal, spiritual fire or central sun. This central sun is God or spirit, and ancient nature magic, or theurgy, is based on an understanding of that spirit's limitless potential to create.

In his treatise *On Hieratic Art (De Arte Hieratica)* Proclus gives the following account: 'The feeling between lovers evolves from simple physical attraction to an attraction between the lovers' inner divine spirits. In much the same way, the ancient priests created a sacred science based on mutual sympathy and similarity. They recognized that the elements of nature had a certain alliance and sympathy to each other. They realized the same sympathy linked the visible world to hidden powers. They discovered that all things are interconnected and rely on one another and these discoveries were the basis of their science. They recognized the higher in the lower and the lower in the higher. They recognized that earthly properties occurred in the rest of the universe, exerting an influence over earthly affairs and they saw that, equally, the properties of the universe existed on earth in a terrestrial form.'

Proclus goes on to discuss the way plants, minerals, and animals respond to the sun. This is familiar to modern naturalists but so far unexplained. For example, he discusses the rotary motion of the sunflower and the heliotrope as they follow the sun's path from east to west. He describes the lotus flower, its petals closed before dawn, expanding gradually as the sun rises and closing again as the sun sets. He discusses the nature of sun and lunar stones, and the mineral called *helioselenus* (a stone that responds to sun and moon equally). He refers to the way the cock crows at dawn and the lion roars at sunrise and sunset. Proclus continues, 'The ancients contemplated this mutual sympathy between celestial and terrestrial things, and applied it for occult purposes, on both the celestial and earthly planes. Through their understanding of this similarity, they were able to perceive the presence of the divine in the material world . . . Everything contains a spark of the divine. Everything on earth is permeated by the celestial and the celestial is permeated in turn by an even greater divine essence. Everything develops gradually as the divine spark descends from the highest spiritual planes to the densest physical realm. Whatever kind of spiritual material exists on the higher planes, it spreads out as it descends to the physical world so that various souls are distributed according to a divine rule or hierarchy.'

Clearly Proclus is not talking here about superstition, but science. Even though it's an occult practice, ignored by the mainstream, magic is still a science. It is based on the interplay between organic and inorganic forms - between the invisible forces of the universe and the mineral, plant, animal and human kingdoms. What science calls gravitation, the ancients and the medieval Hermeticists called magnetism, attraction, affinity. Plato understood it to be a universal law. In the *Timaeus*, he described it firstly as the attraction of smaller bodies to larger ones and secondly as the attraction of similar sized bodies to each other. In the second case, the attraction is due to magnetism rather than gravitation. There is a theory, contrary to Aristotle's view, that gravity causes all bodies to descend at an equal rate, regardless of their weight, and when different bodies appear to fall at different speeds, this is caused by some other unknown force. This theory points to magnetism instead of gravitation as the underlying cause, given that magnetic attraction is dependent on what a body is made of, not what it weighs. The basis of magic was and is a thorough familiarity with nature's occult properties both visible and invisible; an understanding of the relationship between these occult properties, how they attract and repel; recognizing that the cause of these relationships is the all-pervading spiritual principle which animates everything and the ability to create the optimum conditions for this spiritual principle to appear. In other words, the basis of magic is a deep and exhaustive knowledge of natural law.

In 1873, the English astronomer Richard Proctor published *The Borderland of Science* which included 'Notes on Ghosts and Goblins.' Proctor examines stories about the existence of spiritual phenomena contributed by Augustus de Morgan, Alfred Russel Wallace, and the American spiritualist author Robert Dale Owen. When it comes to Owen's supernatural story, Wallace provides a defense of it which Proctor describes as unconvincing. Wallace's defense goes as follows: 'How is such evidence as this refuted or explained away? Hundreds of equally proven facts are on record but no attempt is made to explain them. They are simply ignored and in many cases, it is agreed that there is no explanation for them at all.' Proctor adds playfully, 'Science decided long ago that these ghost stories are all delusions and can simply be ignored. But scientists worry that fresh evidence will be found and fresh converts will be made. They worry that some of these converts will have the nerve to ask for a retrial on the grounds that the original verdict did not take into account this new evidence.'

Proctor continues, 'All this shows exactly why the 'converts' shouldn't be ridiculed for their belief. But scientists will need a good reason before they devote their time to the retrial suggested above. They need to be shown that the wellbeing of the human race is at stake even though all paranormal activity recorded so far has been trivial, and even converts admit as much!'

The English spiritualist Emma Hardinge Britten has collected examples from both secular and scientific journals showing how those papers avoid the tricky subject of 'ghosts and goblins' and pursue more 'serious questions' instead. She quotes a report, published in a Washington paper, from a meeting held on 29 April 1854 by the American Scientific Association. The chemist Robert Hare 'was bullied into silence' by Professor Joseph Henry the moment he touched on the subject of spiritualism. It's important to note that Hare was universally respected for his character and for his contribution to science. Emma Hardinge Britten writes, 'This poor behavior from a member of the 'American Scientific Association' was accepted by the other members present and later endorsed by the Association as a whole in its report.' The following morning, the *Spiritual Telegraph* reported the incident as follows:

'The topic (presented by Hare) was entirely appropriate for scientific investigation. But the American Association for the Promotion of Science decided either it wasn't worth considering or that taking it seriously posed a risk to the Association's reputation. Either way, they voted not to debate it . . . Instead the

Association held a very scholarly, sophisticated and profound discussion on why roosters crow between midnight and 1 a.m.' This was clearly an excellent topic for scientific investigation and essential to 'the wellbeing of the human race!'

Anyone will be made a laughing stock if they say they believe in a mysterious connection between certain plants and human beings. But there are many cases proving that this type of connection does exist. People have fallen ill when a tree, planted on the day they were born, was uprooted. And when the tree died, they died. The reverse has also been known to happen where a person has fallen ill and the tree has withered and died simultaneously. Richard Proctor would explain the first example as an 'effect of the imagination' and would attribute the second example to a 'curious coincidence.'

In his essay 'On Manners and Customs,' Max Müller describes cases like this in Central America, India, and Germany. He traces the tradition throughout Europe and finds examples in British Guyana, in Asia, and among Maori warriors. The English anthropologist Edward Tylor collected several examples in his book *Researches into the Early History of Mankind and the Development of Civilization*. Müller reviewed Tylor's work saying if the tradition 'occurred only in Indian and German folk tales, it could be seen as a particular trait of ancient Aryan mythology. But we also find it in Central America. Either European settlers must have passed the folk tale on to native American storytellers or there is, in fact, a genuine connection between the life of plants and the life of man.'

The present generation have been raised as materialists, only believing in what they can see and touch. No doubt they would struggle to accept the idea of a mysterious connection between plants, animals, and even stones. Their inner sight is obscured and they can only see what's in front of them. Hermes Trismegistus explains this tendency in his dialogue *Asclepius*: 'It's a sad fact that divinity has left mankind so that nothing about the divine is heard or believed, and every divine voice is necessarily silenced.' Or, as the Emperor Julian puts it, the skeptic's 'little soul is undoubtedly perceptive but sees nothing of real importance.'

We are halfway through an evolutionary cycle and in a state of transition. The universe progresses intellectually in cycles and Plato states that every cycle includes fertile and barren periods. The influences of the different elements are always in perfect harmony with divine nature. But on the physical plane, their proximity to the earth has a negative effect on aspects of them. They become polluted with earthly matter (matter being the domain of evil). Consequently, as Plato puts it: 'Sometimes parts of the elements work with divine nature and sometimes they work against it.' The universal ether contains every element. When the circulations within it take place in harmony with divine spirit, earth and everything on it enters a fertile period. Eliphas Levi calls these circulations in the ether 'currents of the astral light.' The occult powers of plants, animals, and minerals connect mysteriously with 'higher' cosmic influences, while the divine soul of man is perfectly aligned with 'lower' earthly influences. But during barren periods, the plants, animals and minerals lose their mysterious connection; the majority of people lose their spiritual sight and they no longer have any sense of the power of their divine spirit. We are in a barren period. Skepticism broke out like a malignant fever in the 18th Century. In the 19th Century it has taken hold like a hereditary disease. It is as if the divine intellect in man is blindfolded. He considers the world with only his animal brain.

Magic was once a universal science administrated by the high priests of antiquity. Knowledge of magic was jealously guarded by the priesthood but its influence inspired the whole of mankind.

This accounts for the extraordinary similarity of 'superstitions,' customs and traditions. The same popular proverbs are repeated all around the world. Exactly the same ideas appear in the folklore of Tartars and Laplanders, the people of southern Europe, the inhabitants of the Russian steppes, and the indigenous peoples of north and south America. For instance, Edward Tylor cites the example of a Pythagorean maxim, 'Do not stir the fire with a sword.' This saying is popular in a number of nations without the slightest connection to each other. Tylor also quotes the Italian diplomat Giovanni da Pian del Carpine, who, as far back as 1246, identified this same tradition among the Tartars. No amount of money would convince a Tartar to stick a knife or any other sharp instrument into a fire for fear of cutting 'the fire's head.'

The people of the Kamchatka Peninsula[20] in the Russian Far East consider this a terrible thing to do. The Sioux Indians of North America will not touch fire with anything sharp. The Kalmucks have a similar tradition; and an Ethiopian would rather bury his arms in blazing coals than use a knife or axe near them. Tylor labels all of these examples as 'simply curious coincidences.' But Max Müller notes that the same Pythagorean idea lies behind them all.

Like most ancient maxims, the sayings of Pythagoras have a dual meaning. Each sentence has its literal meaning and also embodies a moral idea. This is explained by Iamblichus in his *Protrepticus*. For example, according to Iamblichus, 'dig not fire with a sword,' is the ninth Pythagorean symbol. He writes, 'This symbol advises caution.' It shows 'it's best not to use sharp words with a man full of fiery anger - it's better to avoid an argument. If you use the wrong words you'll provoke an ignorant man's rage and the person who'll suffer most is you . . . The philosopher Heraclitus also notes the wisdom of this symbol. He says, 'It's very difficult not to give in to anger. But whatever you can do to avoid it is good for the soul.' People who give in to anger corrupt their souls so badly that death is preferable to life. But by holding your tongue, friendship can come from strife. The fire of anger can be put out and you will appear wise to others.'

The present author has asked herself sometimes, is she being fair? Does she have the right to criticize the work of leading scientists like John Tyndall, Thomas Huxley, William Carpenter or the English philosopher Herbert Spencer? She respects the 'men of old' - the ancient sages - so much that she may not always give modern science credit where it is due. These concerns went away when she read a number of well-written magazine articles published in periodicals around the country. These reassured her that she was simply echoing public opinion. For example, an article called 'Our Sensational Present Day Philosophers' appeared in the *National Quarterly Review* in December 1875. It scrutinizes the new discoveries scientists claim to have made about the nature of matter, the human soul, the mind, the universe and how the universe came into existence etc. The author of the article writes, 'The work of men like Spencer, Tyndall, Huxley, Proctor and others has brought modern science into conflict with religion.' He acknowledges the importance of their work but refuses to accept that they have made any original discoveries. Even their most advanced theories contain nothing that was not known and taught in one form or another thousands of years ago. He writes, 'Scientists put forward their theories and the newspapers fill in the gaps, implying they are modern discoveries . . . The public don't have the time or the interest to check the facts. They believe what the newspapers tell them . . . and wonder what will come next! . . . The hapless scientists are attacked by the Church. Sometimes they try to defend themselves but they never stand up and say outright, *Don't blame us*

- we are only recycling ideas that are as old as the hills.' This is the simple truth 'but even scientists will let people believe a lie if they think it will secure their place in history.'

Huxley, Tyndall and even Spencer have all been put on a pedestal because of their research into protoplasm, molecular and atomic theory and the origins of life. They have received more accolades for their work than Lucretius, Cicero, Plutarch and Seneca had hairs on their heads. But the works of these earlier Roman and Greek thinkers contain countless references to protoplasm and life's origins while Democritus' work on atomic theory earned him the title 'the atomic philosopher.' The article 'Our Sensational Present Day Philosophers' criticizes Tyndall and Huxley as follows:

'Recent discoveries about the nature of oxygen have astonished the public. In particular, Tyndall and Huxley have caused a stir, simply by quoting ideas previously discovered by the German biochemist Justus von Liebig. As early as 1840, Liebig's most advanced work had been translated into English by the British scientist Lyon Playfair.'

The article continues: 'Another recent theory surprised many members of the public by suggesting that every thought we think produces a change in the substance of the brain. But scientists only have to refer to Liebig's earlier work to find this theory and many others like it. For instance, Liebig states: *The field of physiology provides enough evidence to support the view that every thought, every sensation is accompanied by a change in the composition of the substance of the brain. It is reasonable to suppose that every motion and every action is the result of a transformation of the brain's structure or its substance.'*

In his sensational lectures, Tyndall appropriates Liebig's ideas almost to the letter, as well as the even earlier theories of Democritus and other Pagan philosophers. He presents a mishmash of old hypotheses as modern scientific ideas - all in his famously overblown style.

The article in the *National Quarterly Review* shows that many of the same ideas appear in the work of the 18th-century English philosopher Joseph Priestley, author of *Disquisitions on Matter and Spirit*. The article proves that Tyndall and Huxley's greatest discoveries first appeared in Priestley's *Disquisitions* and even in Johann Gottfried Herder's *Philosophy of History*.

The article continues, 'Because Priestley was discreet about his atheistic views, he was not hounded by the authorities. He was the author of between 70 and 80 books and the discoverer of oxygen.' In his books 'he outlines ideas that have been described as 'startling' and 'bold' when put forward by today's scientists.

'Our readers will remember the stir caused by recent theories about the origin and nature of ideas. But those theories, like all the others, contain nothing new.' In *On the Opinions of Philosophers (De Placitis Philosophorum)* Plutarch writes, 'An idea is a disembodied being. It has no substance itself but shapes matter and brings it into existence.'

It's true to say that no modern atheist, including Thomas Huxley, can outdo Epicurus when it comes to materialism. He can only imitate him. Isn't Huxley's 'protoplasm' simply a rehash of the beliefs held by the Svabhavika School of Buddhism[21] or the pantheists? Both groups maintain that all things, gods as well as men and animals, come from 'Svabhava' or their own essential nature. In his poem *On the Nature of Things (De Rerum Natura)*, Lucretius gives the following lines to the philosopher Epicurus: 'Because the soul comes from a material source (is produced within the body), it must be material. It exists only within the body's material system. It is nourished by material food. It grows as the body grows. It matures as the body does and declines with its decay.

Whether it belongs to man or animal, it must die with the body's death.' All the same, it's important to remember that Epicurus is talking about the astral soul, not the divine spirit. If the above is understood correctly, Huxley's idea of 'protoplasm' is very old. It originated in Athens and was conceived by Epicurus.

The author of the article in the *National Quarterly Review* is careful to make his points clearly and not to appear to undervalue the work of modern scientists. He concludes, 'We want to show that anyone who considers himself intelligent should make an effort to remember the 'advanced' thinkers of the past. This is particularly important for anyone involved in any kind of teaching. The result would be less fear, less fraud and, most importantly, less plagiarism.'

The English clergyman Ralph Cudworth is absolutely right when he says the biggest mistake the ancients made, according to so-called modern experts, was believing in the immortality of the soul.

Like Epicurus, scientists are afraid to acknowledge the existence of spirits and apparitions because then, in the words of Cudworth, they must also acknowledge the existence of God. He adds that they'll believe almost anything rather than let God in. On the contrary, the materialists of the ancient world, though they seem skeptical to us now, did let God in. Epicurus rejected the idea of the soul's immortality, but still believed in a God and Democritus wholeheartedly accepted the existence of apparitions. Almost all of the ancient sages believed in the pre-existence of the human spirit and that it had godlike powers. The machagistia (the divine theologic magic of Babylon and Persia) was based on this view of the human spirit. The Byzantine philosophers Gemistus Pletho and Michael Psellus observed that the *Chaldean Oracles* explained and enlarged on this idea further. Far from dismissing the soul's immortality, a great many important thinkers emphasized it: Zoroaster, Pythagoras, Psellus, the Greek philosophers Epicharmus, Empedocles, Plato, and Kebes, the Greek playwright Eurypides, the Greek mathematician Euclid, the Roman philosopher Boëthius, the Roman poet Virgil, the Roman politician Marcus Cicero, the Hellenistic philosophers Philo Judaeus and Plotinus, the Neoplatonist philosophers Iamblichus and Proclus, the Greek theologians Synesius and Origen, and finally, Aristotle himself. Henry More writes in *The Immortality of the Soul* that the Italian philosopher Pietro Pomponazzi is 'no friend to the soul's immortality' but acknowledges the soul's pre-existence nevertheless. He then turns to Pomponazzi's fellow Italian, the philosopher Gerolamo Cardano. According to More, 'Cardano expressly concludes that the rational soul is both a distinct being from the soul of the world, though of the same essence,' and that 'it does pre-exist before it comes into the body.' Ultimately, More calls on the authority of Aristotle, saying that Aristotle was of the same opinion in his treatise *On the Soul (De Anima)*.[22]

Many years have passed since the philosopher and diplomat Joseph de Maistre wrote his philosophical commentary on the human condition, *The St. Petersburg Dialogues (Les Soirées de St. Petersburg.* If his ideas were relevant then they are even more so today. He wrote, 'I have heard and read many good jokes about the ignorance of the ancients and their habit of seeing spirits everywhere. But I think it's us who are the fools for failing to see spirits anywhere.'

Notes

Chapter One

(1) Hermetic, concerning Hermeticism, (also Hermetism). Hermeticism is a religious, philosophical, and esoteric tradition based primarily on writings attributed to Hermes Trismegistus. These writings have greatly influenced the western esoteric tradition and rose to prominence during both the Renaissance and the Reformation. The tradition claims descent from a *prisca theologia*, a single, true theology present in all religions given by God to mankind in antiquity.

(2) The *Phaedrus* by Plato is a dialogue which takes place between Plato's protagonist, Socrates, and Phaedrus, an Athenian aristocrat. It was written c. 370 BC. Although ostensibly about love, the dialogue covers the art of rhetoric, metempsychosis (the Greek tradition of reincarnation) and eroticism.

(3) The Popol Vuh is the sacred book of the K'iche' Indians, descendants of the Mayan people, who live in what is now Guatemala. It contains the K'iche's cosmology, mythology, traditions and history. Popol Vuh means the Book of the People. Blavatsky maintains that the Popol Vuh contains the esoteric history of mankind, including a description of the early 'root races.' Blavatsky states that it parallels the creation accounts of Genesis and the Kabbalah. The mythology of the Popol Vuh consists of four periods, three of which have ended and the fourth of which is current. This may refer to the theosophical idea of 'rounds,' the fourth of which is said to be our current round or it could refer to four of theosophy's root races.

(4) The Kalmucks are a Buddhist people of Mongolian origin. They created the autonomous region known as the Kalmyk Khanate (1630-1724) in Russia's North Caucasus territory. Today they form a majority in the republic of Kalmykia on the western shore of the Caspian Sea.

(5) Knossos, the ancient city on the Greek island of Crete is the location of King Minos' palace. In Greek mythology, Minos had a labyrinth built beneath the palace to conceal his son, the Minotaur.

(6) The Ptolemaic era began in 305 BC when Ptolemy I Soter declared himself pharaoh of Egypt. His family ruled for 275 years, the last dynasty of Ancient Egypt.

(7) The British Museum's Egyptian collection expanded dramatically in 1801 when the British defeated the French at the battle of the Nile. The British were able to acquire many fine examples of Egyptian sculpture but it is alleged that none of these was superior to the wooden statues excavated by Mariette.

(8) The Troad, now called the Biga Peninsula, is situated in the northwestern part of Anatolia, Turkey. It is the location of the ruins of Troy, now a UNESCO world heritage site. It was first excavated by Heinrich Schliemann in 1870.

(9) The Chaldeans were an ethnic group that lived in Mesopotamia, modern day southern Iraq. The Bible contains many references to the Chaldean people. They are associated with the city of Ur and the Biblical patriarch Abraham. Nebuchadnezzar II, king of Babylon, may have been of partial Chaldean descent.

(10) Kabbalah or Kabbala which means 'parallel / corresponding,' or 'received tradition,' is a form of Jewish mysticism. Central to Kabbalah is an illustration of the Tree of Life, a mystical symbol used to describe the path to God. Its ten interconnected spheres represent the ten archetypal numbers of the Pythagorean system.

(11) *The Magicon* is a book of prophecy, full title: *Wonderful Prophecies Concerning Popery And Its Impending Overthrow And Fall, Together With Predictions Relative to America, the End of the World and the Formation of the New Earth; Also, Concerning the True Beginning and Future of the New Church, Called the New Jerusalem.* The book's author, Dr. Paulus, is an obscure figure. Apart from his name nothing further is known. The quote attributed to him by Blavatsky does not appear in the original text of *The Magicon.*

(12) The Musaeum of Alexandria (or Greek 'Mouseion,' meaning 'Seat of the Muses') was a center of classical learning including the famous Library of Alexandria. It was founded c. 280 BC by the Egyptian pharaoh Ptolemy I Soter.

(13) The radiation of spiritual material from God. In theosophy the manifest universe is the product of seven rays that emanate from the 'central spiritual sun' or life source.

(14) Emanationism is a system of thought that maintains all things are derived from a first reality, or first principle.

(15) *Timaeus*, written c. 360 BC, is a Platonic text structured primarily in the form of a monologue by the title character, Timaeus of Locri. The work describes the creation of the world by the demiurge, the divine agent that turns chaos into form.

(16) The Hindu Vedas are a collection of religious texts from ancient India. Written in archaic Sanskrit, they are the oldest of all Hindu scriptures. They are regarded as divine revelations and form the foundation of Hinduism. The Vedas are based on seven major poetic meters, complex syllable patterns which could conceivably form the basis of a mathematical system.

(17) The Aitareya Brahmana is one of the Hindu Brahmanas, commentaries written to aid understanding of the sacred texts, the Vedas. The Aitareya Brahmana comments on the Rigveda, the oldest of the Vedas dealing with cosmology, philosophy and the nature of God.

(18) The Rigveda is an ancient collection of Vedic Sanskrit hymns along with associated commentaries on liturgy, ritual and mystical exegesis. It is one of the four sacred canonical texts of Hinduism known as the Vedas.

(19) The demiurge is a subordinate god responsible for fashioning and maintaining the physical universe. The word comes from Ancient Greek meaning 'craftsman' or 'artisan.' In Plato, the demiurge turns chaos into forms initially conceived in the mind of God.

(20) Tetraktys, HPB: tetractys, is a triangular figure consisting of ten points arranged in four rows: one, two, three, and four points in each row. The Tetractys is a geometrical representation of the fourth triangular number. It was an important mystical symbol in the philosophical school known as Pythagoreanism. The Pythagoreans believed reality was fundamentally mathematical in nature and the Tetractys was a master key to understanding metaphysical and religious truths.

(21) The Serpent Mantra appears in the Aitareya Brahmana commentary on Rigveda V, ch ii, verse 23.

(22) Agnishtoma from Agni, a Sanskrit word meaning fire, which connotes the Vedic fire god of Hinduism.

(23) *Shu-King*, The Book History, is one of the Five Classics of ancient Chinese literature. It is a collection of rhetorical prose attributed to figures of ancient China, and it served as the foundation of Chinese political philosophy for over 2,000 years.

(24) *Shi-King*, The Book of Odes, is the oldest existing collection of Chinese poetry, comprising 305 works dating from the 11th to 7th Centuries BC. It is one of the Five Classics traditionally said to have been compiled by Confucius (551 BC - 479 BC).

(25) The Brahmanas are a collection of ancient Indian texts. They are commentaries written to aid understanding of the four Vedas, the sacred writings of Hinduism.

(26) Brahmin, a member of the highest caste or varna in Hinduism. The Brahmins are the caste from which Hindu priests are drawn.

(27) Gnostics are followers of Gnosticism, a name first coined by the English philosopher Henry

More (1614-1687). The term 'Gnosticism' refers to a variety of ancient religious ideas and systems originating in the 1st and 2nd Centuries AD.

(28) Archeus is the vital force permeating the universe and the source of spiritual energy in the physical world. In alchemy it refers to the densest aspect of the spiritual plane, that margin where spirit condenses into matter.

(29) A psychometer is someone able to discover facts about events or people by contact with inanimate objects associated with them. Because this ability is intuitive, Blavatsky suggests even a child psychometer could channel information more accurately than any scientific instrument.

(30) Pangenesis is Charles Darwin's theory of heredity. It proposes that an organism produces small particles or 'gemmules' of itself. These gemmules collect in the sex organs and determine the configuration of subsequent offspring.

(31) The Delphic commandments are a set of 147 aphorisms inscribed at the ancient sanctuary of Delphi on the south-western slope of Mount Parnassus in Greece. The oracle of Delphi, also known as the Pythia, was a woman over fifty who channeled the counsel of the Greek god Apollo.

(32) The Essenes were a religious group that flourished in Palestine from the 2nd Century BC to the 1st century AD. They lived in seclusion in monastic communities devoted to asceticism, manual labor and strict observance of religious ritual.

(33) The Psammetic Dynasty (664 BC - 525 BC), also known as the Saite or Twenty-sixth Dynasty of Egypt, was ruled over by the three pharaohs Psammeticus I, II, and III.

(34) Ein Sof, HPB: En-Soph, in Kabbalah refers to God prior to His self-manifestation. It can be translated as 'unending' or 'infinity.

(35) Positivism is a philosophical system in which information derived from sensory experience, interpreted through reason and logic, forms the exclusive source of knowledge. It excludes any form of metaphysics.

(36) The Talmud is a set of books regarded as sacred in Jewish religious tradition, second in importance only to the Old Testament of the Bible. It contains commentary on topics including astrology, mathematics, metaphysics and theosophy.

(37) Voilers or Valas are female shamans and seers in Norse religion and a recurring motif in Norse mythology.

(38) Oracle of Amphiaraus or The Amphiareion of Oropos was a

sanctuary situated in the hills southeast of the Greek port of Oropos. It was dedicated in the late 5th Century BC to the hero Amphiaraus.

(39) The precession of the equinoxes refers to the movement of the equinoxes along the plane of the earth's orbit. The Greek astronomer Hipparchus noticed that the positions of the stars appeared to have shifted compared with earlier Babylonian (Chaldean) observations. He realized this was not caused by the stars moving but by a shift in the earth's movement. This shift is called precession, a wobbling in the orientation of the earth's rotational axis, one whole cycle of which takes 25,772 years.

(40) Saros is a period of approximately 18 years, 11 days, 8 hours. It can be used to predict eclipses of the sun and moon. One saros after an eclipse, the sun, earth, and moon return to approximately the same relative geometry and another eclipse will occur.

(41) Phrygian Dactyls are mythological beings from the ancient kingdom of Phrygia located by the Sangarios River in what is now Turkey.

(42) Theurgy means 'divine working.' The term describes a set of ancient magical nature rituals performed to call forth benign spirits to assist in the practice of magic.

(43) Heliopolis was a major city and religious center in ancient Egypt. It was the capital of the 13th or Heliopolite province located in Lower Egypt.

(44) Sais was an ancient Egyptian town in the Western Nile Delta. Herodotus wrote that Sais is where the grave of Osiris was located.

(45) *Berliner Monatsschrift* was a monthly magazine published in Berlin between 1783 and 1796. It discussed the major questions of the intellectual and philosophical movement which became known as the Enlightenment.

(46) The Magi (from Latin *magus*) are followers of the ancient Persian prophet Zoroaster.

(47) A mobed or mobad is a Zoroastrian cleric of a particular rank, qualified to serve as a celebrant and to train other priests.

(48) Pehlvi, Pahlavi or Pahlevi denotes a particular and exclusively written form of various Middle Iranian languages.

(49) The Hyksos, HPB: Hyk-sos, were a people of Palestinian origin who settled in the eastern Nile Delta c. 1650 BC. Ultimately, the Hyksos 15th dynasty ruled most of lower Egypt and the Nile valley.

(50) Brothers of the Rose Cross are members of the worldwide

Rosicrucian brotherhood which originated in Europe in the early 17th Century. The order was allegedly founded by the (almost certainly fictional) Christian Rosenkreuz. It is claimed that Rosicruciansim is based on esoteric insights 'concealed from the average man,' which 'provide insight into nature, the physical universe and the spiritual realm.' Rosicrucian teachings draw on references to Kabbalah, Hermeticism and mystical Christianity.

(51) Delta of Enoch is an important narrative in Masonic Legend. Enoch, a prophet and descendent of Adam, had a vision of a mountain with a golden triangle showing the sun's rays. This became known as the 'Delta of Enoch.' Enoch created a physical representation of the vision - a triangular plate of gold bearing the secret name of God. He concealed it in the deepest of nine vaults he built, one on top of another, below the floor of what would ultimately be the Temple of King Solomon.

(52) The Egyptian Rite of Memphis is a variation of masonic ritual, constituted by Jean-Étienne Marconis de Nègre (3 January 1795 - 21 November 1868), masonic grand master general of France.

(53) The Rathbone Sisters of the World, HPB: RSW, also known as the Pythian Sisters of the World, were a female auxiliary to the Freemason group, the Knights of Pythias. The creation of the female auxiliary was approved by the Supreme Lodge of the Knights of Pythias in 1888.

(54) A neros is a period of 600 years in the ancient Chaldean system of measurement.

(55) Ecpyrosis (ancient Greek: conflagration) describes the belief that the world is destroyed by fire every 'great year' (every 21,600 yrs).

(56) The Brhaspati, HPB: Vrihaspati, refers to Jupiter and astronomical observations of its orbit relative to the 'fixed' stars and the sun. From the Brhaspati Hindu scholars developed a system of time measurement using Jupiter's sidereal orbit. Jupiter completes one orbit in relation to the 'fixed' stars in approximately twelve years and reaches the same conjunction with the sun approximately every solar year. Therefore any solar year can be identified as a certain 'month' in the twelve-year cycle of Jupiter.

(57) A yuga is an age of mankind in Hindu cosmology. Each yuga is shorter than the one before it as mankind declines and the cosmos is eventually destroyed. The four yugas Krita, Treta, Dvapara and Kali all make up a mahayuga, which means 'great yuga.'

(58) Kalpa is the principal cosmic cycle in Hindu cosmology. 2,000

mahayugas make up a kalpa which is the period of time between the creation and the destruction of the cosmos.

(59) Manvantara or age of a Manu, the Hindu progenitor of humanity, is an astronomical period of time measurement. Manvantara is a Sanskrit word, a compound of manu and antara, manu-antara or manvantara, literally meaning the duration of a Manu, or his life span.

(60) *The Hermetica* or *Books of Hermes* are Egyptian-Greek wisdom texts from the 2nd Century AD. They are attributed to the mythological figure Hermes Trismegistus (thrice-great Hermes). The majority of the texts are presented as dialogues in which a teacher (Trismegistus) enlightens his pupil about the nature of the divine, the cosmos, mind, and nature. The books can be divided into two groups: 'popular' Hermeticism dealing with astrology, alchemy and magic and 'learned' Hermeticism exploring theology and philosophy.

(61) Ecliptic plane. The plane on which the earth travels around the sun.

(62) Equatorial plane. The plane passing through the equator of the earth perpendicular to the axis of rotation.

(63) Ptolemaic system refers to a geocentric model of the universe created by the Egyptian astronomer Claudius Ptolemaeus (c.100 AD - 170 AD). Ptolemaeus placed the earth at the center of the universe and proposed that each body orbiting the earth was attached to its own sphere.

(64) It was in Rochester, New York State, US at the Corinthian Hall on 14 November 1849, that three mediums, the Fox sisters, first demonstrated spiritualist rapping for a paying public.

Chapter Two

(1) The UK's National Academy of Sciences is known as The Royal Society, formerly The Royal Society of London for Improving Natural Knowledge. The Society's royal charter was signed by Charles II on 15 July 1662. The Society fulfills a number of purposes: promoting science and its benefits, supporting and recognizing excellence in science, providing scientific advice for policy, fostering international and global co-operation, education and public engagement.

(2) The St. Petersburg Scientific Committee or Commission for the Investigation of Spiritualist Phenomena was set up by the Physical Society at St. Petersburg University on 6 May 1875. Under the leadership of the Russian chemist Dmitri Ivanovich Mendeleev, the committee published

its conclusions on 25 March 1876 in the newspaper *Golos* (*The Voice*). It came to the conclusion that 'spiritualist phenomena arise from unconscious movements or deliberate deception and the spiritualist doctrine is superstition.'

(3) *Tales of the Impious Khalif*. It has not been possible to establish the provenance of this story or the origin of the quote. The English occultist Thomas H. Burgoyne uses the same quote in his text book of esoteric knowledge *The Light of Egypt* but does not identify the source.

(4) The London Dialectical Society was a British professional association founded in 1867. Its purpose was to investigate the claims of spiritualism. Thirty-three of its members were later appointed to a committee in 1869 'to investigate the phenomena alleged to be spiritual manifestations and to report thereon.'

(5) Institute of Paris or the French Academy of Sciences is a learned society, founded in 1666 by Louis XIV. One of the earliest Academies of Sciences, it was at the forefront of scientific developments in Europe in the 17th and 18th Centuries.

(6) Samarkand, (Samarqand or Samarcand) is a city in modern-day Uzbekistan and is one of the oldest inhabited cities in Central Asia. There is evidence of human activity from the late Paleolithic era, though there is no direct evidence of when Samarkand itself was founded. Some theories suggest it was founded between the 8th and 7th Centuries BC.

(7) In alchemy the alkahest is a hypothetical universal solvent with the power to dissolve all substances, including gold.

(8) Aether or ether, also called quintessence, according to ancient and medieval science, is the material that fills the region of the universe above the terrestrial sphere. Late 19th-century scientists theorized the existence of 'luminiferous ether,' the medium through which light traveled. This theory was discarded when it was discovered that light travels through a vacuum.

(9) The *Orphic Hymns* are a collection of 87 short religious poems. They are associated with the Orphic religion, based on the teachings and songs of the legendary Greek musician Orpheus.

(10) The Upanishads are ancient Sanskrit texts, among the most important literature in the history of Indian religion and culture. In the Katha Upanishad a small boy meets the Hindu god of death. Their conversation sheds light on the nature of man, knowledge and the soul.

(11) Purusha in the Katha Upanishad is the cosmic soul, the ultimate reality. It is eternal,

indestructible, without form and all pervasive.

(12) French Academicians are members of the French Academy of Sciences (see note 5 above).

(13) Table turning, also known as table tapping, table tipping or table tilting, is a phenomenon in which a table is said to be turned, knocked or tilted by a spiritual entity acting through the attendees at a seance.

(14) IAO, ιαω, is the Greek equivalent of the Hebrew YHWH, the name of God (Yahweh) transliterated into four letters. The four Hebrew consonants were revealed to Moses and are also known as the tetragrammaton.

(15) The odic force or od is the name given by the German chemist Carl von Reichenbach to a hypothetical vital energy or life force. Von Reichenbach derived the name from Odin, the Norse god.

(16) An elementary spirit is a residual presence, shell or echo of a deceased person which displays reverberations of the deceased's personality. Although an elementary may seem intelligent, it is not directed by the consciousness of the deceased and its apparent intelligence is illusory.

(17) An elemental spirit can take over the shell of an elementary spirit (see note 16). It can reproduce the characteristics of the elementary in order to make mischief and deceive. An elemental can be manipulated by magicians and mediums.

(18) Spirit trumpets were horn-shaped speaking tubes said to amplify the whisper-like voices of spirits to make them clearly audible during a seance. In the latter half of the 19th Century, many spiritualist mediums used specialized tools. As well as spirit trumpets, mediums worked with spirit slates consisting of two chalkboards bound together, said to reveal spirit writing when opened. Spirit cabinets were used to confine mediums, who were often also bound hand and foot, to demonstrate that manifestations were authentic.

(19) *The Medium and Daybreak* was a journal devoted to the history, philosophy, and teachings of spiritualism. Published in London from 1870 to 1895, it was edited by James Burns (1833-1894).

(20) Umbra (shade or shadow) is one of the three spirits (umbra, anima and manes) that every man possesses according to ancient Roman beliefs. Umbra remains behind after death, hovering near the body's resting place. Anima is pure soul material and rises into the heavens. Manes descends into Hades.

(21) Bone of Horus. The name given by the Ancient Egyptians to the magnetic ore magnetite, after the principal Egyptian hawk-god Horus.

Chapter Three

(1) The *Eocene Orohippus* is one in the sequence of species believed to have evolved into the horse. The sequence, from *Eohippus* to *Orohippus* to the modern horse (*Equus*), was popularized by Thomas Huxley and became one of the most widely known examples of a clear evolutionary progression. The horse's evolutionary lineage became a common feature of biology textbooks, and the sequence of transitional fossils was assembled by the American Museum of Natural History into an exhibit that emphasized the gradual, 'straight-line' evolution of the horse.

(2) The Egyptian Hall, Piccadilly, London, built 1812, was an exhibition space designed by the English architect Peter Frederick Robinson in the ancient Egyptian style. It was demolished in 1905.

(3) Saint-Simonianism was a French social ideology of the first half of the 19th Century. It was based on the ideas of the political and economic theorist Claude Henri de Rouvroy, Comte de Saint-Simon (1760-1825). Saint-Simon maintained that the needs of the working class (all people engaged in productive work) must be recognized and fulfilled in order to create an effective society and efficient economy.

(4) Nihilism (from the Latin *nihil* meaning 'nothing') is a philosophical position that challenges belief in anything. Friedrich Nietzsche used the term to imply the rejection of all religious and moral principles. Existential nihilism argues that life is without objective meaning, purpose, or intrinsic value.

(5) Obeah is a system of spiritual and healing practices developed among enslaved west Africans in the West Indies. It is difficult to define as it is not a single unified set of practices. In common with other Afro-American religions like Palo, Haitian Vodou, Santería, and Hoodoo, it includes communication with ancestors and spirits, and healing rituals. However it differs from Vodou in that no one canon of deities is worshiped. Obeah practice tends to be individual rather than collective.

(6) Prajnaparamita is a Sanskrit word and a term in Mahayana Buddhism meaning 'the Perfection of (Transcendent) Wisdom.' It also refers to a body of sacred texts on the subject of that wisdom. The Prajnaparamita proposes that central to understanding the true nature of reality is the concept of emptiness or nothingness.

Chapter Four

(1) *Annales Médico-psychologiques, Revue Psychiatrique* is a peer-reviewed

medical journal covering the field of psychiatry. It was established in 1843 and is published by the Dutch publisher Elsevier on behalf of the Société Médico-psychologique. Articles are published in French with abstracts in English.

(2) The 40 members of the Académie Française (the Immortals) are primarily concerned with the French language. Blavatsky appears to have confused this body with the French Academy of Sciences.

(3) *Revue des Deux Mondes* is a French literary and cultural affairs magazine published in Paris since 1829.

(4) Valeyres-sous-Rances is a small village in the canton of Vaud, Switzerland. Here, from September to December 1853, the French psychical researcher Count Agénor de Gasparin conducted a major investigation into the phenomenon of turning tables.

(5) Spirit operator, a spirit that works or operates through the mental and physical energies of a medium to cause phenomena on the physical plane. Once the spirit operator is given control of the medium, through the process of trance, the phenomena can begin.

(6) The Peculiar People, a Christian movement named after a passage in Deuteronomy: 'For thou art an holy people unto the LORD thy God, and the LORD hath chosen thee to be a peculiar people unto himself, above all the nations that are upon the earth.' The movement was founded in 1838 in Rochford, England by the preacher James Banyard. The Peculiar People declined medical treatment, relying instead on prayer. This led to the death of some children during a diphtheria outbreak in 1910 and their parents were imprisoned as a consequence.

(7) Sadducees were members of a Jewish sect at the time of Christ and are often compared to similar groups including the Pharisees and the Essenes. Their religious responsibilities included the maintenance of the Temple in Jerusalem. They had high social status because of their role in the priesthood. They did not believe in the immortality of the soul or the possibility of an afterlife and they denied the resurrection of the dead.

(8) Brahmans, this passage is quoted from the German magazine *Der Katholik Volume 30, issues IX-XII* published in 1828. The word 'Brahman' is used in the German text. In Hinduism, Brahman connotes the highest universal principle. The context in which the word is used, together with the inclusion of the line 'the entire Hindu priesthood', casts doubt over the accuracy of the original German and perhaps the word intended was 'Brahmin', denoting the priesthood, the highest caste in Hinduism.

(9) Edda (Icelandic: grandmother) is the name given to two books of Icelandic mythology. The older Poetic Edda consists of 39 poems drawn from Icelandic oral tradition. The younger Prose Edda is a detailed compendium of Norse mythology, customarily ascribed to Snorri Sturluson (born 1178) but probably the work of several writers.

(10) The Scandinavian Holy Trinity or the Mysterious Three, guard Valhalla, the hall of Heaven, in Norse Mythology. They are Harr, HPB: Har, the High One; Jafnharr, HPB: Jafuhar, the Equally High One; and Thridhi, HPB: Tredi, the Third.

(11) Titans, in Greek mythology, a race of powerful giant deities that preceded the Olympians. There were twelve Titans, the sons and daughters of heaven and earth.

(12) *The Christian World* was a religious periodical founded in 1857 by the Baptist minister Jonathan Whittemore. Under the editorship of James Clarke, it was able to compete successfully with its secular counterparts in the coverage of current affairs. Clarke ensured *The Christian World* became successful as an 'undenominational and progressive religious weekly.'

(13) The British Association for the Advancement of Science is a charity and learned society founded in 1831. Since 2009 it has been known as The British Science Association (BSA). The Association aims to popularize science, increasing the number and variety of people actively involved and engaged in it.

Chapter Five

(1) Fire is of central importance in Zoroastrian worship. A sacred fire is kept burning continually in Zoroastrian temples making manifest the presence of God. Fire's qualities of warmth, protection and transformation represent those same qualities in the deity.

(2) Antus-byrum is the sacred fire of the Parsis. When the Parsis fled persecution in Persia they carried the antus-byrum with them to India. The fires burning in all Parsi temples are descended from this original sacred fire.

(3) The Parsis, HPB: Parsee, whose name means Persians, are followers of the Persian prophet Zoroaster. They are of Persian descent living in India.

(4) Elmes-fire of the ancient Germans - this reference is obscure and may refer to the practice among ancient Germanic tribes of keeping a sacred fire permanently lit to represent the life force.

(5) Cybele was adopted as a goddess by the Romans following a series of bizarre lightning strikes. In 3 BC,

lightning struck the temple of Jupiter and the sacred grove of the nymph Marica in the city of Minturnae (modern Minturno, Italy).

(6) The two brightest stars in the constellation of Gemini are named after the twin half-brothers Castor and Pollux. In Greek and Roman mythology they are known as the Dioscuri. Castor was mortal but Pollux was the divine son of Zeus. Pollux asked Zeus to let him share his immortality with Castor so they could be together forever. They were transformed into the constellation of Gemini.

(7) Algol is a bright multiple star in the constellation of Perseus and its Bayer classification is Beta Persei. The name Algol derives from Arabic meaning 'the demon's head' which refers to its supposed resemblance to the head of the Gorgon Medusa.

(8) Pallas is an asteroid discovered by the German astronomer Heinrich Wilhelm Matthäus Olbers on 28 March 1802. It is named after Pallas Athena, an alternative name for the Greek goddess Athena. It is the third largest asteroid in the solar system.

(9) The Greek astronomer Hipparchus named a star group in the southern constellations 'Caduceus' after the staff carried by Hermes in Greek mythology and Hermes Trismegistus in Greco-Egyptian mythology. The location of the star group is no longer known.

(10) Tongues of fire refers to the Bible, Acts 2:1-4: 'When the day of Pentecost came, they were all together in one place. Suddenly a sound like the blowing of a violent wind came from heaven and filled the whole house where they were sitting. They saw what seemed to be tongues of fire that separated and came to rest on each of them. All of them were filled with the Holy Spirit and began to speak in other tongues as the Spirit enabled them.'

(11) See Bible, Revelation 20:1-3: 'And I saw an angel come down from Heaven, having the key to the bottomless pit and a great chain in his hand. And he laid hold on the dragon, that serpent of old, who is the Devil and Satan, and bound him for a thousand years. And he cast him into the bottomless pit, and shut him up and set a seal upon him, that he should deceive the nations no more till the thousand years should be fulfilled; and after that he must be loosed a little season.'

(12) In Rosicrucianism the sidereal light (Latin: *sidereus*, of the stars) refers to the inner seat of all memory, a record of all that has happened. In Kabbala the term 'astral light' is more common.

(13) Rosicrucians - see Chapter One, note 50.

(14) Akasha or aether, in Hindu cosmology, is the basis and essence of all things in the material world.

Akasha was the first element to be created.

(15) Elephantine is an island on the Nile, forming part of present-day Aswan in southern Egypt. In Ancient Egypt, the island of Elephantine stood at the border between Egypt and Nubia. It is 75 miles from Heliopolis (Cairo).

(16) The Eumolpidae are a dynasty of priests drawn from the Eumolpidae family at the town of Eleusis. They presided over the Eleusinian Mysteries, the most famous of the secret religious rites of Ancient Greece. The Eumolpidae were descendants of Eumolpus, one of the first priests of Demeter, goddess of the harvest.

(17) Temple of Demeter and Persephone, HPB: Persephoneia, at Athens, also known as the Eleusinion. According to Pausanias, 'On entering the city (of Athens) there is a building for the preparation of the processions, which are held in some cases every year, in others at longer intervals.' In this building all the sacred objects associated with the Eleusinian Mysteries were kept between ceremonies. Any initiates who revealed the secrets of the Mysteries would be put to death, as would any non-initiates who dared enter the sanctuary.

(18) *Theages* is a dialogue attributed to Plato, featuring Socrates, a young man called Theages and his father Demodocus. Demodocus asks Socrates for advice regarding his son. Theages wants to become wise and his father thinks this is dangerous. Socrates speaks directly to Theages asking him what he means by 'wisdom.' Theages says it is the ability to govern men. Socrates says this is best learned by associating with someone who has this skill.

(19) Garden of the Hesperides is an orchard belonging to the Greek goddess Hera. It's golden apples grant immortality. The Hesperides are nymphs given the task of tending the orchard, but occasionally they take apples for themselves. To discourage them, Hera placed in the garden a hundred-headed dragon named Ladon.

(20) The Samothracian Mysteries took place on the Greek island of Samothrace in the northern Aegean. They were second in importance only to the Eleusinian Mysteries (see note 16 above). Pilgrims came from afar to seek protection (especially from the sea), moral improvement, a long life, and a better afterlife.

(21) Agathodaemon, HPB: Agatho-daimon, was a spirit of the vineyards and grainfields in ancient Greek mythology. Agathodaemons were personal companion spirits, comparable to the Roman genii, who ensured good luck, health, and wisdom.

(22) The word 'cacodaemon,' HPB: kakodaimon, is derived from the Ancient Greek kakodaimōn, meaning an evil spirit. It was believed to be a shapeshifter.

(23) Yggdrasil is an immense mythical tree that connects the nine worlds in Norse cosmology. It appears in both the Poetic Edda and Prose Edda (see Chapter Four, note 9). In both sources, Yggdrasil is the sacred center of the cosmos.

(24) The Silurian Period is a geological period which began 443.8 million years ago and ended 419.2 million years ago. During the Mid-Silurian Period animals first appeared on land.

(25) The Mammalian Period (Cenozoic) began 66 million years ago and continues to the present day. During this period the continents settled into their present shapes and positions; plants and animals evolved into their present form.

(26) King of Ophir - Ophir appears in 1 Kings 11: 'Hiram's ships brought gold from Ophir...' In the Old Testament, Ophir was famous for its gold but its location is unknown. Presumably the King of Ophir was the ruler of this unidentified region.

(27) Travancore is a former principality in southwestern India now part of the state of Kerala. It came under British protection in 1795. Following independence, Travancore merged with Cochin and was renamed Kerala in 1956.

(28) Caduceus is the staff carried by Hermes in Greek mythology and consequently by Hermes Trismegistus in Greco-Egyptian mythology. It is a short staff entwined by two serpents, sometimes surmounted by wings. In the present day it is most familiar as a symbol of medicine.

(29) The Sanskrit word 'pitris' means fathers. There are two classes of pitris in Hinduism - the human and the divine. Human pitris are the spirits of departed ancestors. Divine pitris are gods of different origins, forms and grades, regarded as the progenitors of mankind.

(30) The Hebrew word 'qlippoth,' HPB: klippoth, means skins, shells, membranes etc. In Kabbalah, the qlippoth are 'shells' surrounding holiness. They receive their existence from God only in an external manner which makes them spiritually problematic. Kabbalah distinguishes between two kinds of qlippoth, the completely impure and the intermediate.

(31) Assiah, HPB: Asiah, describes the material world in Kabbalah. It is also known as the world of action, effects or making.

(32) Afrits are powerful demons in Islamic mythology. In later folklore

they appear as spirits of the dead inhabiting desolate places such as ruins and temples.

(33) In Zoroastrianism, devs were created by the spirit Ahriman. He manifested six arch-devs and innumerable devs of lower rank. Ahriman and his creatures live in the kingdom of darkness.

(34) Ilus is a primordial slime or mud. It is a term used by the Chaldean priest Berossus for the raw material out of which the cosmos was built.

(35) Chemmis was described by the Roman geographer Pomponius Mela as a floating island in Egypt. It had sacred groves, a temple of Apollo and it drifted wherever the wind took it. According to Plutarch, the Egyptian goddess Isis loosened the island of Chemmis from its foundation and set it afloat to protect her son Horus from her brother Set, the god of war. The island floated sometimes on the Nile and sometimes on the sea.

(36) Book of Jashar, HPB: Jasher, is a collection of Hebrew poems described in the Old Testament (Joshua 10:13 and 2 Samuel 1:18). The word 'Jashar' may mean victorious / upright though its origin and precise meaning are uncertain.

(37) Aesir, in Old Norse, refers to any member of the principal pantheon of gods in Norse religion. This includes Odin, Frigg, Thor, Baldr and Týr.

(38) Vanr, plural Vanir. The Vanir are the second pantheon of gods in Norse religion. They are associated with fertility, wisdom, and prophecy. The Vanir and the Aesir waged war against each other resulting in a single, unified pantheon.

(39) The Greek philosopher Pherecydes of Syros describes the marriage between Chthonia, the unformed earth, and Zeus. Zeus dresses Chthonia in a mantle embroidered with land, rivers, mountains and cities. This brings order to chaos and Chthonia becomes the earth.

(40) The od, ob and aour are explained by Eliphas Levi in his work *The Great Secret or Occultism Unveiled*: 'These strange but incontestable facts lead us to the necessary conclusion that there is a common life shared by all souls; or at least a common mirror for every imagination and every memory, in which it is possible for us to gaze at one another like a crowd of people standing before a glass. This reflector is the odic light of Baron Reichenbach, which we call the astral light, and is the great agency of life termed od, ob and aour by the Hebrews. The magnetism controlled by the will of the operator is Od; that of passive clairvoyance is Ob: the pythonesses of antiquity were clairvoyants intoxicated with the

passive astral light. This light is called the spirit of Python in our holy books, because in Greek mythology the serpent Python is its allegorical representative. In its double action, it is also represented by the serpent of the caduceus: the right-hand serpent is Od, the one on the left is Ob and, in the middle, at the top of the hermetic staff, shines the golden globe which represents Aour, or light in equilibrium. Od represents life governed by free choice, Ob represents life ruled by fate. This is why the Hebrew Law-giver said: 'Woe to those who divine by Ob, because they evoke fate, which is an offense against the providence of God and the liberty of man.' Certainly, there is a wide difference between the serpent Python, which crawled in the mud of the deluge and was shot by the sun's arrows, and that which coils around the rod of Asclepius, just as the tempter serpent of Eden differs from the brazen serpent which cured those who were poisoned in the desert. These two antagonistic serpents really stand for those contrary forces which may be connected but never confused. Hermes' scepter, while keeping them apart, also reconciles them, and even unites them in a way; and this is how, under the penetrating eyes of science, harmony arises from the analogy of contraries. Necessity and Liberty, these are the two great laws of life; and properly speaking these two laws only make one, because they are both indispensable.

Necessity without liberty would be fatal, even as liberty without its necessary curb would go insane. Privilege without obligation is folly, and obligation without privilege is slavery. The whole secret of magnetism lies here: to rule the fatality of the ob by intelligence and the power of the od so as to create the perfect balance of aour.'

(41) Sefirot, HPB: Sephira, meaning emanations, are the ten attributes in Kabbalah, through which Ein Sof (The Infinite) reveals Himself and continuously creates both the physical realm and the chain of higher metaphysical realms.

(42) Pneuma is an ancient Greek word for breath and, in a religious context, for spirit or soul.

Chapter Six

(1) Electrochemical dualism is an obsolete scientific theory pioneered by the Swedish chemist Jöns Jacob Berzelius between 1800 and 1830. The theory held that all molecules are salts composed of basic and acidic oxides.

(2) Avogadro's law (sometimes referred to as Avogadro's hypothesis or Avogadro's principle) states that 'equal volumes of all gases, at the same temperature and pressure, contain exactly the same number of molecules.'

(3) Blavatsky gives the name of Hénin de Cuvillers' journal as the *Annales de Magnétisme Animal* but this appears to be incorrect. A bi-monthly journal the *Annales du Magnétisme Animal* was launched in 1814 and, after a short interruption, reappeared as the *Bibliothèque du Magnétisme Animal*. This title became defunct in 1819 and was then replaced by the *Archives du Magnétisme Animal* under the editorship of Hénin de Cuvillers.

(4) Smyrna was an ancient Greek city located on the west coast of modern-day Turkey. The modern city occupying the original site of Smyrna is called Izmir.

(5) Nineveh was an ancient Assyrian city on the outskirts of what is now the city of Mosul in northern Iraq. Located on the eastern bank of the Tigris River, Nineveh was the capital of the Neo-Assyrian Empire.

(6) *L'Ami des Sciences* was a Sunday paper founded by the French science writer Victor Meunier in Paris in 1855. It promoted general interest in scientific topics and was part of the popular science movement.

(7) Caesar's *Commentaries* may refer to one of two works written by the Roman emperor Julius Caesar. The first is *Commentarii de Bello Gallico* and concerns Caesar's campaigns in Gaul and Britain fought between 58 BC and 50 BC. The second is *Commentarii de Bello Civili* describing his participation in the Roman Civil War 49 BC - 48 BC.

(8) A Leyden jar, or Leiden jar, was the original form of the capacitor. It stores a high-voltage electric charge from an external source between electrical conductors on the inside and outside of a glass jar. Metal foil is cemented to the inside and the outside surfaces, and a metal terminal projecting vertically through the jar lid makes contact with the inner foil.

(9) Perispirit, in spiritism, is the subtle body used by the spirit to connect with the perceptions created by the brain. The term is found in the extensive nomenclature originally devised by Allan Kardec in his books about spiritism.

(10) Planchette, from the French 'little plank,' is a device used in automatic writing. It is a small, flat piece of wood, usually heart shaped, with two castors and a pencil holder.

Chapter Seven

(1) The first spheres of astral existence: Neo-Platonic philosophy, and later, theosophy, suggested that there are several spheres of non-physical existence on the astral plane. These spheres must be traversed by the soul as it incarnates or following the death of the physical body.

(2) Mr. Vincent is described in the original Blavatsky text as a government engineer. It appears from the de la Loubère text (quoted below) that this is incorrect and Vincent was in fact a physician from Provence (see *Vincent, Mr.* page 453) The Blavatsky text goes on to claim that de la Loubère could verify the truth of the fish story but the source text indicates that it was Vincent who vouched for the truth of the phenomenon: *Amongst the Fresh-water Fish, they have some little ones of two sorts, which do here deserve to be mention'd. They call them Pla out, and Pla cadi, that is to say the Fish out, and the Fish cadi. To free me from all doubts, some have assur'd me, that after they have salted them together, as the Siameses us'd to do, if they leave them in an earthen Pot in their Pickle, where they soon corrupt, by reason they salt ill at Siam, then, that is to say when they are corrupted, and as it were in a very liquid Paste, they do exactly follow the flux and reflux of the Sea, growing higher and lower in the Pitcher as the Sea ebbs or flows. Mr. Vincent gave me a Pot thereof at his arrival in France, and assur'd me that this Experiment was true, and that he had seen it; but I cannot add my Testimony thereunto, by reason I was too late advertised thereof at Siam, to have an occasion of ascertaining it by my own Eyes; and that the Pot which Mr. Vincent gave me, and which I brought to Paris, perform'd this Effect no more: perhaps because the Fish were too much corrupted, or that their virtue of imitating the flux and reflux of the Sea continues only a certain time... The External does so exceedingly weaken the Natural Heat, that*

here are not seen almost any of those Distempers, which our Physicians do call Agues: and this is so throughout India, and also in Persia, where, of an hundred sick persons, Mr. Vincent the Provençal Physician, whom I have already mention'd, declar'd that he scarce found one which had the Fever...

(3) The Chukchi Peninsula is the easternmost peninsula of Asia and is located on the edge of Siberia. The indigenous Chukchi people were fishermen, hunters and reindeer herders. In the Chukchi religion, every object, whether animate or inanimate, is assigned a spirit which can be either harmful or benevolent.

(4) 'Talapoin' is a 16th-century French word for a Buddhist monk from the Portuguese 'talapão,' which is derived from 'mon tala pōi' meaning 'our lord.'

(5) Cevennes and Morzine: outbreaks of religious fervor occurred in both towns beginning with convulsions among the towns' children. The first outbreak occurred at Cevennes in 1707, the second in the Alpine town of Morzine in 1857.

(6) The Convulsionnaires of Saint-Médard were a religious sub-group of the Catholic theological movement known as Jansenism. Their spiritual practice was characterized by fits of religious convulsions which began at the tomb of François de Pâris, a

Jansenist deacon, buried at the cemetery of the parish of Saint-Médard in Paris.

(7) Andrew Jackson Davis believed that no sudden or radical change takes place in the character and disposition of an individual at death. Those who were mischievous, unprincipled, or promiscuous during their lives remained so, for a time at least, after they died. He referred to these residual presences as 'Diakka.'

(8) 'Temple of Jupiter Amun at Libya' refers to the temple built at the Oasis of Siwa to the Egyptian deity Amun. Worship of Amun had spread beyond Egypt to include Nubia, Sudan, Greece and ancient Libya. The temple was so renowned for its oracle that even Alexander the Great is said to have crossed the desert to consult it.

(9) 'A Temple of Venus' may refer to the Temple of Venus and Roma, the largest temple in ancient Rome, or the Temple of Venus in Djémila, Algeria. In *Mysteries of Ancient South America*, Harold T. Wilkins writes, 'If we are to believe St. Augustine and Cedrenus, the old Byzantine chronicler, 'perpetual lamps', or lights, were by no means unknown to the ancient Egyptians, Romans and Greeks. St. Augustine says that such a lamp was in a fane of Venus in Africa.'

(10) Carystus was a city-state on the Greek island of Euboea, situated on the south coast, close to the site of modern Karystos. Asbestos is still mined in the northeastern part of the city in the Okhi mountain.

(11) Cabeirian Mysteries, HPB: Kabeirian, is a mystery cult devoted to deities in Greek mythology called the Cabeiri. The mysteries were centered on the north Aegean islands of Lemnos and possibly Samothrace. Like all mystery schools the details of initiation, rituals and deities have been kept secret. Presumably, the image referred to by Blavatsky depicts an aspect of ritual associated with this particular mystery tradition.

(12) Luxor Temple is a large ancient Egyptian temple complex located on the east bank of the river Nile. Constructed c. 1400 BC, it was the major religious center of the ancient city of Thebes (present-day Luxor).

(13) Damascus steel is named after Damascus, the capital of Syria. It was made using a secret process of carburization in which wrought iron was heated with carbon-containing materials in sealed vessels. The metal can be recognized by a distinctive light and dark pattern on its surface. Damascus steel was favored in the production of blades because it was strong but remained flexible.

(14) Karnak Temple Complex covers more than 100 hectares on the east bank of the Nile. The great hall is the highlight of the Karnak

Temple and one of the wonders of the ancient world.

(15) Angkor Wat is a temple complex in northwestern Cambodia covering more than 162 hectares. It is the largest extant religious structure in the world.

(16) Palenque, also known as Lakamha, was a Mayan city state in southern Mexico that flourished in the 7th Century. One of the best-preserved structures is the Temple of Inscriptions which houses the second longest glyphic text in the Mayan world, recording approximately 180 years of the city's history.

(17) Uxmal, Mayan for thrice built, is an ancient Mayan city in Yucatan state in Mexico. The majority of hieroglyphics at Uxmal appear on stone slabs called stelae depicting the ancient rulers of the city.

(18) Nimrud, HPB: Nimroud, is the site of the ancient Assyrian city, Calah, located 20 miles south of the city of Mosul in northern Iraq. Blavatsky may be referring to the Nimrud lens, also called Layard lens, a 3000-year-old piece of rock crystal, unearthed in 1850 by the English archeologist Austen Henry Layard. It may have been used as a magnifying glass, or as a burning-glass to start fires by concentrating the sun's rays.

(19) Sibylline Oracles are a collection of oracular prophecies attributed to the Sibyl, a prophetess in Greek legend and literature. The Sybil was a woman of extreme old age who was able to enter an ecstatic frenzy in order to make predictions about the future.

(20) The people of the Kamchatka Peninsula are the Koryaks. Their origin is unknown. Shamanism and fire rituals are important aspects of Koryak spiritual life. Before hunting, seal blubber and meat, tobacco, tea, and sugar are offered to the fire. This is because fire is regarded as a living entity able to influence the outcome of the hunt. If the fire flares up when the hunter speaks to it, it is thought that the fire is answering positively and the hunt will be a success.

(21) The Svabhavika (or Swahabvika) School of Buddhism is thought to be one of the oldest Buddhist schools. Svabhava means 'own-being' or 'own-becoming'. It describes the intrinsic, essential nature of living beings.

(22) Blavatsky's original text is confused. She indicates that she is quoting from Aristotle's *De Anima* but the text quoted actually appears in Henry More's work *The Immortality of the Soul* Book 2, Chapter 7. She also attributes comments on the nature of the soul to Aristotle when they should be attributed to Gerolamo Cardano.

Who's Who

A.

Abbott, Henry *(1812-1859) was an English physician. He traveled to Egypt where he practiced medicine, settling in Cairo. He amassed a collection of over 1000 ancient artifacts and went on to open the Egyptian Museum on Broadway, New York City, in 1853.*

Adelon, Nicolas-Philibert *(20 August 1782 - 19 July 1862) was a French physician and physiologist. He was Professor of legal medicines at the University of Paris and Vice Dean of the Medical Faculty. In 1823 he obtained his teaching diploma for physiology, and in 1826 succeeded Antoine-Athanase Royer-Collard as chair of forensic medicine at the University of Paris, a position he held until 1861. In 1825, he was part of a special committee supporting Pierre Foissac's call for a new inquiry into mesmerism by the French Academy of Medicine.*

Ady, Thomas *(fl. 17th Century) was an English physician and humanist. He is best known for his book* A Candle in the Dark: Or, A Treatise Concerning the Nature of Witches & Witchcraft. *He challenged the idea that the Bible justifies the persecution of witches.*

Aëtius of Amida *HPB: Æetius Amidenus (mid-5th Century to mid-6th Century) was a Byzantine Greek physician and medical writer. He studied at Alexandria, the most prestigious medical school of the age. His work is a compilation of writings by many authors of antiquity whose texts would otherwise*

have been lost with the destruction of the Library at Alexandria.

Agassiz, Jean Louis Rodolphe *(28 May 1807 - 14 December 1873) was a Swiss-American biologist, geologist and natural historian. In 1839, Agassiz wrote an account of being mesmerized by the English clergyman and eminent mesmerist Chauncy Hare Townshend. In 1857, the* Boston Courier *offered $500 to any medium who could prove that spirit communication was genuine. Evidence was scrutinized by a group of four Harvard professors chaired by Agassiz. The committee concluded that there was no such thing as spirit communication.*

Agni, *(Sanskrit: fire) connotes the Hindu fire god of that name. In classical Indian cosmology, Agni is one of the five inert impermanent elements (Dhatus). The other four are space (Akasa/Dyaus), water (Jal/Varuna), air (Vāyu) and earth (Prithvi). The five combine to form material existence (Prakriti). In ancient Hindu texts, Agni is said to exist on three levels: on earth as fire, in the atmosphere as lightning, and in the sky as the sun.*

Agrippa, Heinrich Cornelius von Nettesheim *(14 September 1486 - 18 February 1535) was a German polymath, physician, legal scholar, soldier, theologian and eminent occult writer. His most influential work is* Three Books of Occult Philosophy *(1533) on the powers of ritual magic, and its relationship with religion.*

Ahura Mazdā HPB: Ormasd *is the sole God of Zoroastrianism. 'Ahura' means mighty or lord and 'Mazdā' means wisdom. He is the just and compassionate creator of the universe.*

Aksakov, Alexander Nikolayevich HPB: *Alexandr Aksakof (27 May 1832 - 4 January 1903) was a Russian writer, translator, journalist, editor, state official and psychic researcher, who is credited with having coined the term 'telekinesis.' He was editor of the* Leipzig Psychische Studien, *a journal published monthly and devoted to exploring the life of the soul.*

Alexander the Great *or Alexander III of Macedon (July 356 BC - 10/11 June 323 BC) was a king of the Ancient Greek kingdom of Macedon. He succeeded his father Philip II at the age of 20. He spent most of his rule on a military campaign in Asia and northeast Africa, creating one of the largest empires of the ancient world from Greece to northwestern India.*

Allchin, William Henry *(1846-1912) was an English physician and lecturer on comparative anatomy, physiology, pathology and medicine. He was Dean of Westminster Hospital, London, and the editor of* A Manual of Medicine.

Almignana, the Abbot of *(1788-1857) was born in Spain and became a parish priest in the Parisian neighborhood of Batignolles. He published a pamphlet presenting 'tables parlantes' (talking tables) as a powerful sign that the age of* miracles had not yet passed. He carried out his experiments with the authorization of the archbishop of Paris. Almignana published a book in 1854 entitled Du Somnambulisme, des Tables Tournantes et des Médiums, Considérés leurs dans Rapports avec la Théologie et la Physique. Examen des Opinions de MM. de Mirville et de Gasparin.

Ampère, André-Marie *(20 January 1775 - 10 June 1836) was a French physicist and mathematician. He is known for his work in the field of electromagnetism. His most important publication was* Mémoire sur la Théorie Mathématique des Phénomènes Électrodynamiques Uniquement Déduite de l'Experience (Memoir on the Mathematical Theory of Electrodynamic Phenomena, Uniquely Deduced from Experience). *This is regarded as the founding treatise of electrodynamics. The ampere, the base unit of electricity more commonly known as the amp, is named after him.*

Amun *was an ancient Egyptian god. He was one of the eight gods worshiped in Hermopolis or the City of Hermes (near the modern Egyptian town of Al Ashmunin). During the rule of the Pharaoh, Ahmose I, Amun acquired national importance. He was identified with the Sun god, Ra, becoming Amun-Ra, regarded as both self-created, and the god of creation.*

Anahita *is the Zoroastrian name for an Indo-Iranian cosmological figure, venerated as the goddess of water. She was* *also associated with fertility, healing and wisdom.*

Anaxagoras *(c. 510 BC - c. 428 BC) was a pre-Socratic Greek philosopher. He was born in the city of Clazomenae (20 miles west of modern-day Izmir in Turkey). He was the first philosopher to live in Athens and is credited with making that city the centre of western philosophical thought.*

Anaximenes of Miletus *(c. 586 BC - c. 526 BC) was a pre-Socratic Greek philosopher. Because none of his works have survived, the details of his life are obscure. What little is known about his ideas and philosophies comes from comments made by Aristotle and other writers on the history of Greek philosophy.*

Angoulême, Duke of *or Louis Antoine of France (6 August 1775 - 3 June 1844) was the eldest son of Charles X of France and the last Dauphin of France from 1824 to 1830. He was technically King of France and Navarre for less than 20 minutes before he himself abdicated, following his father's abdication during the July Revolution in 1830. He never reigned over the country, but after his father's death in 1836, he was the pretender as Louis XIX.*

Anthon, Charles *(19 November 1797 - 29 July 1867) was an American classical scholar. He was the author of* A Dictionary of Greek and Roman Antiquities *amongst other educational titles. He was widely admired for his work as an educationalist.*

Antipater, Lucius Coelius *was a Roman jurist and historian (not to be confused with Coelius Sabinus, the Coelius of* The Digest of Roman Law*). He taught the Roman statesman and orator, Lucius Crassus, and was described by the historian Valerius Maximus as* certus Romanae historiae auctor *(a reliable authority on Roman history).*

Apollo, *son of Zeus, is one of the most revered of all gods in Greek and Roman mythology. He was associated with prophecy, the protection of crops and herds, and later known as god of the sun.*

Apollonius of Tyana *(c.15 - c.100 AD) was a Greek Neopythagorean philosopher and orator. He was likened to Christ in disposition and it was believed he could perform miracles.*

Appian of Alexandria *(c. 95 BC - c.165 AD) was a Greek historian with Roman citizenship who flourished during the reigns of the emperors Trajan, Hadrian, and Antoninus Pius. He was the author of* Romaica, *a history of Rome in 24 volumes.*

Aquinas, Thomas *(1225 - 7 March 1274) was an Italian Dominican friar, Catholic priest, and Doctor of the Church. In his book* Summa Theologiae *he outlined The Five Ways (Latin:* Quinque viæ*) sometimes called the five proofs: five logical arguments for the existence of God. Aquinas is recognized by the Catholic church as its foremost philosopher and theologian.*

Arago, Dominique François Jean known simply as François Arago (26 February 1786 - 2 October 1853), was a French mathematician, physicist, astronomer, freemason and politician. He advised his pupil Urbain Le Verrier to investigate anomalies in the motion of Uranus. This led to the discovery of the planet Neptune.

Arcet, Jean de (7 September 1724 - 12 February 1801) was a French chemist. He was a member of the 1784 Franklin committee, convened by the French Academy of Sciences, to investigate mesmerism. He was one of the first people to manufacture porcelain in France, ultimately becoming director of the porcelain works at Sèvres.

Areopagita, Dionysius (fl. 1st Century AD) was a judge at the Areopagus Court in Athens. He converted to Christianity and went on to become the first Bishop of Athens. He is venerated as a saint in both Roman Catholic and Eastern Orthodox churches.

Aristides also Aristides the Just (530 BC - 468 BC) was an Athenian statesman and general. The historian Herodotus described him as the best and most honorable man in Athens.

Aristotle (384 BC - 322 BC) was a Greek philosopher and scientist. He was the founder of the modern scientific method and developed the study of zoology. His writing on ethics, metaphysics and science form a significant part of western philosophical tradition.

Armstrong, William George 1st Baron Armstrong (26 November 1810 - 27 December 1900) was an English engineer and industrialist. He was the inventor of high-pressure hydraulic machinery. He was also an eminent scientist and philanthropist.

Arnobius of Sicca (died c. 330 AD) was an early convert to Christianity. He taught rhetoric at Sicca Veneria in Africa during the reign of the Roman Emperor Diocletian (284 AD - 305 AD). He was the author of seven books in defense of Christianity called Against the Pagans.

Asclepiades (c. 124 or 129 BC - 40 BC) sometimes called Asclepiades of Bithynia or Asclepiades of Prusa, was a Greek physician practising in Rome. He developed a new theory of disease, based on the idea that atoms flow through the body and diseases are caused by disturbances in the flow. He aimed to restore harmony through the use of fresh air, light diet, massage, exercise, bathing and music.

Astarte is a Middle Eastern goddess and principal deity of the Mediterranean ports Tyre, Sidon and Elat. She was connected with fertility, sexuality, and war. Her symbols were the lion, the horse, the sphinx, the dove, and a star within a circle indicating the planet Venus.

Augustine of Canterbury (died c. 26 May 604 AD) was a Benedictine monk and the first Archbishop of Canterbury. He is considered the English Apostle and a founder of the English Church.

Aura *is a minor deity in Greek and Roman mythology. Her name means breeze. According to the Greek poet Nonnus, she was the daughter of the Titan Lelantos and the mother of Iacchus, a minor deity connected with the Eleusinian Mysteries.*

Aurelianus, Caelius *was a Roman physician and medical writer. He is best known for his Latin translation of* On Acute and Chronic Diseases *by the Greek gynecologist Soranus of Ephesus. Aurelianus probably flourished in the 5th Century, although some historians place him two or even three centuries earlier.*

Avogadro, Amedeo Carlo *(9 August 1776 - 9 July 1856) was an Italian scientist. He is noted for the formulation of Avogadro's law: equal volumes of gases at the same temperature and pressure contain equal numbers of molecules.*

B.

Baader, Franz von *(27 March 1765 - 23 May 1841) born Benedikt Franz Xaver Baader, was a layman in the Roman Catholic church who became an influential mystical theologian. Formerly a mining engineer, he helped found a 'holy alliance' or security pact between Russia, Austria, Prussia, and France.*

Babbage, Charles *(26 December 1791 - 18 October 1871) was an English polymath. A mathematician, philosopher, inventor and mechanical engineer, Babbage originated the concept of a digital programmable computer.*

Babinet, Jacques *(5 March 1794 - 21 October 1872) was a French physicist, mathematician, and astronomer. He is best known for his contributions to meteorology and optics. He was an accomplished popularizer of science, an engaging lecturer and an entertaining writer of popular science articles.*

Bacon, Francis, *1st Viscount St Alban (22 January 1561 - 9 April 1626) was an English author, philosopher and statesman. He served as Attorney General and Lord Chancellor of England. He was a proponent of the modern scientific method and has been described as 'the father of empiricism.'*

Bacon, Roger *also Frater Rogerus (c. 1219/20 - c. 1292) also known as Doctor Mirabilis (Latin:* Wonderful Teacher*) was an English Franciscan philosopher and educational reformer. He was one of the earliest European advocates of the modern scientific method.*

Bailey, Nathan *(died 27 June 1742), was an English philologist and lexicographer. He was the author of several dictionaries, including his* Universal Etymological Dictionary, *which appeared in some 30 editions between 1721 and 1802.* Bailey's Dictionarium Britannicum *(1730 and 1736) was the primary resource used by Samuel Johnson for his* Dictionary of the English Language *(1755).*

Bailly, Jean Sylvain *(15 September 1736 - 12 November 1793) was a French astronomer, mathematician, freemason, and political leader. He was a* member of the 1784 Franklin committee, convened by the French Academy of Sciences, to investigate mesmerism and admitted to the Académie Française in the same year, becoming one of les Immortels.

Baphomet is the idol or other deity thought to have been worshiped by the Knights Templar. The image of Baphomet as a man with a goat's head was created by the French occultist Eliphas Levi. It first appeared as an illustration in his book Dogme et Rituel de la Haute Magie (Dogma and Ritual of High Magic).

Barbaro, Ermolao HPB: Hermolaus Barbarus (21 May 1454 - 14 June 1493) was a Venetian humanist scholar. He edited and translated a number of classical works including Aristotle's Ethics and Politics and his Rhetorica.

Barrachias-Hassan-Oglu is an obscure reference. It may refer to the father of Zechariah, a priest who ministered at the Altar of Incense and was father to John the Baptist.

Barrett, William Fletcher (10 February 1844 - 26 May 1925) was an English physicist and parapsychologist. While investigating mesmerism, he became interested in the phenomena of spiritualism. He conducted his first spiritualist research in 1874. Two years later he submitted a paper, 'Some Phenomena Associated with Abnormal Conditions of Mind,' to the British Association for the Advancement of Science. The paper reported Barrett's experiments in telepathy and his view that

it was the result of some kind of nervous induction. Barrett called a conference in the offices of the British National Association of Spiritualists in January 1882 which led to the formation of the Society for Psychical Research (SPR).

Bart, C.C. is the author of The Cabiri in Germany published c. 1836. His text presents evidence that magnets were used in healing practices on the island of Samothrace c. 600 BC.

Bartholin, Thomas HPB: Thomas Bartholini (20 October 1616 - 4 December 1680) was a Danish physician, mathematician, and theologian. He is best known for his description of the human lymphatic system.

Batria was the wife of the pharaoh Seti I or Rameses II and the mother of Thermuthis. According to tradition, Thermuthis found the baby Moses in the reeds of the Nile and Batria taught him the wisdom of the ancients.

Bayle, Pierre (18 November 1647 - 28 December 1706) was a French philosopher and writer. His seminal work is The Historical and Critical Dictionary, an encyclopedia of historical figures, published in 1697.

Beaumont, Élie de (25 September 1798 - 21 September 1874) was a French geologist. His is remembered primarily for his theory of the origin of mountain ranges presented to the French Academy of Sciences in 1829, and later published as Notice sur le Système des Montagnes.

Beccaria, Giovanni Battista
(3 October 1716 - 27 May 1781) was
an eminent Italian natural philosopher,
and a member of the Order of the Pious
Schools. His principal work was the
treatise Dell' Elettricismo Naturale ed
Artificiale *(1753).*

Bede, the Venerable *(672/3 AD - 26*
May 735 AD) also Saint Bede was an
English monk and historian. He is known
for his work Historia Ecclesiastica
Gentis Anglorum (Ecclesiastical
History of the English People).

Bell, Alexander Graham *(3 March*
1847 - 2 August 1922) was a Scottish-
born scientist, inventor and engineer. He
patented the first mass-produced telephone,
founding the American Telephone and
Telegraph Company (AT&T) in 1885.

Bentinck, William, 2nd Duke of
Portland *HPB: Duke of Portland, (1*
March 1709 - 1 May 1762) was a
British peer and politician. According to
an article in the Gentleman's Magazine
of July 1757: 'The Duke of Portland's
powder was brought over by a friend of
the duke's from Switzerland, where he
copied the receipt from a domestic
collection which was his fathers. By his
persuasion, the duke, who had been
severely treated by an hereditary gout
several years, had the medicine prepared,
and took it. In his case it proved of great
efficacy, and he therefore published the
receipt for the good of others.'

Bergelmir *(Old Norse: Mountain Yeller*
or Bear Yeller) is a frost giant in Norse
mythology. He is the son of the giant

Thrudgelmir and the grandson of the first
giant Aurgelmir (Ymir).

Bernadette of Lourdes, Saint
full name: Marie-Bernarde Soubirous
(7 January 1844 - 16 April 1879) was
a miller's daughter who had visions of the
Virgin Mary. Her visions occurred at the
Massabielle grotto at Lourdes between 11
February and 16 July 1858. According
to Bernadette, a 'beautiful lady',
identifying herself as 'The Immaculate
Conception' told her a chapel should be
built at the grotto.

Berossus *HPB: Berosus (fl. c. 290*
BC) was a Chaldean priest and author.
His three-volume work Babyloniaca
(History of Babylonia) *preserved the*
culture and history of Babylon.

Berti, Domenico *(17 December1820 -*
22 April 1897) was an Italian essayist,
politician and academic. He was professor
of Moral Philosophy at the University of
Turin and History of Philosophy at
Rome. He wrote the Vita di Giordano
Bruno da Nola (Life of Bruno).

Bertrand Castel, Louis *(5 November*
1688 - 11 January 1757) was a French
mathematician and Jesuit priest. He was
science editor of the Journal de Trévoux,
an academic journal that appeared
monthly from 1701 to 1782.

Bestla *HPB: Besla is the wife of Bor*
and the mother of Odin, Vili and Ve. Her
children were the first of the Æsir, the
principal pantheon of Norse gods. Bestla
and Bor planted the seed that grew into
the Yggdrasil, the tree of life.

Blumenbach, Johann Friedrich
*(11 May 1752 - 22 January 1840)
was a German physiologist and
anthropologist. He is widely regarded as
the founder of physical anthropology.*

Boehme, Jakob *(24 April 1575 - 17
November 1624) was a German
shoemaker who became famous as a
Christian mystic and philosopher. He had
visions revealing the spiritual structure of
the world and the unity of the cosmos.
His first book* Aurora *provoked
accusations of heresy. Hegel described him
as 'the first German philosopher.'*

**Boëthius, Anicius Manlius
Severinus** *(c. 477 AD - 524 AD), was
a Roman senator, consul, and philosopher
of the early 6th Century. In his best
known work* De Consolatione
Philosophiae (Consolation of
Philosophy) *he argued that everything is
subject to divine providence despite the
apparent inequality of the world.*

Bois-Robert *is an obscure reference. It
may indicate Louis-Joseph Lavallée
Marquis de Boisrobert, also called Joseph
Lavallée (23 August 1747 - 28
February 1816) He was a French
polymath and man of letters.*

Bölþorn *HPB: Bolthara (Old Norse:
evil thorn) is a frost giant in Norse
mythology. His parentage is unknown. He
is the maternal grandfather of the god
Odin. In English, his name is also
written as Bolthorn or Boelthor.*

Bonelli, Gaetano *(1815-1867) was
an Italian inventor. He made several*

*inventions related to telegraphy and
photography. He was the director of
telegraph services in Turin. With English
inventor Henry Cook, he formed Bonelli's
Electric Telegraph Company in 1860.*

Bordj *is a volcano, according to
Blavatsky, the father of the Zoroastrian
deity of light Mithra. As far as it has
been possible to ascertain, this reference to
Bordj as volcano/father appears
exclusively in the writing of Blavatsky.
No third party source has been found
for verification.*

Borie, Jean-François *(died 21 May
1784) was a French physician. He was
appointed to the 1784 Franklin
committee, convened by the French
Academy of Sciences, to investigate
mesmerism but unfortunately died before
he could begin work. He was replaced at
the king's request by the physician Michel-
Joseph Majault.*

Borr *HPB: Bör (sometimes anglicized
Bor or Bur) was the son of the first Norse
god Búri, HPB: Bur, and the husband of
Bestla, HPB: Besla. He is the father of
Odin, Vili and Ve.*

Bory, Gabriel de *HPB: De Borg
(11 March 1720 - 8 October 1801)
was a French naval officer and physicist.
He was a member of the French Academy
of Sciences and appointed to the 1784
Franklin committee, convened by the
Academy, to investigate mesmerism*

Bosco, Giovanni Bartolomeo
*(3 January 1793 - 7 March 1863) was
an Italian illusionist born in Turin. He*

became one of the greatest conjurers of the 19th Century.

Boucher de Perthes or *Jacques Boucher de Crèvecœur de Perthes (10 September 1788 - 5 August 1868) was a French archaeologist notable for his discovery of flint tools in the gravels of the Somme valley c. 1830. This find made him the first to establish that Europe had been populated by early man. Subsequent archeological investigation has shown the tools to be at least 500,000 years old.*

Boudin, Jean-Christian-Marc *(1806-1867) was an army physician, medical geographer and anthropologist. He was a prolific author of articles on medicine and anthropology. He contributed the article 'Histoire Physique et Médicale de la Foudre et de ses Effets' (Physical and Medical History of Lightning and its Effects) to the second volume of* Annales d'Hygiène Publique et de Médecine Légale (Annals of Public Health and Forensic Medicine) *published in 1854.*

Boué, Ami *(16 March 1794 - 21 November 1881) was a geologist of French origin. He traveled extensively in Germany, Austria and southern Europe, investigating various geological formations. He is acknowledged as one of the pioneers of geological research. He was a founder of the Société Géologique de France in 1830, and subsequently its president.*

Bourdois de la Motte, Edme-Joachim *(14 September 1754 – 7 December 1835) was a French physician*

and an early member of the French Academy of Medicine. He served as its chair in 1822, 1823 and 1829. He was a member of the Academy's 1826 Husson commission, convened to investigate mesmerism.

Boussingault, Jean-Baptiste Joseph Dieudonné *(1 February 1801 - 11 May 1887) was a French chemist. He made significant contributions to agricultural science, petroleum science and metallurgy. He was a member of the French Academy of Sciences.*

Boyle, Robert *(25 January 1627 - 31 December 1691) was an Anglo-Irish natural philosopher, chemist, physicist, and inventor. Boyle is regarded as one of the founders of modern chemistry and a pioneer of the modern experimental scientific method. He formulated Boyle's law, which describes the inversely proportional relationship between the absolute pressure and volume of a gas, if the temperature is kept constant within a closed system. Among his works,* The Skeptical Chymist *is seen as a seminal text in the field of chemistry. A devout Anglican, he is also noted for his writings in theology.*

Brahma *is the creator god in Hinduism. His consort is the goddess Saraswati. He is one of the trinity of great Hindu gods which includes Shiva and Vishnu. He is depicted with four faces and is also known as Svayambhu (self-born) and Vāgīśa (Lord of speech and the creator of the four Vedas, one from each of his mouths).*

Brasseur de Bourbourg, Abbé Charles-Étienne *(8 September 1814 - 8 January 1874) was a noted French writer, ethnographer, historian and archaeologist. His French translation of the Popol Vuh included a grammar of the K'iche' language and an essay on Central American mythology.*

Brewster, David *(11 December 1781 - 10 February 1868) was a Scottish physicist, mathematician, astronomer, inventor, writer, and science historian. He was the author of* A Treatise on Optics *published in 1853.*

Brière de Boismont, Alexandre Jacques François, HPB: Brierre de Boismont *(18 October 1797 - 25 December 1881) was a French physician and psychiatrist. He was the author of numerous publications in different medical fields including hygiene, forensic medicine and anatomy. He is best known for his work in psychiatry. In 1845 he published* Des Hallucinations, ou Histoire Raisonnée des Apparitions, des Visions, des Songes, de l'extase, du Magnétisme et du Somnambulisme (Hallucinations: or the Rational History of Apparitions, Dreams, Ecstasy, Magnetism, and Somnambulism). *This landmark study examined hallucinations and their role in the psychological history of mankind.*

Bruno, Giordano *(1548 - 17 February 1600), born Filippo Bruno, was an Italian Dominican friar, philosopher, mathematician, poet, and cosmological theorist. He proposed that the stars were distant suns surrounded by their own planets. He raised the possibility that these planets could foster life (a philosophical position known as cosmic pluralism). He also insisted that the universe is infinite and could have no celestial body at its center. He believed the cross was a symbol that first appeared in ancient Egypt as the ankh. Bruno was murdered by the Roman Inquisition for his beliefs. His trial lasted seven years. On 17 February 1600 in Rome's Campo de' Fiori he was hung upside down naked before finally being burned at the stake. His ashes were thrown into the Tiber.*

Buchanan, Joseph Rodes *(11 December 1814 - 26 December 1899) was an American physician and professor of physiology at the Eclectic Medical Institute in Covington, Kentucky. Buchanan came to prominence in the 1840s as mesmerism and spiritualism became popular. He is credited with coining the term 'psychometry' and was author of the* Manual of Psychometry: The Dawn of a New Civilization *published in 1893.*

Büchner, Ludwig *(29 March 1824 - 1 May 1899) was a German philosopher, physiologist and physician. In 1881 he founded The German Freethinkers League (Der Deutscher Freidenkerbund) to oppose the power of state churches. He is the author of* Die Stellung des Menschen in der Natur *published in English as* Man in the Past, Present and Future *in 1872.*

Buffon, Georges-Louis Leclerc, Comte de *(7 September 1707 - 16 April 1788) was a French naturalist,* mathematician, cosmologist, and encyclopedist. He was the principal author of Histoire Naturelle, Générale et Particulière (Natural History, General and Particular) a compendium of all contemporary knowledge of the natural sciences published in 1749.

Bulwer-Lytton, Edward George Earle Lytton 1st Baron Lytton (25 May 1803 - 18 January 1873) was an English novelist, poet, playwright, and politician. He wrote a string of bestselling novels including The Last Days of Pompeii, Vril: the Power of the Coming Race, and Zanoni. The novels in particular had a great influence on theosophical writers. Annie Besant and Blavatsky incorporated many of his thoughts and ideas in their own works.

Bunsen, Christian Charles Josias von also Baron von Bunsen (25 August 1791 - 28 November 1860) was a German diplomat and scholar. He is the author of Ägyptens Stelle in der Weltgeschichte (Egypt's Place in Universal History) published in five volumes 1844-57.

Burattini, Tito Livio (8 March 1617 - 17 November 1681) was an Italian inventor, architect, Egyptologist, scientist, instrument-maker, traveler, engineer, and nobleman. He explored the Great Pyramid of Giza with the English mathematician John Greaves in 1639.

Burdin, Jean (c. 1768 - 26 July 1835) was a French physician. He was a founding member of the Société Anatomique de Paris in 1803. He

became a member of the French Academy of Medicine in 1821. In 1825, he was part of a special committee supporting Pierre Foissac's call for the Academy to mount a new inquiry into mesmerism. He became the Academy's president in 1831.

Burges, George (1786 - 11 January 1864) was an English classicist. He translated the works of Plato for Bohn's Classical library. He is noted as a competent scholar but overly fond of introducing arbitrary revisions or corrections into classical texts.

Búri HPB: Bur was the first god in Norse mythology. He is the father of Borr and grandfather of Odin, Vili and Ve. He was formed by the cow Audhumla licking the salty ice of Ginnungagap during the time of Ymir. The only extant source of this myth is Snorri Sturluson's Prose Edda. (See Chapter Four, note 9.)

Butler, Samuel (baptized 14 February 1613 - 25 September 1680) was an English poet and satirist. He is remembered for his long satirical poem Hudibras (1663-1678) ridiculing religious infighting.

Butlerov, Alexander Mikhaylovich, HPB: Butleroff (15 September 1828 - 17 August 1886) was a Russian chemist. He was a member of the Imperial Academy of Sciences and creator of the theory of chemical structure. His wife's cousin, the journalist Alexander Aksakov introduced him to spiritualism. Butlerov published his seminal article Mediumistic Phenomena in the Russian Herald in 1875.

Buttmann, Philipp Karl *(5 December 1764 - 21 June 1829), was a German historical philologist. He was a major contributor to the scientific study of the Greek language. His* Griechische Grammatik (Greek Grammar) *published in 1792 went through many editions, and was translated into English.*

C.

Cabanis, Pierre Jean Georges *(5 June 1757 - 5 May 1808) was a French physiologist and materialist philosopher. His most famous work* Rapports du Physique et du Moral de l'Homme (Relations of the Physical and the Moral in Man) *was published in 1802. Cabanis attempted to explain the psychic, mental, and moral aspects of man in terms of pure materialism. He proposed that life was nothing more than the organization of physical forces. He maintained that thought was a secretion of the brain just as bile is a secretion of the liver. The soul was superfluous because consciousness was the result of mechanistic processes. Toward the end of his life, he regarded the ego as immaterial and immortal and believed this to be compatible with his earlier worldview.*

Caesar, Gaius Julius *(13 July 100 BC - 15 March 44 BC) was Dictator of the Roman Republic from 29 October 49 BC to 15 March 44 BC. During his lifetime, he was regarded as one of the best orators and prose authors in Latin; even Cicero spoke highly of Caesar's rhetoric and style. For more information about his* Commentaries, *see Chapter Six, note 7.*

Caesar, Tiberius *(16 November 42 BC - 16 March 37 AD) was Roman emperor from 14 AD to 37 AD. He was the son of Tiberius Claudius Nero and Livia Drusilla. According to Isidore, Archbishop of Seville, Tiberius had the inventor of flexible glass beheaded, fearing the new material could undermine the value of gold and silver.*

Cagliostro, Count Alessandro di *real name Giuseppe Balsamo (2 June 1743 - 26 August 1795) was an Italian adventurer and magician. He became a glamorous figure associated with the royal courts of Europe where he pursued various occult arts, including psychic healing, alchemy and scrying. He was tried by the Roman Inquisition in December 1789 and originally sentenced to death. The sentence was later commuted to life imprisonment at the Forte di San Leo, where he would eventually die.*

Calcidius *HPB: Chalcidius (fl. 4th Century AD) was a medieval philosopher. He translated the first part of Plato's* Timaeus *from Greek into Latin and provided an extensive commentary. His translation was the only extensive Platonic text known to scholars in the West for approximately 800 years. Little else is known about him.*

Callimachus *(fl. 5th Century BC) was a Greek sculptor. Reputedly, he invented the Corinthian capital after seeing acanthus leaves growing on a tomb. According to Pausanias, Callimachus was the inventor of an ingenious golden lamp hanging in the cellar of the Erechtheion, the temple of Athena and Poseidon on the*

Acropolis. It needed to be refilled with oil only once a year as the asbestos wick did not burn.

Callisthenes of Olynthus *(c. 360 BC - 328 BC) was a Greek historian in Macedon. He was the official historian of Alexander the Great's Asiatic expedition recommended by his uncle Aristotle, Alexander's former tutor.*

Campanella, Tommaso *real name Giovanni Domenico Campanella (5 September 1568 - 21 May 1639) was an Italian philosopher, Dominican friar, astrologer and poet. He was tried by the Inquisition for his heterodox views and interests in astrology and metaphysics. He eventually escaped by fleeing to France.*

Capel, Monsignor Thomas John *(28 October 1836 - 23 October 1911) was an Irish priest, later Monsignor. He is reputedly the first Irish clergyman to meet Bernadette Soubirous (St Bernadette of Lourdes), meeting her in 1859.*

Cardano, Gerolamo *(24 September 1501 - 21 September 1576) was an Italian mathematician, physician, philosopher and gambler. He was one of the most influential mathematicians of the Renaissance, and a key figure in the development of the theory of probability. His principal philosophical work* De Subtilitate Rerum (On Natural Phenomena), *published in 1550, includes the concept of the world soul.*

Carpenter, James *(1840 - 17 October 1899) was a British astronomer. He was an assistant at the Royal Observatory,* *Greenwich. With James Nasmyth he was the author of* The Moon: Considered as a Planet, a World, and a Satellite *(1874). The lunar crater 'Carpenter' is named for him.*

Carpenter, William Benjamin *(29 October 1813 - 9 November 1885) was an English physician. He was the author of* Mesmerism, Spiritualism, Etc: Historically and Scientifically Considered *(1877). He believed that spiritualist phenomena could be explained by psychological factors such as hypnotism and suggestion. He is reported as having described the paranormal and spiritualism as 'epidemic delusions.'*

Casalius, Joannes Baptista *(1578-1648) was an Italian cleric, historian and doctor of law. He was the author of several works examining ancient sacred rites including* De Veteribus Aegyptiorum Ritibus (the Rites of the Ancient Egyptians) *published in 1644.*

Cassian, John *John the Ascetic or John Cassian the Roman (c. 360 AD - 435 AD) was a Christian monk and theologian. He was celebrated in both western and eastern churches for his mystical writings. Cassian brought the ideas and practices of Christian monasticism to the early medieval West.*

Caussidière, Marc *(18 May 1808 - 27 January 1861) was a wine broker and French revolutionary. He took part in the Lyon insurgency of 1834 (in which his brother died). He was subsequently sentenced to 20 years in prison but was pardoned in 1837.*

Cebes of Thebes *(c. 430 BC - 350 BC) was a Greek philosopher. According to Xenophon of Athens he was a member of Socrates' inner circle. He is one of the speakers in Plato's dialogue* Phaedo. *The dialogue takes place in the final hours before Socrates' death and its subject is the immortality of the soul.*

Censorinus *(fl. 3rd Century AD) was a Roman grammarian and writer. He is the author of* De Die Natali (On His Birthday) *written in 238 AD for his patron Quintus Caerellius, a Roman knight, on his 49th birthday. The treatise examines the natural history of man, the influence of the stars and genii, music, religious rites, astronomy, and the ideas of the Greek philosophers.*

Cerise, Laurent Alexis Philibert *(27 February 1807 - 5 October 1869) was a French physician. He was one of the founders of the psychiatric journal* Annales Médico-psychologiques. *He became a member of the Accademia delle Scienze de Turin in 1853 and a member of the Académie de Médecine in Paris in 1864.*

Champollion, Jean-François *(23 December 1790 - 4 March 1832) was a French scholar, philologist and orientalist, known primarily as the decipherer of Egyptian hieroglyphs. He is considered the founder and father of Egyptology.*

Chevreul, Michel Eugène *HPB: Dr. Chevreuil (31 August 1786 - 9 April 1889) was a French chemist. In 1854 he published* De la Baguette Divinatoire (On Diving Rods) *a treatise debunking psychic phenomena. He maintained that involuntary muscular reactions were responsible for phenomena like telekinesis. He was one of the first proponents of the ideo-motor principle.*

Cicero, Marcus Tullius *(3 January 106 BC - 7 December 43 BC) was a Roman statesman, lawyer and philosopher. His treatise* De Divinatione (Concerning Divination) *examined the credibility of divination. It is notable as a primary source of information about the workings of ancient Roman religion.*

Citois, François *HPB: Citesius, Franciscus (1572-1652) was personal physician to Cardinal Richelieu.*

Clare of Assisi, Saint *full name: Chiara Offreduccio (16 July 1194 - 11 August 1253) was one of the first followers of Saint Francis of Assisi. She founded the Order of St. Clare (the Clarissines), a monastic religious order for women in the Franciscan tradition, and wrote their Rule of Life, the first set of monastic guidelines known to have been written by a woman.*

Clement of Alexandria *Titus Flavius Clemens HPB: Clemens Alexandrinus (c. 150 AD - c. 215 AD) was a Christian theologian and apologist. He was leader of the Catechetical School of Alexandria.*

Comte, Isidore Marie Auguste François Xavier *(19 January 1798 - 5 September 1857), was a French philosopher and the founder of positivism. Positivism is a philosophical system in* which information derived from sensory experience, interpreted through reason and logic, forms the exclusive source of knowledge. It excludes any form of metaphysics. Comte conceived a particular role in the positivist era for women. His ideas are difficult for a modern reader to accept because they included a utopian vision of women as virgin mothers and artifical insemination.

Comte, Louis Apollinaire Christien Emmanuel , also simply Comte, 'The King's Conjurer' (22 June 1788 - 25 November 1859) was a 19th-century Parisian magician. He was greatly admired by the famous French illusionist Jean-Eugène Robert-Houdin.

Cooke, Josiah Parsons (12 October 1827 - 3 September 1894) was an American chemist and Erving Professor of Chemistry and Mineralogy at Harvard University. He is the author of The New Chemistry a series of lectures given at the Lowell Institute in Boston, published in 1874.

Copernicus, Nicolaus (19 February 1473 - 24 May 1543) was a Polish mathematician and astronomer. He formulated a model of the universe placing the sun rather than the earth at its center. The publication of his book De Revolutionibus Orbium Coelestium (On the Revolutions of the Celestial Spheres), just before his death in 1543, was a major event in the history of science, triggering the Copernican Revolution and making a pioneering contribution to the Scientific Revolution.

Cory, Isaac Preston (1802-1842) was a British barrister, antiquarian and book collector. He compiled fragments from ancient writers and published them in a compendium with the title Cory's Ancient Fragments. The first edition appeared in 1826.

Costeo, Giovanni HPB: Costæus (1528-1603) was an Italian physician, botanist and chemist. He taught medicine at Turin and Bologna.

Covindasamy HPB: Kavindasami was an Indian fakir. He became well known in the West through the writing of the French author Louis Jacolliot. His miraculous feats were described in detail in Jacolliot's Occult Science in India and Among the Ancients (1884). Covindasamy's abilities were also noted by other European authors in the German monthly journal, Psychische Studien.

Cox, Edward William (1809-1879) was an English lawyer, legal writer and successful publisher. He was a member of The London Dialectical Society's committee to investigate spiritualism and assisted William Crookes in his examination of mediumship. He coined the term 'psychic force' to describe the mechanism that gives rise to spiritualist phenomena.

Crookes, William (17 June 1832 - 4 April 1919) was a highly respected English chemist and physicist. His experimental work was known for the originality of its design and he was considered a superb experimentalist. His interests, ranging from pure to applied *science to psychic research, made him a well-known personality and generated a substantial income. He received many public and academic honors. His interest in spiritualism led him to join the Theosophical Society and he became president of the Society for Psychical Research. He was notable for his investigation into the spirit entity known as Katie King. Crookes believed that spiritualism and mediumship were genuine phenomena.*

Cudworth, Ralph *(1617 - 26 June 1688) was an English Anglican clergyman, Professor of Hebrew at Cambridge University and Master of Clare College. His book* The True Intellectual System of the Universe *(1678) set out to prove the existence of God and the reality of human freedom.*

Cuvier, Georges *real name: Jean Léopold Nicolas Frédéric Cuvier (23 August 1769 - 13 May 1832) was a highly influential French naturalist and zoologist. In his* Essay on the Theory of the Earth *(1813) he proposed that now-extinct species had been wiped out by periodic catastrophic floods. He became the most influential proponent of catastrophism in geology in the early 19th Century.*

D.

Dagon *is a Mesopotamian deity. The similarity of his name to the Hebrew word for fish has led to his identification as a fish god. Dagon's name was more likely derived from a word for 'grain',*

suggesting that he was originally associated with fertility and agriculture. Dagon is often equated with the amphibious deity Oannes in Mesopotamian mythology described in the writings of Berossus.

Dante *or Durante di Alighiero degli Alighieri (c. 1265-1321) was an Italian poet. His* Divine Comedy *is widely considered the most important poem of the Middle Ages and the greatest literary work in the Italian language.*

Darwin, Charles Robert *(12 February 1809 - 19 April 1882) was an English naturalist. In 1859 he published* On the Origin of Species *presenting his theory of evolution by natural selection. This revolutionized western scientific thinking. His earlier theory of pangenesis had attempted to explain the mechanism of heredity, proposing that the tissues of an organism threw off fragments of themselves which accumulated in the sex organs and determined the inherited characteristics of offspring.*

Davis, Andrew Jackson *(11 August 1826 - 13 January 1910) was an American mesmerist and spiritualist. Largely uneducated, he came to believe he had clairvoyant powers after attending lectures on animal magnetism. He became a successful mesmerizer and healer. He published* The Diakka and their Earthly Victims *in 1873.*

Davis, Samuel *(1760-1819) was an English soldier, diplomat, and a director of the East India Company. He read both*

Sanskrit and Hindi and was a member of the Asiatic Society. He studied Indian astronomical tables obtained by the French astronomer Guillaume Le Gentil. These tables demonstrated accurate scientific knowledge of astronomy dating back to the 3rd Century BC. His essay on the advanced nature of Indian astronomy appeared in the journal Asiatic Researches in 1790.

Deleuze, Joseph Philippe François
(1753 - 31 October 1835) was a French naturalist. He became assistant naturalist at the Muséum National d'Histoire Naturelle in 1795. He was a member of the Société des Observateurs de l'Homme, described as the birth place of French Anthropology.

Delrio, Martin *HPB: Delrius (17 May 1551 - 19 October 1608) was a Jesuit theologian. He gained a master's degree in law from Salamanca in 1574. After a period of political service in the Spanish Netherlands, he became a Jesuit in 1580. He wrote many books, including classical commentaries and works of biblical exegesis. He is best known for his six-volume* Magical Investigations *(1599–1600), a work on magic, superstition, and witchcraft.*

Demeter *is the Greek goddess of corn, grain, the harvest and fertility. She also presides over sacred law and the cycle of life and death. She is the central deity in the Eleusinian Mysteries. (See also Chapter Five, notes 16 and 17.)*

Democritus *(c. 460 BC - c. 370 BC) was a pre-Socratic philosopher in ancient*

Greece. He was known as the 'laughing philosopher' because he stressed the value of cheerfulness. He formulated an atomic theory of the universe, developing the ideas of the earlier Greek philosopher Leucippus. According to Bertrand Russell, the worldview of both Leucippus and Democritus 'was remarkably like that of modern science, and avoided most of the faults to which Greek speculation was prone.'

Denton, Elizabeth Melissa Foote
(2 May 1826 - 1916) was an American psychometrist and author, and the wife of the geologist William Denton. She and her husband studied her considerable psychometric abilities and published their findings in 1863 in The Soul of Things or Psychometric Researches and Discoveries.

Denton, William *(January 1823 - 1883) was an American naturalist, explorer and geologist. (See also **Denton, Elizabeth Melissa Foote**.)*

Descartes, René *(31 March 1596 - 11 February 1650) was a French philosopher, mathematician, and scientist. His seminal philosophical statement 'I think, therefore I am' (Je pense, donc je suis, Latin:* cogito, ergo sum*) appears in* Discourse on the Method *(1637) and* Principles of Philosophy *(1644). In* Meditations on First Philosophy *he attempted to demonstrate the existence of God and the distinction between the human soul and the body suggesting that mind and body are distinct but closely joined.*

Deslon, Charles Nicolas *(6 December 1738 - 21 August 1786) was a French physician. He was a professor at the Faculty of Medicine in Paris and member of the Royal Society of Medicine. He was a follower and supporter of Franz Mesmer's theories on animal magnetism. Like Mesmer, Deslon claimed to be able to cure certain diseases by the laying on of hands. He wrote many works on the subject, the most important of which was* Observations on Animal Magnetism *published in 1780. In 1784 Louis XVI appointed two commissions to investigate the phenomenon. They studied Deslon's application of magnetism and found no basis for belief in its existence.*

Diana *was the Roman goddess of the hunt. She is associated with wild animals, woodland and the ability to communicate with animals. Her equivalent in Greek mythology is the goddess Artemis.*

Dionysius of Halicarnassus *(c. 60 BC - c. 7 BC) was a Greek historian and teacher of rhetoric. He is the author of the highly influential history of Rome* Roman Antiquities *which is one of the primary sources of the myth of Romulus and Remus.*

Dolgorukov, Alexei Vladimirovich, Prince. *HPB: Dolgorouky (1813-1869) was a prominent Russian mesmerist. He treated patients in several Moscow institutions. From April 1859 he was a consultant at hospitals in St. Petersburg. He published* Organon of Animal Mesmerism *in 1860 with the subtitle* Practical study, methods of using it to treat diseases and a

chronicle of the historical course of animal mesmerism in Russia.

Donkin, Horatio Bryan *known simply as Bryan (1 February 1842 - 26 July 1927) was a British physician, political radical, and member of the prison service.*

Double, François-Joseph *(11 March 1776 - 12 June 1842) was a French physician and the co-founder of the French Academy of Medicine in Paris in 1820. He was a member of the Academy's 1826 Husson commission, convened to investigate mesmerism.*

Dozous, Pierre Romaine *(1799-1883) was a French physician. He was the first doctor to take an interest in Bernadette Soubirous and her visions of the Virgin Mary at Lourdes. In 1874 he published* La Grotte de Lourdes. Sa Fontaine, ses Guérisons *(The Grotto of Lourdes, its Spring and its Cures).*

Draper, John William *(5 May 1811 - 4 January 1882) was an English-American scientist, philosopher, physician, chemist, historian and photographer. He is credited with producing the first clear photograph of a female face (1839–40) and the first detailed photograph of the moon (1840). He is the author of* History of the Conflict Between Religion and Science *(1874) an immensely successful book popularizing Draper's conflict thesis - the idea that there is an intrinsic hostility in the relationship between religion and science.*

Drummer of Tedworth, the *refers to a story about an unlicensed vagrant* *drummer called William Drury. It appears in the book* Saducismus Triumphatus *(1681) by Joseph Glanvill. In 1661 John Mompesson, owner of a house in the town of Tedworth in Wiltshire, brought a lawsuit against William Drury accusing him of collecting money by false pretenses. Mompesson won the case and Drury's drum was turned over to him by the local bailiff. Subsequently, Mompesson's house was disturbed by mysterious nightly drumming noises. It was alleged that William Drury had used witchcraft to create the phenomenon.*

Drummond, William James Charles Maria of Logiealmond
(baptized 26 September 1769 - 29 March 1828) was a Scottish diplomat, Member of Parliament, poet and philosopher. He is the author of Oedipus Judaicus (The Jewish Oedipus) *published in 1811. It gives an allegorical interpretation of passages from the* Book of Genesis *and the* Book of Joshua *and includes detailed arguments based on astrology.*

Dufferin, 1st Marquess of *Frederick Temple Hamilton-Temple-Blackwood (21 June 1826 - 12 February 1902) was a distinguished British diplomat, Governor of Canada and Viceroy of India. He wrote many successful travel books including* Journal of the Journey from Government House Ottawa to British Columbia and Back *(1877).*

Dunlap, Samuel Fales *(1825-1905) was an American religio-mythology scholar. He is the author of* Sōd: the

Mysteries of Adoni *(1861) which connects Christianity with the much earlier Mystery Tradition and explores the hypothesis that 'the Old Testament is the first offshoot from the Mysteries.'*

Dupuis, Charles-François
(26 October 1742 - 29 September 1809) was a French scholar, scientist and politician. In 1795, he published Origine de Tous les Cultes, ou la Religion Universelle (The Origin of All Cults, or Universal Religion). *Drawing on extensive comparative work, he aimed to demonstrate the common origin of the religious and astronomical ideas of the Egyptians, Greeks, Chinese, Persians and Arabs.*

E.

Eberhard, Johann Peter *HPB:* Eberhart *(2 December 1727 - 17 December 1779) was a German doctor, theologian, mathematician and physicist. He became professor of philosophy at the royal Friedrich University in Halle in 1753, and was appointed professor of medicine in 1756. He became chair of physics at the University of Halle in 1769 and was inducted into the Leopoldina Academy of Scholars in 1753.*

Ebers, Georg Moritz *(1 March 1837 - 7 August 1898) was a German Egyptologist and novelist. In the winter of 1873-74 he discovered an Egyptian medical papyrus at Luxor. Dated c. 1550 BC, it is one of the oldest medical documents in the world. It was*

subsequently named for him as The Ebers Papyrus and is now housed in the Leipzig University Library.

Eddy, William and Horatio *the Eddy Brothers (Horatio 1842-1922 / William 1832-1932) were American mediums. Both brothers claimed to have had strong psychic abilities from an early age. The Eddy Farm in Chittenden, a small hamlet near Rutland, Vermont was the scene of regular seances for visitors from around the world.*

Edison, Thomas Alva *(11 February 1847 - 18 October 1931) was an American inventor and businessman. His inventions included the phonograph, the movie camera, and the electric light bulb. In 1875, he thought he had identified a new force, which he called 'etheric'. But it was later discovered to be radio waves. Edison was a member of the Theosophical Society and is widely regarded as America's greatest inventor.*

Elihu *is a man, described in the Book of Job, who comforts Job in his suffering. His monologue includes discussion of the wisdom and mercy of divine providence, the supremacy of God, and the benevolence of creation. The lines quoted by Blavatsky appear in Job 32:9.*

Emeph *is the prince and ruler of all the celestial gods in ancient Egyptian mythology. According to Iamblichus in* De Mysteriis (On the Mysteries) *Emeph is 'an intellect thinking himself.' There is some confusion about Iamblichus' use of 'Emeph' because there is no record of an Egyptian god with this name. Several*

scholars have suggested that Emeph is actually the god Kneph, variously a winged egg, a globe surrounded by one or more serpents, or Amun in the form of a serpent.

Emerson, Ralph Waldo *(25 May 1803- 27 April 1882) was an American essayist, lecturer and poet. He was the leader of the 19th-century transcendentalist movement, which emphasized a belief in the spiritual potential of every individual.*

Empedocles *(c. 490 BC - c. 430 BC) was a pre-Socratic philosopher. He originated the idea that everything is composed of four essential elements: air, earth, water and fire. He proposed that nothing is created or destroyed, things are merely transformed and believed in the transmigration of souls.*

Ennemoser, Joseph *(15 November 1787 - 19 September 1854) was a Tyrolean physician and scientist. In 1819, he became a professor of medicine at the University of Bonn. He was a supporter of Anton Mesmer and his theory of animal magnetism and went on to gain a great reputation in Munich as a 'magnetic physician.' He is the author of* Geschichte der Magie (The History of Magic) *published in 1844.*

Enoch *is a figure from the Antediluvian period in the Bible, an ancestor of Noah. According to the Book of Genesis, 'When Jared had lived 162 years, he became the father of Enoch. When Enoch had lived 65 years, he became the father of Methuselah. After he became the father of*

Methuselah, Enoch walked faithfully with God 300 years and had other sons and daughters. Altogether, Enoch lived a total of 365 years. Enoch walked faithfully with God; then he was no more, because God took him away.' This Enoch is not to be confused with Cain's son Enoch who appears in Genesis 4:17.

Epicharmus (c. 550 BC - c. 460 BC) was a Greek dramatist and philosopher. Plato described him as 'the prince of comedy.' He is thought to have written more than 50 plays in the Sicilian dialect but just the titles of 35 works survive. Only fragments of his texts exist today.

Epicurus (341 BC - 270 BC) was an ancient Greek philosopher. He founded the highly influential school of philosophy now known as Epicureanism. He proposed an ethical philosophy of simple pleasure, friendship, and non-involvement in political and public life. Based on radical materialism, he believed he could disprove the immortality of the soul, so liberating his followers from the threat of punishment in an afterlife.

Eriugena, John Scotus HPB: John Erigena (c. 815 AD - c. 877 AD) was an Irish theologian, Neoplatonist philosopher, and poet. He is regarded as the most important Irish intellectual of the early monastic period. He proposed that all causes are in actuality one single principle in the divine One. God is the One or the highest principle, which transcends all.

Eslinger, Elizabeth was a 38-year-old widow, held in Weinsberg prison,

Germany in 1835 for offenses connected with digging for buried treasure. Her story is recounted by the English novelist and collector of spirit stories, Catherine Crowe in The Night Side of Nature or Ghosts and Ghost Seers (1848). Eslinger was troubled by an apparition whilst at Weinsberg and placed under the care of a Dr Justinus Kerner. As many as 50 reliable eyewitnesses testified that they had seen the apparition that plague her.

Euclid (fl. c. 300 BC) was a Greek mathematician. He is often referred to as the father of geometry. He was active in Alexandria during the reign of the Egyptian Pharaoh Ptolemy I (323 BC - 283 BC). His mathematical treatise in 13 volumes, the Elements is one of the most influential works in the history of mathematics.

Eupolemus (fl. c. 150 BC) was a Jewish historian. He wrote many works in Greek of which only fragments survive. His popular history of the Jews On the Kings in Judaea was quoted by both Clement of Alexandria and Eusebius. The fragment of his writings usually known as Pseudo-Eupolemus claims that the Assyrian city of Babylon was built by giants who escaped the Flood.

Euripides (c. 484 BC - 406 BC) was a Greek dramatist and the last of classical Athens' great tragic dramatists. The lines quoted by Blavatsky appear in Plato's dialogue Ion. Ion is a professional reciter of Homer's poems. Plato has Socrates say to him, '...talking well about Homer is not some skill within you - as I was just saying - but it is a divine power that *moves you, just as in that stone which Euripides calls a 'Magnet' but which most people call Herakleian.'*

F.

Faraday, Michael *(22 September 1791 - 25 August 1867) was an English physicist and chemist. His work with electricity and magnets laid the foundations for modern electromagnetic technology and he is regarded as one of the greatest scientists of the 19th Century. In the 1850s, the spiritualist craze was at its height. Because the phenomena were thought to be associated with magnets and electricity, Faraday was inundated with requests for his views on the subject. He observed a number of seances and concluded that table turning was caused by the involuntary muscular spasms of the participants. He reported his findings in letters to* The Times *dated 28 June 1853 and* The Athenaeum *dated 2 July 1853. Despite Faraday's intervention, public interest in the paranormal continued to grow. In response to this, he organized a series of lectures at The Royal Institution in 1854 to demonstrate the value of scientific education.*

Faust *is the protagonist of a classic German legend, based on the historical Johann Georg Faust also known in English as John Faustus (c. 1480 - 1540). He was a German itinerant alchemist, astrologer and magician of the German Renaissance. Doctor Faust became the subject of folk legend in the decades after his death, adapted by*

Christopher Marlowe in his play The Tragical History of the Life and Death of Doctor Faustus *(1604) and the legend was again adapted in Johann Wolfgang von Goethe's drama* Faust *(1808). Faust is a charlatan who is highly successful yet dissatisfied with his life. He makes a pact with the Devil, exchanging his soul for unlimited knowledge and worldly pleasures.*

Favre, Jules Claude Gabriel *(21 March 1809 - 20 January 1880) was a French statesman. After the establishment of the Third Republic in September 1870, he became one of the leaders of the Moderate Republicans in the National Assembly. He began his career as an advocate.*

Felix, Lucius Cornelius Sulla *known simply as Sulla (c. 138 BC - 78 BC) was a Roman general and statesman. He was the victor in the first Roman civil war (88 BC - 82 BC) and Dictator of Rome from 82 BC - 79 BC.*

Felt, George Henry *(born 21 September 1831) was an American engineer, Egyptologist, and theosophist . On 7 September 1875, he lectured on the 'Lost Proportion of the Egyptians' in Blavatsky's apartment in New York. Felt described the symbolic content of ancient Egyptian geometrical figures and he also claimed to have discovered how Egyptian priests made contact with the elementary systems of earth, water, fire, and air by means of evocation.*

Ficino, Marsilio *HPB: Ficinus (19 October 1433 - 1 October 1499)* was an Italian scholar and Catholic priest who was one of the most influential humanist philosophers of the early Italian Renaissance. He was an astrologer, a reviver of Neoplatonism and the first translator of Plato's complete extant works into Latin.

Fiske, John *(30 March 1842 - 4 July 1901) was an American philosopher and historian. In his collection of essays,* The Unseen World *(1876), he criticizes the argument presented in John Draper's* History of the Conflict Between Science and Religion *saying 'in reality there has never been any conflict between religion and science, nor is any reconciliation called for where harmony has always existed.'*

Flammarion, Nicolas Camille *known as Camille Flammarion (26 February 1842 - 3 June 1925) was a French astronomer and author of more than 50 titles, including popular science works on astronomy, several science fiction novels, and works on psychical research.*

Flourens, Marie-Jean-Pierre *(13 April 1794 - 6 December 1867) was a French physiologist and founder of experimental brain science. As a creationist, he believed species were fixed and he opposed Darwin's theories of evolution.*

Fludd, Robert *also known as Robertus de Fluctibus HPB: Robertus di Fluctibus (17 January 1574 - 8 September 1637) was a prominent English Paracelsian physician. He is remembered as an astrologer, mathematician, cosmologist,*

Kabbalist and an apologist for the Rosicrucian movement.

Foissac, Pierre *(1801-1886) was a French physician. He was Chief Medical Officer of the Legion of Honor and a member of the French Meteorological Society. In 1825, he lobbied the French Academy of Medicine to convene a second inquiry into mesmerism.*

Forsyth, James *known as J.S. Forsyth (fl. 1824-1833) was a British surgeon and the author of* Demonologia or Natural Knowledge Revealed *(1827). Forsyth's book is subtitled* An Exposé of Ancient and Modern Superstitions. *It covers topics including apparitions, demonology, magic, predestination and talismans.*

Fortin, Dr. *(dates unknown) was described by Blavatsky as 'a great physician, and a gentleman profoundly versed in the old Hermetic Philosophy and Astrology.' In 1882, he established the first theosophical group in France, La Société Théosophique des Occultistes de France, and served as its president. The group's charter was later revoked by the Theosophical Society's president, Henry Steel Olcott, because they 'did not follow the rules!'*

Foucault, Jean Bernard Léon *(18 September 1819 - 11 February 1868) was a French physicist. He demonstrated the earth's rotation using a device known as Foucault's pendulum. He made an early measurement of the speed of light and is credited with naming the gyroscope. He became a member of the*

Royal Society of London in 1864. The asteroid 5668 Foucault is named after him and his is one of the 72 names of French scientists, engineers and mathematicians inscribed on the Eiffel Tower.

Fouquier, Pierre Eloy (26 July 1776 - 5 October 1850) was a French physician. He became a member of the French Academy of Medicine in 1820 and served on its 1826 Husson commission to investigate mesmerism. He was elected president of the Academy of Medicine in 1842.

Fourier, François-Marie-Charles (7 April 1772 - 10 October 1837) was a French philosopher and social theorist. He was an influential early socialist thinker and later associated with utopian socialism. In his new utopia, people would live for 144 years, new species of friendly and pacifistic animals such as 'anti-lions' would emerge, and human beings would evolve long and useful tails. He also believed in reincarnation. In the last 15 years of his life he set these ideas aside to concentrate on putting his economic and social ideas into practice.

Fournié, Germain Célestin Édouard (4 March 1833 - 24 March 1886) was a French surgeon, physician, anatomist and physiologist. He was a prominent specialist in neuroanatomy and neurophysiology.

Fox sisters, the Leah (1831-1890), Margaret or Maggie (1833-1893) and Catherine or Kate (1837-1892) were three sisters from New York. They played an important role in popularizing spiritualism. Margaret and Kate were mediums whose seances were highly publicized and profitable. They were managed by their sister, Leah. Their sensational demonstrations at Leah's home in Rochester became known throughout the world as the 'Rochester rappings.'

Francis of Assisi, Saint full name: Giovanni di Pietro di Bernardone (1181 or 1182 - 3 October 1226) was an Italian friar, deacon and preacher. He founded the Franciscan order of the Friars Minor (Ordo Fratrum Minorum) and the lay Third Order.

Franklin, Benjamin (17 January 1706 - 17 April 1790) was one of the Founding Fathers of the United States. He was a renowned polymath and a leading author, political theorist, politician, scientist, inventor, statesman, and US Ambassador to France. As a scientist, he made important discoveries about the nature of electricity. As an inventor, he is known for the lightning rod, bifocals, and the Franklin stove. He chaired the 1784 Franklin committee, convened by the French Academy of Sciences, to investigate mesmerism.

Fulton, Robert (14 November 1765 - 24 February 1815) was an American engineer and inventor. He developed the first commercially successful steamboat, the North River Steamboat (later known as the Clermont). It carried passengers between New York City and the state capital Albany. The Clermont made the 150 mile (240 km) trip in 32 hours.

G.

Gabalis, Comte de *is the eponymous hero of a 17th-century French text by Abbé Nicolas-Pierre-Henri de Montfaucon de Villars (1635-1673). The Comte de Gabalis is an occultist who explains the mysteries of the world to the book's author. The text first appeared anonymously in Paris in 1670 with the title* Le Comte de Gabalis, Ou Entretiens sur les Sciences Secrètes (The Count of Gabalis, Or Dialogues on the Secret Sciences).

Gale, Theophilus *(1629-1678) was a Puritan Calvinist. In his multi-volume work* The Court of the Gentiles *(published between 1669 and 1676) he maintained that all ancient language, knowledge, and philosophy was derived from the Jews, who had received it as divine revelation.*

Galen *(September 129 AD - c. 216 AD) was a Greek physician, writer and philosopher. He was influential in the fields of anatomy, physiology, pathology, neurology and pharmacology.*

Galileo, Galilei *(15 February 1564 - 8 January 1642) was an Italian astronomer and mathematician. His astronomical observations led him to believe that the sun was at the center of the solar system and the earth was a planet orbiting the sun, as Copernicus had theorized. Consequently he was summoned by the Roman Inquisition. He was declared 'suspect of heresy', condemned to life imprisonment, and required to disavow his theories.*

Galvani, Luigi Aloisio *(9 September 1737 - 4 December 1798) was an Italian physician and physicist. He was the first to discover that muscular contractions are caused by electrical stimuli and is now recognized as a pioneer in the field of bioelectromagnetics.*

Gangleri *HPB: Gangler. Gangleri is a pseudonym adopted by King Gylfi (HBP: Gylfe) the earliest recorded king of Scandinavia according to Norse legend. The Prose Edda describes Gylfi's journey in search of wisdom. He adopts the identity of a common man - Gangleri - when he travels to Asgard, the dwelling place of the gods, comparable to the Greek Mount Olympus. (See Chapter Four, note 9.)*

Gasparin, Agénor Étienne, Comte de *(12 July 1810 - 4 May 1871) was a French politician and author. In 1853 he conducted investigations into turning tables. Seances were held at his home over a period of five months. He concluded that the table was moved by a physical force emanating from the bodies of the participants. He called this 'ectenic force' and believed it explained the phenomena he observed. He recorded his findings in* Des Tables Tournantes, du Surnaturel en Général et des Esprits *published in 1854.*

Gassner, Johann Joseph *(22 August 1727 - 4 April 1779) was an Austrian Catholic priest and a noted exorcist. In c. 1761 his health began to fail. None of the physicians he consulted was able to* *help him. He came to believe that his ill health was due to the influence of evil spirits and could be cured by spiritual means. He cured himself successfully through prayer and went on to cure others in the same way. Soon thousands came to him for healing.*

Gesner, Konrad von *(26 March 1516 - 13 December 1565), was a German-Swiss physician, zoologist, and naturalist. His wrote prolifically on subjects ranging from fossils to theology. He held a semi-religious view of nature. His ideas were based on an eclectic mixture of Aristotle, scripture, and direct observation of nature.*

Gibbon, Edward *(8 May 1737 - 16 January 1794) was an English historian, writer and Member of Parliament. His most important work* The History of the Decline and Fall of the Roman Empire *was published in six volumes between 1776 and 1788 and is known for its use of primary sources, and its open criticism of organized religion.*

Gilbert, William *(24 May 1544 - 30 November 1603) was an English physician and physicist. His most important work is* De Magnete, Magneticisque Corporibus, et de Magno Magnete Tellure (On the Loadstone and Magnetic Bodies and on the Great Magnet the Earth) *published in 1600. He concluded that a compass needle points from north to south because earth acts as a bar magnet. He coined the terms 'electric attraction,' 'electric force,' and 'magnetic pole.'*

Glanvill, Joseph *(1636 - 4 November 1680) was an English writer, philosopher, and clergyman. In his works* Blow at Modern Sadducism *(1668) and* Saducismus Triumphatus *(1681) he defended the reality of witchcraft and apparitions, and supported the pre-existence of the soul.*

Glauber, Johann Rudolf *(10 March 1604 - 16 March 1670) was a German-Dutch alchemist and chemist. He discovered sodium sulfate in 1625 and the compound was named after him as 'Glauber's salt.'*

Godwin-Austen, Robert Alfred Cloyne *(17 March 1808 - 25 November 1884) was an English geologist. He was prominent among early British geologists, and made notable contributions to geological science.*

Goldschmidt, Hermann Mayer Salomon *(17 June 1802 - 26 April 1866) was a German astronomer and painter. He discovered a total of 14 asteroids and was awarded the Gold Medal of the Royal Astronomical Society in 1861. According to the French astronomer Camille Flammarion, Goldschmidt accepted 'the objective reality of the (spiritualist) phenomena' but was 'not fully convinced of the intervention of spirits.'*

Görres, Johann Joseph von *(25 January 1776 - 29 January 1848) was a German writer, journalist and theologian. He studied mystical writers of the Middle Ages and observed, partly in person, young women subject to religious* *visions like Maria von Mörl. He wanted to explore the fundamental nature of Christian mysticism. His conclusions were published in the five volumes of* Christliche Mystik (On Christian Mysticism) *between 1836 and 1879.*

Greatrakes, Valentine *(14 February 1628 - 28 November 1682) was an Irish faith healer. He toured England in 1666 curing people by the laying on of hands. The celebrated Anglo-Irish chemist Robert Boyle, president of the Royal Society, stated, 'Many physicians, noblemen, clergymen, etc., testify to the truth of Greatrakes' cures, which he published in London. The chief diseases which he cured were blindness, deafness, paralysis, dropsy, ulcers, swellings, and all kinds of fevers.'*

Greene, Robert *(11 July 1558 - 3 September 1592) was an English writer. He was the most successful pre-Shakespearean playwright in comic theatre. His play* The Honorable Historie of frier Bacon, and frier Bongay *(written c. 1591 and published in 1594) became the first successful romantic comedy to be performed on the English stage.*

Greenhill, Thomas*(1669 - 1740) was an English surgeon. In 1705 he published* Nekrokedeia or The Art of Embalming *covering all aspects of burial, cremation, funeral rites, mortuary practice and mummification.*

Gregory, William *(25 December 1803 - 24 April 1858) was a Scottish physician and chemist. He studied under*

the German chemist Liebig and translated some of Liebig's works. He was also interested in mesmerism and phrenology.

Grew, Nehemiah *(baptized 26 September 1641 - 25 March 1712) was an English botanist and physician. His most popular work* The Anatomy of Plants *(1682) included many fine illustrations of the microscopic structure of plant tissue. In 1681, he published a catalogue of the Royal Society's collection under the title* Musaeum Regalis Societatis, or, A Catalogue & Description of the Natural and Artificial Rarities Belonging to the Royal Society and Preserved at Gresham College.

Gross, Joseph B. *(died 1891) was an American Lutheran clergyman and author. He wrote many works with the aim of describing the original and progressive development of religious ideas. His books include* The Heathen Religion in Its Popular and Symbolical Development *(1856) and* Old Faith and New Thoughts *(1881).*

Grove, William Robert *(11 July 1811 - 1 August 1896) was a Welsh judge and scientist. He anticipated the general theory of the conservation of energy, and was an important pioneer in fuel cell technology.*

Guéneau de Mussy, François *HPB: Guénau de Mussy (11 June 1774 - 30 April 1853) was a French physician. He qualified in 1803 and went on to practice medicine at the Hôtel-Dieu in Paris. He was physician to King Charles X and* became a member of the Academy of Medicine in 1823. He was part of the Academy's 1826 Husson commission, convened to investigate mesmerism.

Guersant, Louis Benoît *(29 April 1777 - 23 May 1848) was a French physician and botanist. He was a member of the French Academy of Medicine and appointed as one of the medical consultants to King Louis-Philippe I. He was a member of the Academy's 1826 Husson commission, convened to investigate mesmerism.*

Guillotin, Joseph-Ignace *(28 May 1738 - 26 March 1814) was a French politician and physician. He was the first Chair of the French Assembly's Health Committee. He campaigned for the abolition of the death penalty and, failing that, called for a more humane method of execution to be devised. An inventor called Tobias Schmidt developed the prototype that became mistakenly associated with Guillotin's name. He was a member of the 1784 Franklin committee, convened by the French Academy of Sciences, to investigate mesmerism.*

Guizot, François Pierre Guillaume *(4 October 1787 - 12 September 1874) was the 17th Prime Minister of France. Between 1864 and 1868 he published three volumes of* Méditations sur la Religion Chrétienne (Meditations on the Christian Religion) *maintaining that belief in the supernatural is the cornerstone of Christianity.*

Gully, James Manby *(14 March 1808 - 1883) was a Victorian*

physician. He was a well-known practitioner of hydrotherapy. In later life, he became a spiritualist and was a friend and supporter of the Scottish medium Daniel Dunglas Home. Gully became President of the British Spiritualist Association in 1874.

H.

Haeckel, Ernst Heinrich Philipp August *(16 February 1834 - 9 August 1919) was a German zoologist and evolutionist. He promoted and popularized Charles Darwin's work in Germany. He created a genealogical tree relating all life forms, and coined many terms in biology, including 'anthropogeny,' 'ecology' and 'stem cell.'*

Hamilton *real name: Pierre Etienne Auguste Chocat (1812-1877) was a French magician. He was the brother-in-law of Jean-Eugène Robert-Houdin who trained him in magic.*

Hamilton, William *(8 March 1788 - 6 May 1856) was a Scottish metaphysician. From 1836 he was Professor of Metaphysics and Logic at Edinburgh University. His influence grew with the posthumous publication of his lectures in four volumes* Lectures on Metaphysics and Logic *(Metaphysics published 1858. Logic published 1860). His 'latent mental modification theory' maintained that the human mind processes thoughts of which it is unconscious.*

Hardinge Britten, Emma *(2 May 1823 - 2 October 1899) was an English* advocate for the early spiritualist movement. She spent a large part of her adult life in the US. Her books, Modern American Spiritualism *(1870) and* Nineteenth Century Miracles *(1884) are detailed accounts of the early history of spiritualism in America.*

Hare, Robert *(17 January 1781 - 15 May 1858) was an American chemist. He published the results of his studies of spiritualist mediums in* Experimental Investigation of the Spirit Manifestations *(1855). He was convinced that the phenomena observed were real and converted to spiritualism in 1854.*

Harr *HPB: Har is one of the Scandinavian Holy Trinity or the Mysterious Three - the three gods that guard Valhalla, the hall of Heaven, in Norse mythology. Harr is the High One, Jafnharr, HPB: Jafuhar, the Equally High One and Thridhi, HPB: Tredi, the Third.*

Hartmann, Karl Robert Eduard von *(23 February 1842 - 5 June 1906) was a German metaphysical philosopher. He was called 'the philosopher of the unconscious' because his philosophical system centered on the role of the unconscious mind. His most influential work is the three-volume* Die Philosophie des Unbewussten (The Philosophy of the Unconscious) *published in 1870.*

Harvey, William *(1 April 1578 - 3 June 1657) was an English physician. He made important contributions in* anatomy and physiology. He was the first to describe in full, and provide evidence for, the circulatory system of the body.

Haug, Martin *(30 January 1827 - 3 June 1876) was a German orientalist. He became superintendent of Sanskrit studies and professor of Sanskrit in the Indian city of Poona in 1859. He was appointed professor of Sanskrit and comparative philology at Munich in 1868. He wrote many important works of scholarship on the literatures of ancient India and Persia including* Essays on the Sacred Language, Writings and Religion of the Parsees *published in 1862.*

Heindorf, Ludwig *(21 September 1774 - 23 June 1816) was a German classical philologist. His research focused on the works of the Greek philosopher Plato. He published many translations and commentaries including* Platonis Dialogi Quatuor (Four Platonic Dialogues) *in 1802.*

Helmont, Jan Baptist van *(12 January 1580 - 30 December 1644) was a Flemish physician, philosopher and chemist. While he accepted theories like the transmutation of metals and the existence of a medical cure-all, he maintained that experimentation was the only reliable way to understand the natural world.*

Hemmann, Johann Alexander *(died 1779) was a German surgeon in the Prussian Army. He wrote* Medicinisch-Chirurgische Aufsätze (Medico-Surgical Essays) *published in 1778.*

Hénin de Cuvillers, Baron Étienne Félix de HPB: Baron d'Henin de Cuvillier *(27 April 1755 - 2 August 1841) was a French mesmerist. He was a follower of mesmerism's originator, Franz Anton Mesmer, but he did not believe in the existence of an underlying 'magnetic fluid.' Instead, he emphasized the role of suggestion. He is credited with popularizing the term 'hypnotism.' In 1820 he became editor of the journal* Archives du Magnétisme Animal.

Henry, Joseph *(17 December 1797 - 13 May 1878) was one of America's greatest early scientists. He discovered several important principles of electricity, including the phenomenon of self-induction. He became professor of natural philosophy at the College of New Jersey (later Princeton University) in 1832 and was appointed first secretary of the Smithsonian Institution in 1846. He became a founding member of the National Academy of Sciences and its second president.*

Heraclitus *(c. 535 BC - c. 475 BC) was a pre-Socratic Ionian Greek philosopher. In his cosmology, fire was the first principle in a rational universe. His expansive definition of fire included fuel, flame and smoke, and extended to the ether of the higher atmosphere.*

Hercules *is the Roman equivalent of the Greek divine hero Heracles, son of Zeus. Hercules is famous for his strength and his 12 labors, a series of challenges he was commanded to undertake by the king of Mycenae, Eurystheus.*

Herder, Johann Gottfried *(25 August 1744 - 18 December 1803) was a German critic, theologian and philosopher. He made important contributions to the philosophy of history and culture published in two major works:* This Too a Philosophy of History for the Formation of Humanity *published in 1774 and* Ideen zur Geschichte der Menschheit (Ideas for the Philosophy of the History of Humanity) *published 1784–91. He theorized that there are radical mental differences between different historical periods.*

Herford, Brooke *(21 February 1830 - 21 December 1903) was a Unitarian minister and preacher. He traveled throughout Britain promoting the ideas of Unitarian Christianity, in particular, the importance of reason in interpreting sacred scriptures. In 1859 he became co-founder and joint editor of the* Unitarian Herald *the first Unitarian newspaper.*

Hermes *is a Greek god. As messenger of the gods, he is able to move quickly and freely between the worlds of the mortal and the divine, aided by his winged sandals. He also serves as a conductor of souls into the afterlife. He is often depicted with a golden staff representing his role as divine herald.*

Hermes Trismegistus *(thrice-greatest Hermes) is a legendary teacher of magic and mysticism. He is probably an amalgamation of the Greek god Hermes and the Egyptian deity Thoth. In early writings, he was accepted as a historical figure. He was later interpreted as a symbolic figure and representative of* *enlightenment. He is supposed to be the author of the* Hermetic Corpus, *a collection of sacred texts that form the basis of Hermeticism. (See also Chapter One, note 1.)*

Hero of Alexandria *also Heron of Alexandria HPB: Hero (c. 10 AD - c. 70 AD) was a Greek mathematician and inventor. The 'aeolipile,' or steam turbine, which he invented in the 1st Century AD, is described in his* Pneumatica.

Herodotus *(c. 484 BC - c. 425 BC) was a Greek historian. He was a contemporary of Socrates and Euripides, and author of the first great work of history in western literature. The* Histories *written in 440 BC documented the culture, politics and conflicts of Greece, western Asia and northern Africa.*

Herschel, Frederick William *(15 November 1738 - 25 August 1822) was a British astronomer. In 1800 he identified infrared radiation in sunlight. He used a prism to split white light, and used a thermometer, held just beyond the red end of the visible spectrum, to verify the presence of infrared radiation.*

Hiarchas, King *also Hipparchus, son of Peisistratos (fl. 527 BC) may refer to a tyrant of the city of Athens, assassinated by the male lovers Harmodius and Aristogeiton in 514 BC.*

Higgins, Godfrey *(30 January 1772 - 9 August 1833) was a religious historian. He is the author of* Anacalypsis: An Attempt to Draw Aside the Veil of the Saitic Isis or an Inquiry into the Origin of Languages, Nations and Religions *a lengthy two-volume treatise published posthumously in 1836.*

Hippocrates *(c. 460 BC - c. 370 BC) was a Greek physician. He is regarded as the father of medicine and the originator of the Hippocratic oath.*

Hiram, *also Hiram Abiff is a possibly mythological figure portrayed as the chief architect of King Solomon's Temple. In* Antiquitates Judaicae (Antiquities of the Jews) *Flavius Josephus refers to Hiram as a craftsman. He writes, 'Now Solomon sent for a craftsman from Tyre, whose name was Hiram...' Hiram is the central character in the allegory enacted by candidates for the third degree in Freemasonry. Hiram is murdered in the Temple by three ruffians as they attempt to force him to divulge the Master Masons' secret passwords. The themes of the allegory are the importance of fidelity, and the certainty of death.*

Hirtius, Aulus *HPB: Ericius (c. 90 BC - 21 April 43 BC) was one of the consuls of the Roman Republic and a writer on military subjects. He almost certainly contributed to Caesar's* Commentaries *specifically the eighth book of the Gallic War, and possibly the history of the Alexandrine War. In* De Facto *Cicero described Hirtius as 'a very close friend of mine and a devoted student of the subjects that have occupied my life from boyhood.'*

Hitchcock, Edward *(24 May 1793 - 27 February 1864) was an American* geologist and the third President of Amherst College (1845–1854). He was an original member of the American Association for the Advancement of Science and a founding member of the National Academy of Sciences. He was interested in the relationship between science and religion throughout his professional life. He is the author of The Religion of Geology and its Connected Sciences *published in 1851.*

Hœnir *HPB: Hönir is a member of the first pantheon of Norse gods, the Æsir. In Norse mythology he plays an important role in the creation of humanity. According to the Prose Edda he gives humanity the gift of reason. (See Chapter Four, note 9.)*

Hofmann, August Wilhelm von *(8 April 1818 - 2 May 1892) was a German chemist. He studied under Justus von Liebig at the University of Giessen and became the first director of the Royal College of Chemistry in London in 1845. He was appointed chemistry professor and laboratory director at the University of Berlin in 1865. He co-founded the German Chemical Society in 1867 and served 14 terms as its president between 1868 and 1892.*

Hohenlohe, Prince Alexander *full name: Alexander Leopold Franz Emmerich of Hohenlohe-Waldenburg-Schillingsfürst HPB: The Prince of Hohenlohe (17 August 1794 - 17 November 1849) was a German priest and reputed faith healer. He performed his first miraculous cure, with the help of a peasant called Martin Michel, on the*

Bohemian Princess Mathilde von Schwarzenberg, who had been paralyzed for years.

Home, Daniel Dunglas *pronounced: 'Hume' (20 March 1833 - 21 June 1886) was a Scottish medium. He was reputed to have many psychic abilities including the power of levitation, communication with the dead, and eliciting spirit rapping at will. His biographer Peter Lamont described him as one of the most famous men of his time. Home conducted hundreds of seances, attended by many eminent Victorians.*

Horus *is one of the most important of all ancient Egyptian deities. He was most often depicted as a falcon or as a man with a falcon's head. The kings of Egypt were believed to be Horus incarnate. The unification of Upper and Lower Egypt was thought to reflect the final resolution of the battle between Horus and his uncle Set.*

Howitt, William *(18 December 1792 - 3 March 1879) was an English writer. He became interested in spiritualism in 1847 and is the author of* The History of the Supernatural in all Ages and Nations, and in all Churches, Christian and Pagan, Demonstrating a Universal Faith *published in 1863.*

Huc, Évariste Régis *HPB: Abbé Huc (1 August 1813 - 21 April 1860), was a French Catholic priest, missionary, and traveler. He became famous for his accounts of Qing-era China, Mongolia (then known as Tartary), and especially the then little-known Tibet in his book*

Souvenirs d'un Voyage dans la Tartarie, le Thibet, et la Chine pendant les Années 1844, 1845, et 1846 (Recollections of a Journey in Tartary, Tibet, and China during the Years 1844, 1845, and 1846) *published in 1850. When he and his companion Joseph Gabet reached Lhasa on 29 January 1846, they were the first Europeans to reach the Tibetan capital since the British-Canadian explorer Thomas Manning in 1812.*

Hufeland, Friedrich *(18 July 1774 - 21 April 1839) was a German physician. In 1812 he became professor of medicine at Berlin.* His Über Sympathie (On Sympathy) *published in 1811 dealt with animal magnetism and the interaction of organic bodies with each other and with nature in general.*

Humboldt, Friedrich Wilhelm Heinrich Alexander von *(14 September 1769 - 6 May 1859) was a German naturalist. From 1799 to 1804 he traveled extensively in Central and South America, covering more than 6,000 miles. His work* Kosmos: Entwurf einer Physischen Weltbeschreibung (Cosmos: A Sketch of a Physical Description of the Universe) *began as a lecture series he gave at the University of Berlin, and was published in five volumes between 1845 and 1862.*

Hume, David *born David Home (7 May 1711 - 25 August 1776) was a Scottish philosopher. He believed that philosophy could only be improved by placing the empirical study of human nature at its heart. He maintained that passions rather than reason govern human behavior, famously declaring, 'Reason is, and ought only to be, the slave of the passions.'* An Enquiry Concerning Human Understanding, *published in 1758, is among his major works. The* Enquiry *included his essay 'On Miracles', a text that became infamous because it denied that miracles could ever be proved by evidence of any kind.*

Hunt, Robert *(6 September 1807 - 17 October 1887) was a British scientist. He worked principally as a mineralogist but became increasingly interested in photography. He investigated the action of light, and published his findings in* Researches on Light in its Chemical Relations *in 1844.*

Hunt, Thomas Sterry *(5 September 1826 - 12 February 1892) was an American geologist and chemist. He published widely on the subject of geology including* Chemical and Geological Essays *in 1875 and* Systematic Mineralogy *in 1891.*

Husson, Henri-Marie *(25 May 1772 - 11 April 1853) was a French physician. He was a pioneer in the field of public health, playing a major role in the French vaccination programme against smallpox. In 1821, he was elected to the French Academy of Medicine. In 1825, he was part of a special committee supporting Pierre Foissac's call for the Academy to mount a new inquiry into mesmerism. He chaired the subsequent investigation from 1826 to 1831 which became known as the Husson commission.*

In 1839, he was appointed the Academy of Medicine's president.

Husson, Nicolas *(active 1772-1807) was a French army officer. In the 1770s he created l'eau medicinale d'Husson, a patent medicine promoted as a panacea for innumerable diseases. Its ingredients were a closely-guarded secret and the subject of fierce speculation. The medication became fashionable but not without controversy. In 1778 its sale was temporarily prohibited in Paris by police order.*

Huxley, Thomas Henry *(4 May 1825 - 29 June 1895) was an English biologist. He championed Darwin's evolutionary theory in public lectures, earning himself the nickname 'Darwin's Bulldog.' He was an effective popularizer of science and played a key role in elevating the position of science in British society.*

I.

Iamblichus *(245 AD - 325 AD) was a Syrian Neoplatonist philosopher. He is credited with transforming Neoplatonism into a pagan religious philosophy. His cosmology was built on the transcendent incommunicable 'One,' the monad, whose first principle is intellect, 'nous.'*

Innocent X *Giambattista Pamfili (7 May 1574 - 7 January 1655) was Pope from 15 September 1644 to his death in 1655. In 1647 he commanded a Jesuit priest, Juan de Lugo, to test the curative effects of Peruvian bark and later endorsed its use.*

Irenaeus *(c. 130 AD - c. 202 AD) was a Greek bishop who served as Bishop of Lyon. His best-known work is* Adversus Haereses (Against Heresies) *written 180 AD. He was one of the first theologians to uphold the central importance of all four gospels.*

Isis *was one of the most important goddesses in ancient Egypt. In the Osiris myth, she resurrects her slain husband, the divine king Osiris, and produces and protects his heir, Horus. She was believed to help the dead enter the afterlife and was regarded as the divine mother of the pharaoh. A goddess of life and magic, she protected women and children, and healed the sick. She was later worshiped by the Greeks and the Romans. The veil of Isis is a metaphor in which nature is personified as the goddess Isis covered by a veil symbolizing the inaccessibility of nature's secrets.*

Itard, Jean Marc Gaspard *(24 April 1774 - 5 July 1838) was a French physician. He is primarily remembered for his work with the deaf and for educating Victor of Aveyron, a feral child discovered in a forest in Aveyron, south of Paris. He became a member of the Academy of Medicine in 1821. He was part of the 1826 Husson commission, convened by the Academy, to investigate mesmerism.*

J.

Jacob, Auguste Henri *known as Le Zouave (6 March 1828 - 23 October 1913) was a French infantryman and spiritual healer. He was discharged from*

the army because his fame drew vast crowds of people, disrupting military discipline. Like modern evangelists, he healed using forceful commands to his subjects to be well. By 1866, he was described as 'the most famous healer of the 19th Century.' He ascribed his powers to 'the spirits of white magnetism.'

Jacobi, Moritz Hermann von *(21 September 1801 - 10 March 1874) was a German physicist. He moved to St. Petersburg in 1837 and became a member of the Imperial Academy of Sciences. His research focused on electricity and its applications. In May 1834 he built one of the first practical electric motors.*

Jacobonus *possibly Johannes Jacobonus or Giovanni Giaccoboni (fl. 1516) is a figure of uncertain identity. He appears in Thomas Greenhill's* The Art of Embalming *published in 1705: '...the superstitious Egyptians... placed burning lamps with the Dead in their Subterranean Vaults, as Jacobonus, Foxius, Scaliger and others relate...' A later reference appears in* Legends of Sepulchral and Perpetual Lamps *published in 1879 by Henry Carrington Bolton: 'Licetus also relates the testimony of Jacobonus, author of the 'Book of the House of Cesi,' who mentions several persons who had seen these lamps still burning.'*

Jacolliot, Louis *(31 October 1837 - 30 October 1890) was a French writer. He worked first as a lawyer then judge before traveling widely and recording his impressions. He described the feats of the Indian fakir Covindasamy extensively in*

Le Spiritisme dans le Monde, l'Initiation et les Sciences Occultes dans l'Inde et Chez Tous les Peuples de l'Antiquité *(Occult Science in India and Among the Ancients with an Account of Their Mystic Initiations and the History of Spiritism) published in 1875.*

Jafnharr *HPB: Jafuhar is one of the Scandinavian Holy Trinity or the Mysterious Three - the three gods that guard Valhalla, the hall of Heaven, in Norse mythology. Harr, HPB: Har, is the High One, Jafnharr, the Equally High One and Thridhi, HPB: Tredi, the Third.*

Janet, Paul Alexandre René *(30 April 1823 - 4 October 1899) was a French philosopher and writer. He was professor of moral philosophy at Bourges from 1845 to 1848 and Strasbourg from 1848 to 1857, and professor of logic at the lycée Louis-le-Grand, Paris from 1857 to 1864. In 1864 he was appointed to the chair of philosophy at the Sorbonne, and elected a member of the Academy of Moral and Political Sciences. He maintained that a whole generation of thinkers had become infatuated by positivism to their detriment and called for a renewal of spiritualism. He presented these ideas in* La Crise Philosophique, MM. Taine, Littré, Renan, Vacherot *(The Philosophical Crisis, Messrs. Taine, Littré, Renan, Vacherot) published in 1865.*

Jennings, Hargrave *(1817-1890) was a British esotericist and prolific author. He is best known for* The

Rosicrucians, Their Rites and Mysteries *published in 1870. He worked on the text for 20 years, researching and recording his findings on Kabbalah, Gnosticism, the Druids, and ancient and medieval cultures.*

Jerome, Saint *Latin:* Eusebius Hieronymus, pseudonym Sophronius *(c. 347 AD - 30 September 420 AD) was a Dalmatian priest, scholar and translator. He experienced life as a hermit, entered the priesthood, and served as secretary to Pope Damasus I. During his time in Rome he devoted himself to biblical scholarship resulting in his commentaries on the four Gospels and his influential translation of the Bible into Latin, the* Vulgate.

Jevons, William Stanley *(1 September 1835 - 13 August 1882) was an English economist and logician. In 1866 he was appointed to a chair of political economy at Owens College, Manchester. He became professor of economics at University College London in 1876. His book* The Theory of Political Economy *(1871) heralded a new period in the history of economic thought. His most important work on logic and scientific methods was* The Principles of Science *(1874). The lines cited by Blavatsky are quoted by Jevons from the* Ninth Bridgewater Treatise (1837) *by Charles Babbage. (See* **Babbage, Charles.***)*

Jobard, Marcellin *full name: Jean-Baptiste-Ambroise-Marcellin Jobard (17 May 1792 - 27 October 1861) was a French-born Belgian lithographer, photographer and inventor. He innovated*

in the areas of lighting, heating, food, locomotion and ballistics, applying for a total of 73 patents in his lifetime. He was the first to develop a prototype electric light bulb. He sealed a carbon rod inside a vacuum and caused it to glow by passing an electrical current through it. Toward the end of his life, he became a follower of spiritualism.

Jobert de Lamballe, Antoine Joseph *(17 December 1799 - 19 April 1867) was a French surgeon. He was elected to the Academy of Medicine in 1840 and to the Academy of Sciences in 1856. According to the Academy's report of its of Session of 18 April 1859, the German scholar invited to speak by Jobert de Lamballe and Rayer was the physiologist Mortiz Schiff (1823-1896).*

Jones, William *(28 September 1746 - 27 April 1794) was an Anglo-Welsh oriental scholar and judge. He was one of the first scholars to generate enthusiasm among westerners for oriental studies. He identified the philological relationship between Indian and European languages. He was a member of the judiciary at the Supreme Court at Fort William in Bengal, India. In 1784 he co-founded the Asiatic Society of Bengal and consolidated his reputation as an expert orientalist with the publication in 1792 of his* Dissertations Relating to Asia.

Josaphat, Saint *full name: Josaphat Kuntsevych (c. 1580 - 12 November 1623) was a Polish-Lithuanian monk and archbishop of the Catholic Church in the east Slavic region of Ruthenia. The story told about his life and work has* strong parallels with the life of the Buddha. Both figures are presented as princes who renounce their privilege and all earthly pleasures to become great spiritual leaders. Josaphat was canonized on 29 June 1867 by Pope Pius IX.

Joseph of Canaan is a biblical figure, one of the sons of Jacob and Rachel. Because Joseph is Jacob's favorite, Jacob gives him a coat of many colors. His jealous brothers sell him into slavery in Egypt. The biblical narrative that follows echoes the Egyptian story The Tale of Two Brothers preserved on the Papyrus D'Orbiney, currently held in the British Museum. The tale includes magical rituals to bring the dead back to life, transformation into animals and trees, and miraculous impregnation.

Josephus, Titus Flavius born: Yosef ben Matityahu (37 AD - c. 100 AD) was a 1st-century Jewish historian. He is the author of Antiquitates Judaicae (Antiquities of the Jews), a 20-volume work, written in Greek. It contains an exhaustive account of Jewish history written for his Greek patrons. One of the best known translations is by the English theologian William Whiston published in 1737 and continuously in print since that time.

Jowett, Benjamin (15 April 1817 - 1 October 1893) was a British classical scholar and teacher. He was a highly respected translator of Plato, an influential tutor, and later he was appointed to the position of Master of Balliol College, Oxford.

Julian, Emperor Flavius Claudius Julianus, also Julian the Apostate (c. 331 AD - 26 or 27 June 363 AD) was a scholar, military leader and Roman emperor from 361 AD to 363 AD. He rejected Christianity and sought to revive paganism as the official religion of the empire. As a consequence, he is remembered as Julian the Apostate.

Jussieu, Antoine Laurent de (12 April 1748 - 12 September 1836) was a French botanist. He was the first to publish a natural classification of flowering plants and much of this system remains in use today. Contrary to the Franklin Committee of 1784, he argued for the efficacy of mesmerism. He agreed with Mesmer that some form of subtle fluid, which he, de Jussieu, termed 'animal heat' played a significant role in maintaining health.

Justin Martyr, Saint (c. 100 AD - c. 165 AD) was an influential Greek philosopher-apologist in the early Christian church. In 150 AD, he wrote his first major apology to the Roman emperors Antoninus Pius and Marcus Aurelius. He argued that both Christianity and Platonic philosophy posited a transcendent and unchangeable God.

K.

Kant, Immanuel (22 April 1724 - 12 February 1804) was a highly influential German philosopher. He argued that humans only ever have direct experience of sense data and never encounter directly the reality of the world in and of itself. Kantian philosophy maintains that the mind creates the structure of human experience and the world exists independently of our concepts of it.

Kapila *(fl. c. 550 BC) is an important Vedic sage. He is often identified by Hindu scholars as one of the founders of the Samkhya school of Hindu philosophy. In Hindu mythology he is presented as a direct descendant of Manu, the primal human being, and a grandson of the creator-god Brahma.*

Kardec, Allan *pen name of Hippolyte Léon Denizard Rivail (3 October 1804 - 31 March 1869) was a French educator, translator and writer. He is the founder of spiritism. He described spiritism as a science dedicated to the relationship between incorporeal beings and human beings. Unlike spiritualism, spiritism accepts reincarnation. Kardec is the author of the Spiritist Codification consisting of five books published between 1857 and 1868:* Le Livre des Esprits (The Book of Spirits), Le Livre des Médiums (The Book of Mediums), L'Évangile Selon le Spiritisme (The Gospel According to Spiritism), Le Ciel et L'Enfer (Heaven and Hell), and La Genèse Selon le Spiritisme (Genesis According to Spiritism). *Spiritism is also known as Kardecism.*

Kedrenos, George HPB: *Cedrenus and Kedrenus (fl. 11th or early 12th Century) was a Byzantine historian. Toward the end of the 11th Century or the beginning of the 12th, a panoramic history from Creation to 1057 was*

compiled. Titled the Synopsis Historion, *it was credited to George Kedrenos. He edited and combined existing histories to create his compilation. For the years 811 to 1057 he reproduced the work of the Greek historian John Skylitzes, also titled* Synopsis Historion. *For the period prior to 811 he extracts the histories of Pseudo-Symeon, Symeon the Logothete, and George the Monk. For the sixth and seventh centuries he used the Chronicle of Pseudo-Symeon, which relies on Theophanes. Kedrenos reports that in the time of Emperor Justinian there was a burning lamp found in an old wall at Antioch which had burnt for 500 years. Note Blavatsky's source appears to be* The Conjuror's Magazine, Or Magical and Physiognomical Mirror Volume II *printed 1791 - 1793.*

Kepler, Johannes *(27 December 1571 - 15 November 1630) was a German astronomer. He identified three laws of planetary motion, outlining the first two in* Astronomia Nova (New Astronomy) *published in 1609 and the third in* Harmonice Mundi (Harmonies of the World) *published in 1619. In* De Fundamentis Astrologiae Certioribus (Concerning the More Certain Fundamentals of Astrology) *published in 1601, he proposed a more secure foundation for astrology by basing it on newly discovered physical and harmonic principles. He proposed that there are strict limits within which the predictions of astrology can be considered reliable.*

Kerner, Justinus Andreas Christian *(18 September 1786 - 21 February 1862) was a German physician and* medical writer. He became the District Medical Officer for Weinsberg in southern Germany in 1818. He wrote books on animal magnetism, somnambulism and clairvoyance. (See also **Eslinger, Elizabeth**.)

King, John was believed to be a spirit control - a powerful and communicative spirit that organized the appearance of other spirits at seances. He was believed to be active from the 1850s to the 1870s and was thought to be the father of the spirit entity Katie King.

King, Katie was the name given by spiritualists in the 1870s to the figure they believed to be a materialized spirit. She first appeared between 1871 and 1874 at seances conducted by Florence Cook in London. Later in 1874 and 1875 she appeared in New York associated with the mediums Jennie Holmes and her husband Nelson Holmes. The question of whether Katie King was genuine or a fraud was a notable public controversy of the mid-1870s. Katie King was believed to be the daughter of the spirit control John King.

Kircher, Athanasius (2 May 1602 - 28 November 1680) was a German Jesuit scholar. While professor of Ethics and Mathematics at the University of Würzburg, Bavaria, he published his first book Ars Magnesia (The Magnetic Art) in 1631. It is a 48 page pamphlet, a printed version of an earlier lecture, describing his research into magnetism. His best-known work is Oedipus Aegyptiacus (the Egyptian Oedipus) published 1652–54. It is a

comprehensive study of Egyptology and comparative religion including references to Kabbalah, alchemy and astrology.

Korndörffer, Bartholomäus HPB: Bartolomeo Korndorf (fl. 15th Century) was a German alchemist. He is the author of Everburning Lights of Trithemius in which he gives two recipes for everlasting lamps attributed to Johannes Trithemius, Abbot of Sponheim in western Germany.

Kutsa, Maharishi is one of the seven sages of ancient India, described in the Vedas as the fathers of the historical Vedic Religion. Many of the hymns of the Rigvedas are attributed to him.

L.

Lactantius, Lucius Caecilius Firmianus (240 AD - c. 320 AD) was an early Christian writer and advisor to the first Christian Roman emperor, Constantine I. He was the author of Institutiones Divinae (The Divine Institutes) written between 303 AD and 311 AD. It was the first defense of Christian theology in Latin. It aimed to undermine paganism and establish Christianity as the superior belief system.

Lane, Edward William (17 September 1801 - 10 August 1876) was a British orientalist and translator. His book An Account of the Manners and Customs of the Modern Egyptians was published in 1836. It contains a description of Egyptian magic, astrology and alchemy. He also published an Arabic-English Lexicon and a translation of One Thousand and One Nights.

Langhorne, John *(March 1735 - April 1779) was an English clergyman translator and author. He worked with his brother William Langhorne on an English translation of* Plutarch's Lives *published in 1770.*

Lankester, Ray *full name: Edwin Ray Lankester (15 May 1847 - 13 August 1929) was a British zoologist and evolutionary biologist. He held chairs at University College London and Oxford University, and was the third Director of the Natural History Museum. In 1876 he attended seances conducted by Henry Slade. He sued Slade for allegedly producing spirit writing fraudulently. In the decades that followed, Lankester continued to argue against the 'superstition' of spiritualism.*

Laplace, Pierre-Simon, Marquis de *(23 March 1749 - 5 March 1827) was a French scientist and mathematician. He was one of the most influential scientists of his time. His* Essai Philosophique sur les Probabilités (A Philosophical Essay on Probabilities) *was first published in 1814 and reprinted many times. The essay is a fundamental work establishing six principles of probability defined in mathematical terms.*

Lavoisier, Antoine-Laurent de *also Antoine Lavoisier (26 August 1743 - 8 May 1794) was an eminent French chemist. He became a member of the Academy of Sciences in 1768. His work* helped to transform chemistry into a rigorous scientific discipline. In 1789 he published Traité Élémentaire de Chimie (Elementary Treatise on Chemistry) *presenting the precise methods chemists should employ when investigating, organizing, and explaining their subjects. He was a member of the 1784 Franklin committee, convened by the Academy of Sciences, to investigate the phenomenon of mesmerism.*

Layard, Austen Henry *(5 March 1817 - 5 July 1894) was a British archaeologist. He carried out excavations at both Nimrud and Nineveh. At Nineveh, he uncovered reliefs in the Assyrian palace and in 1851 discovered Nineveh's Royal Library of Ashurbanipal, named for the last great king of the Assyrian Empire.*

Lazius, Wolfgang *or Wolfgang Laz (31 October 1514 - 19 June 1565) was an Austrian physician, historian and cartographer. He was appointed professor in the medical faculty at the University of Vienna in 1541. He later became official historian to Emperor Ferdinand I and traveled widely, amassing (and sometimes stealing) documents from monasteries and other libraries.*

Le Conte, Joseph *or Joseph LeConte (26 February 1823 - 6 July 1901) was an American physician and geologist. He became a member of the National Academy of Sciences in 1874 and was president of the American Association for the Advancement of Science in 1892.*

Le Roy, Jean-Baptiste *HPB: Leroi (15 August 1720 - 20 January 1800)* was a French physicist. He defended Benjamin Franklin's single-fluid theory of electricity and offered experimental evidence in support of it. He was director of the French Academy of Sciences in 1773 and 1778, and a member of the 1784 Franklin committee, convened by the Academy, to investigate mesmerism.

Leander of Seville, Saint (c. 534 AD - 13 March 600 or 601 AD) was a Benedictine monk and became Bishop of Seville in 579 AD. De Institutione Virginum et Contemptu Mundi (The Training of Nuns and the Contempt of the World) is his most well-known written work, a monastic rule book for nuns.

Lepsius, Karl or Carl Richard (23 December 1810 - 10 July 1884) was a Prussian Egyptologist. He was president of the German Archaeological Institute in Rome from 1867 to 1880 and head of the Royal Library at Berlin from 1873 until his death. In 1842 he led an expedition to Egypt and the Sudan to explore and record the remains of the ancient Egyptian civilization. He recorded his discoveries in Denkmäler aus Aegypten und Aethiopien (Monuments from Egypt and Ethiopia) a twelve-volume work including 900 plates of ancient Egyptian inscriptions, accompanying commentaries and descriptions. His plans, maps, and drawings of temple and tomb walls remained the chief source of information well into the 20th Century.

Leroux, Jean-Jacques des Tillets (17 April 1749 - 9 April 1832) was a

French physician. He was dean of the Faculty of Medicine in Paris and author of Cors sur les Généralités de la Médecine Pratique et sur la Philosophie de la Médecine (Course on the Generalities of Practical Medicine and on the Philosophy of Medicine) a multi-volume work published c. 1825. He was a member of the 1826 Husson commission, convened by the French Academy of Medicine, to investigate mesmerism.

Leucippus (fl. 5th Century BC) was a Greek philosopher. Aristotle and Theophrastus credit him with developing the theory of atomism.

Levi, Eliphas real name: Alphonse Louis Constant (8 February 1810 - 31 May 1875) was a French occult author and ceremonial magician. Dogme et Rituel de la Haute Magie (Dogma and Ritual of High Magic) was his first treatise on magic published in two volumes Dogma in 1854 and Rituel in 1856.

Lewes, George Henry (18 April 1817 - 30 November 1878) was an English philosopher and critic. In 1868 he wrote a savage attack on mediumship and spiritualists published in the Pall Mall Gazette. He was invited to join the London Dialectical Society's 1869 committee to investigate spiritual manifestations but declined. The line quoted by Blavatsky is his argument against participation.

Leymarie, Pierre-Gaëtan (2 May 1827 - 10 April 1901) was a French publisher and spiritist. He was editor of the spiritist journal Revue Spirite. *In 1875 he was found guilty of fraud for suggesting in the* Revue *that the French medium and spirit photographer Édouard Buguet could photograph family members with the spirits of their deceased relatives.*

Libavius, Andreas *born Andreas Libau(c. 1555 - 25 July 1616) was a German professor, alchemist and early chemist. His* Alchemia (Alchemy) *published in 1597 was a compendium of alchemical knowledge and one of the first chemistry text books. Its publication was criticized by his fellow alchemists who believed alchemical knowledge should remain secret.*

Liceti, Fortunio *HPB: Licetus (3 October 1577 - 17 May 1657) was an Italian physician and philosopher. He is the author of* De Lucernis Antiquorum Reconditis (On the Mystery of Ancient Lamps) *published in 1621. The book focuses on so-called perpetual lamps setting out to prove the truth of the phenomenon. Liceti provides thirty examples including lamps associated with the Oracle of Delphi, the ceremonies of Jupiter Amun, and the Vestal Virgins. He cites the lamp of Demosthenes in the Temple of Minerva at Athens as proof that an inextinguishable fire is possible.*

Liebig, Justus Freiherr von *(12 May 1803 - 18 April 1873) was a German biochemist and innovative teacher. In 1825 he became professor of chemistry at Ludwigs University in Gießen and in 1852 professor of Chemistry at Munich. He was appointed President of the Bavarian Academy of Sciences in 1859.*

He specialized in organic chemistry as a means of investigating living processes. He wrote Die Organische Chemie in Ihrer Anwendung auf Agricultur und Physiologie (Chemistry in Its Applications to Agriculture and Physiology) *published in 1840.*

Linnaeus, Carl *HPB: Lumæus (23 May 1707 - 10 January 1778) was a Swedish botanist. His* Systema Naturæ *(Systems of Nature) published in 1735 introduced Linnaean taxonomy, a system of classification for plants, animals and minerals. Linnaeus' taxonomy is still in use today.*

Linus *is a poet in Greek mythology. The original source of Blavatsky's text about Linus and the heliacal year appears to be* De Die Natali (On His Birthday) *a treatise on human life, the influence of the planets and the divisions of time. It was written in 238 AD by the Roman grammarian Censorinus and dedicated to his patron Quintus Caerellius, a Roman knight, on his 49th birthday.*

Littré, Paul-Émile *(1 February 1801 - 2 June 1881) was a French lexicographer and philosopher. He was a close friend of Auguste Comte and a committed follower of positivism, promoting Comte's philosophy in a series of publications including* Analyse Raisonnée du Cours de Philosophie Positive (Reasoned Analysis of the Course of Positive Philosophy) *published in 1845 and* L'Application de la Philosophie Positive au Gouvernement des Sociétés (The Application of Positive Philosophy in

Government) *published in 1849. Littré's first attempt to join the French Academy was blocked by Félix Dupanloup, Bishop of Orleans on the grounds that his publications were immoral. He was finally elected to the Academy in 1871 and Dupanloup resigned in protest.*

Livy *or Titus Livius HPB: Titus Livy (64 or 59 BC - 12 or 17 AD) was a Roman historian. His History of Rome,* Ab Urbe Condita (From the Founding of the City) *consisted of 142 books, recording 377 years of Roman history.*

Lóðurr *HPB: Lodur is a god in Norse mythology. In the Poetic Edda poem 'Völuspá' he helps animate the first humans but apart from this, he is hardly ever mentioned and remains obscure. (See Chapter Four, note 9.)*

Longfellow, Henry Wadsworth *(27 February1807 - 24 March 1882) was the most popular American poet of the 19th Century. His best-known works include* The Song of Hiawatha *(1855)* and Paul Revere's Ride *(1863).*

Lothar I *or Lothair I, HPB: Lotharius (795 AD - 29 September 855 AD) was Roman Emperor from 817 AD to 855 AD, co-ruling with his father until 840 AD. 'Times change and we change with them (Tempora mutantur, nos et mutamur in illis)' is a late 16th-century proverbial saying. In William Harrison's* Description of Britain, *published in 1577, it is mis-attributed to Lothar I.*

Loubère, Simon de la *(21 April 1642 - 26 March 1729) was a French*

diplomat and writer. He was the French Ambassador to Siam, arriving in Bangkok in October 1687. Louis XIV ordered him to record everything of interest about his time in that country and the result was Du Royaume de Siam (On the Kingdom of Siam) *published in two volumes in 1691. Blavatsky refers to the first English translation which appeared as* A New Historical Relation of the Kingdom of Siam *in 1693.*

Louis XV *(15 February 1710 - 10 May 1774) was King of France from 1 September 1715 until his death. He paid a large sum for Madame Nouffleur's Receipt for Worms. The formula is given in* The Study of Medicine Volume I *by John Mason Good published in 1822. Good writes, 'It will probably either kill the worm or kill the patient!'*

Lucretius, Titus Lucretius Carus *(c. 15 October 99 BC - c. 55 BC) was a Roman poet and philosopher. He is known for a single philosophical poem* De rerum natura (On the Nature of Things). *In the poem he sets out to explain the materialist philosophy of Epicurus.*

Lugo, Juan de *also John de Lugo HPB: Cardinal de Lugo (25 November 1583 - 20 August 1660) was a Spanish Jesuit theologian and cardinal. On the orders of Pope Innocent X, he organized an investigation into the medicinal properties of Peruvian bark, also known as Jesuit's bark or cinchona bark. The bark was analyzed by the Pope's physician Gabriele Fonseca and found to be an effective treatment for malaria.*

Luna is the Roman goddess of the moon, counterpart to the Greek moon goddess Selene. She is often depicted driving a silver chariot across the sky drawn by two horses or oxen.

M.

MacEnery, John HPB: McEnery (27 November 1797 - 18 February 1841) was a Roman Catholic priest and early archaeologist. In 1825 he discovered human fossil remains and tools alongside skeletons of extinct mammals in Kent's Cavern, a cave system near Torquay in South Devon. He believed his find indicated that humanity is much older than the Bible suggests so calling into question Christian doctrine.

Macrinius HPB: Macrinus (but Paschal Beverly Randolph refers to 'Macrinius' in Blavatsky's source Pre-Adamite Man.) It has not been possible to establish which name is accurate. Randolph's 'Macrinius' may be Gaius Macrinius Decianus (fl. 260 AD) Roman governor under the emperors Valerian and Gallienus. HPB's 'Macrinus' is likely to be the Roman emperor Marcus Opellius Severus Macrinus Augustus (c.165 - June 218).

Maffei, Raffaello also Raphael Volaterranus or Maffeus Volaterranus, or Raffaello Volterrano HPB: Volateranus (17 February 1451 - 25 January 1522), was an Italian humanist, historian and theologian. He was a member of the Order of the Servants of Mary and a native of Volterra, Italy.

Magendie, François (6 October 1783 - 7 October 1855) was a French physiologist. He was elected to the French Academy of Sciences in 1821 and appointed professor of medicine at the Collège de France in Paris in 1831. He served as the president of the French Academy of Sciences in 1837. He was a member of the 1826 Husson commission, convened by the Academy of Medicine, to investigate mesmerism but he did not add his name to the commission's report.

Magnes was first king of Magnesia in Greek mythology. He was the son of Zeus and Thyia of Thessaly, Prometheus' granddaughter.

Magnus, Albertus also Saint Albert the Great or Albert of Cologne (c. 1200 - 15 November 1280) was a German Catholic Dominican friar and bishop. He describes the particular qualities of asbeston (asbestos) in his work De Mineralibus (Book of Minerals).

Maimonides, Moses (30 March 1135 - 13 December 1204) was a Jewish scholar and philosopher. He was one of the most prolific and influential Torah scholars of the Middle Ages. His 14-volume code of Jewish law, the Mishne Torah (The Torah Reviewed) is an accessible examination of the whole of Jewish law.

Maistre, Joseph-Marie, Comte de (1 April 1753 - 26 February 1821) was a French author and diplomat. He was appointed envoy to St. Petersburg in 1803 and remained at the Russian court for 14 years, writing Les Soirées de

Saint-Pétersbourg (The St. Petersburg Dialogues) *published in 1821. He was devoutly Catholic and opposed the advance of science.*

Majault, Michel-Joseph *(c. 1714 - c. 1790) was a French physician. He practiced at Hôtel-Dieu, one of Paris' main hospitals. He was a member of the Faculty of Medicine in Paris and served on the first of Louis XVI's commissions investigating mesmerism. The commission of 12th March consisted of four physicians: Majault (replacing Jean-François Borie who died on 21 May 1784) plus Jean-Charles-Henri Sallin, Jean d'Arcet , Joseph Ignace Guillotin; and five members of the Royal Academy of Sciences: the naval officer Gabriel de Bory, the physicist Jean-Baptiste Le Roy , the astronomer Jean Sylvain Bailly , the chemist Antoine Lavoisier and the United States ambassador Benjamin Franklin.*

Majoli, Simone *also Bishop Simone Majolo HPB: Maiolus (1520 - 9 January 1597) was an Italian lawyer and author. He became Bishop of Volturara and Montecorvina in 1572. His encyclopedic work* Dies Caniculares (Dog Days) *was published in 1588 covering a wide range of topics in natural history, demonology and other subjects including werewolves.*

Mallet, Paul Henri *(20 August 1730 - 8 February 1807) was a Swiss writer. In 1756 he published* Monuments de la Mythologie et de la Poesie des Celtes, et Particulièrement des Anciens Scandinaves *which appeared in English as* Northern Antiquities *in 1770. The*

book was the first translation of the Edda into French. (See Chapter Four, note 9.)

Manu *also Manu the Great is the Chaldean god of fate.*

Marc, Charles Chrétien Henri *(4 November 1771 - 12 January 1840) was a French psychiatrist. He specialized in the study and treatment of manias and was the first to describe a number of conditions including kleptomania and pyromania. In 1825, he was part of a special committee supporting Pierre Foissac's call for a new inquiry into mesmerism by the French Academy of Medicine. Foissac's lobbying was successful, resulting in the Husson commission, which Marc joined in 1826. He became a member of the Academy in 1830 and was appointed its president in 1833.*

Marcellinus, Ammianus *(c. 330 AD - c. 391 to 400 AD) was a Roman soldier and historian. His work* Res Gestae (Achievements) *is a major historical account in Latin of the history of Rome from the accession of the Emperor Nerva in 96 AD to the death of the Emperor Valens at the Battle of Adrianople in 378 AD. Only the texts covering the period 353 AD - 378 AD have survived.*

Mariette, August *full name: François Auguste Ferdinand Mariette HPB: Mariette-Bey (11 February 1821 - 19 January 1881) was a French archaeologist. He joined the Egyptian department of the Louvre in 1849. In 1850 he traveled to Egypt and discovered* a large number of painted statues from c. 2000 BC at Memphis the first capital of Ancient Egypt. He settled permanently in Egypt in 1858 becoming conservator of monuments for the Egyptian government, and later founder and first director of the Department of Antiquities in Cairo.

Mariotte, Edme (c. 1620 - 12 May 1684) was a French physicist. He was a Roman Catholic priest and prior of the abbey of Saint-Martin-sous-Beaune. In 1666 he was a founding member of the French Academy of Sciences in Paris. In the Academy's 1669 debate on the causes of gravity, he defended Plato's view that gravity was a natural tendency of parts of the same whole to join together.

Martial or Marcus Valerius Martialis (c. 40 AD - c. 103 AD) was a Roman poet. He wrote twelve books of Epigrams published in Rome between 86 AD and 103 AD, satirizing city life.

Martineau, James (21 April 1805 - 11 January 1900) was an English religious philosopher. He was appointed professor of mental and moral philosophy at Manchester New College in 1840 and became principal in 1869.

Marvin, Frederic Rowland (1847 - 1918) was an American physician. He was one of several figures who attempted to pathologize mediumship. In 1874 he published The Philosophy of Spiritualism and The Pathology and Treatment of Mediomania: Two Lectures read before the New York Liberal Club. In these lectures, he suggested that mediomania was the consequence of a neurosis that originated in the uterus.

Mateer, Samuel (1835-1893) was an English clergyman and missionary. He founded the Mateer Memorial Church in 1838 in Travancore, South India. In 1871 he published a descriptive account of Travancore and its people with the title The Land of Charity.

Matteucci, Carlo HPB: Matteuci (21 June 1811 - 25 June 1868) was an Italian physicist. In 1840 he was appointed professor of physics at the University of Pisa. He was the first to detect an electrical current in the heart. Later research established the role of electrical impulses in heart rhythm, leading ultimately to the invention of defibrillation.

Maturanzio, Francesco HPB: Maturantius (1443 - 20 August 1518) was an Italian humanist and writer. He was appointed chair of poetry and rhetoric at Vicenza in 1493. He wrote a number of influential commentaries on the works of Cicero, most notably on De Officiis (On Duties). According to Liceti he wrote to a friend about his acquisition of a perpetual lamp and its fuel cells: 'Both the vases... have fallen into my hands. If you saw them you would be astonished. I would not part with them for a thousand crowns of gold.'

Maudsley, Henry (5 February 1835 - 23 January 1918) was a British psychiatrist. He was elected a Fellow of the Royal College of Physicians in 1870 and delivered a series of lectures called

Body and Mind. *In his book* Natural Causes and Supernatural Seemings *published in 1886 he wrote that so-called supernatural experiences were disorders of the mind.*

Maxwell, William *(1581-1641) was a Scottish physician. He was appointed royal physician to Charles I of England. In his work* De Medicina Magnetica (On Magnetic Medicine) *published posthumously in 1679, he claimed that human disease could be cured by magnetically transferring it to animals and plants.*

Mayer, Alfred Marshall *(13 November 1836 - 13 July 1897) was an American physicist. In 1871 he became professor of physics at Stevens Institute of Technology, New Jersey and was elected to the National Academy of Sciences in 1872. He is the author of* The Earth a Great Magnet: a Lecture Delivered Before the Yale Scientific Club, February 14, 1872.

Medusa *is one of the three gorgons in Greek mythology. She is usually represented as a winged woman with snakes in place of hair. She is the only mortal gorgon. Consequently Perseus, son of Zeus, was able to kill her by beheading.*

Mendeleev, Dmitri Ivanovich *HPB: Mendeleyeff (8 February 1834 - 2 February 1907) was a Russian chemist and inventor. He became a professor at the St Petersburg University in 1865. He instigated the university's 1875 commission for the investigation of spiritualism. Although similar* commissions were established, this was the first to draw its members exclusively from the ranks of scientists. The commission's declared aim was to investigate, not necessarily to debunk, the phenomenon.

Menippus *appears in the* Life of Apollonius of Tyana *by the Greco-Roman author Flavius Philostratus. Menippus is described as a 25-year-old student of Apollonius. Blavatsky may be alluding to the story in which Menippus is beguiled by a beautiful woman only to discover on his wedding day, and with Apollonius' help, that she is a vampire.*

Mercury *is the Roman god of shopkeepers and merchants, travelers, fraudsters and thieves. He is often presented as an equivalent of the Greek god Hermes, messenger of the gods.*

Mesmer, Franz Friedrich Anton *(23 May 1734 - 5 March 1815) was a German physician. He is the founder of mesmerism, an early system of energy healing. He proposed that the gravity of the planets affected health by influencing an invisible 'magnetic fluid' found in all living things. In 1775 he replaced the term 'animal gravitation' with 'animal magnetism' suggesting that the invisible fluid obeyed the laws of magnetism. He proposed that animal magnetism could be controlled using magnets or the will of a trained mesmerist. Mesmerism attracted a wide following between 1780 and 1850 and continued to have some influence until the end of the century. In 1843 the Scottish physician James Braid proposed the term 'hypnosis' for a technique derived from Mesmer's work.*

Mesue *(c. 777 - 857) was a Persian or Assyrian physician from the Academy of Gundishapur. He became director of a hospital in Baghdad and was personal physician to four caliphs. He composed medical treatises on a number of topics, including ophthalmology, fevers, leprosy, headache, melancholia and the testing of physicians.*

Milton, John *(9 December 1608 - 8 November 1674) was an English poet. He is best known for* Paradise Lost, *published in 1667. The epic poem, widely regarded as the greatest in the English language, deals with The Fall of Man and the expulsion of Adam and Eve from the Garden of Eden.*

Mirandola, Giovanni Pico della *HPB: P de la Mirandolla (24 February 1463 - 17 November 1494) was an Italian scholar and Platonist philosopher. He was the first to use Kabbalistic doctrine in support of Christian theology, a key development in western esotericism.*

Mirville, Jules de, *full name: Charles Jules Eudes de Catteville de Mirville HPB: Comte de Mirville (24 April 1802 - 11 September 1873) was an esotericist and writer. He is author of* Question des Esprits (On the Question of Spirits) *published in 1855. In his text, de Mirville highlights, amongst other phenomena, the history of the haunted house of Cideville. (See Chapter Four.)*

Mithra *is a Zoroastrian goddess. In Roman mythology: Mithras. She is the goddess of sun, justice, war and contracts.*

Mocenigo, Giovanni Zuane *HPB: Zuane Mocenigo (2 August 1531 - 22 June 1598) was a Venetian civil servant and the accuser of Giordano Bruno. Initially, he wanted to learn Bruno's memory system and invited him to Venice. When Mocenigo's expectations were not met, he decided to denounce Bruno who was then arrested by the Venetian Inquisition on 22 May 1592. The Roman Inquisition demanded Bruno's extradition from Venice and on 23 January 1593, he was imprisoned in Rome. He was held for 7 years before his trial finally took place.*

Mochus the Sidonian, *or Mochus the Phoenician was a Phoenician writer. Nothing is known about his life, other than that he flourished before the Trojan Wars (13th Century BC). The Greek geographer and philosopher Strabo cited Mochus as the originator of atomic theory. The English scholar John Selden believed that Mochus was, in fact, Moses.*

Molitor, Franz Joseph *(7 July 1779 - 23 March 1860) was a German philosopher and Kabbalist. His greatest work* Philosophie der Geschichte oder Über die Tradition (Philosophy of History and Traditions) *was published anonymously in four volumes between 1827 and 1853. The first volumes were devoted to the principles of Judaism in the light of Kabbalah.*

Moncel, Théodose Achille Louis du *HPB: Moncal (6 March 1821 - 16 February 1884) was a prominent French physicist. He wrote many works popularizing the science and application* *of electricity. He was elected to the French Academy of Sciences in 1874 and in 1879 founded the scientific journal* La Lumière Électrique.

Monck, Francis Ward *(born c. 1842) was a British clergyman and spiritualist medium. During a seance in Huddersfield, he was challenged by a magician H. B. Lodge who insisted that Monck should be searched. Monck ran away, managing to escape through a window. A pair of stuffed gloves used to create the illusion of spirit hands was found among his possessions. Monck was arrested and tried for fraud. The naturalist Alfred Russel Wallace had investigated a number of mediums and took the stand as a witness for the defense. He claimed to have seen Monck manifest a genuine spirit woman with no hint of fraud. His testimony was overshadowed by the evidence of the physicist William Barrett (presumably Blavatsky's 'so-called scientist') who claimed he had caught Monck simulating a partially materialized spirit using a piece of white muslin. Monck was found guilty and sentenced to three months in prison.*

Montesquieu, Charles-Louis de Secondat, Baron de La Brède et de, *referred to as simply Montesquieu (18 January 1689 - 10 February 1755) was a French lawyer and political philosopher. His major work was* Esprit des Lois (The Spirit of the Law), *a treatise on political theory and comparative law, published in 1748.*

Morcillo, Sebastián Fox, *also Sebastanius Foxius Morzillus (or*

Morzillo), also Foxius of Seville, HPB: Foxius (c. 1528 - c. 1560) was a Spanish scholar and philosopher. He published commentaries on Plato and Aristotle, attempting to reconcile their teachings. In 1559 he was appointed tutor to Don Carlos, son of Philip II, but was lost at sea en route to Spain to take up the post.

More, Henry *(12 October 1614 - 1 September 1687) was an English poet and religious philosopher. He studied at Christ's College Cambridge becoming a fellow in 1639. He was one of a group of thinkers at the university known as the Cambridge Platonists. He is the author of many works including* The Immortality of the Soul, So Far Forth as It Is Demonstrable from the Knowledge of Nature and the Light of Reason *published in 1659.*

Morgan, Augustus de *(27 June 1806 - 18 March 1871) was a British mathematician and logician. He became interested in spiritualism, investigating the paranormal with the American medium Maria Hayden. He published his results, using his wife's name, Sophia, to avoid any backlash from the scientific community.* From Matter to Spirit: The Result of Ten Years Experience in Spirit Manifestations *was published in 1863.*

Morin, Alcide *(fl. mid-19th Century) was a French occult author. Blavatsky quotes from his book* La Magie au Dix-neuvième Siècle (Magic in the 19th Century) *published in 1854.*

Morse, Samuel Finley Breese
(27 April 1791 - 2 April 1872) was an American painter and inventor. He contributed to the invention of a single-wire telegraph system and was a co-developer of the code that bears his name.

Moses *is a prophet in the Abrahamic religions. According to the Hebrew Bible, he was adopted by an Egyptian princess and became the leader of the Israelites. Also called in Hebrew Moshe Rabbenu, he is the most important prophet in Judaism. He is the lawgiver and the acquisition of the Torah from Heaven is traditionally attributed to him. He is also a significant prophet in Christianity.*

Mousseaux, Roger Gougenot des,
also Chevalier Gougenot des Mousseaux (22 April 1805 - 5 November 1876) was a French polemic journalist and writer. Blavatsky quotes extensively from his books La Magie au Dix-neuvième Siècle (Magic in the Nineteenth Century) *published in 1860 and* Moeurs et Pratiques des Démons (The Habits and Practises of Demons) *published in 1854.*

Movers, Franz Karl *(17 July 1806 - 28 September 1856) was a German Roman Catholic priest, theologian and orientalist. His principal work* Die Phönizier *is a comprehensive history of the Phoenicians. The first volume published in 1840 covers religion and spirituality. The second addresses Phoenician political and colonial history and was published in two parts, the first in 1849, the second in 1850.*

Müller, Max *full name: Friedrich Max Müller (6 December 1823 - 28 October 1900) was a German scholar of comparative language, religion, and mythology. He specialized in Sanskrit philology and the religions of India.*

N.

Napier, Charles James *(10 August 1782 - 29 August 1853) was an officer in the British Army. He became a Major General of the Bombay Army, later serving as the Governor of Sindh and Commander-in-Chief in India.*

Naudé, Pierre Poiret *(15 April 1646 - 21 May 1719) was a French mystic and Christian philosopher. He collected the autobiographical and spiritual writings of the French-Flemish mystic Antoinette Bourignon and published them in 19 volumes from 1679 to 1686. Presumably the evidence that Naudé was a supporter of magnetism is contained in one of these books.*

Newton, Isaac *(25 December 1642 - 20 March 1726/27) was an English mathematician, astronomer and physicist. He is acknowledged as a key figure in the scientific revolution. His book* Philosophiae Naturalis Principia Mathematica (Mathematical Principles of Natural Philosophy) *published in 1687, laid the foundations of classical mechanics.*

Newton, James Rogers *(8 September 1810 - 7 August 1883) was an American magnetic healer. He believed the* *healer's vital magnetic energy could produce an instantaneous cure. He treated Olivia Twain (wife of Mark) who had suffered from paralysis since she was a teenager. He prayed over her, opened the curtains in her room and said, 'Now we will sit up my child.' He then aided her in walking a few steps.*

Nicodemus *appears in the Gospel of St John. 'Now there was a Pharisee, a man named Nicodemus who was a member of the Jewish ruling council. He came to Jesus at night and said, 'Rabbi, we know that you are a teacher who has come from God. For no one could perform the signs you are doing if God were not with him.' Jesus replied, 'Very truly I tell you, no one can see the kingdom of God unless they are born again.' 'How can someone be born when they are old?' Nicodemus asked. 'Surely they cannot enter a second time into their mother's womb to be born!' Jesus answered, 'Very truly I tell you, no one can enter the kingdom of God unless they are born of water and the Spirit. Flesh gives birth to flesh, but the Spirit gives birth to spirit. You should not be surprised at my saying, 'You must be born again.'*

Niðhöggr *also Nidhogg, HPB: Nidhögg is a dragon in Norse mythology. Niðhöggr means 'he who strikes with malice'. He is the foremost of several serpents that live beneath the world tree, the Yggdrasil, and eat its roots.*

Nobili, Leopoldo *(5 July 1784 - 22 August 1835) was an Italian physicist. In 1825 he successfully improved the galvanometer by inventing the more*

sensitive astatic galvanometer to detect and measure small amounts of current in an electrical circuit. The astatic galvanometer has two needles with opposite polarities, canceling out inaccuracies caused by the earth's magnetic field.

Nonnus *also Nonnus of Panopolis (fl. 5th Century AD) is the most notable Greek epic poet of the Roman period. Nothing is known of his life. His most important work is the* Dionysiaca, *a hexameter poem of 21,286 lines in 48 books and the longest surviving poem from ancient Greece. Its principal subject is the expedition of the god Dionysus to India.*

Nouffleur, Madame *(fl. 1770) was a French quack. She was famous for a cure for tapeworm. The recipe is given by the English physician John Mason Good in* The Study of Medicine Volume I *published in 1822: 'Powder very finely, for one dose, 3 drams of the male fern, Aspidium Filix Mas, and after the patient has been prepared the previous night by an emollient clyster, and a supper of pananda, this is to be taken early in the morning, fasting: two hours after, a bolus is to be given made of 12 grains each of chloride of mercury and scammony, and 5 grains of gamboge.'*

O.

Oannes *often equated with Dagon is an amphibious deity in Mesopotamian mythology. He is described by the Babylonian writer Berossus as a creature with the body of a fish but the head of a man. (See also* **Dagon**.)

Odin is the king of the Æsir, which is the principal pantheon of deities in Norse mythology.

Ogyges also Ogygos or Ogygus is the first king of Thebes in Greek mythology. During his reign a great flood, called the Ogygian deluge, inundated his kingdom.

Olybius HPB: Maximus Olybius (fl. c. 1st Century) was an early Italian philosopher, chemist and wealthy citizen of Padua. It is alleged that peasants digging at Ateste near Padua discovered his tomb containing an elaborate perpetual lamp. It was claimed that he had found out the secret of transmuting metals and this had enabled him to prepare two vials. One contained transmuted gold and the other, transmuted silver which served as the fuel for the everlasting lamp. The lamp's discovers mistook the liquid for water and tipped it out, losing the secret of transmutation for ever.

Oporinus, Johannes also Johannes Herbster or Herbst (25 January 1507 - 6 July 1568) was a Swiss printer and later a professor of Greek at Basel University. Aged 20, he was apprenticed to Paracelsus for the short time Paracelsus lived in Basel. Oporinus wrote a letter after Paracelsus' death describing him as irritable, ostentatious, and dangerous. Very little is known for certain about the letter including when it was written (c. 1555 or 1565) or who it was intended for.

Oribasius or Oreibasius (c. 320 AD - 403 AD) was a Greek medical writer and the personal physician of the Roman emperor Julian.

Origen (c. 185 AD - c. 254 AD) was a Greek scholar, ascetic and early Christian theologian. He was a prolific writer in multiple branches of theology, including textual criticism, biblical exegesis and hermeneutics, philosophical theology, preaching, and spirituality. He is now regarded as one of the most important theologians and biblical scholars of the early Greek church.

Orioli, Francesco (18 March 1783 - 5 November 1856) was an Italian scientist and professor of physics at the University of Bologna. With the physician Angelo Cogevina, he published in 1842 Fatti Relativi a Mesmerismo e Cure Mesmeriche (Facts Relating to Mesmerism and Mesmeric Cures). Their book called for an examination of the phenomenon, aimed at promoting liberal acceptance of magnetism.

Orpheus is a legendary musician and poet in ancient Greek mythology. In Orphic myths he is able to charm the world with his music. When his wife Eurydice dies of a snakebite, he travels to the underworld. He so moves Hades, king of the underworld, with his music and his grief that Hades allows him to take Eurydice back to the world of the living. There is also an ancient tradition that Orpheus was educated in Egypt and brought Egyptian Mysteries to Greece.

Ørsted, Hans Christian HPB: Oersted (14 August 1777 - 9 March 1851) was a Danish physicist and chemist. In 1806 he became a professor at the University of Copenhagen. During a lecture in April 1820 he noticed that a wire carrying an electric current deflected a compass needle. This discovery led to the development of electromagnetic theory.

Osiris is the ancient Egyptian god of the dead and ruler of the underworld. He is the brother/husband of Isis and the father of Horus. He is the god of resurrection and fertility.

Owen, Robert Dale (7 November 1801 - 24 June 1877) was a Scottish-born American politician and social reformer. He converted to spiritualism in 1854. He published Footfalls on the Boundary of Another World in 1859. In his own words he collected 'the most noted old works containing narrative collections of apparitions, hauntings, presentiments and the like.'

P.

Palissy, Bernard (1509 - 1590) was a French Huguenot potter and scientist. He was appointed King's Inventor of Rustic Ceramics in 1563. From 1575 he gave public lectures in Paris on natural history and published them in 1580 as Discours Admirables (Admirable Discourses). His writing demonstrated that he was a scientific pioneer whose ideas were more advanced than those of his peers.

Pan is the god of nature and the companion of the nymphs in Greek mythology. Similar to a faun or satyr, he is depicted as a man with the hindquarters, legs and horns of a goat. In Periegesis Hellados (Description of Greece) the

Greek geographer Pausanias describes a perpetual fire burning at the temple dedicated to Pan on mount Parthenius at Megalopolis near Acacesium (16km east of Tripoli).

Panciroli, Guido HPB: Pancirollus (17 April 1523 - 5 March 1599), was an Italian antiquarian, historian, and renowned professor of law. In 1599 his student Heinrich Salmuth translated into Latin and published Panciroli's work Rerum Memorabilium, Iam Olim Deperditarum (The History of Many Memorable Things Lost). The work is a comparative survey of natural philosophy, alchemy and medicine, highlighting the lost knowledge of the ancient world. It contains a section on perpetual lamps.

Pantatem is cited as an author knowledgeable about the alkahest by the British surgeon James Forysth in his book Demonologia or Natural Knowledge Revealed (1827). Forsyth writes, 'The Alkahest is a subject that has been embraced by many authors; e.g. Pantatem, Philalettes, Tachenius, Ludovicus, etc.' This is clearly Blavatsky's source and it is the only reference to Pantatem it has been possible to locate.

Paracelsus full name: Philippus Aureolus Theophrastus Bombastus von Hohenheim (c. November 1493 - 24 September 1541) was a Swiss physician and alchemist. He challenged the medical orthodoxy of the time, valuing instead traditional healing lore. He wrote 'a doctor must seek out old wives, gypsies, sorcerers, wandering tribes, old robbers, and such outlaws and take lessons from them.' He gained practical knowledge of alchemy to help him create effective treatments. This made him one of the first to see the significance of chemistry to medicine. Even though he was an unorthodox figure, he laid many of the foundations for modern medicine.

Pariset, Étienne HPB: Parisey (5 August 1770 - 3 July 1847) was a French physician and psychiatrist. In 1819 he became head of the department for mental illness at Bicêtre Hospital, Paris. In the same year he joined the Commission pour l'amélioration du sort des aliénés (Commission for improving the lot of the insane). He was appointed perpetual secretary of the French Academy of Medicine in 1822. In 1825, he was part of a special committee supporting Pierre Foissac's call for the Academy to mount a new inquiry into mesmerism.

Parmenides also Parmenides of Elea (fl. early 5th Century BC) was a pre-Socratic Greek philosopher. His reputation as one of the most profound and challenging thinkers of early Greek philosophy rests on a single poem On Nature. The poem's middle section proposes that all reality is one. Change is impossible, and existence is timeless, uniform and necessary.

Paul III, Pope also Paulus III (29 February 1468 - 10 November 1549) was head of the Roman Catholic church from 13 October 1534 until his death. The tomb of Cicero's daughter Tullia was discovered in 1540 during his papacy.

Paulus, Dr is an obscure figure. Apart from his surname little else is known. He was the author of The Magicon published in New York in 1869 but the lines cited by Blavatsky do not appear in his text.

Pausanias (c. 110 AD - c. 180 AD) was a Greek traveler and geographer. In Periegesis Hellados (Description of Greece) he recounts his travels across ancient Greece, visiting major cities and religious sites. The accuracy of his descriptions is supported by archeological evidence found throughout the country.

Peisander also Peisander of Rhodes (fl. c. 645 BC) was a poet from Cameirus on the Greek island of Rhodes. His poem The Heracleia recounts the Labors of Hercules. It's probable that Peisander was the first to fix the number of labors at twelve. He also introduced a new depiction of Hercules dressed in a lion's skin and carrying a club.

Perdonnet, Jean Albert Vincent Auguste (12 March 1801 - 27 September 1867) was a French railroad engineer. He was instrumental in the construction of the French rail network. He was director of the École Centrale des Arts et Manufactures (Central School of Arts and Manufacturing) in Paris between 1862 and 1867.

Persephone is the goddess of grain and vegetation in Greek mythology. She is the daughter of Zeus and Demeter, the goddess of the harvest. She is married to Hades, king of the underworld, and rules that shadowy realm by his side.

Perty, Maximilian *full name: Josef Anton Maximilian Perty (17 September 1804 - 8 August 1884) was a German naturalist and entomologist. In 1834 he became professor of zoology and comparative anatomy at the University of Bern. He is the author of many works on spiritualism and the supernatural including* Die Mystischen Erscheinungen in der Menschlichen Natur (Mystical Manifestations of Human Nature) *published in 1861.*

Peter *is a mournful gentleman spirit well known in spiritualism in the 19th Century. He often appeared at seances together with the spirit control John King and John King's spirit daughter Katie.*

Peter, Saint *also Simon Peter or Simeon (died 64 AD) was a Jewish fisherman and one of the twelve disciples of Jesus Christ. The early Christian church recognized him as the leader of the disciples and he was the first in the line of Roman Catholic popes.*

Petrarch *full name: Francesco Petrarca (20 July 1304 - 18 or 19 July 1374) was an Italian scholar and poet. He is most well known for his collection of vernacular poems called* Canzoniere (Song Book). *The narrator of the poems dedicates his lines to Laura, a woman he loves but cannot be with.*

Pfaff, Johann Wilhelm Andreas *(5 December 1774 - 26 June 1835) was a German mathematician, physicist and astronomer. He founded the Tartu Observatory, the largest astronomical observatory in Estonia. From 1818 until*

his death he was professor of mathematics at the University of Erlangen. He took a personal interest in the interpretation of the stars publishing Astrologie (Astrology) *in 1816 and* Der Mensch und die Sterne - Fragmente zur Geschichte der Weltseele (Man and the Stars - Fragments of the History of the World Soul) *in 1834.*

Phanes *HPB: Eros-Phanes, is the primeval deity of procreation in the Orphic religion. Orphism is a Hellenistic mystery religion, thought to have been based on the teachings and songs of the legendary Greek musician Orpheus. Phanes is represented as a golden-winged, hermaphroditic deity wrapped in the coils of a serpent. His name means 'bring to light' or 'make appear' from the Greek verbs phanaô and phainô.*

Pherecydes of Syros *(fl. 6th Century BC) was a Greek writer. He is regarded as the originator of metempsychosis - the belief that the human soul is immortal and passes into another body, human or animal, after death. He is the author of* Heptamychos (Seven Recesses) *in which he suggests the world originated from a holy trinity comprised of* Zas (Zeus), Chronos or Kronos, and Chthonie or Ge (Mother Earth).

Philalethes, Eugenius *is the pseudonym of Thomas Vaughan (17 April 1621 - 27 February 1666) a Welsh philosopher and alchemist. He believed that spiritual grace was the first prerequisite for attaining the alkahest or universal solvent. Inner development of the soul was necessary in addition to the* *preparation of the appropriate chemical elements. He published two major works in 1650* Anthroposophia Theomagica (Discourse on the Nature of Man and the After Death State) *and* Anima Magica Abscondita (Discourse on the Universal Spirit of Nature).

Philip IV *also Philip the Fair or the Iron King, HPB: Philippe le Bel (c. May 1268 - 29 November 1314) was King of France from 1285 until his death. When his wife Queen Joan died in April 1305, he considered abdicating the throne of France and becoming ruler of the Holy Land at the head of a consolidated crusading order. Grief and greed are the likely motivators behind his persecution of the Knights Templar. They opposed his wish to unite all crusading orders and he retaliated by seizing all Knights Templar in France.*

Phillips, Wendell *(29 November 1811 - 2 February 1884) was an American abolitionist and attorney. He turned his back on a lucrative legal career to oppose slavery. He became president of the American Anti-Slavery Society in 1865. Blavatsky quotes extensively from the text of his lecture* The Lost Arts. *Beginning in 1838, he gave this lecture more than 2,000 times over a period of 45 years. It was his most famous and lucrative lecture earning him $150,000.*

Philo *also Philo Judaeus, Philo of Alexandria, HPB: Philo Judæus (c. 15 BC - c. 45 BC) was a Greek-speaking Jewish philosopher. He was the first to attempt a synthesis of philosophic reason and religious belief. Plato, Aristotle, and the Neo-Pythagoreans all had an influence on his philosophy. In particular, the Neo-Pythagoreans inspired his ideas about the mystical significance of numbers, especially the number seven. He advocated a state of mysticism or 'sober intoxication' as a prerequisite for escaping the material world and experiencing the eternal.*

Philolaus *(fl. c. 475 BC) was a Greek philosopher of the Pythagorean school. He was the first to argue that the earth was not the stationary center of the cosmos but revolved around a central fire as did the stars, planets, sun, moon, and a mysterious 'counter-earth.'*

Phipson, Thomas Lamb *(1833 - 1908) was a British scientist, violinist and writer. He obtained his doctorate from the University of Brussels and became a member of the Chemical Society in Paris and London. He was author of* Phosphorescence or The Emission of Light by Minerals Plants and Animals *published in 1862.*

Pian del Carpine, Giovanni da *also John of Pian de Carpine, John of Plano Carpini, Joannes de Plano, HPB: De Plano Carpini (c. 1185 - 1 August 1252) was an Italian member of the Franciscan Order, a diplomat and explorer. He was sent to Mongolia in 1245 by Pope Innocent IV to demand and end to the persecution of Christians. He returned to Europe in 1247 and published a chronicle of his travels titled* Ystoria Mongalorum (History of the Mongols) *also know as the* Book of the Tartars.

Piérart, Zéphyr-Joseph *HPB: Pierrard (15 May 1818 - 14 February 1879) was a leading French spiritualist, author and historian. He was a professor at the College of Maubeuge in northern France and went on to found a branch of spiritualism to rival Allan Kardec's spiritism. Piérart's spiritualism rejected the principle of reincarnation. In 1858, he founded the spiritualist journal* La Revue Spirtualiste *and spent his later years as secretary to the famous mesmerist Jules du Potet.*

Pius IX *Giovanni Maria Mastai-Ferretti, HPB: Pio Nono (13 May 1792 - 7 February 1878) was Pope from 16 June 1846 to his death in 1878. His was the longest running papacy in history. Blavatsky alludes to his epilepsy which may have been triggered by a near-drowning incident in his youth.*

Planty, Marquis du *possibly Louis Joseph de Godart, HPB: Chevalier Duplanty (1808 - 1876). Blavatsky's 'Duplanty' is obscure. He may be Louis Joseph de Godart, Marquis du Planty who presided over a commission for the Philanthropomagnetic Society of Paris. His name appears on the report titled:* Rapport de la Commission Nommée par la Société Philanthropo-magnétique de Paris pour Rendre Compte du Triple-électro-galvanique, Appareil Inventé par M. Em. Rebold. (Report of the Commission Appointed by the Philanthropomagnetic Society of Paris to Report on the Triple-electro-galvanic Device invented by Mr. Em. Rebold.) *The publication date is unknown.*

Plato *(428/427 BC or 424/423 BC - 348/347 BC) was a Greek philosopher and the founder of the Academy in Athens, the first institution of higher learning in the western world.*

Playfair, Lyon, *1st Baron Playfair of St Andrews (21 May 1818 - 29 May 1898) was a Scottish chemist. He studied in Gießen under the renowned German biochemist Justus von Liebig. He became professor of chemistry at the Royal Institute, Manchester and at Edinburgh. (See also* **Liebig, Justus von.***)*

Pleasonton, Augustus James *HPB: General Pleasonton (21 January 1801 - 26 July 1894) was a militia general during the American Civil War. He originated the theory that the sun's rays, when passed through blue glass, stimulated the development of crops and contributed to the health and growth of animals. He published his theory in 1876 in* The Influence of the Blue Ray of the Sunlight and of the Blue Color of the Sky. *He delivered numerous lectures at scientific societies and his theory attracted widespread attention, producing a 'blue glass craze.'*

Pletho, Georgius Gemistus *(c. 1355 - 1450/52), was a Byzantine philosopher. He studied in Constantinople and at the Ottoman Muslim court in nearby Adrianople. He believed the gods directed the human soul to reincarnate into successive bodies to fulfil divine will.*

Pliny the Elder *full name: Gaius Plinius Secundus, HPB: Pliny (23 AD - 24 August 79 AD) was a Roman author,* *naturalist and natural philosopher. His major work* Naturalis Historia (Natural History) *consisted of 37 volumes investigating 'the nature of things, that is, life.' It is one of the largest single works to have survived from the Roman Empire.*

Plotinus *(c. 205 AD - 270 AD) was a Greek-speaking ancient philosopher and a founder of the Neoplatonic school. He was the principal classical exponent of the theory of emanationism. In his treatise the* Enneads, *he describes matter as 'the last, lowest and least emanation of the creative power of the All-Soul.'*

Plutarch *(c. 46 AD - after 119 AD) was a Greek biographer. He is the author of more than 200 works including* Bioi Parallēloi (Parallel Lives *also* Plutarch's Lives), *biographies of Greek and Roman soldiers and statesmen, and* Moralia (Morals), *essays on ethical, religious, political, and literary topics. He served as a priest at Delphi for the last 30 years of his life.*

Pluto *was god of the dead and ruler of the underworld in Roman mythology. His Greek equivalent, the god Hades, is more commonly associated with the underworld.*

Podocattarus *is an obscure reference. Blavatsky's source is almost certainly Thomas Greenhill's* The Art of Embalming: *'One Podocattarus, a Cyprian Knight, who wrote* de Rebus Cypriis (On Matters Concerning Cyprus) *in the Year 1566, had both Flax and Linen of this kind with him at Venice, which Porcacchius says, in his* Book of Ancient Funerals, *he and many others that were with him, saw at that Knight's House.' Greenhill in turn could have sourced the quote from any number of books that cite the story but fail to provide biographical information about the mysterious knight.*

Polier, Marie Elisabeth de *(1742 - 1817) was the Swiss author of* Mythologie des Indous (Hindu Mythology) *published in 1809. The book drew on the manuscripts of her late husband Colonel Antoine-Louis Henri de Polier (1741-1795), a Swiss adventurer and soldier who made his fortune in India in the 18th Century.*

Polk, Leonidas HPB: *Bishop Polk also Bishop of Louisiana (10 April 1806 - 14 June 1864) was an American episcopal bishop of Louisiana and a major general in the Confederate army. He resigned his ecclesiastical position to enter the military and became famous as 'Sewanee's Fighting Bishop.'*

Pompilius, Numa HPB: *Numa (fl. c. 700 BC) was the second of the seven kings to rule Rome before the founding of the republic, according to Roman legend. He reigned from 715 BC to 673 BC, succeeding Romulus.*

Pomponazzi, Pietro *or Petrus Pomponatius,* HPB: *Pompanatius (16 September 1462 - 18 May 1525) was an Italian philosopher. In 1516 he published* Tractatus de Immortalitate Animae (Treatise on the Immortality of the Soul). *He maintained that the immortality of the soul cannot be proven by reason but must be taken on faith.*

Pope, Alexander *(21 May 1688 - 30 May 1744) was an English poet. He is best known for his satirical verse and for his translations of the works of Homer.*

Porcacchi, Tommaso *HPB: Porcacchius (1530 - October 1576) was an Italian writer, scholar, geographer and translator. In 1574 he published an ethnographic work on funeral rites called* Funerali Antichi di Diversi Popoli, et Nationi *(Ancient Funerals of Different Peoples and Nations).*

Porphyry *HPB: Porphyry and Porphyrius (c. 234 AD - c. 305 AD) was a Syrian philosopher. He studied philosophy in Rome under Plotinus and wrote many works on philosophy, religion, philology, and science. He lectured on the work of Plotinus and tutored the Syrian philosopher Iamblichus.*

Porta, Giambattista della *known as Baptista Porta (c. 1535 - 4 February 1615), was an Italian scholar and playwright. His major work is* Magia Naturalis *(Natural Magic) published in 1558. His text explores occult philosophy, astrology, alchemy, mathematics, meteorology, and natural philosophy.*

Potet, Baron Jules Denis du *or Dupotet de Sennevoy (12 April 1796 - 1 July 1881) was a French esotericist and became a renowned practitioner of mesmerism. From 1826 he ran a free school of magnetism in Paris. Between 1837 and 1845 he practiced magnetic healing in London, successfully treating epileptics. He also pursued occult applications of mesmerism. He believed that the trance state facilitated contact with the dead or with spirits that had not yet incarnated. He was a member of the Theosophical Society and Blavatsky regarded him as an adept. He published and edited the* Journal du Magnétisme *from 1845 to 1861. His books include* An Introduction to the Study of Animal Magnetism *(1838) and* La Magie Dévoilée ou Principes de Science Occulte *(Magic Unveiled or the Principles of Occult Science) published in 1852.*

Priestley, Joseph *(13 March 1733 - 6 February 1804) was an English clergyman, political theorist and chemist. He discovered ten new gases and was awarded the Royal Society's prestigious Copley Medal in 1773 in recognition of his work. His lasting reputation in science is founded on his discovery of oxygen on 1 August 1774. He published* Disquisitions on Matter and Spirit *in 1777 quoting Saint Paul: 'The bodies with which we shall rise from the dead; when from earthly they will become spiritual; from corruptible, incorruptible; and from mortal, immortal.'*

Proclus *(c. 410 AD - 485 AD) was the last major ancient Greek philosopher. He was a pivotal figure in the dissemination of Neoplatonic ideas throughout the Byzantine, Islamic, and Roman worlds.*

Proctor, Richard Anthony *(23 March 1837 - 12 September 1888) was an English astronomer. He was a prolific writer of popular astronomy books and in 1867 produced one of the earliest*

maps of Mars. In The Borderland of
Science published in 1873 he puts
forward the idea that the greatest difficulty
faced by science is 'determining how far it
is reasonable or likely that any of the
common ideas about the supernatural have
any basis of fact whatever.'

Psellus, Michael (1018 - c. 1078)
was a Byzantine philosopher, theologian,
and statesman. He maintained that
Platonic philosophy and Christian
doctrine were compatible. One of his most
important works is Commentary on
Plato's Teachings on the Origin of
the Soul.

Ptah HPB: Phtha was the supreme
creator-god in ancient Egyptian religion.
Originally a regional deity of Memphis,
his cult grew with the city's political
importance until he was worshiped
throughout Egypt. He was depicted as a
mummified man with a skullcap and a
short, straight beard.

Ptolemy Latin: Claudius Ptolemaeus
(c. 100 AD - c. 170 AD) was an
Egyptian astronomer, mathematician, and
geographer. His geocentric model of the
universe - the Ptolemaic system - is
regarded as one of the pinnacles of Greco-
Roman scientific achievement.

Ptolemy I Soter (367/366 BC -
283/282 BC) was a Macedonian
general under Alexander the Great, then
ruler of Egypt from 323 BC to 285 BC.

Putnam, Israel popularly known as
Old Put (7 January 1718 - 29 May
1790) was an American army general

who served in the American Revolutionary
War. In 1742 he shot and killed
Connecticut's last known wolf. Putnam
and others tracked the wolf to a cave at
Pomfret after it had killed 70 sheep on
Putnam's farm. He entered the cave by
torch light, shot the wolf, and was pulled
free by a rope tied to his ankles, dragging
the wolf behind him.

**Puységur, Amand-Marie-Jacques
de Chastenet, Marquis de** (1 March
1751 - 1 August 1825) was a French
magnetizer and aristocrat. When he
magnetized a 23-year-old peasant, the
man unexpectedly entered a strange form
of sleeping trance. Noting the similarity to
somnambulism, Puységur named the new
trance state 'artificial somnambulism'.
Today the more familiar term is
'hypnosis'. Puységur's Société
Harmonique des Amis Réunis, an
institute for training magnetizers, grew
rapidly until the French Revolution
in 1789.

Pythagoras (c. 570 BC - c. 495 BC)
was a Greek philosopher, mathematician,
and the founder of Pythagoreanism.
This philosophical and religious school
gave rise to important principles
influencing both Plato and Aristotle.
Pythagoreanism informed the later
development of western rational
philosophy and mathematics.

R.

Ra is the ancient Egyptian sun god and
god of creation. He is depicted as a man
with the head of a falcon. In Egyptian

myth he rose from an ocean of chaos creating himself and giving rise to eight other gods.

Rader, Matthew *HPB: Matthaeus Raderus (1561 - 22 December 1634) was a Jesuit philologist and historian. He taught the humanities for 21 years in different Jesuit institutions. He published an improved and expurgated edition of the works of the Roman poet Martial in 1599.*

Randolph, Paschal Beverly *(8 October 1825 - 29 July 1875) was an African American physician, spiritualist and writer. He believed that humans existed on earth before the biblical Adam. In 1863, under the name of Griffin Lee, he published* Pre-Adamite Man: Demonstrating the Existence of the Human Race upon the Earth 100,000 Thousand Years Ago! *The book drew on a wide range of different world traditions, esoterica and ancient religions. According to the poet A. E. Waite, Randolph established the earliest known Rosicrucian order in the United States, the Fraternitas Rosae Crucis, in 1858.*

Raoul-Rochette, Désiré *(6 March 1790 - 3 July 1854), was a French archaeologist. His first major work was* Histoire Critique de l'Établissement des Colonies Grecques (Critical History of the Establishment of the Greek Colonies) *published in 1815. He was superintendent of antiquities at the Bibliothèque at Paris from 1819 to 1848, and professor of archeology at the Bibliothèque from 1826.*

Rawlinson, Henry Creswicke, 1st Baronet *(11 April 1810 - 5 March 1895) was a British army officer, orientalist and cryptographer. He decoded the Old Persian in the inscription of Darius I the Great, at Mount Behistun in the Kermanshah province in Iran. This work provided the key to understanding Mesopotamian cuneiform script in its entirety.*

Rayer, Pierre François Olive *(8 March 1793 - 10 September 1867) was a French physician. He made important contributions in the fields of pathological anatomy, physiology, comparative pathology and parasitology. He was a member of the French Academies of Medicine and Science. According to the Science Academy's report of its of Session of 18 April 1859, the German scholar invited to speak by Rayer and Jobert de Lamballe was the physiologist Mortiz Schiff (1823-1896).*

Raynal, Guillaume Tomas François *(12 April 1713 - 6 March 1796) was a French historian and philosopher. His major work is* L'Histoire Philosophique et Politique des Établissements et du Commerce des Européens dans les Deux Indes (Philosophical and Political History of the Two Indies) *published in 1770. The book provoked strong opposition from the establishment because it criticized religion, colonization and slavery.*

Rāzī *full name: Abū Bakr Muḥammad ibn Zakariyyā al-Rāzī, HPB: Rhasis (c. 854 - c. 925) was a Persian physician,* *alchemist and philosopher. He was an early proponent of experimental medicine and is considered to be the Islamic world's greatest physician.*

Regazzoni, Antonio *(died 1870) was an Italian magnetizer. In Paris in May 1856 he blindfolded strangers and demonstrated how they were constrained by a 'Kabbalistic' line drawn across the floor. In another case, he caused a blindfolded girl to fall, as if struck by lightning. The German philosopher Arthur Schopenhauer discussed Regazzoni's work in* Über den Willen in der Natur (On the Will in Nature) *published in 1836. Schopenhauer believed Regazzoni's demonstration confirmed aspects of his own theory of will.*

Reichenbach, Baron Carl Ludwig von *(12 February 1788 - 22 January 1869) was a German chemist, meteorite expert and the discoverer of kerosene, paraffin, and creosote. He spent the last decades of his life researching a force he called 'od' (also known as odic force). This hypothetical field of energy was generated by all living things and comprised of electricity, magnetism and heat. The od had its theoretical origins in mesmerism.*

Reuchlin, Johann *also Johannes (22 February 1455 - 30 June 1522) was a German humanist and Hebrew scholar. His book* De Arte Cabalistica (On the Art of Kabbalah) *published in 1517 argues there is a profound connection between the Kabbalah and Pythagoreanism. He maintained that the Pythagorean tradition was also*

an expression of Hebreo-Christian religious wisdom.

Richardson, Benjamin Ward *(31 October 1828 - 21 November 1896) was a British physician. He was admitted to the Faculty of Physicians and Surgeons of Glasgow in 1850 and became a member of the Royal College of Physicians in London in 1856. In all, he brought 14 anaesthetics into clinical use; the best known was methylene bichloride. Richardson's* Popular Science Monthly *article referred to by Blavatsky is 'The Physiology of Sleep'.*

Richelieu, Cardinal *full name: Armand Jean du Plessis, Duke of Richelieu and Fronsac (9 September 1585 - 4 December 1642), was a French clergyman and statesman. He rose to prominence in both the Catholic church and the French government, becoming a cardinal in 1622 and King Louis XIII's chief minister in 1624. He sought to consolidate royal power and crush domestic factions. Blavatsky's text does not name Richelieu directly, referring to him obliquely as 'a minister.'*

Robert-Houdin, Jean-Eugène *born: Jean-Eugène Robert (6 December 1805 - 13 June 1871) was a French magician. He is widely acknowledged as the originator of the modern conjuring style. He exposed fraudulent mediums and magicians who claimed the effects they produced were supernatural.*

Roger, Madame *(dates unknown) is an obscure figure in spite of Blavatsky's description of her as a 'famous* *clairvoyant.' Given that she was often mesmerized by Dr. Fortin, the President of the Société Théosophique des Occultistes de France, it seems reasonable to assume she belonged to that group. (See also* **Fortin, Dr.***)*

Ruscelli, Girolamo *HPB: Ruscellius (c. 1500 - 1566), was an Italian mathematician and cartographer. It is generally assumed that he also wrote pseudonymously as the alchemist Alessio Piemontese. He claimed that his most popular book* The Secrets of Alessio Piemontese *contained the experimental results of an 'Academy of Secrets' founded in Naples in the 1540s.*

S.

Saccas, Ammonius *(fl. early 3rd Century AD) was a Greek philosopher from Alexandria. He was the founder of Neoplatonism and teacher of Plotinus from 232 AD to 243 AD. Because Ammonius wrote nothing down, his philosophy is known only through his famous pupil whose writings were arranged and published by Porphyry.*

Sallin, Jean-Charles-Henri *(dates unknown) was dean of the Faculty of Medicine in Paris from 1784 to 1786. He investigated Mesmer as a member of the 1784 Franklin committee, convened by the French Academy of Sciences, to investigate mesmerism.*

Salverte, Eusèbe *full name: Eusèbe Baconnière de Salverte (18 July 1771 - 27 October 1839) was a French poet and*

politician. He was deputy of the 3rd arrondissement of Paris from 1828 to 1831 and deputy of the 5th arrondissement from 1831 to 1839. He published Des Sciences Occultes; ou, Essai sur la Magie, les Prodiges et les Miracles (The Occult Sciences: The Philosophy of Magic, Prodigies and Apparent Miracles) *in 1829. He explores the link between the belief in miracles and ancient religious practices. The book was translated into English in 1846 by the Scottish physician and writer, Anthony Todd Thomson. Thomson described Salverte's work as a significant study of miracles and sacerdotal power. Unfortunately, Thomson edited any passages on Christianity and changed 'miracles' in the original subtitle to read 'apparent miracles.'*

Samuel *(fl. 11th Century BC) is a Hebrew prophet. The Old Testament presents him as a religious hero in the history of Israel.*

Sanchuniathon *HPB: Sanchoniathon (fl. 13th Century BC?) was an ancient Phoenician writer. Only fragments of his work survive in Greek translation by the Lebanese historian Philo of Byblos. These fragments constitute the most important source concerning Phoenician religion.*

Santanelli, Ferdinand *(dates unknown) was a professor of medicine at the University of Naples. He is the author of* Occult Philosophy or Magical-Magnetic Science *published in 1723. He proposed the presence in all material things of a magnetic radiating element. By manipulating this element, the progress* *of disease could be affected. Santanelli aimed to defend magic as a natural science, dedicating his book, in a letter dated 8 May 1723, to the Royal Society in London.*

Saraswati *is the Hindu goddess of knowledge and the arts. Blavatsky does not name Saraswati directly, referring to her only obliquely as the 'prolific consort' of 'Brahma, the fire-god.'*

Sargent, Epes *(27 September 1813 - 30 December 1880) was an American poet and playwright. He was editor of two Boston newspapers and the* New-York Mirror. *He published three books concerning spiritualism:* Planchette, or the Despair of Science *(1869),* The Proof Palpable of Immortality *(1875), and* The Scientific Basis of Spiritualism *(1880).*

Sarpa-Rajni *(Sanskrit meaning serpent queen) is a deity described in the Aitareya-Brahmana. The consort of the Sun God, she sheds her seven skins, symbolizing, according to Blavatsky, the seven geological changes that accompany the evolution of the seven root races.*

Saul *(fl. 11th Century BC) was the first king of Israel (c. 1021BC - 1000 BC). According to the First Book of Samuel, Saul was chosen king by the judge Samuel supported by public opinion.*

Scardeone, Bernardino HPB: *Scardeonius (1482 - 29 May 1574) was an Italian priest and writer. He was appointed by Pope Paul IV as canon of the Cathedral of Padua in 1556. He*

published his most important work in 1560: De Antiquitate Urbis Patavii (The Ancient City of Padua), *a biographical dictionary of the personalities of Padua, from the Roman era to 1559.*

Schatta, Michael *(fl. mid 17th Century) was an Egyptian linguist and lexicographer. He assisted the German Jesuit scholar Athanasius Kircher in the preparation of* Oedipus Aegyptiacus (the Egyptian Oedipus), an *ambitious study of Egyptology and hieroglyphs published between 1652 and 1654.*

Schenk, August Joseph *(17 April 1815 - 30 March 1891) was a German botanist and paleontologist. He was appointed professor of botany at the University of Würzburg in 1850 and became a professor at Leipzig University in 1868.*

Schleiermacher, Friedrich HPB: *Schleirmacher (21 November 1768 - 12 February 1834) was a German theologian and philologist. He is widely acknowledged as the founder of modern Protestant theology. Between 1804 and 1828 he published* Platons Werke, *his translations of Plato's dialogues.*

Schliemann, Heinrich *full name:* Johann Ludwig Heinrich Julius Schliemann *(6 January 1822 - 26 December 1890) was a German businessman and pioneer in the field of archeology. He was the excavator of the ancient cities of Troy, Mycenae, and Tiryns.*

Schopenhauer, Arthur *(22 February 1788 - 21 September 1860) was a German philosopher. His most important work is* Die Welt als Wille und Vorstellung (The World as Will and Idea) *published in 1819. Schopenhauer theorizes that the world we perceive is the product of a blind and insatiable metaphysical will.*

Schwarz, Berthold, *HPB: Schwartz (fl. early 14th Century) was a German monk and alchemist. The claim that he invented gunpowder is supported by entries of dubious authenticity in the town records of Ghent. Very little is now known about his life. He appears to have been a canon at Konstanz Cathedral c. 1300 and a teacher at the University of Paris during the 1330s.*

Schweigger, Johann Salomo Christoph *(8 April 1779 - 6 September 1857) was a German chemist and physicist. He became professor of physics and chemistry at the University of Erlangen in 1817 and at the University of Halle in 1819 where he remained until his death. In* Einleitung in die Mythologie auf dem Standpunkte der Naturwissenschaft (Introduction to Mythology from the Standpoint of Natural Science) *published in 1836, he argued that ancient myths can be interpreted as symbolic representations of scientific truths.*

Scot, Reginald *also Scott (c. 1538 - 9 October 1599), was an English Member of Parliament and author. In 1584 he published* The Discoverie of Witchcraft, *debunking then prevalent*

beliefs about witchcraft, magic and other superstitions. He provided non-supernatural explanations for apparently magical phenomena and incidents of witchcraft. He maintained that anyone executed for witchcraft was innocent and he blamed the Catholic Church for encouraging superstitious belief.

Seneca *also Seneca the Younger, full name: Lucius Annaeus Seneca (c. 4 BC - 65 AD) was a Roman philosopher and statesman and the leading intellectual figure in Rome. His* Naturales Quaestiones (Natural Questions) *investigates aspects of physics and meteorology including meteors, thunder and lightning, water, the Nile, earthquakes and comets.*

Servius, Petrus *(died 1648) was an Italian physician from Spoleto and professor of medicine at Rome. In* Dissertatio de Unguento Armario (Dissertation on the Weapon-Salve) *published in 1642, he described the theoretical ointment thought to cure a wound when applied to the weapon that caused it.*

Settala, Manfredo *HPB: Septalius (1600-1680) was an Italian inventor and collector. He was founder of the Museum Septalius in Milan. Inheriting his father's library, he added strange objects, paintings by great masters, and exotica to make up his collection.*

Sheba, Queen of *(fl. 10th Century BC) was ruler of Saba' (or Sheba) in southwestern Arabia in Jewish and Islamic tradition. According to the Bible,* *she brought a caravan of valuable gifts for the Israelite King Solomon and tested his wisdom by asking him a number of riddles.*

Shiva *(Sanskrit meaning auspicious one) is one of the principal deities of Hinduism. He is the Supreme Being within Shaivism, a major tradition in contemporary Hinduism. Shiva is the destroyer of evil and the transformer. He is one of the Trimurti, the Hindu trinity, with Brahma and Vishnu.*

Siculus, Diodorus *(fl. 1st Century BC) was an ancient Greek historian. He is the author of* Bibliothēkē (Library) *also* Bibliotheca Historica *in Latin, a monumental history of mythology to the year 60 BC.*

Slade, Henry *(1835-1905) was a famous American medium found guilty of fraud. In 1876 Ray Lankester and Bryan Donkin attended one of Slade's seances in London. Slade was best known as a slate-writing medium. During his seances he would place a small slate with a piece of chalk under the table, claiming that spirits would use it to write messages. On this occasion, Lankester snatched up the slate before the spirit writing had supposedly taken place. There was already writing on the slate. On 1 October 1876 Slade was prosecuted for fraud and sentenced to three months in prison. Slade appealed on the grounds that the original indictment had omitted the words 'by palmistry or otherwise'. Before he could be rearrested on a new summons, he fled to Europe.*

Socrates *(c. 470 BC - 399 BC) was a Greek philosopher. His character, his ideas and the way he lived his life had a profound effect on the development of ancient and modern western philosophy.*

Solinus, Gaius Julius *(fl. early 3rd Century AD) was a Latin grammarian and compiler. He was the author of* De Mirabilibus Mundi (The Wonders of the World) *which also circulated under the title* Collectanea Rerum Memorabilium (Collection of Curiosities)*. In his text he refers to the perpetual fires of the temple of Minerva at Aquae Sulis (the English city of Bath in Somerset).*

Solomon, King *was one of the kings of Israel according to the Bible. He is portrayed as great in wisdom, wealth and power, and the builder of the first Temple of Jerusalem.*

Solon *(c. 638 - c. 558 BC) was an Athenian statesman and poet. According to Plato's dialogues* Timaeus *and* Critias *he traveled to the Egyptian town of Sais to visit the temple of Neith, the goddess of war and the hunt. There, the priests recounted to him the history of the lost continent of Atlantis.*

Sophia *is a feminine figure in Gnostic tradition. She is analogous to the human soul and one of the feminine aspects of God.*

Sosigenes of Alexandria *(fl. 1st Century BC) was a Greek astronomer and mathematician. According to Pliny the Elder, he was consulted by Julius Caesar* on the design of the Julian calendar. He modified the 365-day Egyptian solar calendar, introducing the leap year.

Spencer, Herbert *(27 April 1820 - 8 December 1903) was an English sociologist and philosopher. He advocated the primacy of the individual over society and of science over religion. He was an early supporter of the theory of evolution and is remembered for his development of social Darwinism in which he applied Darwin's theory of evolution to society and social classes. He coined the term 'survival of the fittest.'*

Spinoza, Benedict de *(24 November 1632 - 21 February 1677), was a Dutch Jewish philosopher. His work* Ethica (Ethics) *published in 1677 describes an ethical vision in which God is identified with nature. Rather than the transcendent creator of the universe, God is presented as nature itself, of which mankind is an integral part.*

Sprengel, Kurt Polycarp Joachim *(3 August 1766 - 15 March 1833) was a German botanist and physician. Between 1792 and 1799 he published the five volumes of* Versuch einer Pragmatischen Geschichte der Arzneikunde (Toward a Pragmatic History of Medicine). *It was the standard work for nearly a century.*

Stallbaum, Johann Gottfried *HPB: Stalbaüm (25 September 1793 - 24 January 1861) was a German classical scholar. He is noted for his studies of Plato:* Platonis Meno (Plato's Meno) *published in 1827 and* Platonis Opera Omnia (The Works of Plato) *published between 1827 and 1860.*

Stewart, Balfour *(1 November 1828 - 19 December 1887) was a Scottish meteorologist, geophysicist and member of the Society for Psychical Research. He became director of Kew Observatory in 1859 and professor of natural philosophy at Owens College, Manchester in 1870. He specialized in the study of the earth's magnetic field. He was co-author of* The Unseen Universe *(1875) with Peter Guthrie Tait. The book proposes the idea that 'the visible universe has been developed out of the invisible.' Blavatsky refers to Stewart and Tait obliquely using the phrase 'the authors of* The Unseen Universe.'

Stowe, Harriet Elisabeth Beecher *HPB: Stow (14 June 1811 - 1 July 1896) was an author and American abolitionist. Her best known work is her anti-slavery novel* Uncle Tom's Cabin *published in 1852. The line cited by Blavatsky is frequently attributed to Stowe but appears as an uncited aphorism in* The Unjust Judge or the Evils of Intemperance on Judges, Lawyers and Politicians *by 'a member of the Ohio bar,' published in 1854.*

Strabo *(c. 64 BC - after 21 AD) was a Greek geographer and historian. His major work is* Geographica (Geography), *a 17-volume encyclopedia of geographical knowledge. It is the only surviving work from antiquity detailing the peoples and countries known to Greeks and Romans in the reign of Augustus (27 BC - 14 BC).*

449

Swedenborg, Emanuel *(29 January 1688 - 29 March 1772) was a Swedish philosopher, scientist and mystic. His theology reflected a long struggle to understand the world of spirit through investigation of the physical world.*

Sydenham, Floyer *(1710 - 1 April 1787) was an English scholar of ancient Greek. He produced many translations including* The Works of Plato: His Fifty-five Dialogues and Twelve Epistles *published in 1804.*

Synesius *(c. 373 - c. 414) was a bishop and philosopher from the ancient city of Cyrene (now Shahhat, Libya). Before he converted to Christianity, he wrote pagan hymns that closely follow the fire theology of the* Chaldean Oracles. *His later Christian writings reveal great similarities between these belief systems.*

T.

Tachenius, Otto *real name: Heinz-Herbert Take (1610 - 1680) was a German pharmacist, physician and alchemist. He is thought to have been the son of a miller and to have been apprenticed to an apothecary. He qualified as a doctor at Padua in 1652, settling in Venice where he sold a 'viperine salt' (*sal viperinum*) as a cure-all. He wrote a commentary on van Helmont's alkahest published as* Epistola de Famoso Liquore Alkahest (Letter on the Famous Alkahest) *in 1655.*

Tait, Peter Guthrie *(28 April 1831 - 4 July 1901) was Scottish*

mathematician and physicist. He became professor of natural philosophy at Edinburgh in 1860 and held the chair until shortly before his death. He was co-author of The Unseen Universe *(1875) with Balfour Stewart. The book proposes the idea that 'the visible universe has been developed out of the invisible.' Blavatsky refers to Tait and Stewart obliquely with the phrase 'the authors of* The Unseen Universe.'

Tasso, Torquato *(11 March 1544 - 25 April 1595) was an Italian poet, regarded as the greatest of the late Renaissance. His most famous work is* Gerusalemme Liberata (Jerusalem Liberated) *published in 1581. This epic poem portrays the Crusaders' capture of Jerusalem.*

Tatian *(c. 120 - c. 180 AD) was a Syrian Christian writer and theologian. He compiled the* Diatessaron *which presented the four Gospels as a single narrative. This text was of central importance to the Syrian church for centuries. In* Oratio ad Graecos (Address to the Greeks), *published c. 177 AD, he argued that 'whatever immortality a man may obtain is thus by participation in the immortality and incorruptibility of God.'*

Taylor, Bayard *full name: James Bayard Taylor (11 January 1825 - 19 December 1878) was an American travel writer. He wrote accounts of his visits to Europe, India, China, Mexico, Russia, Egypt, Palestine, Iceland, Africa, Scandinavia, and Japan. Blavatsky appears to be paraphrasing his book*

Egypt and Iceland *published in 1874: 'Mariette Bey found... wonderful painted statues... and they are the most excellent specimens of Egyptian art.'*

Taylor, Thomas *(15 May 1758 - 1 November 1835) was an English translator and Platonist. He was the first to translate the complete works of Aristotle and Plato into English.*

Tertullian *full name Quintus Septimius Florens Tertullianus (c. 155 - c. 240 AD) was an important early Christian theologian and moralist. As the first Christian author to write in Latin, he had a profound influence on the vocabulary of western Christianity.*

Teste, Joseph-Alphonse *(1814 - 1888) was a French physician, homeopath and mesmerist. He was a member of the Faculty of Medicine in Paris and several scientific societies including the French Academy of Medicine and the Society of Homeopathic Medicine. Blavatsky quotes Teste from* Manuel Pratique du Magnétisme Animal (A Practical Manual of Animal Magnetism) *published in 1840.*

Thales of Miletus *(c. 624 BC - c. 546 BC) was a Greek philosopher. He proposed a cosmology based on water as the primary substance of matter and conceptualized the earth as a flat disk on an immense ocean.*

Thermuthis *(fl. 1500 BC) was the daughter of the Egyptian pharaoh Seti I or Ramses II who discovered the baby Moses in the reeds of the Nile. In the Old Testament she is identified as the foster mother of Moses, raising him as her own son in the pharaoh's palace. Her story is also recounted by the Roman-Jewish historian Josephus in his work* Antiquitates Judaicae (Antiquities of the Jews).

Thillaye *is difficult to identify definitively. He was a member of the 1826 Husson commission, convened by the French Academy of Medicine, to investigate mesmerism. Unfortunately, the Husson commission's report is signed only 'Thillaye.' As far as it has been possible to determine, he is most likely to be Auguste Jean Thillaye (dates unknown), keeper of the collections of the Faculty of Medicine in Paris.*

Thilorier, Adrien-Jean-Pierre *(16 February 1790 - 2 December 1844) was a French inventor. He was the first person to produce solid carbon dioxide or dry ice. It has not been possible to determine why Blavatsky refers to him in connection with electricity.*

Thomson, Anthony Todd HPB: *Todd Thomson (7 January 1778 - 3 July 1849) was a Scottish doctor and pioneer of dermatology. He translated and edited Eusèbe Salverte's* Des Sciences Occultes; ou, Essai sur la Magie, les Prodiges et les Miracles (The Occult Sciences: The Philosophy of Magic, Prodigies and Apparent Miracles) *published in English in 1846.*

Thomson, William 1st Baron Kelvin *(26 June 1824 - 17 December 1907) was a Scottish engineer,* *mathematician and physicist. He played a major role in the development of the second law of thermodynamics and the absolute temperature scale, measured in kelvins, is named for him.*

Thor *is the Norse god of thunder, the sky, and agriculture. He is the son of Odin, chief of all the Norse gods. His mother is Jord (Earth).*

Thouret, Michel-Augustin *(c. 1749 - 19 June 1810) was a French physician. He was appointed director of the Paris School of Medicine in 1795. He was a proponent of vaccination and an opponent of Anton Mesmer.*

Thury, Marc Antoine *(18 April 1822 - 1905) was a Swiss professor of physics and natural history at the University of Geneva. In a small pamphlet,* Les Tables Tournantes Considérés au Point de Vue de la Question de Physique Générale qui s'y Rattachées (The Physics of Turning Tables) *published in 1855, he reviewed Count de Gasparin's investigations into spiritualism. He also detailed his own observations of seances conducted with a small circle of friends under strict test conditions. He gave the name 'psychode' to a hypothetical substance that he believed served as a link between the soul and the body. He theorized that psychode was controlled by 'ectenic force.' This force was subject to the willpower of the medium. He maintained that wills may exist in the world other than those of men and animals. These other wills were capable, he believed, of acting on matter.*

Trediakovsky, Vasily Kirillovich *HPB: Tretiakowsky (5 March 1703 - 17 August 1769) was a Russian poet, literary theorist and playwright. In 1748 he published* Razgovor ob Ortografii (A Conversation on Orthography) *the first study of the phonetic structure of the Russian language. He argued it was essential for Russians to cultivate their own language. He cited educated Romans who chose to write in Latin rather than Greek, even though Greek was the language of learning at the time. He maintained it was possible to be a progressive and also imitate the ancients.*

Trithemius, Johannes *real name: Johann Heidenberg, born in Tritheim, HPB: Tritenheim (1 February 1462 - 13 December 1516), was a German Benedictine abbot and writer. He entered the order in 1482 and became abbot of Sponheim in western Germany three years later. He is remembered for two celebrated works on magic* Polygraphia (1507) and Chronologica Mystica (1508). *Because of his interest in occult sciences he was eventually removed from office. He had a profound influence on Heinrich Cornelius Agrippa and Paracelsus.*

Trogus, Pompeius *HPB: Trogus Pompeius (fl. 1st Century BC) was a Roman historian. He is the author of* Historiae Philippicae (Philippic Histories) *after Philip II founder of the Macedonian empire. This work surveys the histories of ancient civilisations. The original is lost but about a sixth of it was preserved by Saint Justin in his* Epitome, *a summary of Trogus' original work.*

Tullia *also affectionately Tulliola (5 August 79 or 78 BC - February 45 BC) was the first child and only daughter of Marcus Tullius Cicero and his first wife Terentia.*

Tylor, Edward Burnett *HPB: Tyler (2 October 1832 - 2 January 1917) was an English anthropologist. In 1865 he published* Researches into the Early History of Mankind and the Development of Civilization. *He theorized that both past and present civilizations must be regarded as parts of a single history of human ideas. He wrote, 'The past is continually needed to explain the present, and the whole to explain the part.'*

Tyndall, John *(2 August 1820 - 4 December 1893) was an Irish experimental physicist. From 1853 to 1887 he was professor of physics at the Royal Institution of Great Britain in London. As president of the British Association for the Advancement of Science, he gave a keynote speech in Belfast in 1874. He suggested that cosmological theory should be the province of science rather than theology and that life could arise spontaneously from matter. In the furore that followed, his references to the limitations of science and to mysteries beyond human understanding were forgotten.*

Typhon *is a monstrous giant in Greek mythology with a hundred dragon heads. He is the youngest son of Gaea (earth) and Tartarus (of the nether world)*

V.

Varley, Cromwell Fleetwood *or C.F. Varley, HPB: Varley (6 April 1828 - 2 September 1883), was an English engineer. He helped develop the electric telegraph and the transatlantic telegraph cable. He was sympathetic to spiritualism and carried out investigations with fellow physicist William Crookes using a galvanometer to make measurements of spiritualist phenomena.*

Vaughan, Thomas *see* **Eugenius Philalethes**.

Vāyu *is the Hindu god of air, wind or life breath.*

Vesta *is the Roman goddess of the hearth. The Temple of Vesta in the Roman Forum housed a perpetual fire attended by the Vestal Virgins.*

Vianney, Jean-Baptiste-Marie *also Saint John Vianney, HPB: Curé d'Ars (8 May 1786 - 4 August 1859) was a French priest later made patron saint of priests. In 1818 he became Curé d'Ars - parish priest in the village of Ars-sur-Formans in eastern France. He suffered attacks believed to be caused by the Devil and by 1827 Ars had become a site of pilgrimage.*

Vincent, Mr. *(forenames and dates unknown) is an obscure figure. He appears frequently in* Du Royaume de Siam (On the Kingdom of Siam) *by the French ambassador, Simon de la*

Loubère. In the original French Vincent is described as 'Mr. Vincent, Medecin Provençal.' Since he is not called 'Monsieur' and Provence had a large anglophone expat community, it seems reasonable to assume he was British or American. According to Loubère, 'Mr. Vincent, the physician, was retained by the King of Siam to work in his mines.' And, 'He understood mathematics and chemistry.' In her text, Blavatsky describes him, erroneously, as an engineer.

Virgil *Latin:* Publius Vergilius Maro *(15 October 70 BC - 21 September 19 BC) was a Roman poet. He is best known for his national epic, the* Aeneid *which he worked on from c. 30 BC and was unfinished at the time of his death.*

Vives, Juan Luis *HPB: Ludovicus Vives (6 March 1493 - 6 May 1540) was a Spanish humanist and educationalist. He refers to a subterranean lamp in his commentary, published in 1522, on Saint Augustine's* De Civitate Dei *(City of God).*

Volney, Comte de *full name: Constantin-François de Chassebœuf (3 February 1757 - 25 April 1820) was a French philosopher and orientalist. In 1783 he traveled to Egypt and Syria 'to acquire new knowledge.' After eight months learning Arabic in a Coptic monastery, he explored both countries on foot for three and a half years. He published an account of his travels entitled* Voyage en Égypte et Syrie *(Travels in Egypt and Syria) in 1787. His style is notable for its objectivity and*

its meticulous descriptions of physical, political, and moral conditions.

Voltaire *pseudonym of François-Marie Arouet (21 November 1694 - 30 May 1778) was a French philosopher and author. He was famous for his wit, his satirical attacks on the established Catholic church and Christianity, and his advocacy of freedom of religion, freedom of speech and separation of church and state.*

W.

Wagner, Nikolai Petrovich *(30 July 1829 - 3 April 1907) was a Russian zoologist and writer. He was professor of zoology at St. Petersburg University between 1870 and 1885. In the spring 1875 edition of* Vestnik Evropy *(Herald of Europe) he became the first Russian scholar to declare a belief in spiritualism.*

Wagner, Rudolf Friedrich Johann Heinrich *(30 July 1805 - 13 May 1864) was a German anatomist and physiologist. He made important contributions to the understanding of ganglia, nerve-endings, and the sympathetic nervous system. In 1854 he gave a talk to a meeting of the Naturforscher-Versammlung (Natural Science Assembly) in Göttingen, declaring that science was not yet advanced enough to answer questions about the nature of the soul.*

Walker, Anne *was a servant who lived in the market town of Chester-le-Street in*

Durham. In 1632, she became pregnant by her master, a Mr. Walker. He arranged for her to be taken away by his associate, Mark Sharp, a local collier, on the pretense that this would enable her to give birth in secret. On Walker's instructions, Sharp murdered her on the moors with a pick. Later, her ghost appeared to James Graham, a local miller, and described how she had been murdered and where the weapon and bloodstained clothes of the collier were hidden. Walker and Sharp were arrested, put on trial for murder and executed.

Wallace, Alfred Russel (8 January 1823 - 7 November 1913) was a British naturalist and spiritualist. In his book Contributions to the Theory of Natural Selection (1870) he eschewed the strict materialism of his fellow scientists and maintained that the higher faculties possessed by a human being could not be explained entirely by the theory of natural selection. He advocated the scientific investigation of spiritualism believing that science should not dismiss it without proper evaluation.

Warring, Charles Bartlett (1825 - 1907) was a specialist in Hebrew and contemporary cosmogony. He taught at the Collegiate School in Poughkeepsie, New York and was a Member of the New York Academy of Science. He was a proponent of concordism - the attempt to align scientific thought with a particular interpretation of Genesis. He refers to Peruvian bark in his book The Mosaic Account of Creation published in 1875.

Webster, John also Johannes Hyphastes (3 February 1610 - 18 June 1682) was an English clergyman, physician and chemist. He supported the foundation of the Royal Society of London because he believed the aim of true natural magic was to uncover the 'secret effects' of nature. In his book The Displaying of Supposed Witchcraft published in 1677, he criticized Joseph Glanvill's writing on witchcraft. Webster wrote that 'supernatural' effects, supposedly caused by witchcraft, would eventually be found to have natural causes.

Weekman, Michael was a poor American laborer who moved into a supposedly haunted house in Hydesville, New York in 1846, living there for a year and a half with his wife and young family. In a statement dated 11 April 1848, he described hearing rapping on the front door and his name called in the middle of the night. The Weekmans fled the house and the Fox family moved in during December 1847. They too were disturbed by rapping (from March 1848). One of the children, Kate Fox, challenged the spirit of the house to respond to her, and this gave rise to the birth of the modern spiritualist movement. (See **Fox Sisters, the.**)

Wilder, Alexander (14 May 1823 - 19 September 1908) was an American physician, Neoplatonist scholar and theosophist. He joined the Theosophical Society in 1875 and served as vice president between 1877 and 1880. He placed the manuscript of Isis Unveiled with the original publishers, J. W. Bouton, New York.

Wilkinson, James John Garth *HPB: Dr. J. J. Garth Wilkinson (3 June 1812 - 18 October 1899) was an English homeopathic physician, translator and biographer of Swedenborg.*

Williams, Charles *(1849-1904) was a British materialization medium. He claimed to be in communication with the spirit control John King. In 1878, in a spiritualist circle in Amsterdam, Williams and his fellow British medium Alfred Richard Rita were exposed. Charlie, a materialized spirit, was seized and found to be Rita. Many handkerchiefs, a bottle of phosphorus oil, several yards of dirty white muslin, a false black beard, and other paraphernalia were found on the two mediums.*

Wirdig, Tenzel *also Sebastian Wirdig or Sebastian Werdenig (1613 - 17 April 1687) was a German physician and occultist. He was the author of* Nova Medicina Spirituum Curiosa (The New Spiritual Medicine) *published in 1675. He was a proponent of 'magnetic sympathy,' a theory of magnetic attraction and repulsion. He believed that everything in the universe possessed a soul, and that the earth itself was merely a larger being.*

Witch of Endor *is a female sorcerer who, at the request of Saul, King of Israel, summons the spirit of the prophet Samuel. The story appears in Samuel I, 28:3 - 25. Saul seeks a prediction of the final outcome of Israel's battle against the Philistines. His servants tell him about the Witch of Endor. She conjures up the spirit of Samuel who tells Saul that he and his three sons are destined to die in*

the following day's fighting, and Israel will fall.

Wright, Thomas *(23 April 1810 - 23 December 1877) was an English antiquarian and author. The comment quoted by Blavatsky appears in his book* Narratives of Sorcery and Magic *published in two volumes in 1851.*

Y.

Ymir *also Aurgelmir, is a giant, the first being in Norse mythology. He was created from the meltwater produced when ice from the world of Niflheim met fire from the world of Muspelheim. He was the father of all the giants and appears in both the Poetic Edda and the Prose Edda. (See Chapter Four, note 9.)*

Youmans, Edward Livingston *(3 June 1821 - 18 January 1887) was an American scientific writer, editor, and lecturer. In May 1872 he founded* Popular Science Monthly, *a journal dedicated to popularizing scientific knowledge aimed at the educated layman. The journal is still published today. Blavatsky refers to him erroneously as 'Professor Youmans.'*

Young, Thomas *(13 June 1773 - 10 May 1829) was an English physician and physicist. He demonstrated that a split beam of light produces interference patterns characteristic of waves. With this work he resurrected the wave theory of light from the previous century. He was also an Egyptologist and contributed to the deciphering of the Rosetta Stone.*

Z.

Zeno of Citium *(c. 335 BC - c. 263 BC) was a Hellenistic philosopher and the founder of the Stoic school of philosophy. He was probably of Phoenician descent from the city of Citium in Cyprus. He taught Stoic philosophy in Athens from c. 300 BC. Stoicism emphasizes abstinence from worldly pleasures in order to develop clear judgment, inner calm and freedom from suffering, Stoicism's ultimate goal.*

Zeus *is the Greek god of sky, lightning and thunder, and ruler of all the gods.*

Zeus Cataibates *means 'Zeus who descends as lightning.'*

Zoroaster *also Zarathustra (c. 628 BC - c. 551 BC) was an Iranian religious reformer and prophet, regarded as the founder of Zoroastrianism, the ancient pre-Islamic religion of Iran.*

Zwingli, Huldrych *or Ulrich Zwingli, HPB: Zuinglius (1 January 1484 - 11 October 1531) was a Swiss religious leader and the most important figure in the Swiss Reformation. In 1520 his preaching stirred revolts against fasting and the celibacy of the clergy. His famous sermons given at the Oetenbach convent in Zurich were printed in 1522 as* The Clarity and Certainty of the Word of God. *Zwingli's belief in the ultimate supremacy of scripture lead to the founding of the Swiss Reformed Church.*

Printed in Great Britain
by Amazon